The Crucified God in the Carolingian Era

The Carolingian "renaissance" of the late eighth and ninth centuries, in what is now France, western Germany, and northern Italy, transformed medieval European culture. At the same time the need to ensure that clergy, monks, and laity embraced orthodox Christian doctrine was a fundamental driving force.

This book offers a new perspective on the period by examining transformations in a major current of thought as revealed through literature and artistic imagery: the doctrine of the passion and the crucified Christ. The evidence of a range of literary sources is surveyed – liturgical texts, poetry, hagiography, letters, homilies, exegetical and moral tractates – but special attention is given to writings from the discussions and debates concerning artistic images, Adoptionism, predestination, and the eucharist. Topics discussed in detail include the miniatures in the Gellone Sacramentary, Hrabanus Maurus' *In honorem sanctae crucis*, and later Carolingian crucifixion images such as the Utrecht Psalter illustration to Psalm 115, the miniature in the Drogo Sacramentary, and the ivory cover of the Pericopes of Henry II.

CELIA CHAZELLE is Associate Professor of History, the College of New Jersey.

THE
Crucified God
IN THE
Carolingian Era

Theology and Art of Christ's Passion

CELIA CHAZELLE

CAMBRIDGE
UNIVERSITY PRESS

PUBLISHED BY THE PRESS SYNDICATE OF THE UNIVERSITY OF CAMBRIDGE
The Pitt Building, Trumpington Street, Cambridge, United Kingdom

CAMBRIDGE UNIVERSITY PRESS
The Edinburgh Building, Cambridge CB2 2RU, UK
40 West 20th Street, New York, NY 10011–4211, USA
10 Stamford Road, Oakleigh, VIC 3166, Australia
Ruiz de Alarcón 13, 28014, Madrid, Spain
Dock House, The Waterfront, Cape Town 8001, South Africa
http://www.cambridge.org

First published 2001

Printed in the United Kingdom at the University Press, Cambridge

Typeface Monotype Dante 11/15 pt   *System* QuarkXPress™ [SE]

A catalogue record for this book is available from the British Library

Library of Congress Cataloguing in Publication data

Chazelle, Celia Martin
    The crucified God in the Carolingian era: theology and art of Christ's passion /
Celia Chazelle.
        p.   cm.
    Includes bibliographical references and index.
    ISBN 0 521 80103 6 (hardback)
        1. Jesus Christ – Passion – History of doctrines – Middle Ages, 600–1500.
    2. Christian art and symbolism – Medieval, 500–1500.   3. Jesus Christ – Passion – Art.
    4. Art, Carolingian.
    I. Title.

    BT431.3.C48   2001
    246'.558–dc21   00-050353

ISBN 0 521 80103 6 hardback

For Bernard

Contents

Illustrations

Preface

This book spans three millennia: it discusses developments in the first, was written in the second, and will be published at the beginning of the third. As this may imply, though in a somewhat misleading fashion, it has taken far longer to complete and undergone more permutations than I have the nerve to admit here. One result is that I have accumulated debts to numerous institutions and innumerable individuals.

My interest in the intellectual history of the Carolingians goes back to my undergraduate years at the University of Toronto, where I was introduced to the field by my long-time mentor, Eugene R. Fairweather. It was nurtured by my teachers and dissertation advisors at Yale, Jaroslav Pelikan and Walter Cahn, and by a year of dissertation research at the Zentralinstitut für Kunstgeschichte and the Bayerische Staatsbibliothek in Munich, funded by a doctoral fellowship from the Samuel H. Kress Foundation.

Initial research beyond the dissertation, which led my understanding of the Carolingian era and my initial plans for a book in new directions, took place at Bryn Mawr College with postdoctoral fellowships provided by the J. Paul Getty Foundation and the Mellon Foundation. Since then, while living in Princeton, I have made ample use of the libraries of the university, the Princeton Theological Seminary, and the Institute for Advanced Study, and the resources of the Index for Christian Art, whose staff has consistently been most courteous in assisting me to track down images and bibliography. I have profited, too, from the stimulating intellectual environment created by my colleagues in the History Department at the

College of New Jersey, who have helped me become more aware of historical developments outside the narrow boundaries of Carolingian Europe. The college's FIRSL program gave me release time from teaching duties and a year-long sabbatical leave in 1998–1999, which made it possible to complete the manuscript of this book, and the Council of Associate Deans of Arts and Sciences has provided generous financial assistance towards the costs of photographs and copyright permissions. During my sabbatical year, spent in Paris, I was able to use the rich resources of the Bibliothèque Nationale de France and the fine holdings of the Bibliothèque de Saulchoir. The Bibliothèque Nationale de France and the Bayerische Staatsbibliothek in Munich, visited in the fall of 1999, allowed me to examine normally inaccessible Carolingian manuscripts and book covers in their collections. I am grateful to both institutions for these opportunities, and to Dr. Patricia Stirnemann (Paris) and Dr. Elisabeth Klemm (Munich) for having helped open the doors.

Among the friends who have assisted in countless ways, special thanks are owed to Lawrence Nees, who read and critiqued a draft of the book, and to David Ganz, who did the same for chapter 5. These scholars' own erudition, the encouragement they have given me over the last years to progress in my research and reconsider my assumptions about the Carolingian era, their unfailing generosity in conversations and letters, far beyond any call of duty, have been a continual inspiration to me. I am most grateful, as well, to Jaroslav Pelikan, who also read and offered comments on the book in draft, but whose guidance of my interest in the Carolingians goes back so much further. Jary's first assignment to me as a beginning graduate student at Yale was to read the *Libri Carolini*. My consequent interest in that treatise has led to friendships with Ann Freeman and Paul Meyvaert, who in writing and through conversations have kindly aided my understanding of its more perplexing aspects.

Since I moved to Princeton in 1986, Peter Brown and William Jordan have been constant sources of encouragement; they have patiently read my work, allowed me to take advantage of their profound knowledge of late antique and medieval Europe, and repeatedly asked probing questions that have compelled me to refine my opinions. In the last decade, numerous other friends and colleagues have provided me with opportunities to deliver lectures and conference papers, commented on drafts of articles connected with this project, pointed out weaknesses in my arguments, and stimulated me to new ideas. Outstanding among them are Elaine Beretz, Mildred Budny, Donald Bullough, John Cavadini, John Contreni, Michael Curschmann, the late Robert Deshman, William Diebold, Jeffrey Hamburger, Alice Harting-Corrêa, Herbert Kessler, Dale Kinney, Genevra Kornbluth, R. Emmet McLaughlin, E. Ann Matter, Karl Morrison, Thomas Noble, Elizabeth Sears, Patrick Wormald. Most recently, two anonymous readers for Cambridge University Press, the press's staff, and my editor, William Davies, have helped me through the publication process. My good friend and colleague, Thomas Allsen, patiently guided me in preparing the index. Because I have not always listened as attentively as I should have to the advice of any of these people, I am alone responsible for errors, misjudgments, and other weaknesses found in the following pages.

Finally, I wish to thank my family. My parents, John and Constance Martin, first gave me a love of scholarship, saw to it that I studied Latin, and have been unflagging in their confidence that this book would one day get done. My children, Damien and Anna, kept me in tune with the practical demands of life in the twentieth century even as my thoughts were rooted in the early Middle Ages. Most of all, however, I am grateful to Bernard. I cannot possibly do justice here to the wise counsel, moral support, and many other forms of assistance he has given me in our almost twenty years of marriage.

Abbreviations

BNF	*Bibliothèque Nationale de France*
CCCM	*Corpus Christianorum, Continuatio Mediaevalis*
CCM	*Corpus Consuetudinem Monasticarum*
CCSL	*Corpus Christianorum, Series Latina*
CSEL	*Corpus Scriptorum Ecclesiasticorum Latinorum*
MGH	*Monumenta Germaniae Historica*
Capit.	*Capitularia*
Conc.	*Concilia*
Epp.	*Epistolae*
PLAC	*Poetae latini aevi Carolini*
SRM	*Scriptorum rerum Merovingicarum*
SS	*Scriptores*
NCMH 2	*The New Cambridge Medieval History*, volume 2: *c. 700–c. 900*
PL	*Patrologia cursus completus, series latina*
SC	*Sources chrétiennes*
ST	*Studi e Testi*

CHAPTER I

Introduction

Between the late eighth and mid ninth century, a series of doctrinal conflicts brought Christ's passion into the focus of Carolingian theological discussion with an intensity that, like so many other phenomena of the era,
was unprecedented in the medieval west. The explosive cultural activity of
these decades has left us abundant artistic depictions of the crucified Christ
and a huge variety of writings that commemorate, praise, and grieve over
the crucifixion, wonder at its mystical significance, and offer explanations
of its function in God's work of salvation. But it was when some of the
period's most tenacious, intellectually energetic scholars debated contemporaries over the role of the artistic image, Hispanic Adoptionism, predestination, and the nature of the eucharistic presence that it became
necessary to think through the theological consequences of their beliefs
about this event and harmonize them with other elements of Christian
doctrine, in order to defend these ideas against teachings considered
heretical.

This book's principal aim is to examine more closely than has been done
in the past the broad spectrum of Carolingian thought about the passion or
crucifixion (words I use interchangeably) and its meaning or purpose. I do
not offer a comprehensive survey of the evidence, which would be impossible to accomplish adequately given the volume of material to survive.
Instead, my focus is on those sources that I think best elucidate the parame-
ters of belief, its evolution and richness, in general oversimplified in earlier
scholarship, and its most striking expressions. Although I will discuss some
artistic representations of the crucifixion, my principal concern is texts:

doctrinal, poetical, homiletic, liturgical, and exegetical works, most of
which recall Christ's experience on the cross without polemical intent –
without openly attacking ideas deemed erroneous on this or another theological issue – even though every work sets out what its author clearly
understood to constitute orthodoxy. Carolingian crucifixion images have
been better analyzed than the literature on the subject, but without sufficient investigation of the written sources, the scope and complexity of
some of the thought has not been fully recognized. This, of course, is part
of the larger problem of the sizable gaps remaining in our overall compre-
hension of Carolingian theology, a fundamental arena of intellectual activity in this period that has received far less attention than deserved. A few
recent studies have shed new light on certain features of eighth- and ninth-
century religious thought and its relation to other cultural and political
developments; but on the whole, as David Ganz has recently observed, the
scholarship in the field has been restricted to chapters in intellectual histories of the entire Middle Ages and monographs on individual theologians.[1]

One probable reason for this apparent disinterest is the continued
weight of the opinion, so often expressed in older histories, that
Carolingian scholars were dependent on the teachings of previous centuries, especially the patristic era, and therefore lacked originality. At best,
their accomplishment consisted in the preservation and transmission of
former traditions of belief, chiefly patristic, while their deviations from
those traditions indicate their inadequate grasp of them and the decline in
intellectual standards. To examine theology in the era, then, is largely to
rehearse what was more clearly formulated by the Carolingians' predecessors. In the last few decades, historians have come to realize that numerous
characteristics of early medieval, European intellectual and cultural life
once cited as testimony to this inferiority – "mistakes" in Carolingian "borrowings" from antique literary and artistic productions, for example – are
better interpreted as signs that a very different society was beginning to
emerge. While it drew inspiration from several cultures, including the
ancient world, it transformed that inheritance into something altogether
new to the west. Carolingian theological writing is not necessarily "unorig-
inal" because it regularly makes use of excerpts, frequently unidentified,

---

[1] David Ganz, "Theology and the Organisation of Thought," *The New Cambridge Medieval
History*, vol. 2: *c. 700–c. 900*, ed. R. McKitterick (Cambridge, 1995), 759. Subsequent references to
this volume as *NCMH* 2.

from older texts. Rather than merely passive followers of their forebears, eighth- and ninth-century writers often selected, edited, and rearranged passages from a variety of sources, and artists often proceeded in a parallel fashion, adapting motifs found in earlier works of art, so that these became the voices and imagery through which they expressed themselves – granted that like some modern intellectuals they often built on ideas suggested by the earlier creations they knew and admired.[2] Yet despite this shift in how specialists now perceive Carolingian intellectual endeavor, few efforts have been made to reevaluate even its major currents. If we are ever to gain a comprehensive picture of the phenomenon known as the Carolingian *renovatio* or "renaissance," however, we must explore more deeply the intellectual world of the society's religious leaders: the beliefs they expressed through or in spite of their sources, and their motivations for doing so, which necessarily differ from those of the patristic and other authorities on whom they drew. Above all, it seems to me evident, we need to attend in these terms to how they interpreted the essential doctrines of their faith, the basis, as they were convinced, of the quest for eternal salvation that at least in theory guided every aspect of their daily lives.

As the foregoing suggests, the next chapters will only occasionally discuss source-analysis or the relation of Carolingian thought to earlier doctrine. I am less interested in these issues than in mapping out clearly the theological trends that occurred in this specific region, between the late eighth and the late ninth century.[3] Some features of Carolingian theology of the crucifixion are already well established. Art historians looking for literary parallels to the first known, western images of the dead or dying crucified Christ, his body slumped on the cross and occasionally his eyes closed, works of art usually dated to the second quarter and second half of the ninth century, have pointed to contemporary Latin writings that suggest a new interest in Jesus' human mortality and its redemptive value – that is, his giving up of life in order to save other human beings.[4] In

---

[2] The recent change in scholarly opinion is well illustrated by the articles on early medieval culture and learning in *NCMH* 2, esp. parts 3, 4.

[3] Where possible, I note in parentheses the names of authorities (usually patristic) quoted or cited in the Carolingian writings. Occasionally I indicate the precise text from which the borrowing occurs, though in general this is not germane to my purposes here.

[4] The fundamental study is Reiner Haussherr, *Der tote Christus am Kreuz: zur Ikonographie des Gerokreuzes* (Bonn, 1963), 215–225. Also see Gertrud Schiller, *Iconography of Christian Art*, trans. of vols. 1–2 only by J. Seligman (Greenwich, CT, 1971–1972), 2.9–10, see 99–107.

contrast, some ninth-century depictions of the crucifixion portray him with open eyes and no signs of physical suffering, as do the fewer, older representations surviving from western Europe. These very different images have been linked, instead, with the poetical and prose literature of both the eighth and the ninth centuries, in Latin and occasionally vernacular languages, that seems to stress the son of God's divine qualities: his eternal kingship, immortality, and omnipotent triumph over evil and death.

Because virtually all interest in Carolingian writing about the crucifixion has come from art historians, though, the extant art has understandably guided the choice of texts investigated. For the most part, they have only been examined to the extent that correspondences with the imagery have been discerned, an approach clearly not conducive to analysis of the broad range of ideas recorded in the written material. One result is a somewhat distorted conception of this facet of Carolingian theology and its development. The greater attentiveness of ninth-century Carolingian scholars to the redemptive role of Jesus' crucified humanity is indeed significant, and it is therefore a primary issue explored in chapter 4. But as I hope to demonstrate, while it is useful to conceive of a spectrum of belief about Christ that sometimes emphasizes his immortal divinity, sometimes his mortal humanity, the diversity of teachings about the passion in the Carolingian church was far greater than this alone suggests. Any attempt to clarify this facet of thought or the connections between doctrinal and artistic developments must not only take into account writings in poetry and prose where the crucifixion is the main subject. It is also necessary to consider the sometimes highly individualistic arguments of Carolingian theologians about the nature and function of the artistic image, Adoptionism, divine predestination, and the eucharist, issues that some of them clearly perceived to involve disputes over the proper understanding of the crucified Christ.

The first two of these concerns are studied in chapter 2, where I analyze the *Opus Caroli regis* (*Libri Carolini*) [5] and contemporary Carolingian tracts directed against Hispanic Adoptionism, the Christology misunderstood by

---

[5] Theodulf, *Opus Caroli regis contra synodum* (*Libri Carolini*), *MGH Conc.* 2, *Supplementum* 1, ed. A. Freeman (Hanover, 1998). (Henceforth cited as Theodulf, *Opus Caroli regis*, with book, chapter, and page from this edition.) A partial exception is the series of fine articles on aspects of early Carolingian theology in Rainer Berndt, ed., *Das frankfurter Konzil von 794: Kristallisationspunkt karolingischer Kultur*, vol. 2: *Kultur und Theologie* (Mainz, 1997).

Charlemagne's theologians to announce that Christ was the adopted rather than true son of God. Both the *Opus Caroli regis*, Charlemagne's great attack on Nicea II, the Byzantine council of 787 that restored image worship in the east after the first period of iconoclasm, and the anti-Adoptionist treatises offer an essentially Christological perspective on the crucifixion. Like other medieval theologians, their authors – Theodulf of Orléans, Alcuin, Paulinus of Aquileia, Benedict of Aniane – recognize the connection of Christology, that is doctrine concerning the second person of the Trinity, with soteriology, doctrine concerning the process by which God grants human beings salvation. Christ's passion saves, not only enabling him to rise from the dead but granting this to other mortals, because he is both God and human, and it was precisely in order to bring other human beings to heaven that the son of God became a man. Nevertheless, although the two areas of thinking are interdependent, the *Opus Caroli regis* and the writings against Adoptionism mainly look to the crucifixion as proof of Christological truth, as an episode that helps explain the relationship between divinity and humanity in a God who dies. The Christology of the passion by no means ceases to be a concern in later Carolingian literature. As shown in chapter 3, some discussion along these lines occurs in the 820s to early 840s in reaction to the renewed image controversy in the east and to the iconoclastic activities of Bishop Claudius of Turin. But the questions relating to the passion that arise in the mid-ninth-century debates over divine predestination and the eucharist have more to do with soteriology. In the first-named conflict, examined in chapter 5, disagreements about whether God willed the salvation of the elect alone or the entire human race, and whether Christ died only for the elect or all mortals, required a clear understanding of the crucifixion's function in the divine plan for the end of time. In the conflict over the nature of the eucharistic presence, examined in chapter 6, a quarrel possibly linked with the predestination controversy, the major issue regarding the crucifixion was sacramental: its capacity to save or redeem through its relation, as a sacrifice once for all time, to the daily mass. Here different interpretations of scripture and the liturgy led scholars to argue over how to reconcile the seemingly contradictory doctrines that, on the one hand, the sacrifice of the cross was unique, and on the other, every eucharist is an oblation of Christ's body and blood.

Given how orthodoxy on the passion emerged as an issue within these four areas of theological development, it is not surprising to find that the writings concerned help clarify some of the most enigmatic and theologically complex artistic representations of the crucifixion from Charlemagne's reign and later in the ninth century. I look at a selection of such images in chapters 3 and 7, not in order to propose definitive readings of their iconography, which in each case would require considering other factors besides contemporary doctrine of the crucifixion. Rather, the intention is to point out ways that my analysis of eighth- and ninth-century theology, in particular of certain texts and the thinking of certain scholars, provides a basis for reassessment of these works of art and possibly others, as well. In the process, it should also become evident that the images provide us another perspective from which to assess the ideas about the crucified Christ expressed in writing. The treatise of figure poems, *In honorem sanctae crucis* that Hrabanus Maurus probably completed in 813/814 (figs. 11–16),[6] and some of the illuminations of the Gellone Sacramentary, a manuscript of 790–c. 804 (figs. 6, 7, 9 and 10),[7] in particular these books' imagery of Christ crucified, seem to reflect doctrinal preoccupations similar to those of Charlemagne's scholarly entourage. Indeed, one concern in the production of both works may have been to offer visual confirmation of court teachings, especially the Christology that evolved through the discussions surrounding the *Opus Caroli regis* and Adoptionism. A very different view of the crucified Christ is suggested by the ivory now serving as the cover to the Pericopes of Henry II, a carved tablet usually dated to 840–870 and assigned to the court school of Charles the Bald (fig. 30).[8] This is the focus of chapter 7, where I first more briefly discuss the illustration to Psalm 115 in the famous ninth-century Utrecht Psalter (fig. 26) and the miniature decorating a Palm Sunday initial of the Drogo Sacramentary (fig. 27);[9] the last two images have important iconographic connections with the ivory and may have directly influenced its design. All three depictions of the crucifixion were most likely in part inspired by the Carolingian liturgy: Holy Week, Easter, the mass. All three offer visual parallels to the interest of ninth-century writers in Jesus'

---

[6] Hrabanus, *In honorem sanctae crucis*, CCCM 100, ed. M. Perrin (Turnhout, 1997). The work is the subject of a recent, excellent study by Michele Ferrari, *Il "Liber sanctae crucis" di Rabano Mauro: testo-immagine-contesto* (Bern, 1999).

[7] Paris, BNF, MS lat. 12048; *Liber Sacramentorum Gellonensis*, CCSL 159–159A, ed. A. Dumas (Turnhout, 1981).   [8] Munich, Bayerische Staatsbibliothek, MS Clm. 4452.

[9] Utrecht, Bibliotheek der Rijksuniversiteit, MS 32, folio 67r; Paris, BNF, MS lat. 9428, fol. 43v.

redemptive suffering and death, and all three may imply agreement with
the doctrine of the eucharistic presence espoused by Pascasius Radbertus
in his *De corpore et sanguine Domini*,[10] the treatise that lies behind the ninth-
century quarrel over the eucharistic presence. But beyond this, the ivory's
more complex pictorial composition, like the simpler scene in the psalter
and possibly that in the Drogo Sacramentary, seems best interpreted by reference to writings of Hincmar of Rheims. Among these – in terms of the
ivory – are his tractates on predestination, his analyses of the eucharistic
presence, some of which show the affect of the controversy over its nature,
and his tracts advising Charles the Bald on the relationship between virtue,
including reception of the eucharist, the redemption offered in the crucifixion, and principles by which he should rule.

The flexibility of and range to Carolingian teachings on the crucifixion
attest writers' and artists' varied aims in recalling its meaning or purpose,
as well as the diverse intellectual inheritance on which they drew. For these
ecclesiastics as for the authorities of earlier centuries who provided the
underpinnings to their thought about the passion, the Bible was the foundation of Christian orthodoxy. Its exposition of divine truth, ritually commemorated in the liturgy that itself both helped shape belief while
constituting a mode for its expression, showed the event's significance to
be as impossible to pin down completely as is the concept that Jesus is
simultaneously God and man. Appropriately, it lent itself to a wealth of
interpretations not seen as necessarily contradictory, so long as proponents
were considered to remain within the realm of orthodoxy laid down in
scripture, mirrored in the church's prayers and rites, and confirmed by the
church fathers.[11] Yet partly as a consequence, the array of ideas about the
crucifixion and the crucified Christ found in the literature, as indeed in the
patristic and other sources from which eighth- and ninth-century authors
borrowed, often seems confused and difficult to disentangle. For this
reason, it is best to conclude this chapter with an outline of the most prominent lines of thought, more systematic than anything actually found in
Carolingian writings, though its relation to the ideas they convey should
become clear in the following pages.

---

[10] Pascasius, *De corpore et sanguine Domini cum appendice epistola ad Fredugardum*, CCCM 16, ed. B.
Paulus (Turnhout, 1969), 1–131.
[11] See Jaroslav Pelikan, *The Christian Tradition, a History of the Development of Doctrine*, vol. 3: *The
Growth of Medieval Theology (600–1300)* (Chicago, 1978), 129–144.

To begin, two concepts need to be mentioned that frequently are not directly acknowledged in the Carolingian sources, but are as central to thought about the crucifixion in that or any other period as is the doctrine that salvation required Christ to possess two natures. One is that, like every truth recorded in the New Testament, the passion was foreshadowed in the Old. Hence it is possible to recall its occurrence, describe its circumstances, and reflect on its meaning through comparisons to episodes in the Hebrew scriptures – for example, the sacrifice of Isaac, the Israelites' escape from Egypt, the story of the brazen serpent – or through references solely to the Old Testament personages and events. To compare Christ to the passover lamb, for example, or to say that he is the new Adam or brazen serpent, expresses certain ideas about the passion's significance. The second, critical concept is that God ordained that the crucifixion happen only once. In spite of its Old Testament prefigurations and God's unceasing interaction with earth from creation to the last day, it has no perfect analogy and will never be repeated. Its salvific impact concerns humanity before the incarnation as well as for the rest of creation's history, therefore, no matter which mortals are thought to be finally saved.

Within the boundaries formed by these two doctrines, as mentioned above in regard to the *Opus Caroli regis* and the anti-Adoptionist tracts, Carolingian scholars may stress the passion's Christological role as a revelation that two natures are joined in Jesus' one person. Sometimes this leads to meditation on the event's continuity with other episodes in his earthly life similarly interpreted as evidence of God's incarnation. The crucifixion, like the nativity, resurrection, and other occurrences, demonstrates that the saving union between a human nature able to suffer and die and immortal, impassible divinity truly took place. This perspective is important not only to the *Opus Caroli regis* and the writings against Adoptionism but also, in a different manner, to exegesis of the gospel accounts of the crucifixion. Carolingian exegetical literature often relies extensively on older sources and can weave together multiple strands of literal and allegorical interpretation. Nevertheless, a basic, underlying refrain is that scripture's narrative of both the passion's most humble aspects and its miraculous displays of divine power proves its salvific nature, because every stage was willed by God, the divinity present in Jesus himself during his suffering and death as well as resurrection.

The doctrine that the crucifixion reveals Christ's divinity as well as his humanity overlaps with the varied interpretations that have been collectively identified as the "classic" theory of the atonement; while sometimes acknowledging his human weakness, torments and dying, particularly as contrasts to his power, they give preeminent place to his divinity and its achievement.[12] Although he endured pain and mortality, what Jesus underwent on the cross constituted his triumph over evil and revelation of cosmic majesty. Frequently imagery of war and treachery is employed; the passion was a battle won through the divine savior's omnipotence, or it was an act of intrigue in which his wisdom and justice bested his enemies. The adversaries he combats are sin, death, and Satan, commonly perceived as synonymous forces external to the human race and besetting it as a whole. In Peter Cramer's words, their conflict with Christ turns on a "disputed possession of rights," the issue of who properly has command of the human race.[13] The idea of sin as an individualized burden within a single human soul and as such distinguishable from death, its consequence, or the devil, its catalyst, is typically weak in these writings. Often, therefore, the crucifixion's effect is closely aligned and even merges with that of the harrowing of hell, resurrection, ascension, and the return for the final judgment, different stages in the same conquest or in a single, long-reaching revelation of the son of God's eternal, divine control of the universe.

In all the literature discussed in the next chapters, one of the most frequently recurring ideas is the saving efficacy of Christ's blood. From the period of Charlemagne's reign this is especially true of prose and verse by Alcuin; the corpus of his work exceeds that extant by any contemporary, although the blood's value is also a theme in some writings by other scholars in the early Carolingian court circle. Where the crucifixion is described as a triumph, both the blood and the cross may be upheld as the instruments of victory and signs of Christ's conquering, divine nature or heavenly rule. Based on a rich Latin tradition of exegesis of John 19.34, Carolingian writers often refer to the liquid from Jesus' side wound – both water and blood but usually with special emphasis on the latter – as the very force that defeated

---

[12] Jaroslav Pelikan, *The Christian Tradition, a History of the Development of Doctrine*, vol. 1: *The Emergence of the Catholic Tradition (100–600)* (Chicago, 1971), 149. Cf. Gustaf Aulén, *Christus Victor: an Historical Study of the Three Main Types of the Idea of the Atonement*, trans. A. G. Hebert (New York, 1956).

[13] Peter Cramer, *Baptism and Change in the Early Middle Ages, c. 200–c.1150* (Cambridge, 1993), 147.

sin/death/the devil. Prefigured in the blood of the passover lamb that freed the ancient Israelites, it broke the chains holding humanity captive, washed the world in its divinely empowered wave, opened paradise, and was the "royal purple" of Christ's kingship. The cross's strength, its own role in that conquest, signification of divine majesty, and offer of continued protection to the faithful are also widely found themes. The cross is a letter (X, the Greek *Tau* or Hebrew *Tav*) signifying the name of Christ and all the power it was believed to possess; it is the weapon by which the son of God slew Satan and tore down the gates of hell. Consecrated by his blood and now glorified in heaven, this is the celestial throne from which he reigns over the universe and his judgment seat, the symbol of his universal dominion that will reappear with him at the eschaton. Such ideas about the cross are echoed in praise of its miracle-working relics, of wonders performed through the sign of the cross made by hand, especially by the saints, and in the occasional early medieval accounts of miracles worked by or near cross images. All such "apparitions" of the cross may be symbols of Christ's omnipotence and channel his power from heaven to earth.

The Carolingian literature that dwells on the redemptive value of the crucified Christ's human nature encompasses an even more varied collection of ideas, though the differences from the texts that dwell on his triumph are often ones of emphasis more than categorical distinctions. In general, in these cases, Jesus' sonship receives more attention than his equality with God the father; the son is the victim provided by and/or sacrificed to God. The conquest of death and the devil may be affirmed, but the passion tends to be more specifically associated with the remission of sins, while sin tends to be viewed as something "personal," a burden within the individual soul more than an external enemy of the entire human race. Correspondingly, the crucifixion's effect is often conceived in personal terms; as Amalarius of Metz remarks in his *Liber officialis*, Christ "suffered for me."[14] Although in other circumstances the blood from the side wound is interpreted as a sign of divinity, when the wound or Jesus' bleeding is recalled in these contexts it is more noticeably as evidence of his suffering and mortal, passible humanity. The principal scriptural model is the blood sacrifice; the victim must be bled as well as killed, and therefore Christ's bloodshed stands as the culmination to his innocent,

---

[14] Amalarius, *Liber officialis* 1.14, *Amalarii episcopi opera liturgica omnia*, 3 vols., ST 138–140, ed. J. M. Hanssens (Vatican City, 1948–1950), ST 139.100–101.

human oblation.[15] Whether the blood indicates the divine defeat of Satan and death or the torment and dying of the atoning victim often becomes evident only from the broader context in which the reference to it occurs.

Exactly what makes Jesus' suffering humanity redemptive, too, is open to different interpretations. One line of thought is that the sinful Christian's contemplation of the suffering of the cross, or of the divine love and mercy demonstrated in this experience, helps cleanse the soul of sins by stirring empathy and hence contrition. The pathos of the event inspires the pious to realize that they need to render something to Christ – faith, penitence, a greater effort at virtue – for what God the son and the father accepted on the human race's behalf. The pain and death of the cross can also be viewed as redemptive because they constitute an alternative to the penalty of death other mortals owe. Christ is the substitutive, sinless human being who agrees to die to offset the debt of the rest of the sinful race. Although certain Latin church fathers rejected the notion that Christ ransomed the human race from the devil, since it implied the devil had a legitimate claim to humanity that required compensation,[16] the term "ransom," which has biblical origins, appears in Carolingian literature. Sometimes it expresses the concept of substitution, at times in conjunction with references to Christ's death or blood as the payment of a "price."[17] Sometimes the payment seems to be received by death or Satan; in other texts, God appears to be recompensed, along the lines of the notion of sacrifice that I will discuss shortly.

A somewhat different soteriological perspective is that Christ was crucified, suffered, and died to set a model that mortals are expected to imitate. To do so brings the soul into conformity with Christ, leading it away from sin and rendering it worthy of imitation of his resurrection and ascension.[18] Especially in later Carolingian literature, imitation is often linked with penance and participation in the liturgy and sacraments. As is occasionally indicated, the model is one Christians are capable of following because of the inherent likeness the human being possesses with God, through Adam's creation in God's image and the sacrament of baptism. Adam fell away from that image through sin, but despite this all mortals

[15] See A. N. Chester, "Hebrews: the Final Sacrifice," in *Sacrifice and Redemption: Durham Essays in Theology*, ed. S.W. Sykes (Cambridge, 1991), 57–72.
[16] Aulén, *Christus Victor*, 49–51, 56; J. N. D. Kelly, *Early Christian Doctrines* (New York, 1978), 375–376. See Pelikan, *Christian Tradition* 1.148–149. [17] See 1 Cor. 6.20, 7.23.
[18] Karl Morrison, *The Mimetic Tradition of Reform in the West* (Princeton, 1982), 134, 155–156.

can imitate Christ – in his life as well as his death – because Christ imitated us in the incarnation, making possible, in baptism, the renewal of the connection lost in the fall. Particularly in writings from the later Carolingian period, though this is hinted in some from earlier decades, the idea emerges that *imitatio Christi crucifixi* is the basis of membership in his "body" the church. The ideal for such behavior is found in the saints, both insofar as their struggles against evil emulated the son of God's conquest, and insofar as they imitate his crucified human nature: his "patience" or endurance of torment, his obedience to God's will, his weakness, humility, love for other mortals, and death with its bloodshed.

Finally, the redemptive significance of Christ's suffering and death may be described in terms of his oblation. Based on the epistle to the Hebrews, the passion is understood to conform with yet surpass its models, pagan and Jewish sacrifices. Christ is the priest / victim who offered his own sinless flesh, a final, perfect oblation prefigured in the repeated sacrifices of the ancients and rendering them obsolete.[19] The exact significance ascribed to the crucifixion as sacrifice, however, and the benefits it is understood to bring differ in ways that generally reflect different facets of ancient sacrificial ritual. Sometimes, the principal consequence seems understood as the atonement of God the father for human sin. By offering a propitiatory sacrifice to God, Jesus made it possible for his father to exercise mercy, remit sins, and release mortals from their owed punishment. At other times, though very often these ideas are fused, the sacrifice of the cross is suggested to be efficacious mainly since it allowed the shedding of Christ's blood.[20] Sometimes, as suggested above, the blood is viewed as the substance that the son offered the father; or what flowed from Jesus' wounds – blood, water, or both – was made available to humanity, a sanctifying agent that washes or heals mortal souls of their sins, particularly when the faithful receive baptism and the eucharist or undertake penance. Often where the blood is stressed, it seems, Christ's death is interpreted as sacrificial less in the sense of a sacrifice made to God than of a joint offering by Jesus and his father. It is the "price" they together paid – Christ his human life, God his only son – for mortals' redemption. The liquid released through this oblation represents its final stage and proof of its completeness. In writings

---

[19] See Gerald Bonner, "The Doctrine of Sacrifice: Augustine and the Latin Patristic Tradition," in *Sacrifice and Redemption*, 101–117.   [20] Cf. Chester, "Hebrews," 65.

that focus on the eucharist, especially from the decades after Charlemagne's reign, the emphasis is on the sacrifice offered by the son, the father, or the faithful in the mass as a source of healing food and drink. The offering on the cross brings redemption because it makes Jesus' body and blood available for mortals' consumption, in line with his speech at the last supper. In keeping with the version of that discourse in John 6, the notion of the crucified Jesus as sacrificial food may be linked with the idea that he is the bread of heaven: the son of God descended to earth and the cross to provide mortals with the celestial bread and drink that the blessed will eternally enjoy in paradise.

The foregoing overview only indicates the most basic teachings that lie behind the texts and artistic productions examined in the remaining chapters. The next task is to clarify the thinking about the crucified Christ of the scholars associated with Charlemagne's court, in particular that which emerges from their writings against Byzantine iconodulism and Spanish Adoptionism.

CHAPTER 2

The passion and Christological inquiry at the court of Charlemagne

Sometime between the late 780s and 800, most likely towards the later part of this period, the Anglo-Saxon scholar, Alcuin, and his pupil, Joseph the Scot, presented their Frankish king, Charlemagne, with a collection of *carmina figurata*, a poetical style in which designs are shaped from the verses so that image and text form a single unit. Originally containing two compositions by Alcuin and four by Joseph, the anthology emulated an earlier collection of panegyric figure poems that Publilius Optatianus Porphyry had made for the fourth-century Roman emperor, Constantine I.[1] Alcuin's opening contribution to the series for Charlemagne, however

---

[1] Alcuin, *Carm.* 6, *MGH PLAC* I, ed. E. Dümmler (Berlin, 1881), 224–225; Joseph, *Carm.* 3–6, *MGH PLAC* I.152–159. Alcuin's second *carmen figuratum* = *Carm.* 7, *MGH PLAC* I.226–227. See Ulrich Ernst, *Carmen figuratum: Geschichte des Figurengedichts von den antiken Ursprüngen bis zum Ausgang des Mittelalters* (Cologne, 1991), 9–11 on the different types of *carmina figurata*, 97–142, 168–188 on Porphyry and the early Carolingian poets. Porphyry's *carmina figurata* are published in *Publilii Optatiani Porfyrii Carmina*, ed. J. Polara (Turin, 1973). Some of Porphyry's poems are *Umrissgedichte*, in which the lengths of verses vary so that the poem creates the shadow outline of a form. The Carolingians preferred to compose geometric *Gittergedichte*, the method used by Porphyry for some of his poems, in which each verse is given the same number of letters; these are evenly spaced on the page to form a square or rectangular grid. Certain letters in the text are highlighted, generally by the use of differently colored ink; thus distinguished, they form new verses that run vertically, diagonally, and in other configurations through the main text, outlining geometric designs. (I take the terms *Umrissgedichte* and *Gittergedichte* from Ernst, *Carmen figuratum*, 9–10.)

The date of the Carolingian collection has been variously fixed at 780–790 (Dieter Schaller, "Die karolingischen Figurengedichte des Cod. Bern. 212," in *Medium Aevum Vivum: Festschrift für Walther Bulst*, ed. H. R. Jauss and D. Schaller [Heidelberg, 1960], 22–47, at 36–42, 47; repr. with additions in idem, *Studien zur lateinischen Dichtung des Frühmittelalters* [Stuttgart, 1995], 1–26, 399–403) and c. 800 (Elisabeth Dahlhaus-Berg, *Nova antiquitas et antiqua novitas: typologis-*

(fig. 1),[2] centers on a theme not occurring in Porphyry's figure poetry, though it is expressed in *carmina figurata* possibly known to the Carolingian poet by the sixth-century writer, Venantius Fortunatus and the eighth-century Anglo-Saxon missionary, Boniface: the cross's glorification through Christ's victory in the crucifixion.[3] Alcuin's verses allude to Jesus' suffering and dying, but this is the tormented, yet heroic warrior whose pain testifies to the paradox of the conquest he and the cross together achieve. The "great victim," shepherd, and highest king triumphs by handing over his life. Evil's defeat comes through the passion, harrowing of hell, resurrection, and final judgment together, as Christ destroys the "harsh war-bearer," "carries off the prize," and heals the ages. The enemy is less sin than death and Satan, a single adversary locked in a cosmic battle with the son of God. The two forces struggle over the human soul, not within it but confronting it from the outside. Jesus prevails because he is armed with the cross. Empowered – "crowned" – by the miraculous substance of his blood (signified by the red ink of the poem's cross figure), the cross is the object through which God revealed heaven to earth, the divine throne and judgment seat of the eschaton.[4]

Poetry, penitence, and prayer

As historians of the Carolingian era have long recognized, the eighth- and ninth-century west witnessed a dramatic growth in the cult of the omnipotent savior and his power-filled cross. Alcuin's *carmen figuratum* is one of

---

che Exegese und isidorianisches Geschichtsbild bei Theodulf von Orléans [Cologne, 1975], 184–186; Ernst, *Carmen figuratum*, 177, 195–197). Summary of the debate in Ferrari, *Liber s. crucis*, 215–216, see 51–69 on the genre.

[2] Burgerbibliothek Bern, cod. 212, fol. 123r. This codex (ninth to tenth century) is the only surviving manuscript. See Schaller, "Karolingischen Figurengedichte," 22–47; Hans Bernhard Meyer, "*Crux decus mundi*: Alkuins Kreuz- und Osterfrömmigkeit," in *Paschatis sollemnia. Studien zu Osterfeier und Osterfrommigkeit*, ed. B. Fischer and J. Wagner (Basel, 1959), 96–107.

[3] See Ernst, *Carmen figuratum*, 149–157, 160–167.

[4] Alcuin, *Carm.* 6, *MGH PLAC* 1.224–225; Ernst, *Carmen figuratum*, 170–174. References to the cross's redness from Christ's blood (line 37) and in the figural verses or *versus intexti* (the verses that create the figure) indicate that the original copy used red ink for the design, as does Burgerbibliothek Bern, cod. 212. Joseph also notes the combination of red and black inks: Joseph, *Carm.* 4, *MGH PLAC* 1.154–155 lines 23–24; *Carm.* 6, *MGH PLAC* 1.158–159 *versus intextus*. This coloring system seems to have been traditional since Porphyry; see Elizabeth Sears, "Louis the Pious as *Miles Christi*: the Dedicatory Image in Hrabanus Maurus' *De laudibus sanctae crucis*," in *Charlemagne's Heir: New Perspectives on the Reign of Louis the Pious*, ed. P. Godman and R. Collins (Oxford 1990), 605–628, at 625.

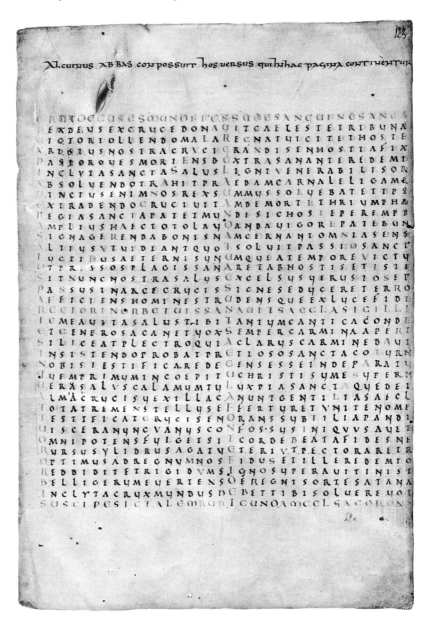

countless works testifying to this devotional focus.[5] Leaving aside the artistic evidence discussed in the next chapter, among the most important sources to which we may turn in order to appreciate the cult's strength in

[5] The contours of this development, with its impact on religious architecture and the liturgy, are traced in Carol Heitz, *Recherches sur les rapports entre architecture et liturgie à l'époque carolingienne* (Paris, 1963), see esp. 145–146.

the early Carolingian period are poems by Alcuin and his contemporaries associated with Charlemagne's court, men from different regions of Europe who enjoyed the Frankish monarch's patronage in the late eighth and early ninth century.[6] The dominant images of Christ presented in the extant verse by this group of writers, both longer compositions and brief inscriptions and dedications for books, paintings, altars, and other objects, center on his status as the one God. Where the subject is the crucifixion or the cross – sometimes only briefly mentioned in short *tituli* or in longer poems mainly concerned with other themes, sometimes explored at length – the focus is usually the destruction of evil and manifestation of his heavenly majesty. As in the famous Anglo-Saxon poem, "The Dream of the Rood," the revelation of divinity that occurs in the passion itself blends into the subsequent demonstrations of power. Even as he died, a *titulus* for a cross by Alcuin announces, Christ the new brazen serpent lifted the world "above the stars," washing away every sin in his blood. He saved mortals from their enemy as the Exodus lamb saved its people, guiding them across the Red Sea.[7] An alphabetic poem by the same author celebrates Christ's membership in the Trinity and his crucifixion as, again, the means by which he drew the human race back with him to God.[8] A figure poem with vertical *versus intexti* by a bishop Bernowin or Angilbert of St.-Riquier hails the lord from David's seed, the source of eternal life, the victor, judge, salvation, hope, redeemer, and king of kings.[9] A poem for Paul the Deacon that Peter of Pisa composed in 783, in Charlemagne's voice, acclaims the powerful Christ who sent Paul to the Frankish court: Jesus is the divine creator and redeemer, the only-begotten son who was clothed in human flesh in order to save mortals and displayed his omnipotence by miracles; he "smashed hell, treading underfoot the dominions of

[6] Mary Garrison, "The Emergence of Carolingian Latin Literature and the Court of Charlemagne (780–814)," in *Carolingian Culture: Emulation and Innovation*, ed. R. McKitterick (Cambridge, 1994), 111–140, esp. 111–117; Peter Godman, *Poetry of the Carolingian Renaissance* (London, 1985), 1–33; idem, *Poets and Emperors: Frankish Politics and Carolingian Poetry* (Oxford, 1987), 38–92; Franz Brunhölzl, *Histoire de la littérature latine du moyen âge*, vol. 1.2: *La Fondation de l'Europe à l'époque carolingienne*, trans. H. Rochais (Leiden, 1991), 7–73.

[7] Alcuin, *Carm.* 116, *MGH PLAC* 1.346. See Arwed Arnulf, *Versus ad picturas: Studien zur Titulusdichtung als Quellengattung der Kunstgeschichte von der Antike bis zum Hochmittelalter* (Munich, 1997), 149 n.645.

[8] Alcuin, *Carm.* 1, *MGH PLAC* 4.3, ed. K. Strecker (Berlin, 1923), 904–907. Cf. idem, *Carm.* 109.10, 114.1, 5, 117, *MGH PLAC* 1.337, 344–345, 346–347.

[9] Bernowin (?), *Carm.* 11, *MGH PLAC* 1.416, see also *Carm.* 10, *MGH PLAC* 1.416. See Arnulf, *Versus*, 151; Ernst, *Carmen figuratum*, 202–209, esp. 203 and Abb. 61; Brunhölzl, *Histoire* 1.2.276.

the dragon whose weapon, death, was devastating the world with hatred," and then led the captives of the underworld to paradise.[10] Verses by the Visigoth Theodulf, who wrote the *Opus Caroli regis (Libri Carolini)* in 790–793 and became bishop of Orléans by 798, describe the eucharist's channeling of the salvation triumphantly achieved on the cross. The sacred banquet of the victorious priest, blood and flesh of the lamb who brings fear to the dragon, conquers the lion, and bears away the world's sins, enables mortals to participate in the heavenly feast.[11]

These notions of the crucifixion's triumph and the sanctity it bestowed on the cross are mirrored in contemporary hagiographical writing, a literary genre strong throughout the early Middle Ages but that increased in popularity during the Carolingian period. *Vitae* in both prose and poetry celebrate the exploits of martyrs and saints who defend the faith against its enemies, bring the pious to heaven, vanquish the devil's troops, reverse the laws of nature, and by a multitude of other means, either directly or through their relics, display supernatural force.[12] Whether or not it is explicitly stated, these heroes were understood to resemble their savior in his own victories over Satan. The *Vita Sturmi* composed by Eigil of Fulda in 794 develops a theme widely found in early medieval hagiography when it describes how Sturm, "through the power of the Holy Spirit," drove demon spirits from the sinful and "cured souls that had been infected with the poisonous doctrines of error."[13] In his poem on the bishops, kings, and saints of York, Alcuin tells how dirt that absorbed water with which King Oswald's bones had been washed forced a demon to flee the man it was tormenting. Often the wonders – healings and conquests of demons in particular – are accomplished through the sign or relics of the cross. Eigil records

[10] Karl Neff, *Die Gedichte des Paulus Diaconus: kritische und erklärende Ausgabe* (Munich, 1908), no. 12.60. Trans. Godman, *Poetry,* 82–87, esp. 82–85, stanzas 1–3.

[11] Theodulf, *Carm.* 58, MGH PLAC 1.554. Cf. idem, *Carm.* 1, 55, MGH PLAC 1.445–452 (esp. lines 257–314), 553; and idem, *Carm.* 69, MGH PLAC 1.558–559, esp. lines 1–22. See Josef Szövérffy, *Die Annalen der lateinischen Hymnendichtung, ein Handbuch,* vol. 1: *Die lateinischen Hymnen bis zum Ende des 11. Jahrhunderts* (Berlin, 1964), 202–205, 184–312 on the hymn tradition of both the early and later Carolingian periods.

[12] See Valerie Flint, *The Rise of Magic in Early Medieval Europe* (Princeton, 1991), 173–199, on the powers associated with the sign of the cross; J. M. Wallace-Hadrill, *The Frankish Church* (Oxford, 1983), 75–93. The classic study remains Peter Brown, *The Cult of the Saints: Its Rise and Function in Latin Christianity* (Chicago, 1981).

[13] Eigil, *Vita Sturmi,* ch. 3, MGH SS 2, ed. G. H. Pertz (Hanover, 1829), 366–367, trans. C. H. Talbot, "The Life of Saint Sturm," in *Soldiers of Christ: Saints and Saints' Lives from Late Antiquity and the Early Middle Ages,* ed. T. F. X. Noble and T. Head (University Park, PA, 1995), 165–187, at 168.

that Sturm, spending the night in the wilderness, protected himself by making the sign of the cross on his forehead before he "went forth to the fray against the devil."[14] The *Vita S. Amandi* recalls that as a boy the saint, walking one day across the Ile d'Yeu, encountered a huge serpent. Amand prostrated himself in prayer, but it was only when he made the sign of the cross before the snake that it fled, never to return to the island.[15] Occasionally manufactured crosses are associated with supernatural events.[16] Such stories, and variations on them, are grounded in the conviction of authors, readers, and listeners that the holy men and women are "soldiers of Christ" whose miracles, virtues, and glorification imitate those of other saints, Old Testament heroes, and of Jesus himself, both the wonders he performed while alive and the triumph of his crucifixion and resurrection.[17]

Other early Carolingian writings invite comparisons between the conquering Christ and lay princes, who are lauded for their divinely blessed governance, virtue, and battles against their and the church's enemies. Probably the most famous early Carolingian document that is viewable in these terms is the prologue that King Pepin III added to an expanded edition of the *Lex Salica* in c. 763/764, a document reissued by Charlemagne in c. 798. Although the crucifixion is not mentioned, the announcement that Christ watches over the Frankish people, soldiers, and their monarch, and the proud description of the Franks' courage, greatness, and successes in battle under his protection, evoke a savior who is himself omnipotent and unconquerable.[18] Much the same can be said of the papal letters to Pepin and his sons asking them to wage war as leaders of God's chosen people, or of the liturgical prayers and services for the Frankish ruler and his army that develop in the eighth century,

---

[14] *Alcuin: the Bishops, Kings, and Saints of York*, ed. and trans. P. Godman (Oxford, 1982), lines 392–426; Eigil, *Vita Sturmi*, ch. 7, *MGH SS* 2, 369, trans. Talbot in *Soldiers of Christ*, ed. Noble and Head, 171–172. Most of the material in Alcuin's poem, which he probably wrote while still teaching at York (before his move to Francia), comes from Bede. See Alcuin, *Carm.* 99.19–21, 109.21, 110.6, 114.5, *MGH PLAC* 1.327, 336, 339, 341, 345.

[15] *Vita S. Amandi*, ch. 1, ed. B. Krusch, *MGH SRM* 5 (Hanover, 1910), 428–449, at 432.

[16] E.g. Alcuin, *Bishops, Kings, and Saints*, lines 243–264, 427–454. Cf. *Vita S. Samsonis*, chs. 48–49, in *La Vie de Saint Simson*, ed. R. Fawtier (Paris, 1912), 144–145, cited in Flint, *Rise of Magic*, 265.

[17] Noble and Head, eds., *Soldiers of Christ*, esp. xiv–xviii, xxxi–xl.

[18] J. N. Hillgarth, ed., *Christianity and Paganism, 350–750* (Philadelphia, rev. edn. 1986), 93; *Lex Salica, 100 Titel-Text*, ed. K. A. Eckhardt, Germanenrechte N. F. (Weimar, 1953), 82–84, 86–90. Discussed in Lawrence Nees, *A Tainted Mantle: Hercules and the Classical Tradition at the Carolingian Court* (Philadelphia, 1991), 128–129.

surviving in ninth-century Carolingian sacramentaries. The most frequent models for the behavior associated with good rulership in these
and other early texts are Old Testament figures like David and Moses;
yet the desire expressed for divine protection of the earthly prince and
the praise of his greatness, especially his military prowess, conform
with and must have encouraged devotion to Christ the powerful king.
Sometimes, the parallel is openly drawn, as in the early Carolingian litanies for rulers and their armies, a custom instigated in Francia under
Pepin III and continued by Charlemagne and his heirs. The appeals of
the *laudes regiae* that heaven guard the glorious Frankish monarch and
liberate his followers from evil, through the cross and the passion, alter-
nate with shouts of acclamation to the Christ who vanquishes and
rules.[19]

In some verse panegyrics, too, references to Charlemagne's military
skills and virtue are interwoven with praise of the triumphant divine
majesty. *De conversione Saxonum*, variously attributed to Lull of Mainz,
Paulinus of Aquileia, and Angilbert of St.-Riquier, juxtaposes Charles'
defeat of the Saxons in 777 with the crucifixion, descent into hell, and resurrection.[20] The three episodes belong to a single victory, by which the son of
God "took away the horrid accusations of infamous death," "washed away
the crime of the world in the waves of the Jordan," "marked the pious with
the purple dye of his precious blood," "snatched the plunder from the jaws
of vile-spewing Celydrus," and "despoiled the hot sands of Cocytus."[21]
Paul the Deacon was probably the author of a cross-figure poem that hails
the omnipotent king Christ as the route to salvation, bringer of peace, and
the sun of salvation; the accompanying commentary indicates that the epi-
thets used for Christ may also apply to Charles.[22] In its entirety, the group of
carmina figurata that Alcuin and Joseph gave Charlemagne links the

---

[19] Of the papal letters, e.g. *Epp.* 10, 11, 17, 32, 33, *Codex Carolinus*, ed. W. Gundlach, *MGH Epp.* 3
(Berlin, 1892), 469–657, at 501–507, 514–517, 538–540. See Susan A. Rabe, *Faith, Art, and Politics at
Saint-Riquier: the Symbolic Vision of Angilbert* (Philadelphia, 1995), 62. On the liturgical texts,
Michael McCormick, *Eternal Victory: Triumphal Rulership in Late Antiquity, Byzantium and the
Early Medieval West* (Cambridge, 1986), 342–384; idem, "The Liturgy of War in the Early Middle
Ages: Crisis, Litanies, and the Carolingian Monarchy," *Viator* 15 (1984), 1–23; Ernst Kantorwicz,
Laudes Regiae: a Study in Liturgical Acclamations and Mediaeval Ruler Worship (Berkeley, 1946),
13–111.

[20] (Attributed to Angilbert), *Carm.* 7, *MGH PLAC* 1.380–381. Discussed with translation in Rabe,
Faith, Art, and Politics, 54–71.

[21] *Carm.* 7, *MGH PLAC* 1.380–381 lines 17–21; trans. Rabe, *Faith, Art, and Politics*, 63.

[22] St. Gall, Stiftsbibliothek, Cod. Sangall. 899, p. 10; Ernst, *Carmen figuratum*, 199–202.

monarch with Christ and the cross as well as the emperor Constantine, to whom Porphyry had presented the collection that likely served as a model for the Carolingian series.[23] While Alcuin's first poem honors the cross and the divine, crucified Christ, his closing poem praises the Frankish king with classicizing terminology reminiscent of Porphyry's acclamations of his Roman ruler (fig. 2).[24] Between these two compositions, Joseph's four *carmina figurata*, the second through fifth pieces in the anthology, laud the passion, the glorified cross, and Christ the ruler, savior, and returning judge together with the virtuous Charles, a source of hope for his people to whom the poet attributes wisdom, faith, love, and truth.[25] The mainly cruciform figures of the Carolingian collection link the cross to both Charles' and Christ's *virtus* and kingship, invoking, without stating directly, its function since Constantine as emblem of both earthly and heavenly imperium.[26] A parallel between Charlemagne and Christ is again implied in a seventh *carmen figuratum* by Theodulf of Orléans evidently added to the collection at Charles' request, after its original presentation to the monarch. This has the same cross figure as Alcuin's *carmen figuratum* to the cross; it imitates the Anglo-Saxon poet's composition, but perhaps with the intention of surpassing it, one of several indications of the known rivalry between the two scholars. Theodulf's work, a prayer for the Frankish king who is a model of piety and source of hope for his people, begins with a startlingly vivid description of the lord's divinity under whom Charles reigns. Christ, bestower of eternal peace, "roars from the summit of the world," the great redeemer and "shining lamp of the Church" who came to earth as "splendor flowing from a lamp" to propitiate the ages and who gives "the heavenly tribunal," the last phrase appropriately written along the cross figure's arm.[27]

[23] See above, n. 1. See Godman, *Poets and Emperors*, 56–59; Ferrari, *Liber s. crucis*, 214–215.

[24] The poem is mistakenly attributed to Joseph in Burgerbibliothek Bern, cod. 212, fol. 125v; see Schaller, "Karolingischen Figurengedichte," 34–36.

[25] Joseph, *Carm.* 4, MGH PLAC 1.154–155. See Godman, *Poets and Emperors*, 58–59; on noble virtue in other literature of the period, Hans Hubert Anton, *Fürstenspiegel und Herrscherethos in der Karolingerzeit* (Bonn, 1968), 80–131.

[26] See Andreas Alföldi, *"Hoc signo victor eris*: Beiträge zur Geschichte der Bekehrung Konstantins des Grossen," in *Pisciculi: Studien zur Religion und Kultur des Altertums, Franz Josef Dölger zum 60. Geburtstage dargeboten von Freunden, Verehrern und Schülern*, ed. T. Klauser and A. Rücker (Münster, 1939), 1–18.

[27] Theodulf, *Carm.* 23, MGH PLAC 1.480–482 lines 1–14, 19, 20, noting Charles' request for the poem at line 40. On the rivalry between Theodulf and Alcuin, Nees, *Tainted Mantle*, esp. 112–120; Dieter Schaller, "Der junge 'Rabe' am Hof Karls des Grossen," in *Festschrift Bernhard Bischoff zu seinem 65. Geburtstag dargebracht*, ed. J. Autenrieth and F. Brunhölzl (Stuttgart, 1971), 123–141.

Figure 2. Alcuin's *carmen figuratum* honoring Charlemagne. Burgerbibliothek Bern, cod. 212, fol. 125 verso

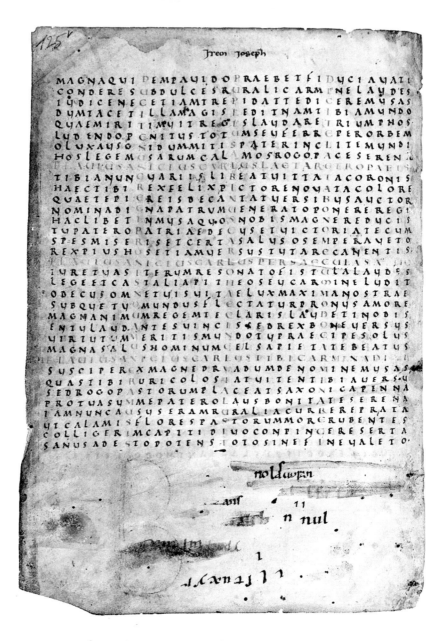

In all the writings mentioned above, whether the principal subject is the passion or the valor of the saints or lay princes, Jesus is remembered as the immortal son of God. Although his human weakness and death on the cross may be remembered for the contrast they present to his omnipotence, the crucifixion is primarily his defeat of sin/death/Satan, a victory continued in his resurrection, ascension, and return, and in the successful combats of his saints and Christian rulers against the adversaries of their faith. The power unleashed through the passion spilled out in Christ's blood and radiated from his cross, signs of his universal dominion that recall his conquest and still protect his followers.

Yet while such themes represent some of the most notable refrains in surviving early Carolingian literature of the crucifixion, it is important to realize that certain writings by members of Charlemagne's court circle develop different lines of thought such as were noted in the last chapter, ones that encourage more direct meditation on the son of God's crucified body and death for sin's redemption. The literature highlighting these concerns is more limited than that celebrating the victorious Christ, and the remembrance of his mortal humanity is typically so imbued with allusions to the divinity that it is impossible to forget this is God. But even so, within the broad boundaries of devotion to the divine savior characteristic of eighth- and early-ninth-century piety, a wider range of ideas about the crucifixion is discernible than is often recognized. A few poems by scholars at one time associated with Charlemagne's court, for instance, seem intended to inspire thoughts about Christ's torments, not only in order to underscore his victory – the focus of Alcuin's *carmen figuratum* on the cross – but because recollection of the crucifixion's sorrows has value in its own right. In the hymn on Lazarus by Paulinus of Aquileia, most likely written after he became archbishop of Friuli in c. 787, Jesus' pierced body is likened to Mary's broken jar, with the water and blood from the side wound prefigured in the ointment she poured on his feet. The reader seems expected to contemplate the bleeding, executed humanity while remaining aware of its significance as the divinely endowed means of the world's salvation. The imagery of suffering is overshadowed in later stanzas by that of the force whereby Christ "struck down death by dying himself," a power contained in the liquid from his side, prefigured in the water from the rock struck by Moses and signifying the "sweet honey" of divine doctrine.[28]

The redemptive purpose of Jesus' sorrowful death is more forcefully evoked in a poetical inscription by Alcuin for an altar containing relics of the cross and saints, though again in verses that also stress the divine nature. Alcuin urges the faithful approaching the altar to turn to the eternal lord who voluntarily suffered for them. Both the wonder of his

---

[28] Paulinus, *Carm.* iv, *L'Œuvre poétique de Paulin d'Aquilée*, ed. D. Norberg (Stockholm, 1979), 103–113, esp. stanzas 4–7; 38–45; trans. Godman, *Poetry*, 90–107. See Szövérffy, *Annalen* 1.197–198.

passion and its pathos should inspire them to weep for their sins, of which they are redeemed through the immaculate blood poured out by the "life of the world." Eternally enthroned in heaven, Christ is the source of saving food and drink, whose agony demonstrated the divine love for humanity that mortals should imitate by humble submission to God's will. In the present and at the last judgment, the penitent Christian's sadness over the sins that made the crucifixion necessary is critical to salvation.[29]

Verses by Theodulf on the wounds of martyrdom, possibly written close to his death in 821 when he was in exile in Angers after having been accused of complicity in the revolt of Bernard of Italy against Louis the Pious, contemplate the "stigmata of death" that the crucifixion left in Jesus' feet, hands, and side. The wounds serve as reminders to the faithful of what God endured on their behalf, and, perhaps, as a source of hope that salvation will be the final outcome of Theodulf's own, sorrowful condition. Asking why the marks remained visible on the "author of life" even after the resurrection, the poet offers a fourfold answer: they served as proof to his disciples that their resurrected lord had indeed died; they inspire God's mercy when the son who "wished to suffer such wounds" for sinful mortals intercedes on their behalf; they lead the elect to sing perpetual praises to God for their salvation through the passion; and on the last day they will cause the wicked to be crushed with sorrow as they see "him whom they transfixed."[30]

The redemption achieved through Christ's human mortality, humility, and willing tolerance of pain are implicitly recalled, as well, where hagiographical texts point to the saints' possession of comparable qualities. While Eigil admired Sturm as the powerful conqueror of demons, he also remembered him as a holy man who aspired to the harshness of the eremetical life, teaching his followers the Christ-like virtues of "patience, mildness, humility, longanimity, faith, hope, and charity."[31] Such writings not only supported the Carolingian tendency to praise the son of God for his divine majesty and to remember his cross's power, by proclaiming the saints' miracles; they indirectly drew attention to the model of virtue Jesus

---

[29] Alcuin, *Carm.* 109.11, *MGH PLAC* 1.337; cf. *Carm.* 2, *MGH PLAC* 4.3.907–910, an alphabetic poem expressing the poet's anxiety as a sinner, his fear of hell and the devil's power.

[30] Theodulf, *Carm.* 11, *MGH PLAC* 1.465–466 esp. lines 10–33, cf. *Carm.* 54, *MGH PLAC* 1.553; Godman, *Poetry*, 15.

[31] Eigil, *Vita Sturmi*, chs. 3–4, *MGH SS* 2, 366–367, trans. Talbot in *Soldiers of Christ*, ed. Noble and Head, 168–169.

established in his human nature. Some early Carolingian penitential literature more clearly affirms the crucifixion's role as an example of patience (in
the sense of both suffering and tolerance) and humility, which all the faithful (not only saints) should imitate. Paulinus of Aquileia's *Liber exhortationis*, completed for Count Henry of Friuli c. 795, draws on the *De vita
contemplativa* of Julianus Pomerius, Gregory I's *Moralia in Job*, and the Latin
translation of St. Basil's *Admonitio ad filium spiritualem* in order to steer the
count towards virtue compatible with his noble station.[32] As in Paulinus'
poetical lament, *Versus confessionis de luctu poenitentiae*, Christ is chiefly
viewed as the judging and fearsome, though merciful lord; the crucifixion's
powerful victory is implied to offer a paradigm for how Henry should combat
vice by pursuing virtue.[33] But the portrayal of the divine warrior-ruler who
leads and protects the count is sometimes intertwined with references to
Jesus' lowliness during his earthly life, including his passion, which should
inspire prayer, confession and penance, obedience to God, and imitation of
his humility and rejection of this world.[34] The count must be aware of the
love displayed in the crucifixion; for "if our sinless lord and savior deigned
to love us sinners with such affection and such love that what we suffer he is
witnessed to have himself suffered, why do we, who are sinful, and who are
able to redeem our sins through charity, not love him with as much perfect
love as he loved us, to the point that he even handed over his own son to
death for us sinners?"[35] For Paulinus, probably mindful of the struggle
against Hispanic Adoptionism contemporary with this treatise, the
mystery of the union of two natures in Jesus' person makes the death of
the universe's creator an even more urgent call to repentance.[36]

Similarly, Alcuin often urges recipients of his correspondence to persevere in faith and virtue by referring to their savior's defeat of Satan. A letter
sent to an anonymous pupil c. 793–795 exhorts him to fight the devil and the
world's temptations, since Christ "conquered the ancient enemy in order

---

[32] Paulinus, *Liber exhortationis*, PL 99.197–282. See Anton, *Fürstenspiegel*, 83–84; Rosamond
McKitterick, *The Frankish Church and the Carolingian Reforms, 789–895* (London, 1977), 166–168.

[33] Paulinus, *Carm.* VI, *Œuvre poétique*, 126–130; see idem, *Liber exhort.* e.g. 8, cf. 51, 58, PL 99.203B-
204A, 254B, 266.

[34] Paulinus, *Liber exhort.* 13, 15, cf. 27–28, 52, 54, PL 99.208A, 209A, 222–225, 257–258, 261B/C. On
Carolingian penitential practices, see Raymund Kottje, "Busspraxis und Bussritus," in *Segni e
riti nella chiesa altomedievale occidentale*, 2 vol., Settimane di studio del Centro italiano di studi
sull'alto medioevo, 33 (Spoleto, 1987), 1.369–403.

[35] Paulinus, *Liber exhort.* 52, PL 99.257B.

[36] See *ibid.* 21, PL 99.215A. Cf. Theodulf, *Carm.* 9, MGH PLAC 1.464.

that we be able to conquer. He triumphed on the cross in order that we should reign in heaven."[37] Writing to Paulinus c. 798, with the Adoptionist controversy in mind, Alcuin reminds the bishop that the son of God's triumph "gave us the power of trampling upon serpents and scorpions and of conquering all heretical depravities," and he asks Paulinus to join him as "comrades on Christ's battlefields and soldiers in one rank under the banner of the holy cross."[38] But in some of the letters, the need for the remission of sins provided by the dying redeemer is a more pronounced theme. Redemption comes through memory that it was "for love of you he hung on the cross, fixed with nails," Aethelhard of Canterbury is told in 793.[39] As other correspondents are informed, attainment of heaven depends first on imitation of Christ's pain, humility, love, and obedience, a model that the clergy emulate by striving for the salvation of sinners and other Christians follow by penitent acceptance of the clergy's judgment of sin.[40] In particular, there is a special urgency to the reminders in numerous letters that Jesus' blood, largely seen in these instances as testimony to his sacrificial death, is the supreme source of purgation, a washing of sin available in confession and penance.[41] Such lines of thought are also implicit to some of the discussion of virtue and vice in the treatise, *De virtutibus et vitiis*, that Alcuin wrote for Count Wido, though, for the most part, specific allusion is not made here to the exemplary status of the crucified Christ.[42]

---

[37] Alcuin, *Ep.* 34, *MGH Epp.* 4, ed. E. Dümmler (Berlin, 1895), 77 lines 4–5.

[38] Alcuin, *Ep.*139, *MGH Epp.* 4.221 lines 5–7. In a letter of c. 800 consoling Charles on the death of Queen Liutgard, Alcuin refers to the divine victory over death and hell, by which "mors mortua est, flammea romphea, custos paradisi, sanguine Christi extincta": *Ep.* 198, *MGH Epp.* 4.328 lines 2–3.   [39] Alcuin *Ep.* 17, *MGH Epp.* 4.45 lines 33–34.

[40] Alcuin, *Ep.* 38, *MGH Epp.* 4.81 lines 19–20; *Ep.* 94, *MGH Epp.* 4.139 lines 12–13; *Ep.* 138, *MGH Epp.* 4.218 lines 9–13; *Ep.* 173, *MGH Epp.* 4.287 lines 4–17; *Ep.* 181, *MGH Epp.* 4.300 lines 22–24; *Ep.* 281, *MGH Epp.* 4.440 lines 15–23; *Ep.* 300, *MGH Epp.* 4.458 lines 33–35.

[41] "Numquid aliquis peccator talis est, qui Christi sanguine purgari non possit; et tam profunda scelerum voragine demersus, ut misericordia Christi eum mederi non possit? Quid aliud sit, qui hoc dicit, nisi ut Christus frustra mortuus sit? Frustra autem mortuus est, si aliquos non potest vivificare, qui nobis veniam cotidie donat": Alcuin, *Ep.* 245, *MGH Epp.* 4.395 lines 6–10. See *Ep.* 58, *MGH Epp.* 4.101 lines 37–39; *Ep.* 125.184 lines 23–25; *Ep.* 223, *MGH Epp.* 4.367 lines 8–11.

[42] Alcuin, *De virtutibus et vitiis liber ad Widonem comitem*, *PL* 101.613–638. This was his most popular work, judging from the number of extant manuscripts: Donald Bullough, "Alcuin's Cultural Influence: the Evidence of the Manuscripts," in *Alcuin of York: Scholar at the Carolingian Court*, ed. L. A. J. R. Houwen and A. A. MacDonald (Groningen, 1995), 1–26, at 3, 20–23 and n. 7 citing Paul Szarmach, most recently in "The Latin Tradition of Alcuin's *Liber de Virtutibus et Vitiis*, cap. xxvii-xxxv," *Mediaevalia* 12 (1989, for 1986), 13–41. See also Luitpold Wallach, *Alcuin and Charlemagne: Studies in Carolingian History and Literature* (Ithaca, NY, 1959), 231–254; Anton, *Fürstenspiegel*, 84–86.

More directly, both the crucified savior's powerful victory and the redemptive, purging effect of Jesus' death and blood are recurring refrains of the tract on the penitential psalms that Alcuin completed in 802. This is based on an abbreviated version of Cassiodorus' commentary on the psalms, but, as Donald Bullough has observed, Alcuin shifts the perspective to "moral-theological" concerns.[43] Christ is the warlord who overcame Satan and damns the devil by his justice, releasing the human race from its chains.[44] But he is also the model of patience who was beaten and mocked yet remained silent before his accusers, whose humility is justly compared to hyssop, the lowliest of herbs; and he is the bleeding sacrifice of propitiation who "offered himself for all, so that the world might receive the salvation it did not merit."[45]

Any assessment of early Carolingian thought about the crucifixion, moreover, must acknowledge that the varied ideas presented in the literature just surveyed were recalled in liturgical prayers, music, and ritual, devotional forms which, as noted in chapter 1, not only helped define the boundaries of doctrine but were means by which belief was expressed. As they joined in the liturgy and received the sacraments, monks, clergy, and laity of both the eighth and ninth centuries engaged in a seasonal journey of remembrance and celebration that encompassed the most humble aspects of Jesus' humanity and his manifestations of eternal divinity.[46] The possible generalizations about ritual practice and its signification in either the eighth or the ninth century are limited by the complicated heritage of Gallican, Roman, and other liturgical sources already in circulation in Frankish territories before Charlemagne's reign; the gradual diffusion of the "Gregorian" sacramentary sent by Pope Hadrian to Charles (the *Hadrianum*); the different interpolations into copies of that book and

---

[43] Alcuin, *Expositio pia ac brevis in psalmos poenitentiales*, PL 100.569–596; Donald Bullough, "Alcuin and the Kingdom of Heaven," in idem, *Carolingian Renewal: Sources and Heritage* (Manchester, 1991), 161–240, at 172–174. Alcuin incorporated the tract into a devotional handbook for Arno of Salzburg. The penitential orientation of the entire work is noted in the preface, where it is remarked that salvation comes "humilitate et misericordia Christi": *In psalmos poenitentiales, PL* 100.574B.

[44] Alcuin, *In psalmos poenitentiales, PL* 100.584A/B (to Ps. 50.6–7), 590D-591A (to Ps. 101.20), 594C (to Ps. 142, title). Cf. *In psalmos graduales* (in the same handbook), *PL* 100.619–638, at 625D (to Ps. 123.6–7), 627A (to Ps. 125, title), 628B/C (to Ps. 126, title), 634A/B (to Ps. 131.1).

[45] Alcuin, *In psalmos poenitentiales, PL* 100.586D-587A (to Ps. 50.21), see 581 (to Ps. 37.15, 18), 584D-585A (to Ps. 50.9) 593B/C (to Ps. 129.4, 5). Note the plea for Christ's mercy in ibid., *PL* 100.583B/C (to Ps. 50.4); cf. *In psalmos graduales, PL* 100.632D (to Ps. 129.4), 637A/B (to Ps. 132.2).

[46] See Donald Bullough, "The Carolingian Liturgical Experience," *Studies in Church History* 35 (1999), 29–64; McKitterick, *Frankish Church and Carolingian Reforms*, 138–142.

different supplements prepared for it; and the continued usage of other liturgical books throughout the ninth century, including non-*Hadrianum* Gregorian sacramentaries as well as "eighth-century Gelasian" sacramentaries.[47] Yet in spite of these factors, the core structures of the main rites conducted in Carolingian churches and many of the individual orations remained the same.[48] The spectrum of belief about the crucified Christ that the liturgy communicated to early as well as later Carolingian faithful, therefore, may be basically understood if we look at the principal characteristics of the feasts and sacraments understood to commemorate the passion, death, and resurrection, insofar as these devotional forms are evident from documents in circulation under Charlemagne but keeping in mind that the ceremonial I discuss was known in the ninth century. Because my interest in this chapter is chiefly in the early Carolingian court, I will also point to literature that suggests how its scholars, specifically, interpreted the crucifixion in light of the same observances.

If we first turn to the Easter liturgy, the feast that most strenuously celebrates Christ's victory against death and Satan, we find that the dominant image it conveyed to Carolingian Christians was the triumphant transition from darkness to light. That transition, they understood, mirrored the movement from the harrowing of hell and Christ's tomb to the resurrec-

---

[47] See Roger E. Reynolds, "The Organization, Law, and Liturgy of the Western Church, 700–900," *NCMH* 2.617–621. Gregorian and supplemental materials published in *Le Sacramentaire grégorien*, 3 vols., ed. J. Deshusses (Fribourg, 1971–1982). The complexity of Carolingian liturgical developments is lucidly discussed in Frederick Paxton, *Christianizing Death: the Creation of a Ritual Process in Early Medieval Europe* (Ithaca, 1990), esp. 154–161. Also worthy of note is Jean Deshusses, "Les sacramentaires: état actuel de la recherche," *Archiv für Liturgiewissenschaft* 24 (1982), 19–46.

[48] Indispensable to tracing these developments in the Carolingian era are the Gregorian sacramentary materials edited by Deshusses (above, previous note); also *Les Ordines romani du haut moyen âge*, 5 vols., ed. Michel Andrieu (Louvain, 1931–1961); Cyrille Vogel, *Introduction aux sources de l'histoire du culte chrétien au moyen âge* (Spoleto, 1966); J. Deshusses and B. Darragon, eds., *Concordances et tableaux pour l'étude des grands sacramentaires*, 3 vols. (Fribourg, 1982–1983). In examining the prayers for the rites and sacraments studied below I have principally relied on the "eighth-century Gelasian" sacramentary type as represented by the Gellone Sacramentary (Paris, BNF, lat. 12048) and on the Gregorian as represented by the *Hadrianum*. For the former, see *Sacr. Gellon.*, *CCSL* 159–159A. The *Hadrianum* is published in *Sacramentaire grégorien* 1, ed. Deshusses, 85–348, based on Cambrai, MS 164, the oldest surviving complete copy and the only one without alterations, made for Notre-Dame at Cambrai in 811–812. I have also consulted Deshusses and Darragon, eds., *Concordances et tableaux*, for parallel orations in older sacramentaries in circulation during the early Carolingian period and in the *Hucusque* supplement of Benedict of Aniane (*Sacramentaire grégorien* 1, ed. Deshusses, 351–605), which gradually, during the ninth century, became the preferred supplement to the *Hadrianum*.

tion, from the old law to the new, sin to redemption and the promise of
future glory. Ritually, this was suggested by performative emulation of
darkness's defeat: the blessing of the baptismal font, the baptism of infants
and adult catechumens, who were then dressed in white robes, their confirmation, the new illumination of the formerly darkened church, the
singing of the *Gloria* and the restoration of Christ's body and blood to the
faithful at the Easter mass, deprived of both since the previous Thursday.[49]
The prayers of the Easter vigil and mass hail the restoration of light to the
world, Christ's eternal kingship and the second Adam's triumph over
sin/death/the devil, and anticipate his return in language echoed in some
of the poetry noted earlier. With chains of death destroyed, the victorious
Christ now ascends from hell, opening the entrance to eternity. According
to prayers in the Gellone Sacramentary, a version of the "eighth-century
Gelasian" sacramentary probably copied in 790–c. 804,[50] the son of God is
the lamb who "destroyed death by dying and repaired life by rising," who
like the passover lamb freed his people by his poured blood.[51] Another
oration in the same sacramentary, decorated with a crucifixion image that I
will examine in the next chapter, describes Christ's death as the vehicle of
his harrowing of hell and defeat of Satan's forces.[52] The celebration of new
life and victory in the Easter ceremonies was reinforced by the lections
from Genesis, Exodus, and the gospel accounts of the resurrection,[53] and in
sermons and homilies designated for the feast. Those identified for Easter
in the homiliary that Charlemagne commissioned from Paul the Deacon,
actually excerpts from patristic sources, present the passion, descent into
hell, and resurrection as together elements of the victory foreshadowed in
the liberation from Egypt.[54] Paulinus of Aquileia's poem, *De resurrectione*

[49] See *Ord.* 12, *Ordines romani* 2.463–464 (last quarter eighth to mid ninth century); *Ord.* 24–28 (c. 750–800), *Ordines romani* 3.287–413, see *Ord.* 31 (c. 850–900), *Ordines romani* 3.491–509.

[50] Jean Deshusses, Introduction, *Sacr. Gellon.*, CCSL 159A. xviii–xxi; idem, "Le sacramentaire de Gellone dans son contexte historique," *Ephemerides liturgicae* 75 (1961), 193–210. Cf. B. Moreton, *The Eighth-Century Gelasian Sacramentary: a Study in Tradition* (Oxford, 1976), 187–191.

[51] *Sacr. Gellon.*, CCSL 159, nos. 721, 2011, see 675–701, 715–737, 2009–2010, 2012; *Hadrianum, Sacramentaire grégorien* 1, ed. Deshusses, nos. 359–391.　　[52] *Sacr. Gellon.*, CCSL 159, no. 2009.

[53] See *Ord.* 31, *Ordines romani* 3.500–501, 504.

[54] See "L'homéliaire de Paul Diacre," in R. Grégoire, *Les Homéliaires du Moyen Age: inventaire et analyse des manuscrits* (Rome, 1966), 71–114, at section 2, "Partie d'été," nos. 1–3, p. 93 (Jerome, Bede, Maximus of Turin), section 2 no. 5, p. 93 (Gregory I). Cf. the Easter homilies in the early ninth-century homiliary of Ottobeuren, Grégoire, *Homéliaires*, 142–160. The classic study of the homilaries remains Henri Barré, *Les Homéliaires carolingiens de l'école d'Auxerre* (Vatican, 1962). On the use of such texts, see Thomas L. Amos, "Preaching and the Sermon in the

Domini, indicates a similar understanding of Easter. The pain and death of the crucifixion are described, but the event appears principally as the first stage in the triumph that climaxed when Jesus rose from the dead, a victory already revealed in the liquid from his side that washed away sins, the "rosy blood" that erased the decree against humanity.[55]

The crucified son of God's victory was also remembered in the feast of the *Inuentio crucis* (May 3), originally a celebration of the pre-Carolingian Gallican liturgy, and in the Roman *Exaltatio crucis* (September 14); both feasts are recorded in Gelasian sacramentaries and the ninth-century Gregorian sacramentaries that include supplements containing Gallican forms. While the prayers of these ceremonies sometimes recall the redemption of sins through Christ's suffering, the emphasis, as in many of the early Carolingian verse inscriptions for the cross altars where such rituals would have taken place, is on the reversal of Adam's fall through the second Adam and the cross's sanctification. Both Christ and the cross are the tree of life, and the cross is his banner that guards the pious against evil.[56] Carolingian baptismal orations, too, stress the devil's defeat, Christ's protection of the faithful from Satan, and spiritual renewal.[57] Carolingian clergy encouraged the restriction of baptism to Easter and Pentecost, including that of infants, though exceptions occurred.[58] As in the rest of the Easter liturgy, here too performance was critical: in the extratemporal

footnote 54 (*cont.*)

   Carolingian World," in *De ore Domini: Preacher and Word in the Middle Ages*, ed. T. L. Amos et al. (Kalamazoo, 1989), 41–60; and the different viewpoint of R. Emmet McLaughlin, "The Word Eclipsed? Preaching in the Early Middle Ages," *Traditio* 46 (1991), 77–122.

[55] Paulinus, *Carm.* xii, *Œuvre poétique*, 150–156, stanzas 3, 6, 7; cf. Theodulf, *Carm.* 55, *MGH PLAC* 1.553.

[56] *Sacr. Gellon.*, CCSL 159, nos. 944–948 (*Inuentio sanctae crucis*); 1448–1451 (*Exaltatio sanctae crucis*); *Hadrianum, Sacramentaire grégorien* 1, ed. Deshusses, nos. 690–692 (*Exaltatio sanctae crucis*); *Gregorianum Paduense, Sacramentaire grégorien* 1, ed. Deshusses, 609–684, nos. 421–423 (*Inuentio sanctae crucis*). Cf. the prayers for the benediction of a cross: *Sacr. Gellon.*, CCSL 159, nos. 2447–2450, e.g. 2447: "Benedic domine hanc crucem tuam per quam eripuisti mundum a potestate[m] demonum et superasti passionem tuam subiessorem peccati qui gaudebat in preuarigatione[m] primi hominis per uetitum lignum. Sanctifica domine istut signaculum passionis tuae ut sit inimicis tuis obstaculum et credentibus in te perpetuum perfici uixillum."

[57] *Sacr. Gellon.*, CCSL 159, nos. 702–714, esp. 704a, 704b, see 2215–2386, e.g. 2217, 2218 (on the sign of the cross), 2220, 2229, 2304, 2317c. See also *Hadrianum, Sacramentaire grégorien* 1, ed. Deshusses, nos. 373–374, 980–981, cf. nos. 985–986; *Ord.* 11, *Ordines romani* 2.417–447, cf. *Ordines romani* 3.81–92; Julia Smith, "Religion and Lay Society," *NCMH* 2.656–660; Arnold Angenendt, "Der Taufritus im frühen Mittelalter," *Segni e riti* 1.275–336.

[58] Smith, "Religion and Lay Society," 657–658; Peter Cramer, *Baptism and Change in the Early Middle Ages, c. 200–c.1150* (Cambridge, 1993), 137–139.

realm of the sacrament, early Carolingian commentaries indicate, the faithful were held to witness and participate in the crucified Christ's experience of both death and resurrection, with the solemnity of the former event subsumed in the glory of the latter.[59] For Theodulf of Orléans and the other respondents to Charlemagne's questionnaire about baptism, in 809–812, performative obedience to the model of Jesus' suffering for human sin leads, as Paul indicated in Romans 6.4, to emulation of his victory over Satan, resurrection, and ascension. The immersion in the baptismal font recalls and imitates the death and entombment and constitutes a washing of sins in Christ's blood. Emerging from the water to a new life as Jesus rose from the tomb, a life that, however imperfectly, foreshadows future beatitude, the new Christian is clothed in white to signify his inner cleansing and regeneration; for Christ, who "was made sin for us and suffered for us," took away our "sordid vestments," deleting our sins so that we may rise with him. The head is anointed with chrism and girded with a white headband, symbolizing again the new purity, and, for the first time, the newly baptized receive the eucharist.[60]

In the mass itself, certain elements of the liturgy were understood in Charlemagne's court circle to remind participants of Christ's power, the source of the sacral efficacy that the eucharist mediates to the faithful. The poem on the eucharist by Theodulf noted near the beginning of this chapter indicates how closely the sacrament could be linked with the divine conqueror.[61] The eighth-century Tassilo Chalice, decorated with the blessing Christ between the *Alpha* and *Omega*, the four evangelists with their symbols, and four busts probably of saints, evokes the eucharist's function to connect the faithful with the holy creatures in heaven and their

---

[59] Cf. Cramer, *Baptism and Change*, 156–158, 160–167.

[60] E.g. Leidrad, *Liber de sacramento baptismi*, PL 99.853–872, esp. 861–863; Magnus of Sens, *Libellus de mysterio baptismatis*, PL 102.981–984; Theodulf, *De ordine baptismi*, PL 105.223–240; Amalarius, *Epistula de baptismo*, in *Amalarii Episcopi opera liturgica omnia*, 3 vols., ST 138–140, ed. J. M. Hanssens (Vatican City, 1948–1950), ST 138.235–251. The response of Odilbert of Mainz is a compilation of patristic sources: Friedrich Wiegand, *Erzbischof Odilbert von Mailand über die Taufe* (Aalen, 1972), 27–37. Cf. Alcuin, *Epp.* 134, 137, MGH *Epp.* 4.202–203, 210–216. For a list and discussion of other Carolingian baptismal expositions, see Susan A. Keefe, "Carolingian Baptismal Expositions: a Handlist of Tracts and Manuscripts," in *Carolingian Essays: Andrew W. Mellon Lectures in Early Christian Studies*, ed. U. Blumenthal (Washington, DC, 1983), 169–237. See also Cramer, *Baptism and Change*, 187–188; Bullough, "Carolingian Liturgical Experience," 57–60. The order of ritual elements could vary: Angenendt, "Taufritus" (discussion), 323–324.

[61] Theodulf, *Carm.* 58, MGH PLAC 1.554. See also Alcuin, *Carm.* 100.1, 104.3, 5, 105.4, MGH PLAC 1.327–328, 331, 332.

supernal lord, engaging them in a feast that anticipates the eschaton.[62] The chapters on the eucharist and liturgical vessels in Theodulf's great treatise, the *Opus Caroli regis (Libri Carolini)* describe both as *res sacratae*, material things, specially consecrated by God in Christ, that parallel Christ's own role as the mediator between God and humanity by channeling divine power to mortals. Through the blood received in the eucharist, Theodulf declares in the chapter on the sacrament, the faithful gain remission of sins and are protected from diabolical attack.[63]

But for early Carolingian scholars as for their ninth-century successors, at its core the mass was a sacrifice made possible by Jesus' oblation of humanity. It was a ceremony that remembered his sacrificial death, a model of patience that mortals imitate in the mass and by penance and good works, even as it acclaimed the power miraculously displayed through his body and blood.[64] Unlike the treatises that will be examined in chapter 6 where the sacramental function of the mass and the eucharist become an explicit concern, the early and later Carolingian *expositiones missae* and other discussions of the mass show relatively little interest in defining the relationship between the eucharistic "body" and "blood" and the flesh and blood of the crucifixion. Nevertheless, an unquestioned doctrine in all of them is that, in the mass, body and blood are offered for mortals' consumption, just as Christ gave those substances to his followers at the last supper and on the cross. The divinely blessed offering of the son of God, granted by heaven to earth and given back to God in the sacrament, is perpetually consumed by the angels at the heavenly altar and simultaneously available to the gathered faithful, whose communion is both the symbol and the accomplishment of their union with one another and their creator. The sacrifice of the mass that commemorates Jesus' death is the foundation of that miraculous joining.

[62] Stift Kremsmünster, Austria; Günther Haseloff, *Der Tassilokelch* (Munich, 1951); Jean Hubert, J. Porcher, W. F. Volbach, *L'Empire carolingien* (Paris, 1968), 210, fig. 191.

[63] Theodulf, *Opus Caroli regis* 2.27.290–296, esp. 291, 2.29.301–302, 4.2.492 lines 11–15. Cf. (for other early *expositiones missae*), *Expositio missae Romanae*, PL 96.1481–1502, esp. 1495–1496; *Primum in ordine*, PL 138.1173–1186, esp. 1180D-1181A; *Dominus vobiscum*, PL 147.191–200; Hanssens, ed., *ST* 138.108, 283–338. Also J. A. Jungmann, *Missarum Sollemnia: eine genetische Erklärung der römischen Messe*, 2 vols. (Vienna, 1958, 4. expanded edn.), 1.113–115 and n. 55; Brunhölzl, *Histoire* 1.2.88, 274–275.

[64] Such themes are already heard in some earlier expositions of the mass: e.g. Gregory I, *Dialogues* 4, esp. 57–62; Germanus, *Quomodo solemnis ordo ecclesiae agitur*, in *Ordo Antiquus Gallicanus: der gallikanische Messritus des 6. Jahrhunderts*, ed. K. Gamber (Regensburg, 1965), 17–21; Isidor, *De ecclesiasticis officiis* 1.14–15, 18, *CCSL* 113, ed. Christopher Lawson (Turnhout, 1989), 16–22. On the history of the *expositiones missae*, A. Wilmart, "Expositio missae," *Dictionnaire d'archéologie chrétienne et de liturgie*, ed. F. Cabrol et al., vol. 5 (Paris, 1922), 1014–1027.

Alcuin's commentary on John 6, based on Augustine, stresses the union of the faithful with God through their consumption of the body of Christ that is the living bread from heaven. The son of God descended from the father to death on the cross in order to provide mortals with flesh that is the source of eternal life. By "spiritually" eating and drinking his body and blood, the Christian becomes one with his savior, who is himself one person with two natures, just as one loaf is made from many grains and wine from many grapes.[65] Such ideas and the even more intricate patterns of meaning that later Carolingian commentators derive from the mass (examined in chapter 4) accord with its complex liturgy: the ritual, lections, music, and prayers leading up to and accompanying the offertory; the subsequent prefaces glorifying the divine majesty (the *Vere dignum* and *Sanctus*); the prayer *Te igitur*, which through the diffusion of supplemented Gregorian sacramentaries in the ninth century gained new significance as the beginning of the mass "canon," that is the actual consecration of the bread and wine as body and blood; and the following oration or sections of the *Te igitur*. Among its multiple themes, this last-named portion of the ceremonial invokes the saints, asks the lord to remember his faithful and to transform the mass elements into blood and body, links the eucharist with the last supper and passion, remembers the resurrection, ascension, and the sacrament's prefiguration in the sacrifices of Abel, Abraham, and Melchisedech, and requests that an angel bear the mass oblation to the heavenly altar.[66]

---

[65] Alcuin, *Commentaria in S. Joannis Evangelium* 3.15, PL 100.834–837. Cf. *Expositio in Epistolam Pauli Apostoli ad Hebraeos* 10, PL 100.1077B/C (Chrysostom); idem, *Ep.* 137, *Epp.* 4.211–212, esp. 212 lines 14–19; cf. Theodulf, *Opus Caroli regis* 2.27.292–293; *Primum in Ordine*, PL 138.1180D-1181A; and the earliest commentary on the mass by Amalarius, *Missae expositionis geminis codex*, 1: *Codex seu scedula prior*, ST 138.255–265. Where the mass is discussed in the early Carolingian tracts on baptism, the union it effects between the recipient and Christ is also emphasized: e.g. Amalarius, *Epistula de baptismo*, ST 138.248; Theodulf, *De ordine baptismi*, PL 105.239C-240; Leidrad, *De sacramento baptismi*, PL 99.866–867; Magnus, *De mysterio baptismatis*, PL 102.984B; Odilbert, in Wiegand, ed., *Erzbischof Odilbert*, 36; cf. Alcuin, *Ep.* 134, MGH *Epp.* 4.203. The concept of the eucharist and hence indirectly of the crucifixion itself as a divinely empowered offering to God lies behind the diffusion of votive masses in the Carolingian period, among them Alcuin's: see Jean Deshusses, "Les messes d'Alcuin," *Archiv für Liturgiewissenschaft* 14 (1972), 7–41; *Sacramentaire grégorien* 2, ed. Deshusses, 25–27; Mayke de Jong, "Carolingian Monasticism: the Power of Prayer," NCMH 2.648. Some of the masses have a clear penitential focus, e.g. Alcuin's *Pro petitione lacrimarum*, in which the *Praefatio* links penitence with memory of Christ's death for sin: Deshusses, "Messes d'Alcuin," no. 40.

[66] *Sacr. Gellon.*, CCSL 159, nos. 1895–1955; *Hadrianum, Sacramentaire grégorien* 1, ed. Deshusses, nos. 2–20; *Ord.* 1–4, *Ordines romani* 2.1–170, cf. *Ord.* 5–9, *Ordines romani* 2.209–336. See Vogel, *Introduction aux sources*, 127–133; on the significance of the *Te igitur*, Jungmann, *Missarum Sollemnia*, 2.128–136, 173–190.

Finally, already under Charlemagne though more noticeable in later decades, some aspects of the liturgy suggest a desire among monks and clergy to meditate on the chronological progression of Jesus' time on earth and on the passion's historicity. One consequence is again, implicitly, attention to his human suffering and dying as temporally distinct episodes from the subsequent triumph in the resurrection. *De sancta cruce*, one of Alcuin's votive masses, includes orations evoking the crucifixion both as a victory by which Christ's blood sanctified the "life-giving cross" and as the sacrifice "on the altar of the cross." Possibly it was to be celebrated on Friday, the day of the crucifixion and annually of the *Adoratio crucis*.[67] For the monks of Tours, perhaps during Alcuin's own time there, the daily offices of terce, sext, and none signified the progression of Jesus' experience of the passion.[68] An impressive effort to commemorate the passion's historical circumstances and, in particular, the instruments of its torment is suggested by the list of relics in Angilbert's Church of the Holy Savior at St.-Riquier – among them relics of the cross, of Jesus' garment, of the sponge from which he drank while on the cross, of the bread he gave to the disciples at the last supper, of the column where he was whipped, of the ropes with which he was tied, of the rock on which the cross was erected, and of the nails. These objects were certainly at St.-Riquier by the end of the ninth century and possibly counted among the relics collected during Angilbert's abbacy from c. 789 to 814. The *capsa major* housing them, Carol Heitz has argued, offered a "summary of Christ's life" much as did the fraction of the host in the mass and the reliefs depicting the nativity, passion, resurrection, and ascension placed in different locations in the church. Together with the altars there dedicated to the cross and various saints, the centers of cult on their feastdays, this ordering of the building's interior recalled the full historical compass from the incarnation to the ascension and the saints' triumphs in Christ's name, within a liturgical space symbolizing the timeless reality of the heavenly Jerusalem.[69]

[67] Deshusses, "Messes d'Alcuin," nos. 15–19; idem, *Sacramentaire grégorien* 2, nos. 1835–1840.

[68] A. Wilmart, *Precum libelli quattuor aevi karolini* (Rome, 1940), esp. 25–26. Cf. the so-called *De psalmorum usu*, PL 101.465–508, at 507; Isidor, *De eccl. offic.* 1.19, CCSL 113.23. See Bullough, "Alcuin's Cultural Influence," 20 and n. 62; idem, "Alcuin and the Kingdom of Heaven," 170, 217 n. 43.

[69] See Heitz, *Recherches*, 102–106, esp. 103 (list of relics), 106. Cf. Angilbert, *Institutio de diversitate officiorum*, in *Corpus Consuetudinem Monasticarum* 1 (= CCM 1), ed. K. Hallinger (Siegburg, 1963), 291–303. On the four reliefs, Rabe, *Faith, Art, and Politics*, 117–119, though cf. Roger Collins, "The Carolingians and the Ottonians in an Anglophone World," *Journal of Medieval History* 22 (1996), 97–114, at 107.

The most dramatic and extended memorial of the passion in the early as well as later Carolingian liturgy, though, occurred in Holy Week, the final days of Lent that kept alive the hope for Easter, reiterated belief in Christ's power, and anticipated the second coming, while remembering the sacrifice for sin that paved the way for the Easter celebration.[70] The climax to the passion's liturgical rehearsal began on Holy Thursday. On that day, Carolingian Christians remembered Jesus' washing of the disciples' feet at the last supper, his betrayal and arrest, and they participated in the ceremonial reconciliation of penitents, the blessing of the chrism for the Easter baptism, and the final mass before Easter, commemorating the last supper and the eucharist's foundation. Certain prayers for the Thursday reconciliation of penitents recall the son of God's divinity, his conquest of the devil, and the terrors of the final judgment.[71] In one oration for the dying penitent found in Gellone, unique to this sacramentary, the passion's grief and its awesome force are remembered in a moving description of nature's fear and horror when Christ died yet simultaneously conquered.[72] But overall the emphasis is on solemn recollection of Jesus' humility, the progression towards his death on the cross, and remorse for the sinfulness that made the crucifixion necessary. Thus prayers for the Thursday vespers reflect on the connection between the last supper, the eucharist, and the crucifixion as sacrifice, on Christ's example of humble innocence, patience, and gentleness in washing the disciples' feet and in his passive, innocent confrontation with Judas.[73] For the seventh-century theologian, Isidor of Seville, whose treatise *De ecclesiasticis officiis* was well known in the early

---

[70] Isidor, *De eccl. offic.* 1.28(27)-31(30), CCSL 113.31–35; *Sacr. Gellon.*, CCSL 159, nos. 565–570 (*In palmas*), 588–640 (*In caena Domini*), 641–666 (*In passione Domini*); see also *Ord.* 23–24, 26–32, *Ordines romani* 3.265–297, 325–524.

[71] See *Sacr. Gellon.*, CCSL 159, nos. 588–610, esp. 596 a,b (unique to *Gellone*).

[72] "Cuius passione cuncta conmota sunt et euentum dominici uulneris elementa tremuerunt. Expauit dies non solida nocte et suas tenibras mundus inuenit. Stetit sub incerte lumine dies [dies] clausus, etiam lux ipsa uisa est mora cum christo. Ad hoc enim omnis claritas migrauit in noctem ne sacrilegium cernere uideretur. Clauserat enim suos oculus celum ne in cruce aspiceret saluatorem. Et mundus ipse testis esse non potuit ut solus aspicerit qui percussit cuius dolore plaga nostra curata est et lapsus nostros aliena ruina suscepit. Tremuerunt elementa mundi sub uno percusso cuius uulnere captiuitas resoluta est. Dum enim occiditur christus cuncta renata sunt, et dum moritur omnia surrexerunt per ipsius maiestatem quem laudant angeli": *Sacr. Gellon.*, CCSL 159, no. 606; cf. Deshusses and Darragon, eds., *Concordances et tableaux* 1, no. 3661.

[73] *Sacr. Gellon.*, CCSL 159, nos. 608, 633–640; *Hadrianum, Sacramentaire grégorien* 1, ed. Deshusses, nos. 328–337. Cf. *Orationes ad reconciliandum paenitentem Feria V in Caena Domini, Sacramentaire grégorien* 3, ed. Deshusses, nos. 3963–3976.

Carolingian period and used in the *Opus Caroli regis*, the Thursday ceremonies celebrate the transition from the Old Testament to the true paschal sacrifice, and the washing of the vessels, altars, and interior of the church recalls and emulates the humility of the footwashing.[74]

The main Good Friday service, typically at sext or none, adumbrated the Easter celebrations in its recitations of Osee 6.3 and verses from Habbacuc 3, while portents of the approaching triumph were also heard in the passion narrative usually read from John.[75] Some of the service's prayers hail the divine victory over death and Satan; others indirectly remember it through appeals to God to crush evil and convert heretics, Jews, and pagans, and, again unique to Gellone, to aid the Frankish king in his battles against the church's enemies.[76] Angilbert of St.-Riquier choreographed the Good Friday *Adoratio crucis* at his abbey to honor the entire Trinity, ritual affirmation that Christ was fully divine as well as human.[77] Nevertheless, the primary aim of the office at St.-Riquier and in other Carolingian churches was to involve the clergy and laity in a solemn, sustained rehearsal of the crucifixion and its sadness that paralleled the individual Christian's inner imitation of Christ's sufferings through penitence and virtue. In both the early and later Carolingian periods, *ordines* show, the Friday afternoon service began with the clergy's silent entrance into the darkened church.[78] The passion according to John, read by a deacon whom an early eighth-century *ordo* notes should be barefoot,[79] usually concluded with the stripping of the altar, so that only a bare altar remained to symbolize the deprivation the crucifixion caused.[80] No

---

[74] Isidor, *De eccl. offic.* 1.29 (28), CCSL 113.32.

[75] See Gerhard Römer, "Die Liturgie des Karfreitags," *Zeitschrift für katholische Theologie* 77 (1955), 39–93, esp. 44.

[76] *Sacr. Gellon.*, CCSL 159, nos. 642–666, esp. 654–655; cf. *Hadrianum, Sacramentaire grégorien* 1, ed. Deshusses, nos. 338–355.

[77] Rabe, *Faith, Art, and Politics*, 124–126; Heitz, *Recherches*, 77–102.

[78] Amalarius notes that it was the Carolingian custom to extinguish all lights from Thursday to Easter, while in Rome the church was darkened only during the Good Friday hours commemorating the crucifixion: *Liber de ordine antiphonarii* 44, ST 140.79–80. Cf. *Ordo Casinensis II*, CCM 1.107–123, at 116–117. Through the Carolingian practice, Amalarius claims, participants are taught "facere de laetitia in tristitiam, de gaudio in moestitiam."

[79] *Ord.* 23, *Ordines romani* 3.271; see Römer, "Liturgie des Karfreitags," 62–63. On the preference for John's passion, A. Chavasse, "La structure du Carême et les lectures des messes quadragésimales dans la liturgie romaine," *La Maison-Dieu* 31 (1952), 76–119, at 95–97.

[80] Some early Carolingian *ordines* specify that the stripping is conducted *in modum furantis*: *Ord.* 27, 28, *Ordines romani* 3.356, 399; cf. *Ord.* 24, 29, *Ordines romani* 3.293, 295, 442.

eucharistic consecration took place between Thursday and the Easter mass. Only a "Mass of the Presanctified Elements" was conducted on Friday, generally after the *Adoratio crucis*, using consecrated bread from Thursday and unconsecrated wine that the clergy and laity received in silence. From then the church stayed dark and without music until Easter.[81] Jesus' sacrifice for sin, the faithful's imitation of his exemplary humility and pain, and their rage at the Jews' iniquity for killing him are also key refrains of the homilies assigned to both Thursday and Friday in Paul the Deacon's homiliary.[82]

These liturgical elements, together with the sources that reveal how scholars associated with Charlemagne's court understood their significa- tion, suggest a general tendency to combine memories of Christ's human suffering and death with proclamations of his divine omnipotence and heavenly rule from the cross. The degree to which attention is brought to crucified, mortal humanity or immortal divinity, however, to the redemp- tive value of the former or the salvation powerfully won by the latter, varies depending on the rite or sacrament in question. Good Friday in par- ticular, and to some extent the mass, engaged the clergy and laity in prayer and ritual that centered on remembrance of the human death for human sin. A comparable range of perspectives is implied by the other literature examined so far in this chapter. Most of these texts directly or indirectly recall Christ as the divine king who defeated sin/death/the devil, but at times the same and other writings, perhaps most markedly certain works by Alcuin, offer different views of the crucifixion's purpose: the redemp- tion effected in Jesus' atoning sacrifice and its purging blood, the model of suffering humility set on the cross, the contrition stirred by memory of his dying, and variations on these themes. Although early Carolingian schol- ars usually tied meditation on the death to celebration of the divine triumph, such different lines of thought attest the divergent purposes for which they wrote, the different contexts in which they remembered their crucified savior, and sometimes, as is especially clear with Alcuin, a per- sonal preoccupation with sin and penitence.

---

[81] *Ord.* 24, 27, 28, 29, 30A, 30B, 32, *Ordines romani* 3.294, 357–358, 400–401, 443, 456, 471, 520; see Römer, "Liturgie des Karfreitags," 86–89.

[82] See "Homéliaire de Paul Diacre," Grégoire, *Homéliaires, section* I, "Partie d'hiver," nos. 104–106, p. 92 (Leo, Bede); "Homiliary of Ottobeuren," ibid., 142–160. Cf. Isidor, *De eccl. offic.* 1.30 (29), *CCSL* 113.34, who stresses Christ's victory yet affirms the function of the Good Friday liturgy to inspire emulation of his "patience."

Byzantine iconodulism and Spanish Adoptionism

The doctrinal tracts to which I now turn were written within this climate
of belief in Charlemagne's entourage, and insofar as they discuss the crucifixion they reflect that climate in important respects. All three major
theological issues that occupied the court in the 790s and early ninth
century – Byzantine doctrines of the artistic image, the *filioque* clause of
the creed, Hispanic Adoptionism – led to the articulation of noticeably
Christocentric teachings. In line with the intense cult of the divine savior
in the Frankish church, all three inspired Carolingian scholars vigorously
to uphold Christ's divinity and kingship against perceived challenges to
this central doctrine of Christian faith. At least initially, however, motivated most likely by both theological predilections and a desire to undermine the Byzantine claims of ecumenicity regarding the second Nicene
council of 787,[83] the errors attributed to the Carolingians' opponents
were defined by reference to the great debates about Christ that had
taken place in the early church. The controversy over the *filioque*, the
phrase that Carolingians inserted into the Nicene–Constantinopolitan
creed to clarify the procession of the Holy Spirit from the son as well as
the father, will not concern us here, since the dispute was principally
Trinitarian – focusing on the relationship among the three persons of the
Trinity – and did not involve significant discussion of the crucifixion. In
the *Opus Caroli regis*, which attacks Greek ideas about images and image
worship, Theodulf identifies Charlemagne's views (the treatise is in the
king's voice) with Trinitarian orthodoxy; yet the critical point of faith on
which the opposition to the east turns here is not simply Jesus' divinity
but his two natures in one person, and this leads to consideration of his
passion's significance. This is also true in the Carolingian tractates against
the Adoptionists. Both the *Opus Caroli regis* and the anti-Adoptionist literature develop arguments based on their adversaries' presumed failure to
accept the early conciliar decrees that, in the son of God, full divinity is
indissolubly and perfectly joined to full humanity. One proof of this
truth, the Carolingian authors thought, was the crucifixion; for that event
could only have been salvific if the human being fixed to the cross was the

[83] See John C. Cavadini, "Elipandus and his Critics at the Council of Frankfort," in *Das frankfurter Konzil von 794*, ed. Berndt, 2.787–807, at 804–807.

one immortal deity, and conversely, if God had indeed become a man, so that God was capable of dying. Like so much other early Carolingian literature, then, the *Opus Caroli regis* and the writings against Adoptionism frame their discussions of the passion with praise of the son of God's eternal impassibility and power. But unlike the texts discussed so far, they offer formal, theological defenses, against opponents believed to have fallen into heresy, of visions of Christ that center on the divine union with passible, mortal flesh.

The *Opus Caroli regis*

In 787, the second council of Nicea met in Byzantium under the empress Irene and her son, Constantine VI, to proclaim the restoration of the cult of images in the Greek empire. Charlemagne's official response to the Byzantine acts was initially written by the Visigoth, Theodulf of Orléans, in 790–793. It was edited by him with the help of other scholars linked with the court, among them probably Alcuin; but the recent publication of the excellent new edition by Ann Freeman makes it clear that even after extensive revisions of some portions, the writing remains essentially Theodulf's, a highly distinctive prose characterized, in particular, by the inflexible, driven quality it gains from the frequent syllogisms.[84] The work had only limited circulation in the Carolingian period. Plans to send a copy to Rome were apparently abandoned when it was learned in 793, from Hadrian's reaction to a list of proposed chapter headings for the *Opus Caroli regis*, that the pope supported Nicea II.[85] Despite Hadrian's acceptance of the Greek council, iconodulism was formally condemned at the synod of Frankfurt in 794; yet only two complete copies of the *Opus* and a

---

[84] See Freeman, ed., *Opus Caroli regis*, esp. 23–50. On Theodulf's authorship and the circumstances of production, also Freeman, "Carolingian Orthodoxy and the Fate of the *Libri Carolini*," *Viator* 16 (1985), 65–108, with references to her earlier articles on the treatise. I have most recently discussed the *Opus'* theology in "Memory, Instruction, Worship: 'Gregory's' Influence on Early Medieval Doctrines of the Artistic Image," in *Gregory the Great: A Symposium*, ed. J. C. Cavadini (Notre Dame, 1996), 181–215, at 188–192; see also my, "Images, Scripture, the Church, and the *Libri Carolini*," *Proceedings of the Patristic, Medieval, and Renaissance Studies Conference* 16/17 (1993), 53–76, and "Matter, Spirit, and Image in the *Libri Carolini*," *Recherches Augustiniennes* 21 (1986), 163–184. On Alcuin's probably limited contribution to the treatise, Bullough, "Alcuin and the Kingdom of Heaven," 182–187.
[85] Freeman, "Carolingian Orthodoxy," 87–92.

fragment of a third have survived from the ninth century, and few echoes of its contents occur in later Carolingian literature.[86] Nevertheless, the *Opus Caroli regis* was the single, most ambitious work of literature from Charlemagne's court, a document intended to show the Frankish king's superiority to the rulers of Byzantium on every possible level. As Theodulf seeks to demonstrate, behind the countless wrongs attributed to the Greeks – regarding not only artistic images but also politics, aesthetics, the liberal arts, and other subjects – lies a thorough-going departure from the biblically grounded orthodoxy to which Rome had remained loyal since the first council of Nicea, most importantly the orthodox doctrine of Christ's mediatorship.[87]

The acts of Nicea II were known to Charlemagne's scholars only through a fault-ridden Latin translation undertaken in Rome that somehow made its way to Francia by 790, one that they mistakenly believed had been produced in the east.[88] This document led them to profound misunderstandings of the Greek decrees, yet even apart from those misinterpretations, Theodulf's assault on the eastern council depends on an entire structure of thought considerably distanced from Byzantine and indeed facets of Rome's intellectual traditions.[89] This is why we cannot speak of a true dialogue or debate between the Carolingians and their opponents in the conflict (Pope Hadrian as well as the Greeks), as occurred among the different participants in the ninth-century quarrels over predestination and the eucharist, even though they, too, tended to distort their

---

[86] *Capitulare Francofurtense, Concilium Francofurtense A. 794*, MGH Conc. 2.1, ed. A. Werminghoff (Hanover, 1906), 165. On the *Opus'* background and copies and the later relatively little evidence of its influence, Freeman, ed., *Opus Caroli synodum*, 1–12, 67–76. Other early Carolingian doctrinal treatises that expressed teachings with which Rome agreed also did not circulate widely in the ninth century. Two of Alcuin's anti-Adoptionist treatises are represented by only one extant copy each, and a third by only two copies, with only a scattering of other, lost copies recorded as having been made in the ninth century: Bullough, "Alcuin's Cultural Influence," 9–12; John Cavadini, "The Sources and Theology of Alcuin's *De Fide Sanctae et Individuae Trinitatis*," *Traditio* 46 (1991), 123–146, at 127. See my review of Freeman's edition, *The Medieval Review* (December 4, 1999), www.hti.umich.edu/b/bmr/tmr.html. One person who copied and studied Theodulf's treatise was Hincmar of Rheims: Nees, *Tainted Mantle*, esp. 210.

[87] The importance of Nicea I to the Carolingian interpretation of Nicea II is made apparent in *Opus Caroli regis* 4.13.515–522, where Theodulf contrasts the two councils.

[88] Freeman, ed., *Opus Caroli regis*, 1–2. See also Stephen Gero, "The *Libri Carolini* and the Image Controversy," *Greek Orthodox Theological Review* 18 (1973), 7–34 at 10–13.

[89] See G. Dumeige, *Nicée II* (Paris, 1978), esp. 123–150. On the relation between Rome's teachings (Hadrian I) and the Carolingian position, Freeman, ed., *Opus Caroli regis*, esp. 3–7; Chazelle, "Memory, Instruction, Worship," 185–188.

adversaries' positions. The *Opus Caroli regis* is so removed from the intellectual presumptions of the Greeks or Rome that it is best read not as a response to contemporary opposing opinions, but an isolated proclamation of theology.[90] It is a masterpiece of argument developing with rigid logic a vision of the relation of heaven to earth, spiritual to mundane that is representative of specifically Carolingian thinking and perhaps, in some ways, thought unique to Theodulf – despite Alcuin's likely input and, as I will discuss in the next chapter, possible connections between the treatise's teachings, the Gellone Sacramentary decoration, and Hrabanus Maurus' *In honorem sanctae crucis*. My concern here, therefore, as is necessary in order to lay the basis for investigation of those works in chapter 3, is solely to analyze the *Opus'* theological "logic," its Christocentric foundation, and the function it assigns to the crucifixion.

Relying on their Latin translation of the Greek decrees, Theodulf and his colleagues erroneously believed that Nicea II had called for the bestowal on artistic images of the worship owed to God, a reverence normally designated in Latin as "adoration" (*adoratio*), though Carolingian literature sometimes uses the term to refer to other forms of worship, as well.[91] Against the doctrine that images should be adored, the *Opus Caroli regis* asserts that the Bible, confirmed by the church fathers, demands adoration uniquely of the divinity. The saints in heaven and their relics may receive "veneration" (*veneratio*), a word Theodulf employs to designate a lesser form of honor; their relics are the only earthly objects to which the treatise admits this privilege.[92] But the image must never be the subject of reverence, either adoration in the sense owed to the Trinity or any other mode of honor, because it is nothing more than a manufactured production that scripture never indicates to have been divinely blessed. The value of images is exclusively material; it depends solely on the goods from which they are made and the skills of mortal, fallible artisans. As purely material objects lacking all reason, sense, and life itself, therefore, they are inferior even to their producers and the beings they represent, whose souls, unlike the artistic depiction, are made "to God's image and likeness." The

---

[90] See Freeman, ed., *Opus Caroli regis*, 25.

[91] Theodulf, *Opus Caroli regis Praef.*, 100, 101–102, ibid. 2.21.273–275, and the comments in 3.17.412–416; cf. *Capit. Franc., MGH Conc.* 2.1.165 lines 26–30. See Chazelle, "Memory, Instruction, Worship," 186–188.

[92] Theodulf, *Opus Caroli regis* 3.24.449 lines 3–5, 451 lines 15–17; cf. ibid. 4.27.555–556.

Christian who reveres an image, beneath him in the order of creation, withdraws from his creator.[93]

As suggested by these teachings, which agree with ideas expressed by Augustine and variations on them by Isidor of Seville, Theodulf's assessment of the value of artistic imagery is for the most part decisively negative.[94] Still, the *Opus Caroli regis* opposes not only iconodulism but also the iconoclasm that had represented government policy in the east before the accession of Irene and Constantine. It therefore notes on several occasions that works of art should not be destroyed, because despite their material status they possess a certain, limited utility. Unlike both the iconoclasts and the iconodules in Byzantium, it is declared in the treatise's preface, the Carolingians hold to the "kingly way, having images in ornamentation of churches and in memory of past deeds and adoring God alone and exhibiting appropriate veneration to his saints, since neither do we destroy with [the iconoclasts] nor adore with [the iconodules]."[95] Both of the two uses admitted to images here and in other passages of the *Opus*, however, are understood to reflect the divide that Theodulf posits between them and the sacred and consequently to be indicative of their inability to bring the true Christian closer to God. Through passages from Pseudo-Augustine's *Categoriae decem* and Augustine's *De diversis quaestionibus* presented in Book 1 chapter 8, the artistic image is defined as a likeness that, as such, only brings something to mind to the extent that it resembles its subject.[96] What is not represented in the strict sense of the term is not recalled through the image. But since nothing fabricated from matter and lacking God's blessing can resemble or "depict" something spiritual, the *Opus* informs its readers, the image's subject is necessarily restricted to the visible, material realm; that which is invisible and spiritual, including individual, imperceptible characteristics of a visible subject, is beyond the reach of artistic representation. Hence it is impossible for the artist to represent the incorporeal God, the virtues of the saints, or any other insensible qualities or beings or abstract truths.[97]

[93] Ibid. 1.7.138–145.

[94] Cf. Augustine, *De doctrina Christiana* 2.25.39; idem, *De magistro*, 12.39; *De consensu evangelistarum* 1.10.16; Isidor, *Etymologiae* 19.16.

[95] Theodulf, *Opus Caroli regis Praef.* 102 lines 14–17, see also 99, 101.

[96] See ibid. 1.8.145–148; 4.16.528–529. On Carolingian interest in the *Categoriae decem*, see John Marenbon, *From the Circle of Alcuin to the School of Auxerre: Logic, Theology and Philosophy in the Early Middle Ages* (Cambridge, 1981), 30–66 for Charlemagne's court.

[97] Theodulf, *Opus Caroli regis* 1.17.185, e.g. lines 17–20 ("cum videlicet in imaginibus non possit sanctae conversationis virtus videri, sed solummodo ille materiae, quibus [ipsa]e imagines formate sunt"); ibid. 2.16.263–264, 3.15.403–404, 3.16.409–410, 4.21.539–540. Cf. ibid. 1.10.155–1.22.209, 2.26.286–2.30.322.

Although Theodulf does not develop the point, it is clearly implied that
works of art are useful as decoration because this function derives from
material features: the quality of their components and the craftsmanship
that contributes to their aesthetic value. The image may also serve as a
reminder of past deeds, since such events, by definition, happened within
the temporal and therefore earthly or material sphere. Past deeds were
once seen on earth despite being no longer visible in reality, so that possessing likenesses in order to remember them is worthwhile. Whatever it
depicts, however, the image cannot in itself assist Christian piety, even if
the beholder may proceed to thoughts of heaven and the exercise of faith
on his own. This does not mean that the *Opus Caroli regis* sets limits to the
appropriate subjects for artistic productions. In general, there is a noticeable lack of discussion of specific artistic media or subject-matter for
Christian imagery for the purposes of either condemnation or praise, even
though certain passages, like other writings by Theodulf and the decoration of his oratory at St.-Germigny-des-Prés (fig. 3), reveal his personal love
for artistic creation. What he wants to make clear in the *Opus*, pursuing its
internal logic to lengths that clearly cause some of its argument to diverge
with his own practice and that of other, contemporary commissioners of
art, is not that certain works of art or types of art should be avoided or forbidden. Rather, it is that no artistic production of any kind available to
Christians can bring the viewer physically, mentally, or spiritually closer to
the heavenly realm. Any depiction may be valued as decoration, then, and
any image of Christ or the saints may recall their past deeds. But according
to the teachings of the *Opus Caroli regis*, no matter the subject of an image,
these are the only two useful roles it conceivably performs. As a result, its
utility remains thoroughly grounded in the material world.[98]

---

[98] Ibid. *Praef.*, 99 lines 10–11, 101 lines 4–5, 102 lines 14–15. See Chazelle, "Images, Scripture, the
Church," 57–58; idem, "Matter, Spirit, and Image," 178–179. On Theodulf's interest in art,
Nees, *Tainted Mantle*, 21–46; on the mosaic at St.-Germigny-des-Prés, Peter Bloch, "Das
Apsismosaik von Germigny-des-Prés: Karl der Grosse und der Alte Bund," in *Karl der Grosse:
Lebenswerk und Nachleben*, 5 vols., vol. 3, ed. W. Braunfels and H. Schnitzler (Düsseldorf, 1965),
234–261; Freeman, ed., *Opus Caroli regis*, 29–30; idem, "Theodulf of Orléans and the *Libri
Carolini*," *Speculum* 32 (1957), 663–705, at 695–703. While there is no evidence that the treatise
encouraged artists with Charlemagne's court to avoid specific media or subjects of artistic representation, it has been suggested that the value Theodulf ascribes to imagery for commemorating past deeds and for their beauty may have encouraged the prominence of
narrative depictions and the role of works of art as gifts in the ninth-century Carolingian
church: Jean Wirth, *L'Image médiévale: naissance et développements (VIe–XVe siècle)* (Paris, 1989),
139–154; see Lawrence Nees, "Art and Architecture," *NCMH* 2.818–820.

Figure 3. Apse mosaic, Theodulf's oratory, St.-Germigny-des-Prés

The Ark of the Covenant is the exception that proves this rule. For Theodulf, divine consecration will necessarily be revealed in scripture, and the Ark, the subject of four chapters of his treatise (as of his oratory mosaic), is enthusiastically declared to differ from all other artistic productions because the Bible announces it, alone, to have been divinely ordained. Thus the Ark is the sole "artistic" production identified in the treatise as a *res sacrata*, a title also given to the eucharist, the cross, liturgical vessels, and the Bible itself. All these objects, Theodulf indicates, are announced in scripture to be distinguished from ordinary, unblessed artistic images because they were or are divinely sanctioned things that serve as contacts with heaven, operating in and through the material world.[99] Unlike artistic depictions, *res sacratae* were "predestined before time by the highest and secret and prophetic judgment of God alone," whereas images "are produced by the vanity of gentile authors and offer to mortals no demonstration of salvation, no prerogative of any sacrament, but favor only the eyes."[100]

The rigidly dualist structure of Theodulf's doctrine of the artistic image that should now be apparent permeates other aspects of his treatise's contents. Whether the subject is iconodulism or another of the many errors attributed to Nicea II, the Carolingian treatise proceeds from the axiom, supposedly forgotten by the Greeks, that in order to seek heaven the mortal must turn from the earthly sphere; for the world of matter is radically different from and inferior to all that is spiritual and heavenly. This perspective seems to have been influenced by a dualist and possibly distinctively Hispanic reading of Augustine mediated through Isidor;[101] its effect is evident in other writings by Theodulf and has been connected with his antipathy towards the culture of pagan imperial Rome, an attitude that recurs, as Lawrence Nees has demonstrated, in the work of the ninth-century archbishop, Hincmar of Rheims.[102] In the *Opus*

---

[99] Theodulf, *Opus Caroli regis* 3.24.448 lines 11–14, 4.13.516 lines 12–14, see 1.15–16.169–181, 2.26–30.286–322. Cf. ibid. 1.19–20.192–203; 4.16.527–528. Although the name *res sacratae* does not apply to relics of the saints, they have equivalent value: ibid. 3.24.448.

[100] Ibid. 2.30.303 lines 13–27.

[101] See Chazelle, "Images, Scripture, the Church," esp. 54–55; Dahlhaus-Berg, *Nova antiquitas*, 190–201; Ann Freeman, "Scripture and Images in the *Libri Carolini*," in *Testo e immagine nell'alto medioevo*, Settimane di studio del Centro italiano di studi sull'alto medioevo, 41 (Spoleto, 1994), 163–195, at 176.

[102] Nees, *Tainted Mantle*, esp. 47–143; Dahlhaus-Berg, *Nova antiquitas*, 196. Hincmar's views on pagan Rome are discussed further in chapter 7.

Caroli regis, another patristic source (besides Augustine or Isidor) offered as broadly representative of the treatise's position, likely both because of the focus on artistic images and because the author was the spokesman of Christian Rome, is the second letter of Pope Gregory I to Serenus of Marseilles. The heading to Book 2 Chapter 23 of the *Opus* announces its doctrine to be that of Gregory; however, the chapter interprets and selects from Gregory's letter in ways compatible with the dualism framed in the Carolingian treatise, by simplifying the pope's complex advice to Serenus in order to focus on the concept that images should be neither destroyed nor adored, and by ignoring Gregory's claim that images help instruct the illiterate.[103] Although the second passage that Theodulf excerpts from the letter to Serenus mentions the didactic value of artistic depictions, the *Opus Caroli regis* offers no independent confirmation of this idea, in spite of a reference in Book 2 Chapter 30 to the notion that the viewer "reads" the image.[104] Theodulf had enormous respect for Gregory, but he must have considered it meaningless to posit a didactic role for any purely material thing, since the knowledge conveyed by that object cannot encompass the invisible, spiritual realm, the only truly valuable focus of learning. In the *Opus Caroli regis*, the one unconsecrated material entity recognized to assist the mortal to that kind of insight is the written word, and the supreme text imparting such knowledge is the Bible.

One of the themes running through the entirety of the *Opus Caroli regis* – it is reflected even in the treatise's impressive length and "wordiness" – is the superiority of words and written language to artistic imagery as forms of communication.[105] Underlying this conviction is apparently the belief that while writing, like the image, signifies an external reality, it does so without any need for a visual similitude between the written text and the subject to which it refers. Resemblance is so critical to an artistic representation that viewers may make mistakes in identifying its subject, Theodulf observes, if the image is badly formed, damaged, or, indicative of the

---

[103] Theodulf, *Opus Caroli regis* 2.23.277–280.

[104] Ibid. 2.30.303 lines 26–29. This and other aspects of Gregory's teachings on images are discussed in my article, "Pictures, Books, and the Illiterate: Pope Gregory I's Letters to Serenus of Marseille," *Word & Image* 6 (1990), 138–153.

[105] Celia Chazelle, "'Not in Painting but in Writing': Augustine and the Supremacy of the Word in the *Libri Carolini*," in *Reading and Wisdom: the De doctrina Christiana of Augustine in the Middle Ages*, ed. E. D. English (Notre Dame, 1995), 1–22.

importance attached to writing, if it has lost its inscription.[106] No such danger, though, is faced with written language. Consequently, writing is a far more reliable means of conveying information and it can signify a much wider range of truths, including abstract qualities and ideas to which no material object can bear a resemblance. Many things that cannot be depicted may be recorded in writing, then, such as the wisdom and eloquence of the saints, their prudence, justice, strength, faith, other virtues residing in the soul, truths about God and the heavenly sphere.[107] As the *Opus Caroli regis* also makes clear, however, among all written work the Bible is unique, because it is a *res sacrata*, blessed by God as the divine word in Christ.[108] Scripture's importance is symbolized by the treatise's organization in four books, which, Theodulf notes, mirror the four gospels,[109] and it lies behind his original plan for Book 2 Chapter 30 to conjoin Book 3 Chapter 1 at the midpoint of the work. The former chapter contains the treatise's principal encomium of scripture, in response to a decree of Nicea II comparing the Bible to images, while the first chapter of Book 3 offers the treatise's major credal summation of Trinitarian doctrine.[110] Book 2 Chapter 30 observes that to compare images to the Bible is less an error than the comparisons the iconodules supposedly drew to the eucharist and the "mystery of the cross," evidently since scripture, like imagery, is composed of signs. Yet the chapter's focus is the contrast the Bible presents to any form of depiction. Whereas artistic imagery is ascribed no significant instructional value, scripture is the resource critical to the attainment of Christian truth, Theodulf argues, one containing the very wisdom needed for salvation. Moses and the other holy authors recorded their teachings "not by painting but by writing," for "not pictures but scriptures are provided in the erudition of our faith."[111] Every orthodox doctrine upheld in the *Opus Caroli regis* has its roots in the Bible, then, and anything not confirmed by scripture, such as (in Theodulf's view) the holiness of artistic images, cannot be part of the church of Rome's teachings.

---

[106] See Theodulf, *Opus Caroli regis* 1.15.170 lines 15–18 (images sometimes deceive, evidently because of their poor quality); ibid. 4.16.528–529; 4.21.540.   [107] Ibid. 1.17.185–189.

[108] Ibid. 2.30.303–322.

[109] Ibid. 4, *Praef.*, 485–486. Each book was originally to contain the same number of chapters. The treatise was meant to present a contrast to the disorder that the Carolingians perceived in the acts of Nicea II: see ibid. 1.5.131–132; 2, *Praef.*, 233–234.

[110] Ibid. 2.30.303, 3.1.336–340; see Ann Freeman, "Further Studies in the *Libri Carolini*, I and II," *Speculum* 40 (1965), 203–289, at 216.   [111] Theodulf, *Opus Caroli regis* 2.30.305 line 2, 311 lines 10–12.

While important truths are recognized to be present in the literal sense of biblical texts, a series of chapters in Book 1 and at the beginning of Book 2, in which Nicea II is criticized for having used Old Testament passages to support the doctrine of the artistic image's sanctity, indicates that biblical wisdom is best discovered at the spiritual level of interpretation.[112] The ability to read scripture at this level, guided by the church fathers whom Rome identifies as authoritative, distinguishes the Carolingians, the "spiritual Israel," from the ancient Jews who remained bound to the material world and scripture's literal meaning.[113] Those who explore scripture's vast repository of learning in this manner can avoid the numerous "mistakes" that the *Opus Caroli regis* finds in the scriptural exegesis of Nicea II, an assembly that, like the iconoclasts, taught things "that neither the savior nor the apostles are known to have supported."[114] Among the many errors supposedly resulting from the council's failure to interpret the Bible accurately are its evident inability (given the Latin translation of Nicea II's acts available to the Carolingians) to understand or write clear, grammatically correct language. The linguistic problems thought to have incited the image quarrels in the east – for example, the iconoclasts' misunderstanding of the difference between "image" and "idol," the iconodules' equally astounding incapacity to distinguish "to possess" from "to adore"[115] – made Theodulf convinced that Byzantium had altogether abandoned the liberal arts; yet these are essential tools for scripture's correct interpretation that are themselves taught in the Bible.[116] In contrast, true Christians, such as Charlemagne, realize the need to search for the knowledge necessary to salvation not in artistic imagery but in scripture, a *res sacrata* that consistently guides its readers from the mutable world of material images to the immutable world of the spirit.[117]

The Christian's ability to proceed from scripture's literal to its spiritual sense and, correspondingly, away from the artistic image is owed to the presence of both humanity and divinity in the son of God. The incarnation provided the bridge between the mundane and sacred realms. This is the basis of

---

[112] See ibid. 1.9–30.148–232, 2.11.238–258.

[113] See ibid. 1.17.183 line 24, 1.19.192–195, 1.30.231–232.   [114] Ibid. *Praef.*, 99 lines 4–5.

[115] Ibid. *Praef.*, 99, 100 lines 11–18.

[116] Esp. ibid. 2.30, 311–317. For another example of early Carolingian theological analysis that hinges on grammatical criteria, see Marcia L. Colish, "Carolingian Debates over *Nihil* and *Tenebrae*: a Study in Theological Method," *Speculum* 59 (1984), 757–795.

[117] Theodulf, *Opus Caroli regis* 1.19.193; 1.30.231–232.

the sanctity of all *res sacratae*, whose blessing by Christ the mediator enables them to channel heavenly power to mortals. By decreeing the worship of images, Nicea II shows its rejection of this doctrine of Christ and, therefore, its departure from the Trinitarian orthodoxy of Nicea I and the other councils of the early church. It is not surprising, however, that although Theodulf repeatedly refers to Christ as mediator[118] and makes numerous, usually brief references to his human nature – for instance, to the sacrifice of the cross, the blood that washes away sins, the body and blood commemorating the passion in the eucharist[119] – the *Opus Caroli regis* directs far more attention to his divine than to his human qualities. In fact, his divine nature is often described in ways that seem to divorce it almost completely from considerations of his humanity. Although this is in keeping with the general emphasis on Christ's divinity and kingship in early Carolingian devotion, it also accords with the logical structure of the argumentation in the *Opus*. An essential point Theodulf sought to make was that the union of two natures in one person, which enables mortals to turn from earthly to spiritual things, means that the son of God may be contemplated not merely in the humanity shown in his artistic representations. More importantly, he can be pondered in the unportrayable, divine nature revealed in the Bible.[120] In many passages of the *Opus Caroli regis*, the reality of Jesus' mortal flesh almost entirely disappears from view. Thus he is hailed as God's image, face, word, and truth,[121] the true rather than adoptive son (reflecting the contemporary concerns over Adoptionism),[122] and, a recurring theme also heard in Theodulf's *carmen figuratum* for Charlemagne, the emanation of light from God. Prefigured in Beseleel, the maker of the Ark, the "ineffable splendor, God from God, light from light" is one substance with the father who spoke

---

[118] See Freeman, ed., *Opus Caroli regis*, 565. On Christ as the juncture between the Old Testament and the New, which sets the same notion on an historical plane, Theodulf, *Opus Caroli regis* 2.27.291–292, 2.29.302; Dahlhaus-Berg, *Nova antiquitas*, 194–196. On the union of two natures in Christ, also Theodulf, *Opus Caroli regis* 1.4.125–128; 2.15.263; 4.14.524. As consecrated material things, the *res sacratae* offer a contact with heaven and the second person of the Trinity that parallels his own mediation of God to the human race: see ibid. 1.15.170–175, 2.27.290–296, 2.28.296–300, 2.29.301–302.

[119] E.g. ibid. 1.1.111, 1.12.162, 1.19.194, 2.15.263 lines 18–19, 2.27.290–291, 3.6.361–363, 4.1.489–491, 4.14.523–524.   [120] Ibid. 2.22.275–276, see 2.16.263–264, 3.15.403–404; 4.14.523.

[121] Ibid. 1.23.210, see 1.5.129, 1.15.172, 175, 4.2.492.

[122] Ibid. 4.1.491 lines 8–10. Freeman has suggested that the worries over Adoptionism and hence the desire to demonstrate Christ's assumption rather than adoption of humanity influenced the choice of creed for Book 3 Chapter 1: ibid. 3.1.336 n. 3; Freeman, ed., *Opus Caroli regis*, 44.

to Moses from the burning bush and sent the fire of the Holy Spirit,[123] who showed to us "sitting in the shadows, the great light of his brilliance."[124] As stated in Book 2 Chapter 22, Christians should seek Jesus by means not of their corporeal senses, therefore, but of the eyes of their minds or souls. Through these, they may "drink in the eternal light" and "cleave to him in whose image [the human mind] is created."[125]

The Greeks' failure to understand Christ and the consequences of his mediatorship, revealed in the decrees of Nicea II, is the basis of the supposed ignorance in the same *acta* of the truth about the crucifixion. To comprehend the passion and the divine work of salvation requires recognition that Christ is both God and man. The centrality of orthodox Christology to the Carolingian treatise's doctrine of the crucifixion is clearest in Book 2 Chapter 28; there Nicea II is attacked for its teachings on the cross, specifically an assertion that images possess equivalent sanctity. The chapter juxtaposes the emptiness of artistic depictions to the cross's magnificence as a *res sacrata*. Acclamations, the text implies, are appropriately rendered both to the weapon of the crucifixion now glorified in heaven and to the spiritual sign that the faithful carry inwardly, which unlike the artistic representation is known only through the "eyes of the heart."[126] Other chapters of the *Opus* affirm that the sign of the cross worn within the soul or made by hand is blessed by God and, like other *res sacratae*, mediates divine power to earth. The treatise's admission that relics of the saints are legitimately venerated suggests that cross relics, too, were probably recognized to be sacred, though they are not actually mentioned.[127] Book 1 Chapter 19, however, draws a distinction between the two cherubim and two tablets of the Ark, on the one hand, and on the other manufactured crosses. As opposed to the divinely blessed objects of the Old Testament, representations of the cross are implied to be unconsecrated material things belonging to the same category as other forms of artistic representation.[128] Although there is a possibility that inconsistency was introduced into the *Opus* by its revisions, which particularly affected Book 2,[129] it seems

---

[123] Theodulf, *Opus Caroli regis* 1.16.177 lines 3–16.

[124] Ibid. 2.8.253 lines 2–4, see 1.23.209–212, 2.16.264–265.   [125] Ibid. 2.22.275–277.

[126] Ibid. 2.28.296–300, esp. 296–298.

[127] Ibid. 1.23.211, 4.16.528 lines 8–26 (probably referring to both the sign of the cross borne inwardly and, more clearly, to the sign made by hand). Cf. ibid. 2.28.297, 3.24.449 lines 3–5, 451 lines 15–17.   [128] Ibid. 1.19.192–193, cf. 1.20.196–203.

[129] Freeman, ed., *Opus Caroli regis*, 39.

best to think that the encomia of the cross in Book 2 Chapter 28 and other chapters do not refer to cross images. Rather, they only concern the forms of the cross just noted that are clearly identified to be holy. Praise is for the sanctity that the cross demonstrates through immaterial means, in contrast to the materiality of Christian artistic images, including man-made renderings of the cross.[130]

The main argument of Book 2 Chapter 28 is that the true cross or its spiritual sign is divinely blessed and thus different from the artistic production, because the crucifixion was the climactic act by which the son of God rejoined earth to heaven. It was the culmination to the reunion of these two, diametrically opposed spheres of existence that began when he joined human to divine nature. Nicea II evidently failed to realize that what Jesus initiated in his one person, the cross and the passion applied to the entire universe.[131] As Theodulf makes apparent, this does not mean that mortals may therefore access the holy through ordinary material objects. Rather, the crucifixion has released Christians from bondage to this world, an imprisonment epitomized in the worship of artistic imagery, by offering them the capacity to move away from that realm and towards their creator.[132] Here as elsewhere in the *Opus Caroli regis*, Christ's divinity and powerful victory over sin/death/Satan are emphasized. It is by the crucifixion that the "ancient enemy was conquered," the "devil was defeated," the "prisons of hell were destroyed," and the human race was redeemed. The cross is the emblem of Christian reform because it served as the triumphal banner, the "hook" on which Satan was captured, Theodulf declares,

---

[130] Perhaps the comments in *Opus Caroli regis* 1.19.192–193 shed light on the relationship between Alcuin's opening and Theodulf's closing *carmina figurata* in the series for Charlemagne. While Theodulf's figure copies Alcuin's, his verses make no direct mention of the cross. In contrast to Alcuin's poem, they do not clearly ascribe representational significance to his figure, and it therefore remains an essentially "abstract" design, possibly additional evidence of his sense that images, including crosses, are inferior to the written word and incapable of communicating spiritual truth. Earlier in the *Opus Caroli regis*, though, Theodulf suggests that even the Ark of the Covenant should not be sought "in depictis tabulis sive parietibus" (ibid. 1.15.175 lines 5–8). This statement needs consideration in efforts to link the treatise with his own mosaic of the Ark at St. Germigny-des-Prés, and it indicates the difficulty of relating the *Opus'* doctrine with complete consistency to what is known about its author's behavior regarding art.   [131] See ibid. 2.28.300 lines 19–21.

[132] The theme of the reunion of earth with heaven through the crucifixion is old and, in particular, has Visigothic precedents: Freeman, ed., *Opus Caroli regis* 1.12.162 n. 2, with references to other places it occurs in the treatise. See also Theodulf, *Opus Caroli regis* 4.1.490 lines 1–3; and (for a non-Visigothic parallel), Alcuin, *Carm.* 1, stanza 15, *MGH PLAC* 4.3.904–907.

echoing Isidor's commentary on Good Friday. Consequently, the "mystery of the Lord's cross" is now the weapon, fortification, helmet, shield, and breastplate by which the faithful are brought within the realm of the sacred and enabled to withstand the wicked powers still threatening to separate them from heaven.[133] They follow the model of the saints, whose lives are symbolized in the cross's form and who inwardly carry its sign, rejecting devotion to mundane things such as images.[134] The language used to defend these ideas gains intensity in the chapter's concluding lines, which describe the ability the passion gave the Christian to engage in an immediate experience of the words of the heavenly, divine Christ contained in scripture, and obey his commandments. The reader is urged to "come to the Lord," sit "with Mary at his feet" and hear "the word from his mouth" – that is, to attend to the Bible where is recorded the command of the "fountain of light" and "origin of goodness" that the faithful deny themselves and "take up the cross" to follow Christ, so as to be "crucified to the world" (Matthew 16.24, Gal. 6.14).[135] They should render to Caesar "the things that are Caesar's," again meaning that they must turn from images in order to adore their savior.[136] It is because the Greeks ignore these doctrines and their significance for understanding earth's relation to heaven that they remain devoted to artistic imagery, unable to comprehend the Bible's wisdom, the treasury of orthodox faith.

The Carolingian responses to Adoptionism

Like Theodulf in the *Opus Caroli regis*, his associates who attacked Hispanic Adoptionism interpreted their opponents' teachings as a deviation from the dogma of Christ's two natures laid down in the synods of the early church, a deviation that, in part, involved a failure to grasp the truth about the crucifixion.[137] But the acts of Nicea II brought Theodulf to think about

[133] Theodulf, *Opus Caroli regis* 2.28.296–297.
[134] Ibid. 2.28.298, see 3.28.470 lines 12–18. Cf. Augustine, *De doctrina Christiana* 2.41; Isidor, *De eccles. offic.* 1.30; Eph. 3.18 ("You may be able to comprehend, with all the saints, what is the breadth, and length, and height, and depth"). All English translations are taken from the Douay-Rheims version.
[135] Theodulf, *Opus Caroli regis* 2.28.299–300.
[136] Theodulf, *Opus Caroli regis* 2.28.300 lines 18–22; see 3.17.415 lines 14–17.
[137] See Gary B. Blumenshine, "Alcuin's *Liber Contra Haeresim Felicis* and the Frankish Kingdom," *Frühmittelalterlichen Studien* 17 (1983), 222–233, esp. 225–226.

how Jesus' mediatorship allowed the faithful to turn from the inferior world of matter to the spiritual sphere, where they might contemplate their savior in his divinity. The quarrel with the Adoptionists led Alcuin and Paulinus of Aquileia, the authors of the main Carolingian tractates stemming from this conflict, to try to explain just how the one person of the mediator united mortal humanity with immortal divinity.

The dispute over Adoptionism began in Spain in the early 780s. It did not gain the attention of Charlemagne's court circle until 791–792, however, when Bishop Felix of Urgel, a city in the Spanish March that had come under Charles' control in 789, began preaching Adoptionism there and consequently within the Frankish king's dominion. Charles summoned Felix to a council at Regensburg, where he was condemned, required to sign a retraction, and sent to Rome under the supervision of Angilbert of St.-Riquier in order to reiterate his abandonment of heresy. He returned to Urgel by 793.[138] Two letters written by the bishops of Spain to protest the decision at Regensburg, one to the bishops of Francia and the other to Charlemagne, provided the occasion for discussion and further condemnation of Adoptionism at the council of Frankfurt in 794.[139] The tractates against the Hispanic Christology from the Frankfurt synod include the *Liber sacrosyllabus*, composed and later revised by Paulinus on behalf of the bishops of Italy,[140] and a letter probably by Alcuin on behalf of the bishops of Germany, Gaul, and Aquitaine to the bishops of Spain. A second letter, probably also by Alcuin but less informative on Carolingian views, was sent in Charlemagne's name to Archbishop Elipandus of Toledo, Adoptionism's first major exponent, and to the other bishops of Spain.[141] Felix's return to Adoptionist doctrine by c. 796 led to correspondence between him and Alcuin, who by this time had left Charlemagne's court for the monastery of St. Martin at Tours. In 799, a debate was held between Alcuin and Felix at Aachen. Once Felix had yielded to his opponent and

[138] John Cavadini, *The Last Christology of the West: Adoptionism in Spain and Gaul, 785–820* (Philadelphia, 1993), 72–73, and *passim* for an excellent analysis of Adoptionist theology; his findings are summarized in idem, "Elipandus and his Critics," 787–807. See also Wilfried Hartmann, *Die Synoden der Karolingerzeit im Frankenreich und in Italien* (Paderborn, 1989), 104–105. [139] Hartmann, *Synoden*, 105–115.
[140] Paulinus, *Libellus Sacrosyllabus Episcoporum Italiae*, Conc. Franc. 794, MGH Conc. 2.1.130–42, identifying himself as author at 131 line 20.
[141] Alcuin, *Epistola episcoporum Franciae*, Conc. Franc. 794, MGH Conc. 2.1.142–157; idem, *Epistola Karoli Magni*, Conc. Franc. 794, MGH Conc. 2.1.157–164.

signed another profession of orthodox faith, he was taken to Lyons and confined there until his death in 818. Although he never changed his opinion,[142] the main Carolingian anti-Adoptionist writings all appeared in the decade after completion of the *Opus Caroli regis* and seek to refute Elipandus' and Felix's assertions during the same period. In addition to those written for the Council of Frankfurt, they are Paulinus' *Contra Felicem*, probably completed c. 799; Alcuin's *Contra Haeresim Felicis*, c. 798; his longer *Adversus Felicem*, dating to 799–800 and possibly influenced by Paulinus' *Contra Felicem*; and Alcuin's last work on the subject, written shortly before he died at Tours in 804, *Adversus Elipandum*.[143]

Where Alcuin comments on Adoptionism in his own words, the language is often more passionate and less closely reasoned than Paulinus', and he is far more reliant on the church fathers to develop his ideas. As a result, there is less careful analysis of the doctrinal implications of Adoptionism but a clearer demonstration of its exponents' failure, as both he and Paulinus believed, to adhere to patristic orthodoxy.[144] Nevertheless, the basic lines of thought that remain constant throughout the work of both theologians mean they are best treated together. While their writings for the synod of Frankfurt suggest only a limited knowledge of Adoptionist theology influenced by the assessment of Pope Hadrian I,[145] Paulinus' *Contra Felicem* and Alcuin's last two tractates against Felix and Elipandus reveal the two scholars coming to grips with the Hispanic churchmen's rejoinders to their earlier rebuttals. Like Theodulf in the *Opus Caroli regis*, however, both worked within doctrinal traditions that separated them from the intellectual milieu to which their opponents belonged, though in this case – as is not true with Theodulf – they held beliefs similar to those of Rome. Again, true discussion or debate was hampered by the fundamentally different starting points of the Hispanic and Carolingian

---

[142] After his death, Agobard of Lyons found a pamphlet by Felix defending his views and wrote a response that again links Adoptionism with Nestorianism: *Adversum Dogma Felicis*, in Agobard, *Opera Omnia*, CCCM 52, ed. L. Van Acker (Turnhout, 1981), 71–111.

[143] Paulinus, *Contra Felicem*, CCCM 95, ed. D. Norberg (Turnhout, 1990); Alcuin, *Liber Alcuini Contra Haeresim Felicis: Edition with an Introduction*, ST 285, ed. G. B. Blumenshine (Vatican City, 1980); idem, *Adversus Felicem Urgellitanum Episcopum*, PL 101.119–230; idem, *Adversus Elipandum*, PL 101.243–300. Norberg argues that Alcuin's *Adv. Felicem* is dependent on Paulinus' *Contra Felicem*: CCCM 95.vii-viii; cf. Cavadini, *Last Christology*, 82 and 191 n. 60.

[144] See Cavadini, *Last Christology*, 103–106. Cf. Alcuin's description of his approach in *Liber contra haeresim*, ST 285.55–56. Paulinus relegates most of his patristic excerpts to the final portion of *Contra Felicem* 3.20–28, CCCM 95.104–121.   [145] Cavadini, *Last Christology*, 77.

arguments. Although I will note a few aspects of the Hispanic teachings, my focus is therefore restricted to the writings of Charlemagne's scholars, which like Theodulf's treatise against Nicea II represent largely isolated expressions of Carolingian thought.[146]

Paulinus and Alcuin were convinced that Elipandus and Felix had revived the early Christian heresies of Arianism and Nestorianism, rejecting the councils of Ephesus (431) and Chalcedon (451),[147] by asserting that Jesus was not the true son of God but rather adopted or adoptive.[148] This in fact misconstrues the Hispanic position, as John Cavadini has demonstrated, because the Carolingians were evidently ignorant of the Adoptionists' understanding of the incarnation, rooted in the Philippians 2 account of the son's self-emptying or -lowering. For Elipandus and Felix, Philippians 2.6–11 described how the fully divine son assumed a perfect human nature into his one person while remaining the immutable God. The word emanated from God and descended to our level, emptying itself of divinity even as it remained consubstantial with the father. In the Adoptionists' belief, the self-emptying of divinity could not be salvific unless it extended to the point that the incarnate word, in its human nature, shared all the limitations of our existence except sin, including Christians' status as adoptive sons of God. Christ saves other mortals because while remaining eternally divine, in the adoptive yet sinless humanity that he assumed through his perfect self-abasement he is the firstborn among brothers.[149]

Like Pope Hadrian, the Carolingians prefer to think of the incarnation as essentially moving in the opposite direction. What is at issue is not the word's self-lowering, but the taking up, "assumption," or exaltation of a complete, though sinless, human nature into union with the Trinity's

---

[146] See ibid. *passim*, on the Hispanic teachings.

[147] See Paulinus, *Libellus sacrosyll.*, MGH *Conc.* 2.1.136; idem, *Contra Felicem* 1.8, CCCM 95.13; Alcuin, *Ep. episc. Franciae*, MGH *Conc.* 2.1.154–155; idem, *Liber contra haeresim* 2, 36, ST 285.55, 74–75; *Adv. Felicem* 1.11, 5.2, 5, 7.11, 15, PL 101.136A/B, 189D, 192A, 223C, 228C; *Adv. Elipandum* 1.14, 2.4, 4.5, 7, PL 101.250C/D, 260C/D, 289D, 291C; Bullough, "Alcuin and the Kingdom of Heaven," 196–199. On Alcuin's sources, especially his usage of Cassian's refutation of Nestorius and extracts from the acts of Ephesus, see Cavadini, "Sources and Theology," 126. As observed by Cavadini ("Elipandus and his Critics," 804–807), these charges occur primarily in Alcuin's writings, as the passages just noted indicate. They may reflect his particular sensitivity to Charlemagne's political role as the west's defender of orthodoxy.

[148] The Carolingian writings treat the words as synonyms. Compare e.g. Alcuin, *Liber contra haeresim* 31, 32, ST 285.71 (Augustine); Paulinus, *Contra Felicem*, 1.9, 26, CCCM 95.15, 31–32. See Cavadini, "Elipandus and his Critics," 803.

[149] See Cavadini, *Last Christology*, 28–29, 31–32, 35–38.

second person. The assumption occurred at the very moment the human
nature was conceived, or better the conception itself constituted this union
with the divine. When the Adoptionists refer to Christ as adoptive or when
Felix uses the term *nuncupativus Deus* to clarify his understanding of the
son's adoptive status,[150] then, Alcuin and Paulinus interpret such statements
in light of their own, very different doctrine of the incarnation. To their
mind, to speak of Christ as the adoptive son is wrong since they think the
term means (as is not the Adoptionists' intention) that in Jesus God adopted
rather than assumed human nature. For Paulinus and Alcuin, however, the
very term "adoption" can only refer to a distinct person that first exists separated from its adopter, before being joined to the latter. When attributed to
Christ, this seems to them equivalent to the heresies of Arianism and
Nestorianism: the former insofar as the fourth-century Arians supposedly
taught that Jesus was not born the true son of God, but was only subsequently promoted to that status, the latter insofar as the early Nestorians
supposedly claimed that the humanity and divinity in Christ constituted
two persons rather than two natures. Looking at Adoptionism from this
perspective, Paulinus and Alcuin argue that it involves two major errors
with a direct bearing on how their anti-Adoptionist tracts present the crucifixion. One is that Christ's full divinity and equality with the other persons
of the Trinity seem to them denied. If the man Jesus is adopted, then he did
not begin existence as God's true son, having become a "son" only after his
conception in Mary's womb as a separate person from the divinity. Hence
he is inferior to God. Or, taking the same error from the opposite vantage
point, if the human nature is only adopted, then God, who remains utterly
superior to Jesus, did not truly become a man.[151] The union of divinity with
humanity is therefore not complete nor is it unbreachable, since an adopted
humanity, forever inferior to God, will always retain the ability to exist apart
from the divinity as a mere human being or *purus homo*, just as is true of
other mortals. Adoption can be undone, just as Christians, who are adopted
sons of God, can fall away through sin into damnation.[152]

---

[150] See ibid., 81–82, 90–91, 107–108.

[151] As Alcuin notes to Elipandus (*Ep.* 166, *MGH Epp.*4.273 lines 29–33), "Si igitur homo, qui
adsumptus est a verbo Dei, deus est nuncupativus, quia alia natura est humanitatis, alia divinitatis, consequens videtur, ut Deus, qui hominem adsumpsit, homo sit nuncupativus, et non
potest stare quod evangelista ait: 'Verbum caro factum est'."

[152] See Paulinus, *Contra Felicem*, 1.26, 2.9, 11, 18, 3.27, *CCCM* 95.32, 59, 61–62, 67, 118; cf. Alcuin, *Adv.
Felicem* 1.15, *PL* 101.140A.

Against such ideas attributed to Elipandus and Felix, both Carolingian scholars insist that the man conceived in Mary is the immutable deity himself. In this conception God did not adopt but instead assumed or exalted human nature – not a person but nature, something with no possibility of existing on its own that therefore could not have been adopted – into an indissoluble union with the divine in the second person of the Trinity.[153] The praise of the Virgin in the treatises of both Alcuin and Paulinus is an important vehicle by which they support this doctrine. Her holiness, absolute virginity, and the acclamations the church has traditionally rendered to her as Mother of God and *Theotocos* are offered as proof that the conception in her womb constituted the human nature's assumption as opposed to adoption, and thus the perfect union of divinity with humanity. The entire Trinity was at work in the womb of Mary, the "inviolate" and "immaculate virgin," Paulinus announces.[154] She who is full of grace is the mother who bore her own maker and father, the true mother of God, not *nuncupativa*, Alcuin declares. Outstanding over all women in her nobility and sanctity, she is a virgin "of royal dignity" born from "royal and free stock," the "immaculate earth" on which the holy spirit operated in the incarnation.[155] From Mary, the Christ who is "God from God, the same man from man" proceeded like the bridegroom from the wedding chamber, "magnificent, with gigantic course, like the rising sun."[156] There are not two distinct persons or two sons, one human and adoptive and the other the true, divine son of God, but a single person with two unconfused natures,[157] so that God was in Christ "not through grace as in other holy and pure men [*puri homines*], but essentially through nature."[158] In the process of the assumption of humanity, that nature was honored. The

---

[153] See Paulinus, *Libellus sacrosyll.*, MGH Conc. 2.1.137; idem, *Contra Felicem*, 1.36, 2.24, 3.27, CCCM 95.43, 75, 118–119 (Gregory I); Alcuin, *Liber contra haeresim* 69–71, ST 285.95–98 (Augustine); *Adv. Felicem*, PL 101.138–142A, 156A.

[154] Paulinus, *Libellus sacrosyll.*, MGH Conc. 2.1.133–134, see 141. See also *Contra Felicem* 1.13, 37, 2.9, 17, CCCM 95.18, 44, 59, 66, 67.

[155] See Alcuin, *Liber contra haeresim* 70, ST 285.96 (Augustine); *Adv. Felicem* 6.6, 9, 7.2, PL 101.207D, 210, 213C; *Ep. episc. Franciae*, MGH Conc. 2.1.152.

[156] Alcuin, *Adv. Felicem* 6.10, 7.4, PL 101.212B, 215D (Gregory I); *Adv. Elipandum* 3.6, PL 101.275B. See Paulinus, *Contra Felicem* 1.14, 15, 2.11, CCCM 95.19, 20, 62. Cf. Alcuin, *Adv. Elipandum* 1.13, PL 101.250A/B; Bullough, "Alcuin and the Kingdom," 197–198; L. Scheffczyk, *Das Mariengeheimnis in Frömmigkeit und Lehre der Karolingerzeit* (Leipzig, 1959), 80–99.

[157] Paulinus, *Libellus sacrosyll.*, MGH Conc. 2.1.136–137. See Alcuin, *Ep. episc. Franciae*, MGH Conc. 2.1.154–155; *Adv. Felicem* 1.11, 5.3–5, 7.11, PL 101.136A/B, 190D-192, 223D-224A; *Adv. Elipandum* 4.6, PL 101.291A/B (Cyril). [158] Paulinus, *Libellus sacrosyll.*, MGH Conc. 2.1.133 lines 5–6.

incarnation created a humanity unlike any other, Alcuin indicates; "in many things we say that he is similar to us, and in many more things dissimilar," noting as examples the human nature's sinlessness, that Jesus' death was unequal to ours because it was redemptive, and, in a letter to Elipandus written in 799, that while Christ is both God and man we are merely human, "born in sins and saved by his grace."[159] To hold that Christ is adoptive and not the true son of God makes it impossible to believe in his uniqueness among men, a quality vital to his ability to make other mortals adoptive sons of God through baptism.[160]

The sense that it was crucial to Christian soteriology to believe the humanity in Christ was assumed or "taken up" and fully, perfectly joined with divinity underlies the difficulties both Carolingian writers seem to experience in finding adequate ways to describe the union. Sometimes their language is almost monophysite in tone, implying the human nature to be little more than a shell housing the deity. For Paulinus, God was hidden beneath the veil of flesh.[161] In other places, the emphasis is on the conjunction of opposites;[162] in still others the two natures blend together, at times to the point that they become virtually indistinguishable, or the characteristics of one nature are attributed to the other.[163] The effort to defend Christ's divinity and its union with humanity provokes in Alcuin, especially, some of his most forceful and eloquent writing against Elipandus and Felix. "Neither disjunction nor any division can occur between Christ and God," Felix is reminded, "since God is wholly in Christ and Christ wholly in God. No separation is possible here, no splitting asunder; there is only one simple, one sound confession, to adore, love, worship Christ God" – one of Alcuin's favorite titles for Jesus.[164] As the doubting Thomas proclaimed, Alcuin observes through a passage from Cassian, "God is the Jesus whom I touched, God whose limbs I felt . . . I touched the body of my lord, I felt flesh and bones, I put my fingers in the wound, and concerning Christ my lord whom I touched, I shouted, 'My

[159] Alcuin, *Adv. Felicem* 1.15, *PL* 101.140–141 (Augustine); *Ep.* 166, *MGH Epp.* 4.270 lines 21–23.

[160] See Alcuin, *Ep. episc. Franciae*, *MGH Conc.* 2.1.157; *Liber contra haeresim* 2, 14, 21, 31, 50, 54–55, 68, 71, *ST* 285.55, 61–62 (Cyril), 64–65 (Atticus of Constantinople), 71 (Augustine), 83–84 (Jerome), 86–87 (Origen, Jerome), 94–95 (Augustine), 97–98; *Adv. Felicem* 1.9, 2.11–12, *PL* 101.134D, 154–156. Cf. Alcuin, *Ep.* 137, *Epp.* 4.211 lines 19–27.

[161] Paulinus, *Contra Felicem* 1.19, 2.5, *CCCM* 95.25, see 54–55.   [162] Ibid. 1.15, 30, *CCCM* 95.21, 35.

[163] Alcuin, *Adv. Felicem* 1.5, 10, 7.11, *PL* 101.132B, 135C, see 223B/C. Cf. idem, *Ep. episc. Franciae*, *MGH Conc.* 2.1.149 lines 21–24.   [164] Alcuin, *Adv. Felicem*, 4.7, *PL* 101.180D.

lord and my God'."[165] "The father thundered from the heavens and named
him his son," the bishops of Spain are reminded, "Christ cried out from the
earth to the heavens, he named himself son; and with the Jews you still do
not believe? The thief on the cross named him lord, the centurion seeing
him die cried out: 'Truly this was the son of God'. Even the demons with
their legion proclaimed him the true son of the highest God, just as is read
in the holy gospels; and Elefantus [*sic*] with his legion still denies that he is
truly the son of God?"[166]

Closely connected to the impossibility of reconciling Adoptionism with
the doctrine of Jesus' full divinity, Paulinus and Alcuin think, is the second
error it seems to entail, that his humanity was necessarily conceived in sin,
the cause of mortals' alienation from God. Human nature that is distanced
from its creator and needs adoption, as do ordinary human beings, must be
sinful. For this reason, too, a perfect union of two natures in Christ is
impossible. Though the Carolingians realize that the Adoptionists understand Jesus' humanity to be free of sin, they are convinced that to refer to
him as adoptive contradicts the concept of his innocence, while the doctrine of his sinlessness requires admitting that the humanity was assumed
rather than adopted. An adoptive Christ cannot be the "adopter" of other
mortals.[167] Separated from God by sin, he would have himself needed
redemption and divine grace. He would have needed baptism in order to
be joined to God as his adoptive son, becoming only then the "son of God"
as do ordinary mortals who receive the sacrament. He would have been
under the obligation of mortality so that he suffered and died for his own
sins, not those of the rest of humanity.[168] Such beliefs are clearly wrong.
For Paulinus and Alcuin, the absence of any potential for alienation from
God in Christ's humanity, and thus any possibility of sin, follows unques-
tionably from the very meaning of assumption, the purity of the Virgin's
womb, and the divine omnipotence that could accomplish the miracle of
incarnation. Linking sin with adoption and sinlessness with assumption,
Alcuin observes to Elipandus, "If you wonder how Christ could be born
from David, who was adopted, and not be adoptive himself, don't you also

[165] Ibid. 2.19, *PL* 101.144A/B.
[166] Alcuin, *Ep. episc. Franciae*, *MGH Conc.* 2.1.155 lines 24–29; see *Liber contra haeresim* 13, *ST* 285.61.
[167] As Paulinus states, "Quo igitur pacto nobis adoptionem filiorum tribuit, si ipse necessarium
eguit, ut sibi haberet?" *Libellus sacrosyll.*, *MGH Conc.* 2.1.133 lines 7–8.
[168] See Paulinus, *Contra Felicem* 1.25–26, 2.18, *CCCM* 95.30–32, 67.

wonder how Christ could be born from David the sinner and himself be
without sin? From the same power by which he could be conceived and
born without sin, from the same strength of the divine will, by the operation of the Holy Spirit, he could be conceived and born without adoption
from someone adoptive [i.e. David]."[169] His baptism was not a purgation,
therefore, because being innocent he did not require cleansing. Rather, like
the annunciation and transfiguration, it was a way for God to proclaim
Jesus his true son, and these events actually demonstrate the sinlessness of
his human nature.[170] According to Paulinus, Jesus' innocence is why it is
wrong to equate his role as advocate (1 John 2.1) with adoption, as
Elipandus supposedly does. Whereas the former term refers to his propitiation of our sins, "adoptive" designates one to whom, because of sin,
"nothing is owed by the adopting father but is granted by the indulgence of
grace."[171] Drawing on Jerome in the last book of *Adversus Felicem*, Alcuin
declares Jesus to be the angel of great counsel sent to purge the entire
world, whose own body was "like wool, clean without the stain of any sin,
and like a most lucid gem more precious than the whole world," a body
shining forth "like gold tested by fire."[172]

As the foregoing remarks suggest, the New Testament occurrences
most discussed in the Carolingian anti-Adoptionist literature are the incarnation, by which the divine and human natures were initially joined, and
the preceding and following scriptural events interpreted as indicative of
that union, in particular the annunciation, Jesus' baptism, and the transfiguration. In Paulinus' *Regula fidei*, a poem directed against Adoptionism and
sometimes copied in manuscripts immediately after his *Contra Felicem*, this
same list of events is singled out as proof that Christ is both God and
man.[173] Nevertheless, the arguments as a whole of Paulinus' and Alcuin's
tractates make it apparent that alongside the incarnation, the critical
episode in Jesus' earthly existence that renders Adoptionist teachings
untenable, as the Carolingians understood them, is the passion; for this is

---

[169] Alcuin, *Adv. Elipandum* 2.6, PL 101.264B; see *Ep. episc. Franciae*, MGH Conc. 2.1.152, *Adv. Felicem*
6.2, PL 101.201A/B.

[170] See Alcuin, *Ep. episc. Franciae*, MGH Conc. 2.1.152–153; *Ep.* 166, MGH Epp. 4.270; *Adv. Felicem*
2.17–20, PL 101.158–162; Paulinus, *Libellus sacrosyll.*, MGH Conc. 2.1.134; idem, *Contra Felicem*
2.18, CCCM 95.68–69.   [171] Paulinus, *Libellus sacrosyll.*, MGH Conc. 2.1.135, esp. lines 32–33.

[172] Alcuin, *Adv. Felicem* 7.8, PL 101.220A-C.

[173] *Carm.* I, *Œuvre poétique*, 91–96 lines 20, 30–50. See Norberg, ed., *Œuvre poétique*, 26; Rabe, *Faith,
Art, and Politics*, 36–40.

the critical event by which humanity is saved. Salvation could only have been achieved if the crucified Christ was the true, not the adopted, son of God. The theology of the crucifixion enunciated in this context, as in the *Opus Caroli regis*, proclaims the event's role as proof of Christ's perfect union of two natures, his mediatorship between God and man. Sometimes, as in the *Opus Caroli regis*, defense of this doctrine focuses on the heavenly kingship and omnipotence of the crucified Christ, a power that Jesus could only have possessed on the cross if he was perfectly divine. At times, along such lines, the crucifixion and resurrection are recalled together; that one man suffered, died, and rose again by his own power, the cause of Satan's destruction and human salvation, shows the man to be God's only begotten son.[174] If the one "who suffered and was crucified in the flesh was not the lord savior and God, and son of the father," Alcuin states emphatically, quoting Athanasius, there is no true salvation.[175] When compared with Theodulf's treatise, though, the striking feature of the crucifixion theology developed in these texts is the attention given to the mortal human nature. For Paulinus and Alcuin, orthodoxy on the crucifixion is critical to their efforts to demonstrate that just as Jesus is truly God, God, through the assumption rather than the adoption of humanity, truly became man, demonstrating his divine love and mercy by embracing every aspect of human existence except sin, including death on a cross.

In Paulinus' *Liber sacrosyllabus*, the discussion of Elipandus' claim that Christ consists of two natures but three substances – divinity, soul, and flesh – brings comments on the completeness of the crucified human nature as proof of the son of God's true humanity.[176] Since the divine nature remains "impassible, inviolable, and forever immutable," unless Christ possesses human nature in its entirety, body and soul, he cannot have known the entire scope of human pain and frailty. Without the soul, the flesh cannot hunger, thirst, and feel the pains of the passion, while without the flesh the soul cannot be hungry, thirsty, or crucified, fastened to the cross at the hands and feet.[177] But two other lines of thought are

---

[174] See Alcuin, *Adv. Felicem* 3.15, 5.4, 11, *PL* 101.171B, 191C, 200B/C; Paulinus, *Contra Felicem* 1.25, 3.5, 24, *CCCM* 95.31, 89 lines 26–28, 113–114.   [175] Alcuin, *Liber contra haeresim* 17, *ST* 285.63.

[176] Paulinus, *Libellus sacrosyll.*, *MGH Conc.* 2.1.137–140; cf. *Epistola Episcoporum Hispaniae ad Episcopos Franciae*, *Conc. Franc. 794*, *MGH Conc.* 2.1.111–119, at 114 lines 34–39; Alcuin, *Ep. episc. Franciae*, *MGH Conc.* 2.1.149.

[177] Paulinus, *Libellus sacrosyll.*, *MGH Conc.* 2.1.140; see *Contra Felicem* 3.5, *CCCM* 95.89 lines 30–32; Alcuin, *Adv. Felicem* 7.11, *PL* 101.223B/C.

more important in the anti-Adoptionist tracts of both Alcuin and Paulinus. Against the Adoptionists' presumed belief that God merely adopted instead of assumed humanity, so that he did not experience all of mortal existence, the Carolingians insist that the suffering and death on the cross occurred to the second person of the Trinity. In order to save the human race, the very word, the immortal son of God, accepted the mortality that is the extreme of the human condition. In emphasizing, therefore, the indissolubility of the union between dying humanity and impassible divine, the recollections of the pain of crucifixion are often permeated with reminders of the divine nature, without sight being lost of the fact that the event involved true suffering. Although both Paulinus and Alcuin are clear that the divinity had no actual share in the torments of the crucified humanity – as Paulinus declares, "Christ God suffered in the flesh, not with the flesh, nor did he co-suffer with the flesh. For Christ God is outside the passion"[178] – they are equally adamant that, since the divine could not desert the human nature, the agony of the cross, like the resurrection, happened on some level to God.[179] Only in this case could it be true that "God so loved the world that he gave his only begotten son" and, in Paul's words, "He that spared not even his own son, but delivered him up for us all."[180] The crucified one was indeed the "lord of glory." The word who according to the divinity cannot be seen, touched, subdued, suffer, or die received flesh that was properly his. The divinity that before the incarnation did not have limbs, now having them could be fixed to the cross. The hand of him who created heaven and earth was pierced with a nail, and "his blood, through whom all things are created, was poured for the salvation of all."[181] For Alcuin, especially, the presence of God in the crucifixion is attested by the power belonging to the blood, a substance

[178] Paulinus, *Contra Felicem* 2.9, *CCCM* 95.59 line 23; see Alcuin, *Adv. Felicem* 4.13, *PL* 101.188C.

[179] See Paulinus, *Libellus sacrosyll.*, *MGH Conc.* 2.1.137 lines 19–20; Alcuin, *Adv. Felicem* 6.9, 7.10, 11, *PL* 101.211B-D (Leo I), 222D-223A, 224A.

[180] John 3.16; Romans 8.32. Alcuin, *Adv. Felicem* 1.15, *PL* 101.139D; *Adv. Elipandum* 3.6, *PL* 101.274D; *Ep. episc. Franciae*, *MGH Conc.* 2.1.145 line 34; Paulinus, *Libellus sacrosyll.*, *MGH Conc.* 2.1.134 line 11.

[181] See Paulinus, *Contra Felicem* 1.17, 37, *CCCM* 95.22–23, 45; Alcuin, *Adv. Felicem* 1.8, 2.4, 5.11, *PL* 101.134B, 149D, see 200B (Leo I). Attacking Felix's usage of the terms, *adoptivus* and *nuncupativus Deus*, Alcuin imagines what Christ might have said to his executioners: "Cur, quaeso, Redemptorem vestrum non agnoscitis? Cur Deum indutum pro vobis carne nescitis? Salvatori vestro necem paratis. Auctorem vitae ad mortem ducitis: Deus vester sum, quem suspenditis: Deus vester, quem crucifigitis. Quis, rogo, hic error, aut quae insania est?" *Adv. Felicem* 2.2, *PL* 101.147C.

that spilled from the dead humanity yet depended on the divine omnipotence for its ability to unify the human race with its creator. Indeed, he
hopes, its power is so great that it may "soften and dissolve" even
Elipandus' hardness of heart, since it was shed for his salvation, as well; for
"he is truly God who redeems you by his blood, and truly the son of God
who rose again from the tomb."[182]

Further, as a corollary to their insistence on God's participation in
mortal flesh through the assumption of humanity, Alcuin and Paulinus
emphasize the passion's voluntary aspect. In their belief, this characteristic
of the passion demonstrates not only Christ's omnipotence but also the
unique sinlessness of his human nature – a nature that in their eyes, consequently, cannot be adoptive. Jesus' death was undertaken of his own will,
they remind their Hispanic opponents, both because he was God and
because unlike other mortals he was under no obligation to die, possessing
a humanity that sin had not separated from God. Sometimes the emphasis
is on his divinity: God assured that Christ's humanity was unlike any other,
and even in death he only did what his power willed for the sake of other
mortals.[183] Elsewhere, though, the focus is more noticeably on the suffering of the cross. As in the following passage in Alcuin's *Adversus Felicem*, this
is suggested to have a certain marvelous or intense quality by being something Jesus chose to experience for humanity's sake that in his innocence he
did not have to accept, even though it is evident that the one who willed
such hardship was God:

> Voluntary and true hunger, since hungering he came to the fig-tree; volun-
> tary and true weariness, since tired from his journey he sat at the well; vol-
> untary and true wound, when he was struck by the soldier's lance in the
> side; voluntary and true death, when on the cross, with bowed head, he
> gave up the spirit; voluntary and true burial, when, having been taken
> down from the cross, Joseph and Nicodemus placed him in the tomb. For
> Christ had all these weaknesses of the flesh as voluntary, but true, since he
> assumed human nature not in fantasy but in truth. Hence he had these pas-
> sions voluntarily in the flesh, in order that in the truth of the flesh, by
> divine power, which was able neither to suffer nor ever to die, he might

---

[182] Alcuin, *Adv. Elipandum* 4.2, *PL* 101.287B/C; see *Adv. Felicem* 2.11, 7.15, *PL* 101.155B/C, 228D-229B
(Cyril); *Adv. Elipandum* 3.11, *PL* 101.278D-279A; Paulinus, *Contra Felicem* 1.25, *CCCM* 95.31.

[183] See Paulinus, *Contra Felicem* 1.18, 28, 37, 2.4, *CCCM* 95.23–24, 33, 45, 52–53; Alcuin, *Liber contra
haeresim* 13, *ST* 285.61.

conquer weakness and death, and raise his flesh into eternal life and power.[184]

The willingness of this suffering, for Paulinus and Alcuin so clearly contradictory to Adoptionist doctrine, shows that Jesus alone acts in perfect harmony with the father. That feature of the passion, Paulinus implies, testifies to the humility that is a necessary counterpart of obedience. All other mortals owe the penalty of death because they are estranged from God by sin, but what Christ undertook in his mortal nature for the rest of the human race, even the model of patience that he set in the suffering, sadness, and death of the cross, was done in full, humble obedience to his father. His will belongs to a humanity completely united with God, without sin's alienation.[185]

It is useful to compare Paulinus and Alcuin's writings against Adoptionism and the theology of the crucifixion developed there with the approach of the Visigoth, Benedict of Aniane. The probable author in 810–815 of the *Hucusque*, the supplement to the *Hadrianum* that gradually became the most popular in Carolingian territories, Benedict was a friend of Alcuin who helped bring Felix to the Aachen debate. He also served as supervisor of monasteries under Charlemagne's son, Louis the Pious, during the latter's governance of Aquitaine.[186] Alcuin's *Adversus Felicem* and *Adversus Elipandum* were meant to be used by Benedict and other orthodox preachers in the border areas of Charlemagne's kingdom, where it seems that Adoptionism spread rapidly in the 790s among clergy as well as laity. Benedict's own tracts are directed against the "Felicians" and the "Felician heresy," suggesting that he has in mind multiple followers of the bishop of Urgel. The teachings Benedict espouses against this group, as Cavadini has demonstrated, show a greater sympathy than do those of Alcuin or Paulinus with some of the theological presuppositions shared by

[184] Alcuin, *Adv. Felicem* 6.4, PL 101.204C/D; see ibid. 5.11, 7.15, 200B/C, 228B/C; *Liber contra haeresim* 38, ST 285.76 (Augustine); *Adv. Elipandum* 1.20, PL 101.256C; Paulinus, *Libellus sacrosyll.*, MGH Conc. 2.1.140.   [185] See Paulinus, *Contra Felicem* 3.3–5, 9, CCCM 95.87–90, 93.

[186] After Louis became the sole Carolingian emperor at Charlemagne's death in 814, he entrusted Benedict with the furtherance of monastic and liturgical reform in the empire. On Benedict's involvement in the Adoptionist controversy, Cavadini, *Last Christology*, 82, 115, 128–130, 184 n.7, 185 n.10; on his role in liturgical reform, Paxton, *Christianizing Death*, 131–133; and Jean Deshusses, "Le 'Supplement' au sacramentaire grégorien: Alcuin ou Saint Benoît d'Aniane?" *Archiv für Liturgiewissenschaft* 9 (1965), 48–71. See also Ardo, *Vita Benedicti abbatis Anianensis*, MGH SS 15.1, ed. G. Waitz (Hanover, 1887), 200–220, trans. Allen Cabaniss, "The Life of Saint Benedict, Abbot of Aniane and of Inde," in *Soldiers of Christ*, ed. Noble and Head, 213–254.

Elipandus and his Hispanic opponent, Beatus of Liebana. In this regard, they are indicative of Benedict's geographical proximity to the Hispanic Christology's strongholds, and possibly of direct knowledge of Beatus' counter-arguments.[187]

Benedict attacks the Adoptionists in two *opuscula*, probably written in the early ninth century, that were incorporated into his collection of doctrinal writings, the *Munimenta fidei*. One is the short treatise, *Disputatio adversus Felicianam impietatem*, the other is a tract or *Testimonia* for a former pupil, Guarnarius, who is charged with Felician beliefs.[188] Like Paulinus and Alcuin, Benedict agrees that the Adoptionists teach that Christ is adopted in his humanity,[189] and he links this idea with Arianism and Nestorianism. The former heresy is emphasized in the *Testimonia*; the emphasis is on Nestorianism in the *Disputatio*.[190] The Adoptionists confuse assumption with adoption, it is noted to Guarnarius and in the *Disputatio*. Christ is the true son of God "by the propriety of power"; the son did not adopt the man, since adoption refers only to the status of mortal Christians. Born from the father before the ages, Benedict declares, quoting the council of Chalcedon, the son of God was also born "from the Virgin Mary *Theotocos* according to the humanity" and now has, "without confusion," two natures or substances in his one person.[191]

In the *Testimonia*, however, Benedict's concern to demonstrate that Christ is fully God brings a sharp differentiation of the two natures. Alcuin and Paulinus also recognize that the humanity and divinity are distinct, but the language they use to uphold the union sometimes seems to compromise this doctrine, such as when they suggest that God participated in the crucifixion. While Benedict struggles with the same linguistic difficulty,

---

[187] See Cavadini, *Last Christology*, 71–72, 128–130.

[188] Benedict, *Testimoniorum nubecula de incarnatione Domini, sancta et individua Trinitate et iteratione baptismatis devitanda pernicie*, PL 103.1381–99 (henceforth = *Testimonia*); idem, *Disputatio Benedicti levitae adversus Felicianam impietatem*, PL 103.1399B-1411B (henceforth = *Disputatio*); on the likely date of the latter, Cavadini, *Last Christology*, 191 n. 64. Despite the title of the *Testimonia*, Benedict's initial remarks indicate that he writes to counter a feared revival of the "Felician heresy," which suggests that this work, too, dates to sometime after Felix's imprisonment: see PL 103.1381D. The opening of the *Disputatio* refers back to the *Testimonia*: PL 103.1399B. The *Munimenta fidei* date c. 804–814; see Jean Leclercq, "Les *Munimenta Fidei* de Saint Benoit d'Aniane," *Analecta Monastica ser.* 1.20 (1948), 21–74.

[189] Benedict, *Testimonia*, PL 103.1382D; *Disputatio*, PL 103.1399C/D; Cavadini, *Last Christology*, 130.

[190] Benedict, *Testimonia*, PL 103.1383D, 1389A, C/D; *Disputatio*, PL 103.1404C/D.

[191] Benedict, *Testimonia*, PL 103.1382D-1383B; *Disputatio*, PL 103.1406A/B (Chalcedon), see 1399C-1400, 1404C/D, 1407C, 1409C/D.

how to affirm the presence of two antithetical natures in a single person, the emphasis, in the *Testimonia*, lies on the other side of the equation. Consider, for example, the following passage, where he takes such care to separate the attributes of the divine and the human that he almost appears to lose sight of their union, as if dealing with two persons:

> For according to the man he hungered, in order that he might show true flesh. But according to the God he satisfied five thousand men with five loaves, in order to demonstrate that he had the power of God. According to the man he thirsted, but according to the God he refreshed the Samaritan with living water. According to the man he climbed into the ship, but according to the God he walked with dry feet on the sea. According to the man he slept on the ship, but according to the God he commanded the winds and the waves. According to the man he hung on the cross, but according to the God he gave paradise to the thief. According to the man, having suffered, he tasted death, but according to the God he raised himself from the dead.[192]

There is no sense here or elsewhere in this tract of Alcuin and Paulinus' concern to promote the exceptional status of Jesus' human nature through its union with divinity. While Christ is fully God his humanity remains, for Benedict, strikingly similar to that of ordinary mortals except in its sinlessness, and even the absence of sin receives noticeably little attention.

In the *Disputatio*, where Benedict focuses on the supposedly Nestorian qualities of Adoptionism, a theology of the incarnation is articulated that, Cavadini has pointed out, resembles the Christology of the Adoptionists and Beatus in its development on the Philippians 2 account of the word's self-lowering. The *Disputatio* again shows little interest in Christ's innocence or other characteristics specific to his humanity that distinguish it from ordinary mortals' existence.[193] Here, though, while Benedict admits that the

---

[192] Benedict, *Testimonia*, PL 103.1383B/C. Benedict continues (C/D): "Si haec et similia vellent sapienter discernere, et unicuique substantiae quod suum est deputarent, facile poterant rectae fidei cursum tenere, et non pro ejus beneficiis, quae pro nobis redimendis in forma servi suscepit vel passus est, divinitati ejus contumelias irrogarent, et ubicunque legunt in Scripturis secundum humanitatem aliquid quod minus loquatur divinitas, sed pro dispensatione carnis assumptae hoc protestetur humanitas, naturae unicuique propria recognoscerent, et divinitatis aequitatem derogare desisterent." See also ibid., PL 103.1388A, 1390A.

[193] Although Benedict recognizes Christ's sinlessness in his humanity, it is not something he stresses. Similarly, while Mary is proclaimed *Theotocos*, he does not dwell on the special qualities that distinguish her from ordinary women. See *Disputatio*, PL 103.1400D, 1406A/B (Chalcedon).

human nature was "assumed,"[194] he declares both that term and adoption ultimately inadequate. Both assumption and adoption in fact denote a similar process, he suggests, and thus assumption, too, implies the Nestorian heresy that the human nature had separate personhood prior to its union with divinity.[195] Against this, Benedict turns to the Philippians 2 theme of the word's descent as the foundation of Christ's mediatorship. Remaining inviolable in its divine nature,[196] the word lowered itself to become incarnate man. It did not assume flesh, but instead was "made flesh," meaning that it became flesh through its descent and self-emptying. This, Benedict claims, is the true meaning of Paul's statement that, "being rich he became poor" (2 Cor. 8.9), the opposite of which is implied by "assumption."[197]

Although the word "assumption" does not apply to Christ's humanity, then, it does denote his relationship with mortals in the body of the church. The son of God's coming to earth and the return to heaven are conceived as a process continuing even in the present through his mediation between the two realms. Insofar as "the plenitude of divinity dwelled corporeally" in the mediator – another way in which Benedict, following Paul, describes Christ's descent – it "fills" mortals, whose nature the son of God received into his person. The church that is Christ's body is replete with his divinity and the word is inseparably united with human nature in one person, making Christ the "assumption" and "refuge" of those who use the power this union gives them to become sons of God "by adoption."[198] They understand their savior's true being, because their hearts are illumined by the light of wisdom that is Christ. For Benedict, the father's begetting of the son is like the radiation of light from a lamp, an image that fits perfectly with this focus on the descent of a word who nonetheless remains God and is contemplated in his divinity. Beatus of Liebana uses a similar light metaphor to describe the incarnation in his treatise against Elipandus. Much the same image as Benedict employs is found in both the *carmen figuratum* for Charlemagne and the *Opus Caroli regis* by Theodulf of Orléans, two works that we may now see to share some of the identical, Christological presuppositions as the writings of fellow Hispanic/Visigothic theologians.[199]

---

[194] E.g. Benedict, *Disputatio*, PL 103.1407C, D.   [195] Ibid., *PL* 103.1401.

[196] Ibid., *PL* 103.1405A, 1408A.

[197] Ibid., *PL* 103.1401. See Cavadini, *Last Christology*, 128–130, cf. 64–66, discussing Beatus' outlook.

[198] Benedict, *Disputatio*, PL 103.1404D-1405 (Col. 2.8–10), 1408.   [199] Ibid., *PL* 103.1406D. See above, n. 197, for Beatus.

Whereas in the *Testimonia* Benedict stresses the differences between the two natures, in the *Disputatio* the notion of the word's self-lowering highlights the continuity of subject in Christ from his "birth" from the father through the entire history of salvation. The smoothly flowing descent and reascent of the word, a process spread out from before time to the ascension and, it is implied, climaxing in the events of the last day, binds Christ's two natures together and renders his mediatorship possible. As Benedict asks in the *Disputatio*, "Is Christ divided so that one is crucified and another Christ is the power and wisdom of God?" To this he answers,

> And since the same one is the one descending and ascending, there is also for us one Jesus Christ son of God and son of man, the word God and the man flesh, having suffered and died and been buried, and rising again having been received into heaven, sitting at God's right hand, having in himself one and the same, through dispensation and nature, in the form of God and in the form of servant, without any separation that which is man and without any division that which is God, without uncertainty, in which sacrament he both suffered and lived.[200]

The references to the crucifixion in the *Testimonia* and *Disputatio* reflect the different emphases in their approaches to Adoptionism. To the extent that the first-named text alludes to the crucifixion, the event is envisioned in terms of Christ's suffering and death as a true man, while his divine nature overcame death as the true God, two distinct sets of experience even though the two natures belong to one person. Alcuin and Paulinus stress God's participation in the crucifixion through the union of the two natures. In the *Testimonia*, perhaps because of his concern here with the Arian features of Adoptionism – perhaps this tells us something about the nature of the "Felicianism" that Guarnarius expounded – Benedict more clearly denies the divinity's involvement in anything related to the humanity's humiliation. Conversely, there is little parallel to the passages by Paulinus and Alcuin recalling the exceptional character of the crucified, sinless humanity.[201] The *Disputatio*, on the other hand, picks up on the theme that God underwent the cross's torments. As Benedict remarks towards the end of the tract, "although there was in the same [person] weakness unto the passion and power of God unto life, there is not one

---

[200] Ibid., *PL* 103.1408D-1409A.   [201] Cf. Benedict, *Testimonia*, *PL* 103.1383B/C, 1388A, 1390A.

being divided from himself who both suffered and lived. For the only-begotten God suffered what men are able to suffer."[202] But the *Disputatio*'s exegesis of the crucifixion is distinguished from that of Alcuin or Paulinus by the concept of the word's descent and ascent: even as the son remains consubstantial with the father, the crucifixion marks the final stage in his self-lowering to the form of servant, a process reversed in the resurrection. This doctrine of self-abasement forms the context in which Benedict reads John 3.16 and Romans 8.32, in particular the opening words of the latter verse, "He that spared not even his own son."[203] What God did not spare his son, for Benedict, was the entire process of descent, continued to death on the cross. As in the passage quoted earlier from the *Disputatio*, the crucifixion of the word is evidence of the perfection of the self-abasement, which went as far as it could go, and hence proof that it was salvific. "The only-begotten God suffered what men can suffer," and yet God remained the subject, as shown by the resurrection, ascension, and return.[204]

The *Opus Caroli regis*, the anti-adoptionist treatises, and their influence

The attacks on Nicea II and Adoptionism by Theodulf, Alcuin, Paulinus, and Benedict all clearly affirm Jesus' divinity, celebrated in so much other, early Carolingian literature and in the early Carolingian liturgies of Easter and the feasts of the cross. At the same time, however, their tracts present formal, theological defenses not simply of the son of God's divine nature, but of its indissoluble union with mortal humanity. Interpreting their adversaries' positions in light of the great councils of the early church, all four theologians view Christological orthodoxy as central to their argumentation. All of them are convinced that their opponents have abandoned Rome's doctrine of two, complete natures united in Christ's one person, the foundation of his mediatorship between heaven and the human race and, therefore, of the divine work of salvation.

Yet these features shared in common should not allow us to overlook the distinctive characteristics of each scholar's thought and of the crucifixion theology he articulates. Theodulf's *Opus Caroli regis* announces the

---

[202] Benedict, *Disputatio*, *PL* 103.1409A, see 1408C/D.
[203] See ibid., *PL* 103.1400B, D-1401A, 1402A/B, 1410B.   [204] Ibid., *PL* 103.1408C/D.

reconnection of the earthly with the heavenly realm through the passion's conquest of evil, an achievement that mirrored and was based on the joining of human with divine in the incarnation. While Jesus' humanity is regarded as crucial to this victory, the reader is encouraged to attend to the redeemer almost exclusively in his divinity. Mortals who leave behind the material world to which artistic images belong in order to study the Bible, both its literal meaning and that discernible through spiritual interpretation, come in contact with the heavenly son of God, the light of the word from the father also contemplated in the writings of other Hispanic and Visigothic scholars of the late eighth and early ninth centuries.

The theology of the crucifixion presented in the anti-Adoptionist treatises of Paulinus and Alcuin, on the other hand, is more concerned with the crucified humanity. This accords with their interest in defending not only the doctrine that Jesus is truly God, immortal and omnipotent, but its corollary, that God truly shared in human experience. In their writings, we find a marked effort to describe the divinity's participation in the suffering and death on the cross, despite the assurances that the divine nature remained impassible; and we find a pronounced effort to recall the passion's voluntary aspect. That Christ willed it to happen affirms the union of his two natures – his humanity acts in harmony with his divinity since it was assumed, not adopted – and indicates that assumption provided for a human nature possessing extraordinary characteristics not shared by ordinary mortals, above all sinlessness. Alcuin and Paulinus take similar approaches to refuting Adoptionism; but Alcuin's writings on the subject are distinctive, first, simply for their volume, much of it intended for Benedict of Aniane and others in the border territories in their struggle against Felicianism, and, second, for the emotional strength of some of his prose, his own comments and his abundant excerpts from church fathers.

Benedict of Aniane himself also looks to the crucifixion as the revelation of the union of two natures in Christ and thus of the divinity's full acceptance of human existence. Whereas the *Testimonia* distinguish between the two natures, though, despite their joining in one person, the *Disputatio* envisions the incarnation as the self-emptying of the word. More clearly than do the tractates by Paulinus and Alcuin, it therefore demonstrates the continuity of subject between the eternally reigning God and the man on the cross. The crucifixion emerges as a stage in the same process that encompassed the incarnation, the culmination to the self-lowering by which the son of God "became poor." One person, born from the father, lowered himself to the death on the cross and then rose again and reascended into heaven. Because the descent was complete, Christ was truly human as well as divine.

Reflections of the anti-Adoptionist struggle and the Christocentric thought it generated seem discernible in a few other writings by Paulinus besides those overtly directed against the Hispanic theology. [205] Possibly, too, as will be discussed in the next chapter, some artistic imagery from Charlemagne's reign offers evidence of the conflict's impact. To conclude this chapter, however, it is worthwhile briefly to consider a few tracts by Alcuin from the last five years of his life that, while not directly opposing Nicea II or Adoptionism, also set forth a Christological view of the passion's significance. Most likely, this perspective was influenced by his deliberations over the Hispanic teachings and, perhaps, by his participation in the editing of the *Opus Caroli regis*. One such text again aimed at defending orthodox doctrine against a Greek opponent. This is the letter that Alcuin composed between 801 and his death in 804 to answer a question raised by Charlemagne about the "ransom" theory of atonement proposed by a Byzantine visitor to the Frankish court. In response to his monarch, I have indicated in an earlier article, Alcuin outlines a redemption theology focused on the crucifixion's role as a sacrifice to atone God for human sin and to release the blood that purges sins;[206] but another noticeable feature of the letter (which I did not sufficiently address in my earlier study) is its insistence on the two natures in the crucified savior – the equality with the other persons of the Trinity of the "victor and victim and therefore victor because victim." One person, human and divine, both suffered and offered himself in sacrifice. Death and divine omnipotence belong to the same being; Jesus' sinless blood offering was achieved with the power by which he alone decided when he would put down his soul and take it up again.[207]

In writing to Charlemagne on the doctrine of ransom, Alcuin surely must have been conscious of the battle against Nicea II as well as the

---

[205] E.g. perhaps Paulinus' *Liber exhortationis* and, more clearly, some of his poetry, esp. *Carm.* 1, 11B, *Œuvre poétique*, 91–96, 99.

[206] Alcuin, *Ep.* 307, *MGH Epp.* 4.466–471; see Celia Chazelle, "To Whom Did Christ Pay the Price? The Soteriology of Alcuin's *Epistola 307*," *Proceedings of the Patristic, Medieval, and Renaissance Studies Conference* 14 (1989), 43–62; Jean Rivière, *Le Dogme de la rédemption au début du Moyen-Age* (Paris, 1934), 263–271.   [207] *Ep.* 307, *MGH Epp.* 4.470 lines 1–18, see 467–469.

more recent struggles against Adoptionism, even though neither issue is mentioned in the letter. The concern about the Adoptionists is clearer in *De fide sanctae et individuae Trinitatis*, a summary of the Catholic faith to guide clergy in their preaching. This treatise, the letter responding to the court's Greek visitor, and Alcuin's last anti-Adoptionist tract, *Adversus Elipandum*, were all written within three years of one another.[208] *De fide*, evidently motivated in part by fear of the spread of heresy from Spain into Carolingian regions, offers, in Book 3, an analysis of the union of two natures in the living, dead, and resurrected Christ that surpasses in completeness, eloquence, and conciseness any other from Charlemagne's court circle. Its basic lines of thought, however, have already been seen in Alcuin's and Paulinus' refutations of Felix and Elipandus.[209]

Alcuin's treatises on the gospel of John and the epistle to the Hebrews also emphasize the Christology of the passion, though to what extent this was his deliberate intention is uncertain, since here he extensively relies on patristic sources to interpret scriptural texts that themselves invite meditation on the relation between Jesus' two natures. Most of the commentary on John, which Alcuin completed in 800–801 for Charlemagne's sister, Gisla, and daughter, Rotrud, is drawn from Augustine; but the abbreviation of material from Augustine's tractates on John, along with the selections from a few other sources, have the general effect of providing for a clearer, partly because simpler, exposition of the gospel's Christology.[210] Alcuin's prefatory letter to Gisla and Rotrud remarks that, more than any other gospel, John's "intends to proclaim the divinity of our lord Jesus Christ, by which he is equal to the father."[211] The exegesis of the passion and resurrection is the first portion of the treatise that Alcuin composed, and to a limited extent it circulated separately from the rest of the com-

---

[208] Alcuin, *De fide sanctae et individuae Trinitatis*, PL 101.13–58; see Cavadini, "Sources and Theology," 124–131; and on the treatise's use of logic, especially the Categories, John Marenbon, "Alcuin, the Council of Frankfort and the Beginnings of Medieval Philosophy," in *Das frankfurter Konzil von 794*, ed. Berndt, 2.603–615, at 609–610. On the treatise's transmission, Bullough, "Alcuin's Cultural Influence," 12–15.

[209] *De fide* 3.9–18, PL 101.43B–51A; Cavadini, "Sources and Theology," 125–131, n. 11.

[210] *Comm. in Joann.*, PL 100.737–1008, prefatory materials also published as Alcuin, *Ep.* 196, MGH *Epp.* 4.323–325 and *Ep.* 213, MGH *Epp.* 4.354–357. On Alcuin's sources, Bullough, "Alcuin and the Kingdom of Heaven," 200–202. Gisela was abbess of the royal foundation of Chelles; Rotrud, whose betrothal to the Byzantine emperor Constantine VI was broken off in 787, was by 800 a nun at Chelles.   [211] *Comm. in Joann.*, *Ep. ad Gislam et Richtrudam*, PL 100.742A.

mentary.[212] A shorter, more succinct version of Augustine's analysis, it highlights the redemptive value of Christ's human suffering and humiliation but also God's ordering of that experience to reveal its true significance, and hence Jesus' divine nature. Every stage of the passion is demonstrated to signify, miraculously, some aspect of the divine accomplishment of salvation. The division of garments is a symbol of the church's diffusion in the world, the undivided tunic denotes ecclesiastical unity; the "width, and length, and height, and depth" of the cross (see Eph. 3.18) are a reminder of the virtues of charity and perseverance, the heavenly reward for good works, and the "profundity of God's grace."[213] The bowl of vinegar symbolizes the Jews, filled by the "world's iniquity" that the crucifixion overcame, the hyssop is symbolic of Jesus' humility, by which the faithful are cleansed of sin. The commentary on the final moments before and encompassing his death (John 19.28–37) notes his obedience, sacrifice, and the redeeming value of his blood, and obliquely identifies the blood and water from his side wound with baptism, the eucharist, and the church's creation, prefigured in Eve's birth from Adam's side.[214] Only the mediator between God and man, Alcuin observes through Augustine, could have so arranged all these episodes.[215] The subsequent discussion of the women's visit to the empty tomb confirms this message. Here Alcuin uses two homilies by Gregory I, adding passages of his own, to stress the God beneath the crucified flesh, a hidden truth offered to both the gentiles and the synagogue but inspiring the former alone to faith.[216]

The commentary on Hebrews 1–10, written c. 802, is the oldest known Latin treatise on this epistle. The exegesis is primarily from John Chrysostom's homilies as transmitted in the Latin version by Mutianus, though borrowings have also been identified from Augustine, Cassiodorus, and Gregory I.[217] Developing on Hebrews' own themes, as do later Carolingian commentators on the letter, Alcuin begins with analysis

---

[212] See esp. *Comm. in Joann.* 7.40, *PL* 100.977D-987B (John 19; Augustine, *In Iohannis Evangelium Tractatus* 116–120); Bullough, "Alcuin and the Kingdom of Heaven," 200; Brunhölzl, *Histoire de la litterature latine* 1.2.37.   [213] Ibid. 7.40, *PL* 100.982, 983B/C.

[214] Ibid. 7.40, *PL* 100.985–986.   [215] Ibid. 7.40, *PL* 100.984D-985A (Augustine, *Tract.* 119.4).

[216] Ibid. 7.41, *PL* 100.987B-992, esp. 988.

[217] *Ad Hebraeos, PL* 100.1031–1084. It is unclear whether the extant chapters represent only a portion of the original or whether Alcuin stopped his commentary at Hebrews 10: Eduard Riggenbach, *Historische Studien zum Hebräerbrief*, vol. 1: *Die ältesten lateinischen Kommentare zum Hebräerbrief* (Leipzig, 1907), 19–25, esp. 22–24. See also Bullough, "Alcuin's Cultural Influence," 19–20.

of Christ's perfect divinity and plays on the paradoxical union of eternal priesthood and kingship with the humanity offered in blood sacrifice. The central thread of the commentary is that the only begotten son of God is mediator between divine and human because he possesses both natures, having assumed flesh that he offered to atone for sin and end the repeated sacrifices of the Old Testament. Especially in the chapters on Hebrews 9–10, the focus is Christ's sinless, one-time oblation, the source of the blood that washes mortals in baptism, penance, and the mass and enables them to become adoptive sons of God.[218]

To refer to Alcuin's *De fide*, the letter responding to the court's Greek visitor, or commentaries on John and Hebrews as expositions of orthodox Christology does not do full justice to the thought expressed in these tracts. Nonetheless, it is important to be aware of how, at the end of the eighth century and beginning of the ninth, Christological doctrine and its ramifications were investigated in writings beyond the *Opus Caroli regis* or those that immediately stemmed from the Adoptionist controversy. While the tractates on John and Hebrews count among several works, not only by Alcuin, indicative of the development of exegetical studies in Charlemagne's scholarly circle,[219] his choice of these biblical texts as subjects of exegesis may have been influenced by a sense that they offered particularly valuable material for analyzing the union of two natures in the son of God.

Within a few years after Alcuin completed his commentary on John, around the time that he wrote the *Adversus Elipandum*, the letter on the atonement, the commentary on Hebrews, and *De fide sanctae et individuae Trinitatis*, his most famous pupil came to study at Tours, one who had already been with him at the court in the early 790s. This was Hrabanus Maurus, whose treatise, *In honorem sanctae crucis*, will be examined in the next chapter.

---

[218] *Ad Hebraeos* 9, 10, PL 100.1070D-1084, see esp. 1074D-1075A, 1077, 1081.
[219] See Michael Gorman, "Wigbod and Biblical Studies under Charlemagne," *Revue Bénédictine* 107 (1997), 40–76; idem, "The Commentary on Genesis of Claudius of Turin and Biblical Studies under Louis the Pious," *Speculum* 72 (1997), 279–329.

CHAPTER 3

The crucified God in the Gellone Sacramentary and Hrabanus Maurus' *In honorem sanctae crucis*

Among the surviving eighth- and early-ninth-century images of Christ from centers north of the Alps are a relatively few representations of the crucifixion, the vast majority if not all depicting him with stiffly erect body and open eyes.[1] The staring savior on the Werden Casket;[2] the enigmatic miniature in the Würzburg Pauline Epistles, where bands and dots of color fill the bodies of the living Christ and two thieves;[3] the solemn, crucified lord in the Durham gospel fragment;[4] the crucifixion watched by angels in the Gospels of St. Gall (fig. 4);[5] the early-ninth-century ivory, attributed to the court, of Mary and John with the loincloth-clad, crucified Christ, who gazes impassively at the viewer as he bleeds from the wounds in his hands and side;[6] the ivory in the cathedral treasury of Narbonne, a work

---

[1] A possible exception in the Gellone Sacramentary is discussed below, this chapter. Generally on Carolingian crucifixion images, see Johannes Reil, *Christus am Kreuz in der Bildkunst der Karolingerzeit* (Leipzig, 1930).

[2] Werden, Abbey Church; *799: Kunst und Kultur der Karolingerzeit, Karl der Grosse und Papst Leo III. in Paderborn: Katalog der Ausstellung Paderborn 799*, 2 vols., ed. C. Steigemann and M. Wemhoff (Mainz, 1999), 2. 479 VII.35; Victor H. Elbern, "Der fränkische Reliquienkasten und Tragaltar von Werden," in *Das erste Jahrtausend: Kultur und Kunst im werdenden Abendland an Rhein und Ruhr*, 3 vols., ed. V. H. Elbern (Düsseldorf, 1962), 1.436–470, see fig. 1.

[3] Würzburg, Universitätsbibliothek, Mp. theol. fol. 69, fol. 7r; Ernst H. Zimmermann, *Vorkarolingische Miniaturen*, 4 vols. (Berlin, 1916), vol. 3, pl. 220 (a).

[4] Durham, Cathedral Library, A.II.17, fol. 38₃ v; Zimmermann, *Vorkarolingische Miniaturen*, vol. 3, pl. 222 (a).

[5] St. Gallen, Stiftsbibliothek, Cod. Sang. 51, p. 266; see Gertrud Schiller, *Iconography of Christian Art*, trans. J. Seligman (Greenwich, CT, 1972), vol. 2.102.

[6] Formerly Berlin, Staatliche Museen No. 601; Adolph Goldschmidt, *Die Elfenbeinskulpturen aus der Zeit der Karolingischen und Sächsischen Kaiser, VIII.-IX. Jahrhundert*, vol. 1 (Berlin, 1914), no. 8.

Figure 4. Crucifixion,
Gospelbook, Stiftsbibliothek
St. Gallen, Cod. Sang. 51, S.
266 (Zumbühl Nr. 20)

Figure 4. Crucifixion,
Gospelbook, Stiftsbibliothek
St. Gallen, Cod. Sang. 51, S.
266 (Zumbühl Nr. 20)

sometimes dated c. 810, depicting the crucifix surrounded by witnesses and scenes from the passion to the pentecost,[7] exemplify artists' efforts in early medieval northwestern Europe to create images that invite contemplation of Jesus' immortality even as he hung on the cross.

[7] Narbonne, Cathedral Treasury; Danielle Gaborit-Chopin, *Elfenbeinkunst im Mittelalter*, trans. Gisela Bloch and Roswitha Beyer (Berlin, 1978), 52 fig. 43, cat. 45, dating the ivory c. 810, but noting that it has also been assigned to the reign of Charles the Bald.

Innumerable depictions of the cross from the same period and region also offer reminders of Jesus' divine omnipotence: cross pages in manuscripts, a mode of decoration that reaches the peak of its popularity in the late eighth century; an increasing number of cross-decorated book covers from the same years, such as the late-eighth-century "first" cover of the Book of Lindau, where four busts of Christ mark the cross's center;[8] crosses decorating church furnishings and walls; gemmed altar and processional crosses such as the splendid one in Brescia, where Christ sits enthroned at the center.[9] Other eighth- and early-ninth-century productions in various media recall his power and kingship by portraying the *Majestas Domini* or lord of the apocalypse, his miracles, the ascension, the enthroned Mary holding her child. On the following page to the crucifixion miniature in the St. Gall Gospels, a bust of Christ holding a cross staff is watched by two angels blowing horns and the apostles, a scene that links the passion with his ascension, enthronement in heaven, and return at the end of time.[10] Several early Carolingian ivories have survived that show the lord treading on the beasts, a motif based on Psalm 90.13, a psalm used in the Roman Good Friday liturgy (fig. 5).[11] Works of art where Christ himself is not represented, such as an ivory of St. Michael spearing the dragon,[12] the illumination of the fountain of life in the Godescalc Gospel Lectionary,[13] and Theodulf's mosaic of the Ark of the Covenant at

[8] New York, Pierpont Morgan Library; Hubert et al., *L'Empire carolingien*, 211 fig. 192; Victor H. Elbern, "Liturgisches Gerät in edlen Materialen," in W. Braunfels, ed., *Karl der Grosse: Lebenswerk und Nachleben*, 4 vols., vol. 3: *Karolingische Kunst*, ed. Braunfels and H. Schnitzler (Düsseldorf, 1965), 115–167, at 154 fig. 26. See Bernhard Bischoff, "Kreuz und Buch im Frühmittelalter und in den ersten Jahrhunderten der spanischen Reconquista," *Mittelalterliche Studien: Ausgewählte Aufsätze zur Schriftkunde und Literaturgeschichte*, 3 vols., vol. 2 (Stuttgart, 1967), 284–303; Frauke Steenbock, "Kreuzförmige Typen frühmittelalterlicher Prachteinbände," in *Das erste Jahrtausend*, ed. Elbern, 1.495–513, esp. 498.

[9] Brescia, Museo Cristiano; *799: Kunst und Kultur, Katalog* 1. xxxvi, pl. 1; Braunfels, ed., *Karl der Grosse*, 3, Color Plate 31. Cf. the manuscripts and other objects reproduced in *799: Kunst und Kultur: Katalog*, esp. vol. 2, e.g. 445 VII.12, 453 VII.15, 626 IX.12, 650 IX.32, 652 IX.33, 653 IX.34, 776 Pl. 3, 783 XI. 2, 798 XI.12.

[10] St. Gall, Stiftsbibl., MS 51, pg. 267; Zimmermann, *Vorkarolingische Miniaturen*, 3, pl. 188 (a).

[11] Oxford, Bodleian Library, MS Douce 176, ivory cover. Also, the Genoels-Elderen diptych in Brussels, Musées Royaux d'Art et d'Histoire, Nr. 1474; the Lorsch Gospels cover in the Vatican, Museo Sacro, A. 62; *799: Kunst und Kultur: Katalog* 2.735 X.22b; Gaborit-Chopin, *Elfenbeinkunst*, cat. 37, 39, 40.

[12] Leipzig, Museum des Kunsthandwerks (Nr. 5350); *799: Kunst und Kultur: Katalog* 2.748 X.30; Gaborit-Chopin, *Elfenbeinkunst*, 50 fig. 40, cat. 42.

[13] Paris, BNF, nouv. acq. lat. 1203, fol. 3v; Hubert et al., *L'Empire carolingien*, 279 fig. 279; Percy Ernst Schramm, Hermann Fillitz, and Florentine Mütherich, *Denkmale der deutschen Könige*

Figure 5. Christ treading on
the beasts, Oxford, Bodleian
Library, MS Douce 176, ivory
cover

St.-Germigny-des-Prés (fig. 3), commemorate in other ways his divine origins, heavenly governance, and victory against death and the devil.

Although it is important not to oversimplify the signification of these varied images, they all generally offer visual testimony to the strength of the cult of the conquering son of God reflected in so much of the early Carolingian literature investigated in the last chapter. In certain ways, the same claim can be made about the decoration of the two books that are my principal concern in the following pages: the Gellone Sacramentary (Paris, BNF, MS lat. 12048), and *In honorem sanctae crucis*, the treatise containing twenty-eight *carmina figurata* honoring the cross that Hrabanus Maurus completed in 813/814, while head of the school at his monastery, Fulda.[14] As I will try to show particularly by reference to their depictions of the crucified Christ, however, these works also provide evidence that their designers expressly sought iconographic means to convey the doctrine not only that Jesus is God, but that he unites two complete natures in his one person.

A unique version of the "eighth-century Gelasian" sacramentary that incorporates borrowings from the *Hadrianum*, the Gellone Sacramentary has been convincingly dated to 790– c. 804 and assigned to a center, possibly Meaux, working for Notre Dame at Cambrai. Cambrai's bishop at the time, Hildoard (790–816), had strong ties to Charlemagne's court and was involved in the efforts at liturgical reform.[15] It is likely that he attended the

footnote 13 (*cont.*)

    und Kaiser, 2 vols., vol. 1: Schramm and Mütherich, *Ein Beitrag zur Herrschergeschichte von Karl der Grossen bis Friedrich II. 768–1250* (Munich, 2nd expanded edn., 1981), 213 pl. 8.

[14] *In honorem sanctae crucis*, CCCM 100, ed. M. Perrin (Turnhout, 1997). Subsequent references to individual texts and figures in this edition indicate section (A, B, C, D) and line numbers. Reproductions are from Biblioteca Apostolica Vaticana, Reginensis Latinus 124; on this manuscript, see Perrin, ed., *In honorem s. crucis*, CCCM 100, esp. xxx, xxxiv–lv. French translation in idem, *Raban Maur, Louanges de la Sainte Croix* (Paris, 1988). On the treatise's date, Ferrari, *Liber s. crucis*, 12–13, and *passim* for an excellent study of the treatise, focusing on its place in the evolution of medieval poetry. See also Ernst, *Carmen figuratum*, 222–292; Herrad Spilling, *Opus Magnentii Hrabani Mauri in honorem sanctae crucis conditum: Hrabans Beziehung zu seinem Werk* (Frankfurt, 1992). Facsimile of a ninth-century copy in *Hrabanus Maurus. Liber de laudibus sanctae crucis. Codex Vindobonensis 652 der Österreichischen Nationalbibliothek, Wien. Vollständige Faksimile-Ausgabe* (Graz, 1972).

[15] Since Gellone includes some Roman Gregorian forms taken from the *Hadrianum*, it could not have been made earlier than 784, when that copy of the Gregorian sacramentary arrived at Charlemagne's court. The Gellone Sacramentary was at the abbey of Gellone (today St.-Guilhem-le-Desert) from its foundation in 804 or shortly thereafter, but Jean Deshusses presented strong arguments that the book was produced for Hildoard of Cambrai, who was also responsible for "l'unique lectionnaire d'Alcuin non supplémenté (Cambrai 553); [et] le plus

Council of Frankfurt in 794;[16] but even if he was not there, his connections
with the court mean he was probably familiar with the doctrinal deliberations that began in the early years of the 790s and continued almost until
Alcuin's death in 804. My focus with the sacramentary is, first, the illumination of the Virgin Mary at the beginning of the codex, and then three
images of Christ, among them the widely published miniature of the crucified lord on the T of the *Te igitur* prayer (fol. 143v; see figs. 6, 7, 9, and 10).
At this point, I can only offer suggestions as to how these miniatures should
be interpreted, which I hope may encourage other historians or art historians to undertake more comprehensive evaluations of the manuscript and
the entirety of its decoration. Yet when the paintings that interest me are
examined in light of contemporary anti-Adoptionist literature, the *Opus
Caroli regis*, and certain other writings by Alcuin, it becomes apparent that
one aim behind their creation may have been to provide visual support for
the Christological orthodoxy being defined precisely at this time, in the
face of the heresies supposedly rampant in Spain and Byzantium. Possibly,
Alcuin's direct influence is discernible here; as Jean Deshusses noted, pro-
posing a connection between Alcuin and the Gellone Sacramentary, the
eighth-century Gelasian was the sacramentary type that the Anglo-Saxon
scholar seems to have preferred.[17] An anti-heretical character to the manuscript's imagery may shed light on why the Gellone Sacramentary went
from Notre-Dame of Cambrai to Gellone soon after the latter's foundation, conceivably as one of the gifts that Louis the Pious and Duke William
of Toulouse gave the monastery. One of the most important new monastic
communities in Louis' kingdom of Aquitaine, Gellone was established in
804 by William and Benedict of Aniane, the supervisor of monasteries in

footnote 15 (*cont.*)

> ancien exemplaire de *l'Hadrianum* non corrigé ni supplémenté (Cambrai 164)": Jean
> Deshusses, "Le sacramentaire de Gellone dans son contexte historique," *Ephemerides liturgicae*
> 75 (1961), 193–210 at 199. See idem, Introduction, *Sacr. Gellon.*, CCSL 159A.vii, xix-xxi, xxv-xxvi.
> An earlier study of the book's decoration was undertaken by B. Teyssèdre, *Le Sacramentaire de
> Gellone et la figure humaine dans les manuscrits francs du VIIIe siècle, de l'enluminure à l'illustration*
> (Toulouse, 1959). I am very grateful to Dr. Patricia Stirnemann and the Bibliothèque Nationale
> de France for arranging for me to examine the manuscript directly.

[16] The synod's capitulary notes that its attendants included bishops and priests from all parts of
Charlemagne's realm: *Capit. Franc.* 1, *MGH Conc* 2.165. Officially, the consensus of the bishops
of Francia is presented in Alcuin's *Epistola episcoporum Franciae*, *MGH Conc.* 2.142–157. See
Hartmann, *Synoden*, 106.

[17] See Deshusses, "Sacramentaire de Gellone," 208–210, though cf. Bullough, "Alcuin and the
Kingdom of Heaven," 204.

Louis' realm.[18] Benedict, it should be recalled, had assisted Alcuin in his campaign against Adoptionism, and his own *Testimonia* and *Disputatio adversus Felicianam impietatem*, probably written in the early ninth century, warn of the dangers that "Felicianism" continued to pose in the Carolingian territories near Spain.[19] At the very least, Benedict would surely have recognized the potential correspondence between the manuscript's decoration and the struggle against Adoptionism (whether or not it had been sent to Gellone for this purpose), both because of his own efforts to refute the Christology and because he was well acquainted with Alcuin's writings on the subject.

With *In honorem s. crucis*, it is also impossible in a single chapter to analyze exhaustively the complex thought suggested by its imagery and poetry as well as prose. Instead, I want to concentrate on one, critical issue: how Poem 1, with its representation of the crucified savior (fig. 11), provides the intellectual foundation for the ideas about Christ, the cross, and the passion set forth in the rest of the treatise, apparently by alluding to some of the same doctrinal developments that seem relevant to understanding the Gellone decoration. There is no evidence that Hrabanus envisioned a polemical purpose for his work or meant it directly to address the threats of Christological unorthodoxy that his master, Alcuin, had confronted. The noticeable connections with Alcuin's teachings, and perhaps with those articulated in the *Opus Caroli regis*, point more to a common climate of opinion than immediate influence. Nevertheless, the image that Hrabanus created of words in Poem 1 of his treatise is possibly the most thorough-going attempt in Carolingian art to express the doctrine of Christ's mediatorship that was so important to both Alcuin and Theodulf. In this respect, it may have no match in earlier or later western imagery.

The Gellone Sacramentary

Gellone has long been recognized as exceptional among early sacramentaries for its rich decorative scheme as much as its text. Throughout the book, margins and initials are adorned with an assortment of ornamental, vegetal, animal, and human figures, some depicted in ways that can only be

---

[18] Ardo, "Life of Saint Benedict," ch. 30, in *Soldiers of Christ*, ed. Noble and Head, 239–241 (this chapter is an eleventh-century addition to the life). See McKitterick, *Frankish Kingdoms Under the Carolingians*, 108.   [19] See chapter 2, at n. 186.

meant as consciously humorous. Clearly, more was involved in designing the book than solely the defense of orthodox Christology.[20] The *Te igitur* miniature (fol. 143v; fig. 7) and the opening depiction of the Virgin, the latter forming the upper half of the I-initial of the sacramentary's *incipit* (fol. 1v; fig. 6), are the two largest images in the codex. Wearing a gold ornamented gown with beaded trim or necklace and a headdress (pointed like the headdress worn by St. Agatha, fol. 17v, and similar to the pointed male head on fol. 35v), Mary holds a processional cross raised in her left hand and a censer dangling from her right. At the bottom of the page, below her feet and the title, "On the vigil of the Lord's birth at None, at St. Mary's" (Rome's stational church used by the pope for the Christmas vigil), appears the beginning of the vigil's first oration: "God, you who make us rejoice in yearly expectation of our redemption, grant that we be unafraid to see coming as judge your only begotten, whom we joyfully receive as redeemer."[21]

The Gellone Virgin lacks the jeweled headdress she wears in depictions commissioned by Pope John VII (705–707),[22] but her decorative robe otherwise recalls the iconography of *Maria regina* that developed in the west in association with the papal court.[23] Other echoes of this iconography have been noted in other early Carolingian depictions, such as the Genoels-Elderen and Bodleian ivories, where Mary is more simply dressed but the *sella curulis* on which she sits offers a different reminder of her authority (fig. 5).[24] In the Gellone miniature, she stands alone without her child, as she evidently appeared in the original setting of the mosaics that John VII ordered for St. Peter's.[25] The arrangement accords with the miniature's placement alongside prayers for the commemoration of the eve of Christ's

---

[20] Note, e.g., the playfully intertwined figures and the contorted figure having his beard snipped by gigantic shears, alongside a prayer for tonsuring (fols. 164v, 209r); *Sacr. Gellon.*, CCSL 159A, figs. 104, 107.

[21] *Sacr. Gellon.*, CCSL 159, no. 1: "Deus qui nos redemptionis nostre annua expectatione letificas, presta ut unigenitum tuum, quem redemptorem leti suscepimus, uenientem quoque iudicem securi uideamus."

[22] Hans Belting, *Likeness and Presence: a History of the Image before the Era of Art*, trans. from the German by Edmund Jephcott (Chicago, 1994), 126–129; Suzanne Lewis, "A Byzantine *Virgo Militans* at Charlemagne's Court," *Viator* 11 (1980), 71–93, at 76.

[23] Her gold robe with beaded trim at the neck or pearl necklace is reminiscent of the Virgin's dress in the mosaic of the triumphal arch in Sta. Maria Maggiore, Rome: Carlo Cecchelli, *I Mosaici della basilica di S. Maria Maggiore* (Turin, 1956), pls. 49, 53.   [24] Above, n. 11.

[25] See Belting, *Likeness and Presence*, 127 and fig. 76; Anna Kartsonis, *Anastasis: the Making of an Image* (Princeton, 1986), 78–80 and fig. 15.

Figure 6. Mary initial, Gellone Sacramentary, Paris, Bibliothèque Nationale de France, cod. lat. 12048, fol. 1 verso

birth, when, as the accompanying prayer declares, the faithful wait in hope
for his appearance. The liturgical instruments she holds (the processional
cross and censer) are uncommon in early medieval Marian imagery, yet a
tradition existed for showing her with a cross scepter, and Mary holds a
censer in some Carolingian images of the women at the tomb, such as that
on the Narbonne crucifixion ivory.[26] Thus the latter detail of the Gellone
painting, and conceivably the empty cross, may be partly meant to
evoke the coming resurrection. They also link the picture with the liturgy
of the Christmas mass celebrated after the vigil, recalling the connection
between Mary's role in Jesus' birth and the "new" incarnation in the
eucharist. But while sense can be made of this image without reference to
the theological deliberations of Charlemagne's court in the 790s, its overall
uniqueness needs to be stressed. Pictorial precedents or liturgical rationale
can be identified for individual features, but taken as a whole the portrayal
of Mary standing alone without the infant Jesus, in royal garb and holding
both a processional cross and a censer, is without close parallel in known
older or contemporary works of art.

Although the early Carolingian cult of the Virgin is attested in non-
Alcuinian sources, the most substantial literary comparisons to the
Gellone depiction of Mary are in his writings, those directed against
Adoptionism and others, as well. Mary's royal lineage, for example, is a
regular theme of Alcuin's comments on her significance. It occurs already
in the relatively early work, *De laude Dei*, which is based on his experience of
the liturgy at York before he joined Charlemagne's court. The section of *De
laude Dei* on the antiphonary contains a group of texts that present striking
acclamations of the Virgin, hailing her as the *porta facta coeli* and *benedicta
imperatrix et gloriosa castitatis regina*, and declaring that she is crowned in
heaven.[27] Comparable praise recurs in poetry by Alcuin, such as a *titulus* for
an altar dedicated to the Virgin that announces her to be the *Dei genetrix,
castissima virgo, lux et stella maris, nostrae regina salutis*,[28] and the notion of

[26] Above, n. 7; Lewis, "Byzantine *Virgo Militans*," 77.
[27] Edited in Radu Constantinescu, "Alcuin et les *Libelli precum* de l'époque carolingienne," *Revue
de l'histoire de la spiritualité* 50 (1974), 17–56, esp. 49–51, nos. 80 ("Porta facta coeli, virgo Maria
facta est filia Dei"), 84 ("Vere benedicta imperatrix et gloriosa castitatis regina, quae dum
honore virginitatis gaudium matris habes"), 93 ("Sancta Maria, nos laudamus te, gloriosa, glo-
rificamus te, corona regni coronata es, intercede pro nobis, quia beata es"). See Bullough,
"Alcuin and the Kingdom of Heaven," 163–166, 197.
[28] Alcuin, *Carm.* 109.4, *MGH PLAC* 1.336, see also *Carm.* 88.2, 89.13, 90.1–2, *MGH PLAC* 1.305, 310,
313–314.

her royal descent is incorporated into the arguments of his anti-Adoptionist treatises. For Alcuin as well as Paulinus, the Adoptionists' supposed rejection of the doctrines that Jesus is completely divine as well as human and that his human nature is sinless rested on a misunderstanding of the incarnation. Elipandus, Felix, and their supporters failed to realize that far from having adopted human nature, the son of God was conceived by both God and man, and hence his mother is the true *Theotocos*. This truth about the incarnation is celebrated in the Christmas liturgy, Alcuin shows in his *Adversus Felicem*, where he quotes the prayer below the Gellone image to defend the two natures' union in Christ.[29] The encomias of the Virgin in the Carolingian anti-Adoptionist treatises are themselves grounded in older Latin literature, as is evident from Alcuin's substantial reliance on excerpts from patristic authorities. But in their tracts attacking the Adoptionists, Paulinus and especially Alcuin take such ideas to new lengths. Mary's cult gains exceptional clarity as they explain the crucial significance of her glory to Jesus' position in the Trinity and, accordingly, to the crucifixion's salvific efficacy. Alcuin, in particular, as indicated in the last chapter, attacks Elipandus and Felix by referring to Mary as the product of a royal line and to her unique magnificence among mortals. [30]

The inspiration that the conflict with Adoptionism gave to devotion to the Virgin, particularly for Alcuin, is also apparent from his votive mass in her honor. Its prayers invoke her role as the powerful intercessor who helps assure that participants in the mass enjoy God's protection from evil and sin, receive a eucharistic oblation that is salvific, and come to future beatitude. A lengthy defense of Mary's uniqueness is also found in the same scholar's *De fide sanctae et individuae Trinitatis*, and she is more briefly praised in the commentary on John.[31] The parallels to these writings in the Gellone painting are evident: the dress suggestive of Mary's royal status; the power suggested by her erect stature and the control she wields over the instruments of the mass (here, too, as in Alcuin's votive mass, she may be the mediator of the eucharistic celebration, and she marks the "entrance" to the liturgy, recalling her praise in *De laude Dei* as the "gate of heaven"); the connection that she, her cross, and her censer imply between

---

[29] Alcuin, *Adv. Felicem* 7.13, *PL* 101.227A. See Bullough, "Alcuin and the Kingdom of Heaven," 204.

[30] Bullough, "Alcuin and the Kingdom of Heaven," 197–198.

[31] Deshusses, "Messes d'Alcuin," nos. 20–23; *Sacramentaire grégorien* 2, ed. Deshusses, nos. 1841–1846; Alcuin, *De fide* 3.14, *PL* 101, esp. 46–47; idem, *Comm. in Joann.* 1.1, *PL* 100.749.

the incarnation, the passion, and the mass; the allusions to the eschaton through the two Christograms with *alpha* and *omega* that appear between the lines of text beside her, where – in the prayer below her feet – Christ's future return is remembered; and, possibly, her identification as a quasi-personification of *Ecclesia*, through her censer and processional cross.

Whereas the Christmas vigil miniature and its oration refer to the passion, resurrection, eucharist, and apocalypse while most directly remembering the incarnation, the *Te igitur* illumination turns attention squarely to the crucified son of God who sacrificed himself on the cross, rules in heaven, and will reappear on the last day, tying these themes again to the church and the mass. The image (fol. 143v; fig. 7) is situated slightly beyond the book's midpoint, at the start of the prayer for the eucharistic sacrifice that, with the diffusion of the supplemented Gregorian sacramentaries, ninth-century Carolingian clergy came to view as the beginning of the canon of the mass. Dressed in a long, front-knotted loincloth or perizoma that leaves his chest bare but covers his navel, a cross-inscribed nimbus encircling the curly hair that frames his head, the bearded Jesus stands rigidly upright on the cross, as he does in the crucifixion images noted at the beginning of this chapter. His eyes stare from an impassive face and his arms extend straight from his body; red blood flows from the wounds in his hands, feet, and right side. The cross behind him, dark blue with a red border, has the abbreviated title on the upper arm and is sprinkled with red and white stars or possibly gems. Above it float two angels in decorated gowns, the seraphim described in the *Vere dignum* prayer as singing the *Sanctus* hymn written above Christ's head in red and black, Latin and Greek letters. Their wings (two each) have green and red feathers spotted with black and white almond motifs, perhaps to suggest peacocks' wings or, more likely, those of the six-winged creatures "full of eyes" who sing the *Sanctus* in Apocalypse 4.8.[32] With their outstretched hands, though, the Gellone angels not only praise the lord sabaoth with the *Sanctus* hymn; probably, too, they witness his ascension and receive his ascending body, in accordance with the request in the *Supplices te* prayer that an angel bear the eucharist to the heavenly altar.[33] On the opposite page (fol. 144r), a head with long wavy hair forms the top of an initial I for the section of the *Te igitur* that begins, *Inprimis quae tibi offerimus pro ecclesia tua sancta*

[32] Schiller, *Iconography*, 2.102.
[33] *Sacr. Gellon.*, CCSL 159, nos. 1932, 1941; see Marie-Christine Sepière, *L'Image d'un Dieu souffrant: aux origines du crucifix* (Paris, 1994), 122.

Figure 7. *Te igitur* initial, Gellone Sacramentary, Paris, Bibliothèque Nationale de France, cod. lat. 12048, fol. 143 verso

catholica. Given the text, it is possible that this represents *Ecclesia.*[34] Although the face looks toward the top of the preceding page, above Christ's head, it is clear that it is to be associated with the imagery of Christ and the angels that marks the start of the *Te igitur* oration.

---

[34] I am grateful to Lawrence Nees for calling this small but clearly significant image to my attention and for suggesting a plausible interpretation. Earlier images of *Ecclesia* exist; on the motif's evolution, see Gertrud Schiller, *Ikonographie der christlichen Kunst,* 5 vols. (Gütersloh, 1966–1991), 4.1.

Most of the individual motifs of the *Te igitur* miniature have known precedents in earlier western or Byzantine art. As has already been noted, the depiction of Christ alive on the cross with open eyes and erect body is typical of surviving crucifixion images from the west before the ninth century, and it was a preferred iconography in early Byzantium, despite the appearance there of the first images of the dead Christ in the seventh to eighth centuries.[35] The gems or more likely stars on the Gellone cross do not seem to correspond to earlier imagery of the crucifixion, but they bring to mind gemmed crosses such as might have been used for processions or placed near an altar in an important early Carolingian church like Notre-Dame at Cambrai. The perizoma, which Christ wears on the court and Narbonne ivories mentioned at the beginning of this chapter, and which was a typical attribute in ninth-century Carolingian crucifixion images, was one of several forms of dress in representations of the crucified Jesus from Byzantium and Italy before the Gellone Sacramentary. The perizoma was originally depicted and later painted over with a colobium on a Sinai icon of the seventh or eighth century, evidence, Kathleen Corrigan has demonstrated, of indecision about the relative signification of the two vestments among Byzantine artists of the seventh to ninth centuries.[36] Christ wears the same garment on the Ursus tablet, a north Italian work of the mid eighth century;[37] he wears a briefer loincloth on the fifth-century London passion tablet and carved door of Sta. Sabina, Rome.[38] Perhaps most significantly, in terms of precedents for the Gellone image, the fresco commissioned by Pope John VII for the triumphal arch over the main apse in Sta. Maria Antiqua, Rome, originally showed a crucified Christ who, like the Gellone figure, had a short beard, open eyes, and curly hair, wore the perizoma, and was accompanied by angels – in the fresco,

[35] Kurt Weitzmann, *The Monastery of Saint Catherine at Mount Sinae: the Icons*, vol. I: *From the Sixth to the Tenth Century* (Princeton, 1976), cat. B.36. On this iconography's development, Kartsonis, *Anastasis*; Hans Belting and Christa Belting-Ihm, "Das Kreuzbild im *Hodegos* des Anastasios Sinaites: ein Beitrag zur Frage nach der ältesten Darstellung des toten Crucifixus," in *Tortulae: Studien zu altchristlichen und byzantinischen Monumenten*, ed. W. N. Schumacher (Rome, 1966), 30–39.

[36] Kathleen Corrigan, "Text and Image on an Icon of the Crucifixion at Mount Sinai," in *The Sacred Image East and West*, ed. R. Ousterhout and L. Brubaker (Urbana, 1995), 45–62, at 46–49 and nn. 7, 14; Weitzmann, *Icons*, cat. B.32.

[37] Museo Archeologico [Arte Sacra, 2]; Gaborit-Chopin, *Elfenbeinkunst*, 43 fig. 34, cat. 36.

[38] Schiller, *Iconography*, 2.6–7 and fig. 323. Gregory of Tours seems to refer to an image of Christ in a loincloth in *De gloria martyrum* 22.

six-winged seraphim or cherubim.[39] Such close correspondences between these two images raise the question of whether the Gellone painting's designer or artist may have seen the apse fresco or received information about it through travels by him or others between Rome and northern Francia.

Other western images predating the sacramentary also show angels alongside the crucifix, as do, for instance, the illuminations of the Durham gospel fragment (fol. 38_3 verso)[40] and the St. Gall Gospels (p. 266) where they stand in attendance at the cross arms, holding books in the St. Gall picture (fig. 4). Flying or hovering two-winged angels, closer to those in Gellone, appear on eighth- and early-ninth-century crucifixion icons from Mt. Sinai.[41] Precedents exist, too, for the representation of Jesus' side wound. A number of early crucifixion images portray him flanked by Longinus (the lance bearer) and Stephaton (the sponge bearer); examples include the reliquary shrine lid of c. 600 from the Sancta Sanctorum in Rome,[42] the Durham and St. Gall gospelbook paintings (fig. 4), the Ursus tablet, and the wall painting in the Theodotus chapel of Sta. Maria Antiqua (fig. 8). In these images, Stephaton lifts the cup or sponge of vinegar to Christ's mouth and Longinus either has just pierced his side or is in the act of doing so. On the crucifixion ivory attributed to the early-ninth-century court, neither Longinus nor Stephaton is shown, but the wounded, peri-zoma-clad Christ is accompanied by Mary, John, and personifications of the sun and moon.[43] The depiction of the bleeding, crucified Jesus without any earthly attendants, however, seems to have no known precedent. In the Gellone miniature, the sole "terrestrial" witnesses of the crucifixion and its bloodshed (excluding therefore the angels) are the "church" on the facing page and the book's user. Furthermore, an exceptional amount of blood relative to other early medieval representations comes from the Gellone Christ's side, pouring out to his right in a long wave.[44]

---

[39] See Per Jonas Nordhagen, "John VII's 'Adoration of the Cross' in S. Maria Antiqua," *Journal of the Warburg and Courtauld Institutes* 30 (1967), 388–390; idem, *The Frescoes of John VII (A.D. 705–707) in Santa Maria Antiqua in Rome*, Acta ad archaeologiam et artium historiam pertinentia, 3 (Rome, 1968), 52–54. Also see Jean-Marie Sansterre, "A propos de la signification politico-religieuse de certaines fresques de Jean VII à Sainte-Marie-Antique," *Byzantion* 57 (1987), 434–440, with references to earlier literature.   [40] Above, n. 4.
[41] Weitzmann, *Icons*, cat. B.36, B.50; Schiller, *Iconography*, 2.101.
[42] See Belting, *Likeness and Presence*, 121 and fig. 72.   [43] Above, n. 6.
[44] Compare Weitzmann, *Icons*, cat. B.32, B.36, B.50, and the images noted above.

Figure 8. Crucifixion, Rome, Sta. Maria Antiqua, Chapel of Theodotus

The Gellone miniature is also apparently without precedent in its combination of a crucifixion image with what seems to be a personification of the church, an arrangement that would anticipate the depictions of *Ecclesia* next to the crucifix in several later Carolingian images, such as two of those studied in chaper 7. And it is clearly unusual for the manner in which the

miniature of Christ crucified is integrated with the accompanying orations. Although the western tradition of decorating scriptural and liturgical books with crosses, including cross initials, reaches its peak in the late
eighth to early ninth centuries, the Gellone picture is the first known
example of a *crucifix* initial. Correspondingly, it is the first known crucifix
painted on the T of the *Te igitur* prayer, a pictorial form that reappears in
the ninth century and, more frequently, in post-Carolingian sacramentaries, though these later representations link the crucified Jesus only with the
Te igitur and not, as well, with the preceding prayers of the mass.[45]

It has been suggested that the importance the Gellone Sacramentary
lends to the *Te igitur* oration is indicative of an early stage in the shift,
within the ninth-century Carolingian church, toward the notion that this
prayer marks the start of the mass canon.[46] It should be noted, however,
that despite the special decoration of the T, rather than separating the *Te
igitur* from the *Vere dignum* and *Sanctus* as occurs in later manuscript illuminations, the Gellone miniature binds these texts together. By means of the
two angels, the crucifixion scene belongs to the prayers before it as well as
to the subsequent orations of the eucharistic consecration. Suspended
between the *Sanctus* and the *Te igitur*, Christ's body and his cross essentially
join the heavenly realm of the angels, who acclaim their eternal, divine
lord, with the mundane sphere of the eucharistic sacrifice, which rehearses
the human oblation on the cross. The large quantity of blood, drawing
attention to the fact of his bleeding, may be a symbol of, at once, the divinity with its cosmic dominion and the humanity's mortality, a death confirmed in both the redeemer's blood offering and the sacrifice of the mass
that the image introduces. The Gellone artist conceivably thought that
other motifs in the painting, too, highlighted this conjunction of opposites
in Christ. The perizoma and bare torso and limbs were perhaps meant to
accentuate his human corporeality, the function the loincloth probably
serves in certain Byzantine images, while his cruciform halo, staring eyes,
erect posture, starry cross, and the reverent angels announce his divine
nature.[47]

---

[45] See Rudolf Suntrup, "*Te igitur*-Initialen und Kanonbilder in Mittelalterlichen
Sakramentarhandschriften," in *Text und Bild: Aspekte des Zusammenwirkens zweier Künste im
Mittelalter und früher Neuzeit,* ed. Christel Meier and Uwe Ruberg (Wiesbaden, 1980), 278–382.

[46] Sepière, *L'Image d'un Dieu souffrant,* 118–124, esp. 121.

[47] See Corrigan, "Text and Image," 45–62.

As a portrayal of the living savior whose crucifixion blends into the resurrection, ascension, and the eschaton, the Gellone illumination agrees with the numerous early Carolingian writings that remember the passion as a triumph unified with the subsequent moments of divine revelation. The cross is the instrument and symbol of Christ's victory and eternal kingship, his throne, and the sign that will accompany him when he redescends from heaven. The depiction is therefore reminiscent, too, of the various contemporary texts noted in the last chapter that link the divine omnipotence displayed in the passion with the sacral power of the eucharistic elements: poems such as Theodulf's verses on the eucharist that praise the conqueror of Satan, or the comments, in late-eighth- and early-ninth-century expositions of the mass, on Jesus' victorious passion and resurrection, the eucharist's heavenly origins, the power of the blood received in the wine, and the earthly sacrament's connection with the celestial feast.

In the focus that the painting brings on Christ's joining of divine with human, heaven with earth, however, the writings it most closely recalls are those by Alcuin and his peers that explore the crucified son of God's mediatorship, among them the anti-Adoptionist treatises. In their efforts to refute Felix and Elipandus, it was observed in the last chapter, Paulinus and Alcuin had to search for language adequate to expressing the simultaneous, unbreachable presence of humanity and divinity in one crucified person. The designer of the Gellone miniatures may have faced a similar artistic dilemma, one that possibly sheds light on the complicated weaving of words with imagery that connects the *Te igitur* painting with more than one mass prayer. A passage in Alcuin's *Adversus Felicem* that identifies the lord of the crucifixion with the eschaton provides an interesting parallel to the Gellone miniature: Christ is the God of gods who has the power of judging, who will be seen in majesty at his return, when the "wounds of the true body will reveal the true son of man, who is about to judge the world; that form will be judge, which stood before the judge [at the passion]."[48]

The anti-Adoptionist texts show greater concern with the significance of orthodox Christology to the baptism of Jesus and ordinary mortals than they do with the eucharist. But still, the liturgical orations that Alcuin quotes against Felix and Elipandus and his votive masses, among them ones for the Holy Trinity and the cross as well as Mary, reflect his convic-

---

[48] Alcuin, *Adv. Felicem* 5.9, PL 101.197–198A, esp. 197D.

tion that the dogma of Christ's two natures was thoroughly expressed in the church's celebrations of the mass.[49] The connection between the son of God's possession of two natures, the eucharist's sacral efficacy, and the church – a connection possibly evoked in the Gellone painting – is an implicit theme of the comments on the mass and the passion as sacrifice in Alcuin's treatise on Hebrews. It is more explicitly examined in the exegesis of the side wound in his commentary on John, where, following Augustine, the church is declared to have been born in the flow of water and blood from Jesus' side.[50]

The text from Charlemagne's court that probably offers the best parallel to the *Te igitur* image, though, is the chapter on the eucharist in the *Opus Caroli regis*.[51] For Theodulf, the sacral efficacy of all the *res sacratae*, among them the eucharist, is founded on and mirrors Christ's mediatorship, the source of their blessing. Through divine consecration, the bread and wine, too, like his person, are both celestial and mundane. The second person of the Trinity assures that the sacrament, consisting of visible, material things, is the body and blood of the mediator, the "true bread of God who descended from heaven," and at the same time a gift from mortals on earth that "angelic hands" bear to the supernal altar. Commemorating not only the passion but also the "resurrection from hell and indeed the most glorious ascension into heaven," the eucharist serves the church as a perpetual bridge between the two spheres made possible by their reunion effected in the triumphant crucifixion. It channels God's power to mortals precisely because the incarnation and passion joined the two realms together.[52] Very similar thinking seems conveyed by the Gellone Sacramentary image. On the one hand, Christ is emphatically part of the earthly sphere to which the mass ceremonial belongs. There the historical events of his last supper and passion are recalled in the church's repeated oblations of his human body and blood, both substances equally important to the sacrament and both clearly displayed in the painting; the dual character of the eucharist elucidates the picture's large quantity of blood. On the other hand, he is the divine king praised by the angels in the timeless *Sanctus* hymn. The body and blood sacrificed in the mass belong to the son of God who physically

[49] Alcuin, *Adv. Felicem* 7.13, PL 101.227A/B; *Adv. Elipandum* 2.9, PL 101.266C-267A; Deshusses, "Messes d'Alcuin," nos. 1–5, 15–23; idem, *Sacramentaire grégorien* 2, nos. 1806–1810, 1835–1846.

[50] Alcuin, *Comm. in Joann.* 7.40, PL 100.986.   [51] Theodulf, *Opus Caroli regis* 2.27.289–296.

[52] See ibid. 2.27.291 lines 1–5, and chapter 2, at n. 118.

Figure 9. Baptism oration initial, Gellone Sacramentary, Paris, Bibliothèque Nationale de France, cod. lat. 12048, fol. 60 verso

mediates between heaven and earth, the "living bread" that comes down to mortals and the gift that the angels bear on high, a reminder of his ascension that looks forward to his return and to the faithful's hoped-for ascent with him to paradise.

Two further images of Christ in the Gellone Sacramentary are simpler compositions than the Virgin and *Te igitur* miniatures. The earlier of the two in the manuscript seems partly to derive from traditional iconography of Christ's baptism, though the combination of forms again has no clear model (fol. 60v; fig. 9). Framed by the small initial O of a prayer for the benediction of the baptismal font for the Easter vigil, the bust of Christ with cruciform nimbus is shown with a dove flying directly downwards over his head. The image evokes the holy spirit's descent in the form of a dove after the baptism in the Jordan, when God's voice was heard to pronounce Jesus his son.[53] Early medieval depictions of Christ's baptism, however, typically portray John the Baptist as well as a full-length Jesus who stands in or near the water with his hands lowered, while the dove flies down towards him (as it does here). Such a scene is represented on the Bodleian Douce ivory of

[53] Matthew 3.16–17, Mark 1.10–11, Luke 3.21–22; see John 1.32–34.

the lord treading on the beasts (fig. 5); this baptism image is modeled on one carved on a diptych of c. 400.[54] On the Douce carving, the diptych, and in other images of the baptism, Christ is naked, though in some ninth-century Carolingian representations he wears the perizoma or the robe that the newly baptized donned when they emerged from the font.[55]

In addition to John's absence in the Gellone painting, the critical departures from the traditional iconography of the baptism are Jesus' hand lifted in benediction and his priestly (it seems) garb of a tunic with stole.[56] The motivation for this unusual representation, I think, may lie in the accompanying prayer's reference to adoption; the "allmighty eternal God" is asked to be present during the baptismal rite of the Easter vigil and to send forth the "spirit of adoption" for the new people to whom the font gives birth.[57] As discussed in the last chapter, Jesus' baptism is one of the key scriptural episodes that Paulinus and Alcuin cite, and seek to explain, in their anti-Adoptionist writings, in order to support their doctrine that Christ is not himself adoptive. Whereas other mortals need adoption because of original sin, they argue, the voice of the father heard at the Jordan (God remained invisible, as in the Gellone image) revealed Jesus' status as innocent man and the true son of God. His baptism was not a purgation of sin, because far from requiring adoption, through baptism he adopts other mortals.[58] Suggesting a similar line of thought, the Gellone depiction is perhaps meant to relate the baptism of Christians to that of Jesus while affirming their distinction. While his divine sonship is being revealed, as it was by the dove that descended over him at his own baptism, Christ, dressed in the vestment of sacerdotal office and with his hand raised in blessing, is the adopter of his faithful.

The last depiction of Christ in Gellone is a second crucifixion miniature near the bottom left corner of folio 152 verso. Smaller than the *Te igitur*

---

[54] Berlin, Staatliche Museen Preussischer Kulturbesitz, Skulpturengalerie; Gaborit-Chopin, *Elfenbeinkunst*, 23, fig. 15, cat. 12.

[55] See Genevra Kornbluth, *Engraved Gems of the Carolingian Empire* (University Park, PA, 1995), 49–54, 56–68, with reproductions of ninth-century baptismal crystals.

[56] Similar vestments are worn by St. Mark, fol. 42r.

[57] "Omnipotens sempiterne deus, adesto magne pietatis tuae misteriis, adesto sacramentis et ad creandus nouus populus quos tibi fons baptismatis parturit, spiritus adoptionis emitte, ut quod humilitatis nostre gerendum est, minesterium tue uirtutis conpleantur effectu": *Sacr. Gellon.*, *CCSL* 159, no. 703.

[58] E.g. see Alcuin, *De fide* 3.17, *PL* 101.49–50; idem, *Ep.* 137, *MGH Epp.* 4.211 lines 19–27; *Adv. Felicem* 2.13–14, 15–17, *PL* 101.156B-D, 157–159. Cf. Paulinus, *Contra Felicem*, 1.9, 26, *CCCM* 95.15, 31–32.

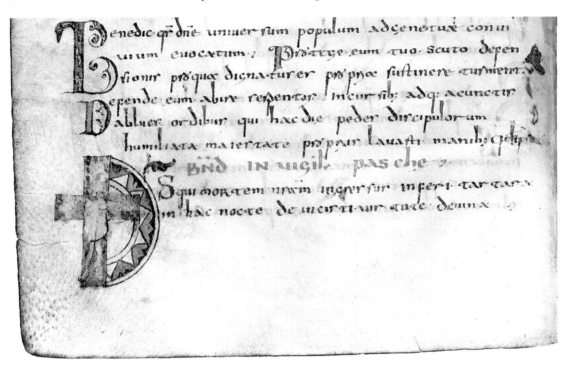

Figure 10. Crucifixion initial, Gellone Sacramentary, Paris, Bibliothèque Nationale de France, cod. lat. 12048, fol. 152 verso

illumination, it forms the vertical bar of the D initial of an episcopal bene-diction for the Easter vigil (fig. 10). The oration commences by addressing God the victor who, "having entered the depths of hell, conquered our death by divine power," and "by your death dragged away as prize the wealth despoiled from the funeral of the many." The remainder of the oration asks that the newly baptized (who received the sacrament at the vigil) remain forever liberated from sin and the devil so that they come to the final judgment deserving of heavenly reward.[59] The crucifixion mini-ature has suffered extensively from moisture; Christ's face, hands, and feet have been almost entirely effaced as have been some details within the outline of his torso. While there are occasional signs of water damage else-where in the manuscript, overall this picture seems more affected than other decoration. Various explanations are possible, one being that the

[59] *Sacr. Gellon., CCSL* 159, no. 2009: "Deus qui mortem nostram ingressus inferi tartara in hac nocte deuicisti uirtute deuina. Et eam multorum funere diuitem morte tua spoliatam traxisti pie uictur in predam. Suscipe propitius familie tue preces humilimas uoto sencere mentes oblatas. Et quos ueteribus maculis baptismatis emundauit unda sacrata per lauacrum, tue pro-tectionis auxilium purgati, tales ante te represententur in iudicium quales nunc processerunt ex baptismo. Et qui te miserante reuocati sunt in paradisum, non patiaris exules fieri renas-cente conmisso. Et qui te simel agnouit principem uniuersitatis et dominum, numquam in suis sensibus in se tyrannizantem sentiat inimicum."

painting's location near the outside corner of a page made it particularly susceptible to moisture that infiltrated the manuscript over the years. But the damage's limitation to the image of Christ and his cross, with the half-circle of the D virtually untouched, may point to other causes. It is perhaps significant that this is the only depiction of Christ or the cross in the sacramentary that accompanies a prayer for the *Triduum*, the period from Good Friday to Easter that brought the Holy Week observances to a conclusion and encompassed the *Adoratio crucis*. Conceivably, the miniature was touched or kissed in reverence during that ceremony or at the Paschal vigil, perhaps as the benediction was recited. Although partially effaced, enough of the image is visible to show that it originally bore some resemblance to the *Te igitur* Christ: Jesus with a cruciform halo stands erect on the cross, legs apart and arms stiffly extended, dressed in a perizoma with blood flowing from the wounds in his hands, feet, and possibly his side. These basic similarities with the *Te igitur* miniature and the tone of the adjoining oration, celebrating the powerful return from hell, favor the assumption that in this second crucifixon image he was portrayed with the open eyes of the living savior. Not enough of the face has survived, though, to be certain. Given the generally innovative nature of the illumination already examined in the sacramentary, together with the prayer's clear declaration that the conquest of hell was accomplished "by your death," it is worth considering whether, as in some earlier Byzantine imagery and a few ninth-century Carolingian works of art, Jesus was depicted with his eyes closed.[60] This may help explain the damage the painting has suffered; Christ's face, hands, and feet, its most eroded portions, might have been the focal points of touching or kissing, possibly long after the manuscript was completed, because his wounded limbs and face of death recalled his human suffering.

Whether the Easter vigil illumination originally portrayed Christ living or dead on the cross, here again the designer may have been concerned to imply the reality of both natures, in keeping with the allusions to both in the prayer – through Jesus' erect posture and cruciform halo, recalling his divine immortality, and yet semi-naked, bleeding body. The importance of Christological doctrine in guiding iconographic decisions is more evident in the larger, better-preserved *Te igitur* image, with its more intricate

---

[60] I thank Lawrence Nees for this suggestion. The two dots of paint in the lower half of the face, well below what remains of the cruciform halo, most likely indicate not the eyes but the line of the cheekbones. Cf. Christ's face, fol. 143v (fig. 7).

intersection of image with written text. The latter painting seems to offer a clear visual expression of the concept that the eucharist's sacrality depends on Christ's mediatorship. Both the figure on the opposite page and the clergy who contemplate the image, as they celebrate the mass, are witness to the two natures shown united in one person, the eternal meeting the temporal that underlies the eucharist's power and is manifested not only in the mass liturgy, but in every other revelation of divine majesty that the image evokes, from the incarnation through the crucifixion to the eschaton. Such ideas may also lie behind the opening image of Mary, the powerful queen, God's chosen vessel for assuming human flesh, and the leader – perhaps again personifying *Ecclesia* – of the eucharistic ritual where his body and blood are in a sense reborn. Perhaps an interest in upholding Christological truth elucidates, too, the miniature of the baptismal oration. As should now be apparent, precisely the same doctrines that these images seem to convey received their fullest, contemporary articulation in the Carolingian texts responding to Adoptionism and Nicea II and in other writings by Alcuin, some probably influenced by his conflict with Elipandus and Felix.

It is possible that the Gellone's decoration also reflects an attentiveness to the anti-iconodulism campaign recorded in the *Opus Caroli regis*. As is perhaps true with Hrabanus' *In honorem sanctae crucis*, contemporary viewers and the designer of the sacramentary's paintings may have associated the conjunction of written letters and artistic representation with the belief, defended in Theodulf's treatise, that writing is superior to images, especially when the text is a holy one such as the prayers designated for the performance of the sacraments. Perhaps this helps explain the seemingly iconic character of the Virgin Mary and *Te igitur* illuminations, the two largest images in the manuscript; each portrait of a single holy figure was possibly meant to inspire feelings of reverence in its Carolingian viewers, much as may have happened with the second crucifixion image. For the sacramentary's designer and its early Carolingian audience, these depictions conceivably appeared to possess a sacral value not normally belonging to works of art, by virtue of their creation from sacred texts. In this regard, we may go on to speculate, they perhaps seemed to present a contrast to the icons that Theodulf and his contemporaries thought were worshiped in Byzantium and Rome, in place of the written word of holy scripture. If the head opposite the *Te igitur* painting is a personification of the church, then this symbol of Roman authority in a "Roman" sacramentary gazes at what may have been understood to constitute a type of icon that, from the Carolingian perspective, appropriately serves as an object of meditation and reverence, because it is itself an integral part of sacred writing. These are among the many facets of the sacramentary's illumination that deserve further study; the affect of theological inquiry on the Gellone decoration cannot be entirely resolved at the present. Nevertheless, the codex's production between 790 and c. 804 at a center with connections to Charlemagne's court; its presence soon thereafter in a region where "Felicianism" was a problem for Carolingian ecclesiastics such as Benedict, to whom Alcuin offered assistance in opposing Adoptionism; and the elements of the book's illumination discussed here accord with the possibility that this exceptional manuscript was informed by a desire to tie church ritual to the related and equally essential task, in Carolingian eyes, of defending orthodoxy against heretical belief.

In honorem sanctae crucis

With *In honorem sanctae crucis*, the Christ-centered deliberations of Charlemagne's scholars may be more distantly remembered than in the Gellone Sacramentary. The passion's Christology is more fully presented, however, partly since the combination of text with artistic design in the treatise's *carmina figurata* (figs. 11–16) allows for further exploration of this issue than do the miniatures of the sacramentary's initials. A dedicatory poem for a copy of *In honorem* sent to the monks of Tours notes that Hrabanus learned the "art of meter" from Alcuin while a student at the abbey, c. 803,[61] and the prologue alludes to the inspiration provided by Porphyry's figure poems for Constantine.[62] But despite some comparability with Porphyry's fourth-century collection and with poetry by other late antique and early medieval authors, including the poems that Alcuin, Joseph, and Theodulf gave Charlemagne, Hrabanus' treatise is unique among writings in this genre.[63] Not only is it longer than any extant series of figure poems since the one Porphyry presented to his emperor; the

---

[61] Ferrari, *Liber s. crucis*, 12. Perrin, *Louanges*, 17.

[62] Hrabanus, *In honorem*, CCCM 100, A7, lines 68–69; see Ferrari, *Liber s. crucis*, 59.

[63] See Massin, *Letter and Image*, trans. Caroline Hillier and Vivienne Menkes (New York, 1970), 158–167, esp. 161–167.

intricacy of most of its figures is unrivaled in ancient or medieval *carmina figurata*. Other Latin poets before Hrabanus – Porphyry, Venantius Fortunatus, Ansbert of Rouen, Boniface, Alcuin and his colleagues – usually created simple geometric "grid-poems," most often with cruciform figures.[64] A few of Porphyry's designs are more complex, but none matches the "image-poems" that Hrabanus produced for most of *In honorem sanctae crucis*, where the figures represent a variety of motifs and three of the original compositions, in addition to the Christ of Poem 1, incorporate human or animal forms.[65] Moreover, as Michele Ferrari has recently shown, *In honorem* is unusual as a collection of figure poetry for its internal coherence. Unlike Porphyry's series for Constantine and that offered to Charlemagne, each individual piece in Hrabanus' treatise was conceived as part of a carefully unified examination of a single set of themes.[66]

Hrabanus recognized the difficulties that even a skilled reader of his poems might encounter because of the need to decipher the words within each figure and the constraints the designs impose on the Latin of the poetry. To clarify the figures' signification, as both artistic forms and lines of verse, he set a prose *declaratio figurae* ("declaration of the figure") on the page opposite each composition; to ease understanding of the poem as a whole that frames each figure, he also provided a prose paraphrase in a second book, possibly written at a later stage.[67] The resulting anthology of verse, prose, and imagery communicates meaning on several levels at once: the immediate one of the poetical texts, Book 2, the crosses, and the other representational imagery of the figures; a less accessible level of figural symbolism, which is unveiled chiefly in the declarations; and a third level at which the figures, their coloring, and numerical and geometric rela-

---

[64] Cf. chapter 2, nn. 1–3.

[65] Hrabanus, *In honorem*, CCCM 100, B4 (two seraphim and two cherubim), B15 (four beasts of the Apocalypse around the lamb), B28 (Hrabanus kneeling beneath a cross). Compare Porphyry, *Carm.* 26, *Carmina* 1.103–105. See Ernst, *Carmen figuratum*, 98–108; Perrin, *Louanges*, 18–19, 25–29.   [66] Ferrari, *Liber s. crucis*, 101–165.

[67] Perrin, ed., *In honorem*, CCCM 100.xviii-xix. For the combination of verse with prose Hrabanus notes his debt to Prosper of Aquitaine and Sedulius, though here he particularly has in mind his treatise's second book, in which the "sense" of the poems is repeated in prose. He also refers to Horace's *Ars poetica*: *In honorem*, CCCM 100, D 0, esp. lines 6–7, 20–23. For the *declarationes figurarum*, he was probably influenced by the transcriptions and explications of the figural verses that Porphyry placed on the facing pages to the poems in his collection. See Ferrari, *Liber s. crucis*, 271–273; Perrin, *Louanges*, 18–20; Spilling, *Opus Magnentii Hrabani Mauri*, 12–14, 22.

tions suggested by them and the verses possess symbolic values not discussed in the poetry or prose, but which the attentive Carolingian reader
might have discerned.[68] Such varied poetry and figures, the interplay
between them, the prose analyses attributing to the poems a polyvalent
symbolism, clearly display Hrabanus' mastery of a classical literary genre
and the encyclopedic knowledge of biblical exegesis, sacred history,
ancient secular and Christian literature that he already possessed in pro-
ducing this, his first work. Its elaborate compendium of art and text was an
achievement of which the poet was justifiably proud for the rest of his life,
and it remained very popular in later centuries. Approximately eighty-one
manuscripts and manuscript fragments of the treatise are extant;[69] numerous copies, some of which survive, are known to have been made under
Hrabanus' own supervision at Fulda and later when he was archbishop of
Mainz (847–856). Among the identified recipients are his friend Hatto, who
evidently helped in the treatise's initial preparation, monasteries, and high-
level personnages such as the previous archbishops of Mainz, Haistulf (d.
826) and his successor, Otgar (d. 847), Louis the Pious (d. 840), the abbeys of
St.-Martin of Tours and St.-Denis, Archbishop Raoul of Bourges, Pope
Gregory IV (who died before his copy reached him, in 844; it was received
by his successor, Sergius II), and Count Eberhard of Friuli (d. c. 865).[70]

The first third of Hrabanus' Poem 1 (fig. 11), the opening of Book 2
Chapter 1, and the figural verses formed by the crucified Christ's body hail
the son of God's powerful victory against his enemies and his revelation of
kingship. This is the eternal lord and "holy creator" come into the world to
seize the prize from the deep, the God placed on the cross who bestowed
the supernal crown.[71] The rest of the poem and Chapter 1 mainly consist of
a list of Christ's names, beginning with those that pertain strictly to his
divinity and membership in the Trinity, then moving to others more
closely related to his assumption of humanity and incarnate existence.
Despite references to his role as the sacrificial victim, though, his human
nature is principally viewed from the perspective of the God who became
man. "For our redemption" he received human nature "like a vestment for
his divinity," a nature that hides the "splendor of his majesty from human
sight and the rays of his brilliance from the eyes of the impious," even as

---

[68] Perrin, *Louanges*, 20–25.   [69] Perrin, ed., *In honorem*, CCCM 100.xxx.
[70] See Ferrari, *Liber s. crucis*, 24–29; Perrin, ed., *In honorem s. crucis*, CCCM 100.xii-xxvi.
[71] Hrabanus, *In honorem*, CCCM 100, B 1, lines 11–14, C 1 lines 111–140, D 1 lines 4–22.

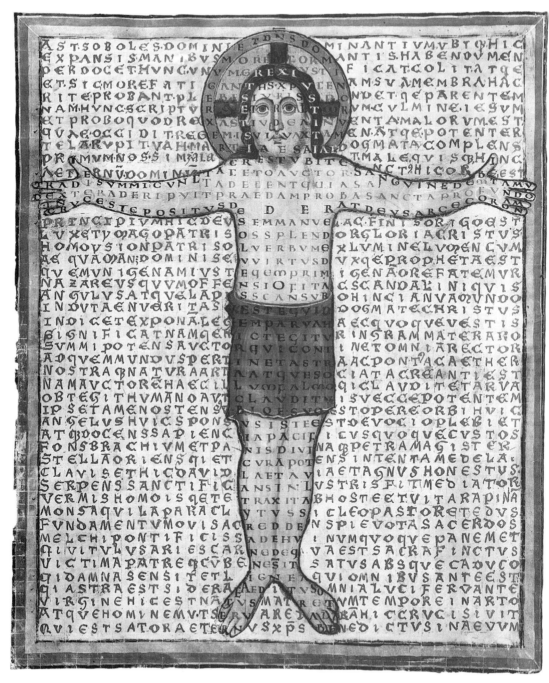

Figure 11. Poem 1, *In honorem sanctae crucis*, Vatican, Biblioteca Apostolica Vaticana, cod. Reg. lat. 124, fol. 8 verso

"by shining miracles and thundering gospel he signifies that he is true God."[72] On the whole, Poem 1 more clearly balances praise of the divinity with remembrance of the incarnate humanity than does the *Opus Caroli regis*, yet dwells less than do the anti-Adoptionist tractates on Christ's experience of suffering and mortality. In line with the acclamations of his divinity and power, the figure, like the Gellone *Te igitur* miniature (fig. 7), portrays the living crucified lord. Dressed in the perizoma, his head framed by a cruciform halo, Jesus stands erect with arms extended straight from his sides, his open eyes designated by two letter O's. In other respects, the depiction that Hrabanus envisioned for the poem – as far as we can judge from the figural verses defining its form in its varied copies – is somewhat closer to the Narbonne crucifixion tablet than to the Gellone painting.[73] Both the *In honorem* and Narbonne Christs wear the perizoma and have open eyes, erect bodies, and cruciform halos; both, too, unlike the Gellone Christ, have shoulder-length hair, navels that are visible above their loincloths (marked by an O in *In honorem*), splayed feet, and weight shifted at the hips so that the right leg is thrust very slightly in front of the left.

One detail clearly distinguishing the *In honorem* Christ from the Narbonne as well as the Gellone depictions, though, is the absence of a cross behind him.[74] In order to understand why he is thus shown, it is necessary to give some thought to the treatise's subsequent textual and visual contents. Throughout the following poems of *In honorem sanctae crucis*, the center of praise is the omnipotent deity who triumphed in the passion and resurrection and, more directly, his cross, the emblem of that conquest and his universal dominion.[75] The power displayed in the passion now radiates from the cross, which itself controls and orders the created universe and all sacred history. Each section of the treatise (poem, *declaratio figurae*, chapter of Book 2) advances some aspect of this theme by lauding the savior, the cross, and the passion and developing an intricate exegesis, often structured around number symbolism, of a single sacred phenomenon or

---

[72] Ibid., *CCCM* 100, D 1 lines 37–43, see 44–62, B 1 lines 27–47.   [73] See above, n. 7.

[74] The wounds, too, are usually not depicted in copies of Hrabanus' poem, though the figural verse along Christ's left hand declares that he washes away sins by his blood; see Hrabanus, *In honorem*, *CCCM* 100, C 1 line 115. The lack of cross recalls the crucifixion scene on the fifth-century door of Sta. Sabina, Rome, an image that otherwise seems unrelated to the *In honorem* figure: see Wirth, *Image médiévale*, 124, and above, n. 38.

[75] The theme is already introduced in Hrabanus, *In honorem*, *CCCM* 100, B 2 and C 2. The cosmic role attributed to the cross is stressed by Ferrari, *Liber s. crucis*, see esp. 132–135, 253.

Figure 12. Poem 4, *In honorem sanctae crucis*, Vatican, Biblioteca Apostolica Vaticana, cod. Reg. lat. 124, fol. 11 verso

group of phenomena with roots in scripture.[76] The readers / viewers of the treatise are expected to contemplate how both figures and texts demonstrate that the Christian teachings set forth there conform to the cross's structure, the primary motif of each figure, and therefore reflect the divine ordering of the cosmos over which Christ reigns.

[76] See Burkhard Taeger, *Zahlensymbolik bei Hraban, bei Hincmar – und im "Heliand"? Studien zur Zahlensymbolik im Frühmittelalter* (Munich, 1970), 3–86.

Yet while Poem 1 and the other *carmina figurata* repeatedly stress Christ's divinity and cosmic majesty, another refrain of their verses is the miracle of his incarnation. He is simultaneously the second person of the Trinity and the redeemer who possessed humanity capable of being fixed to a cross, in order to vanquish sin / death / Satan and restore the universe to God. Poem 4, for example (fig. 12), depicts an equal-armed cross flanked by two, six-winged seraphim above (so identified in the texts) and two, two-winged cherubim below.[77] The poem, *declaratio figurae*, and chapter announce that Isaiah's vision of seraphim, and the cherubim who stood next to the Ark of the Covenant in the tabernacle and Temple, foreshadowed the glory of the conquering cross, the "likeness of our redemption" that Christ the king wished to be visible even before his incarnation. The angelic creatures sing the praises of the cross, the "royal throne" and "conciliation of the world" to which the creator and heavenly king was fastened, the structure that the reader is asked to behold in the poem's figure. They hail, too, the lord who used the cross as his weapon in order to defeat the devil, the savior who rules in heaven and will return as judge. The seraphim prefigure the "image of Christ's cross" with their wings reaching up, down, and to their sides; their *Sanctus* hymn (Isaiah 6.1–3) is the threefold voice that exhorts the elect before and after the incarnation, since all are redeemed in Christ's one passion, by which he "conquered sadness," "burned up iniquity," and "put the evil powers to flight." The cherubim next to the Ark and propitiatorium – next to the cross in the poem's figure – foreshadow the propitiation that occurred in the incarnation, their wings forever extended to signify that the redemption brought in Christ's passion is for all time.[78]

Poem 15 (fig. 13) is decorated with the four evangelist symbols arranged around the lamb of God, suggesting the four arms of an equal-armed cross with the lamb at its center. The verses hail Christ, "born of the highest father," for his victory that "broke the fearsome weapons," and they laud the four gospel writers and symbols for their accounts of his incarnate humanity and divinity: John (the eagle) describes the son "forever with the father" who was the universe's creator yet assumed a human soul and body; Mark (the lion) recalls Christ's conquest, his priest-hood and offering of himself as sacrifice; Luke (the calf) remembers that Jesus is both king and saving victim, the "admirable infant" born of Mary

---

[77] Hrabanus, *In honorem*, CCCM 100, B 4, C 4, see esp. lines 18–64.

[78] Ibid., CCCM 100, B 4, C 4.

Figure 13. Poem 15, *In honorem sanctae crucis*, Vatican, Biblioteca Apostolica Vaticana, cod. Reg. lat. 124, fol. 22 verso

and the "ancient of days" who, although "suspended on the cross, sustained the stars"; Matthew describes his descent from David, the one from that line promised as the world's savior.[79] The *declaratio figurae* announces the "likeness" of the cross that the figure reveals in the apocalyptic vision of the four beasts around the lamb. While the lamb signifies the one who, fixed to the cross, "bore away the world's sins," the four beasts signify the evangelists, all of whom "agree in witnessing to the lord's passion and res-

[79] Ibid., *CCCM* 100, B 15, D 15.

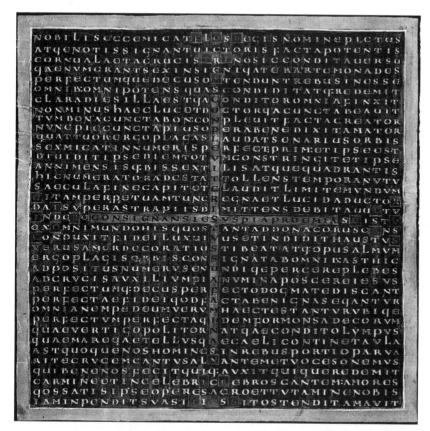

Figure 14. Poem 23, *In honorem sanctae crucis*, Vatican, Biblioteca Apostolica Vaticana, cod. Reg. lat. 124, fol. 30 verso

urrection" and reveal different mysteries of his humanity and divinity along with other secrets pertaining to the number four.[80] Poem 23 (fig. 14) opens by referring to its figure of a cross, the ends formed of triangles composed of six squares each, as the "noble flower" here "painted" with the name of Christ the king. The words *Jesus* and *Christus* intersect at the S marking the figure's center.[81] The remaining verses, *declaratio figurae*, and chapter explore the mysteries of the numbers four and six, symbolic of the beauty of the universe that the omnipotent God created and then saved through the crucifixion. The numbers refer to the "perfection of Christ's passion and our redemption," since on the cross "the maker of all things provided a sign of his own consummation, when, having received the cup, he said, 'It is consummated'." They also signify the "concourse of

---

[80] Ibid., *CCCM* 100, C 15, esp. lines 31–37.

[81] Ibid., *CCCM* 100, B 23 lines 1–2. The *declaratio figurae* states that the cross's arms spread like the petals of a lily: C 23 lines 59–61.

Figure 15. Poem 28, *In honorem sanctae crucis*, Vatican, Biblioteca Apostolica Vaticana, cod. Reg. lat. 124, fol. 35 verso

people from the four regions of the world praying to their redeemer" for their salvation; the "twenty-four books" of the Old Testament; David's division of the tribe of Levi and the priesthood of the sons of Aaron, prefiguring the priesthood of Christ who was also the sacrifice; the twenty-four elders of the apocalypse, designating the church; and, ultimately, all the "perfected" works of God that point towards the perfect creator, "who made us and multiplied us, [and] freed us from the enemy's power by his own blood."[82]

The climax of these encomia of the incarnate, divine lord occurs in

[82] Ibid., *CCCM* 100, B 23, C 23, D 23, esp. lines 41–44.

Poem 28 (fig. 15), where Hrabanus is depicted kneeling in veneration, beneath an equal-armed cross that floats above his head. The poem praises Christ as the high majesty, sabaoth, creator, and with other names that allude to his work of salvation. Everything written on the preceding pages, it is claimed, was directed to the honor of the savior whom the poet now adores. Hrabanus prostrates himself in order to "adore" his lord and, he adds in Book 2, the cross as well;[83] he prays that Jesus will receive him as a new sacrifice, and that the crucifixion will burn up all sinfulness in him, in preparation for the terrifying return on the last day. The *declaratio figurae* announces that twenty-eight poems are contained in the treatise because the number represents the perfection and consummation of all things, [84] and it confirms that the poet's adoration is directed to the "eternal and perpetual and inseparable God, Trinity and unity" who inspired and assisted him to prepare his work. The treatise is variously described as honoring the cross, the passion, and Christ the redeemer and savior, who, "having been born the only begotten from [the father] before the ages, wished temporally to assume human flesh and soul and undergo the cross for the salvation of the human race."[85]

The prologue of *In honorem sanctae crucis* states that Hrabanus composed his treatise in order to honor God by fulfilling the injunction of Exodus 25.2 to bring to him the "first fruits," in this instance the author's first published work.[86] The reverence paid to the cross is indicated to be synonymous with worship of Christ and remembrance of his incarnation and saving passion.[87] The accomplishment of the Exodus command gave Hrabanus the opportunity to demonstrate his prowess as a poet, his familiarity with classical literary forms, his command of the large fund of biblical and patristic learning that provides the core of each poem and *declaratio figurae*. In a sense, the "first fruits" of Charlemagne's educational reforms are seen here, one of the earliest works of literature from the second generation of scholars who would dominate Carolingian intellectual and cultural activity during the first half of the ninth century: a son of Frankish

---

[83] Ibid., *CCCM* 100, B 28 line 15, D 28 lines 22–26.

[84] Ibid., *CCCM* 100, C 28 lines 67–69. See Ferrari, *Liber s. crucis*, 128–129; Perrin, *Louanges*, 20–23.

[85] Hrabanus, *In honorem*, *CCCM* 100, C 28 lines 1–4.

[86] Ibid., *CCCM* 100, A 7 lines 4–6, 9–10.

[87] Ibid., *CCCM* 100, A 7 lines 17–28. Perhaps, as Herrad Spilling has proposed, the gift was meant to parallel the one Hrabanus would offer when celebrating his first mass as priest: Spilling, *Opus Magnentii Hrabani Mauri*, 10. See also Ferrari, *Liber s. crucis*, 27.

aristocracy, educated at the court and Tours by the Anglo-Saxon, Alcuin. Thus the treatise implicitly pays respect not only to God but to Alcuin, dead only a decade when it was completed, with whom Hrabanus studied scripture and the church fathers and who taught him how to write *carmina figurata*. That Hrabanus believed the work a fitting memorial to his teacher is evident from the dedication poem composed for the copy sent to Tours, where Alcuin is imagined asking St. Martin to assure that God accepts this gift from the pupil.[88]

The size of *In honorem*, the large prose apparatus provided to assist the reader, and the sheer volume of information about sacred history and Christian dogma communicated by both literary and artistic means attest the educational function the treatise was also designed to fulfill, as was appropriate for a work by the master of the Fulda school. Hrabanus' didactic intentions may underlie, too, the decision to write in the form of the *carmen figuratum*, in spite of the difficulties the genre creates for reading his verse. At the simplest level, he perhaps thought, the intriguing integration of figures with texts would encourage readers to closer study of the meaning of both and the mysteries embedded in each poem, figure, and each poem plus figure. By such means, they would arrive at a better understanding of the doctrines communicated in the different sections of his treatise than if they were to meditate on images alone, concerning whose utility Hrabanus was hesitant, as will be discussed shortly, or simply on the written word.[89]

Furthermore, a series of *carmina figurata* may have seemed especially well suited to educating readers about, specifically, the cross's signification of divine majesty, the divinely ruled cosmos, and of God's work of salvation. While these are traditional themes of exegesis of the cross in early medieval literature, including other *carmina figurata*, Hrabanus develops them to unprecedented lengths, both textually and visually. A certain tension is apparent between the heavy load of ideas that the figures and texts of *In honorem* together teach and the relatively simple shape of the

---

[88] Hrabanus, *In honorem*, CCCM 100, A 2, see esp. lines 1–14. Perrin has suggested (*Louanges*, 25) that Hrabanus may have begun work on the treatise while still at Tours, under Alcuin's direction. As Ferrari notes, Hrabanus does not specifically mention the *carmina figurata* of Alcuin, Joseph, and Theodulf as models for his work: *Liber s. crucis*, 407.

[89] See Ferrari, *Liber s. crucis*, 315–316. The comments of Giselle de Nie, Sabine MacCormack, and others who heard my paper on Hrabanus' treatise at Kalamazoo, May 1998, have helped me enormously to develop these ideas.

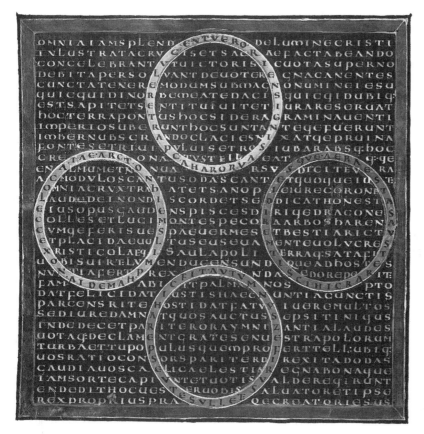

Figure 16. Poem 7, *In honorem sanctae crucis*, Vatican, Biblioteca Apostolica Vaticana, cod. Reg. lat. 124, fol. 14 verso

cross. In the *carmina figurata* by Alcuin, Joseph, and Theodulf and in earlier examples of such poetry, the usually geometric figures merge into the verses, so that the eye moves easily from one to the other and each poem can be studied as a single unit. In contrast, the more intricate designs of *In honorem sanctae crucis* present visual expressions of quite involved teachings that may require the reader to consult the prose *declarationes figurarum* on the opposite pages, or the chapters of Book 2 – to turn away from text plus image and consult pure text – in order to grasp the full weight of this thought. Moreover, although each figure of *In honorem* purportedly represents the cross, most in fact consist of arrangements of quite different motifs that, in many cases, barely bring to mind the cross's appearance, or that suggest a cruciform design on the verge of disintegrating into individual components. According to the *declaratio figurae* of Poem 7, for example (fig. 16), the figure designates the presence of the cross's form in the fourfold ordering of nature, yet what we actually see are four, separate circles that can be identified as "cruciform" only from what is said in poetry and prose.[90]

Nonetheless, regardless of these problems, *carmina figurata* honoring the cross quite possibly appeared to Hrabanus exceptionally acute demonstrations of its sanctity and Christ's majesty, precisely because of the nature of the literary genre. Three factors need here to be borne in mind. The first is the cross's special status, in its own right, as both representational form and written language, through its traditional association with the letter Tau or Tav and the first letter, symbol, and abbreviation of the name of the savior who, himself, is the word and image of God. For Hrabanus and contemporary readers, the poems of *In honorem*, like other cross-figure poetry, may have announced the cross's holiness by both depicting and also writing its "sign."[91] Second, the extant verses of another poem that Hrabanus wrote for his friend, Hatto, echoing ideas espoused in the *Opus Caroli regis* and earlier by Augustine and Isidor, declare that artistic representations are inferior to the written word. Images are "empty" (*vana in imagine forma*) and deceptive (*falsa colorum*), incapable of showing the "figures of things" (*rerum . . . figuras*) correctly or contributing beauty to the soul.[92] A passage in the *declaratio figurae* of Poem 11 of *In honorem* stresses the value of the "figure" (*figura*) in leading thoughts to sacred truth. The reference is to Old Testament typology, but in Hrabanus' mind it was clearly applicable to his *carmina figurata*, as well. This should probably be read not as contradicting the verses for Hatto, but as an expression of essentially the same idea from another perspective. Artistic images do *not* show the "figures of things" correctly, and therefore do not convey holy teachings; the *carmen figuratum*, however, guides the viewer's thoughts to the spiritual realm, and hence to awareness of the glory of the savior and his cross, because it presents not images but indeed figures, by joining visual forms with words praising Christ.[93]

---

[90] Hrabanus, *In honorem*, CCCM 100, B 7, C 7.

[91] On the early history of this doctrine, F. J. Dölger, "Beiträge zur Geschichte des Kreuzzeichens, I–IX," *Jahrbuch für Antike und Christentum* 1–10 (1958–1967).

[92] Hrabanus, *Carm.* 38, MGH PLAC 2.196 lines 1–7. Cf. Ferrari, *Liber s. crucis*, 19–21.

[93] Hrabanus, *In honorem*, CCCM 100, C 11 lines 1–13; cf. Ferrari, *Liber s. crucis*, 314–316, with a different interpretation. A poem by Hrabanus on an image of Christ in a chapel of Fulda implicitly distinguishes the artistic representation from the sacral realm to which Christ belongs: *Carm.* 61, *MGH PLAC* 2.222; see Herbert L. Kessler, "Real Absence: Early Medieval Art and the Metamorphosis of Vision," *Morfologie sociali e culturali in Europa fra tarda antichità e alto medio-*

Third, as Giselle de Nie has observed, early medieval churchmen conceived of miracles as repetitions of patterns established in the Bible. The
ability to recognize a miracle as such depends on knowledge of the scriptural paradigm. For the sixth-century bishop, Gregory of Tours, the effort is
comparable to that needed in order to read scripture. Developing a doctrine of Augustine's, Gregory suggests that while heretics read or see the
same texts as true believers, lack of faith impedes them from recognizing
the marvel – the divine truth – contained there.[94] The supreme, biblical
pattern for miracles was the creation and its corollary, the incarnation, the
re-creation through Christ, and any extraordinary occurrence was
regarded as, to some measure, a drawing out of the conjunction of nature
and miracle in those two events.[95] Given these ideas, it is reasonable to ask
whether Hrabanus and Carolingian readers of *In honorem sanctae crucis*
might have considered its intersection of text and figure – words fashioning
images and images fashioning words, despite their contradictory natures –
as possessing a special value through its analogy to the miracle pattern of
the incarnation. The cross's holiness is announced in the repeated union of
word and image that honors and depicts its form. Thus these *carmina figurata* mirror, on a lower plane, the miraculous joining of divine and human
in the second person of the Trinity – a renewal of creation echoing through
the universe that, because it is divinely ordered, as Hrabanus' treatise demonstrates, conforms to the cross's shape.

Hrabanus probably knew the existence of the *Opus Caroli regis* when he
composed his treatise, yet it is uncertain to what degree he would have
been acquainted with its contents. Although he was associated with the
court at the time of its preparation, he was most likely a boy less than ten
years old. While he may have learned something about its argumentation

---

evo, Settimane di studio del Centro Italiano di Studi Sull'Alto Medioevo, 45 (Spoleto, 1998),
1157–1211, at 1195–1196.

[94] Giselle de Nie, "Word, Image and Experience in the Early Medieval Miracle Story," in *Language
and Beyond/Le langage et ses au-delà, Text: Studies in Comparative Literature* 17, ed. P. Joret and A.
Remael (Amsterdam, 1998), 97–122, at 101. De Nie has explored this issue in several other
important articles, as well, e.g. "Iconic Alchemy: Imaging Miracles in Late Sixth-Century
Gaul," *Studia Patristica* 30 (Leuven, 1997), 158–166; and "Seeing and Believing in the Early
Middle Ages: a Preliminary Investigation," in *Word and Image: the Pictured Word, Interactions* 2,
ed. M. Heusser et al. (Amsterdam, 1998), 67–76. Pope Gregory I, too, implies a correspondence
between the seeing of an artistic image and of a miracle, when he draws on Augustine's ideas
about the latter activity in order to explain art's value to Serenus of Marseilles: see Chazelle,
"Pictures, Books, and the Illiterate," 146–147.

[95] Benedicta Ward, *Miracles and the Medieval Mind* (Philadelphia, rev. edn., 1987), 3–5.

from Alcuin, there is no direct allusion to the *Opus* in the writings of either scholar, just as there is no evidence of continued discussion of its teachings on images among Charlemagne's scholars after the council of Frankfurt in 794.[96] Still, by presenting views related to those of the *Opus Caroli regis*, as in some ways may be true of the decoration of the Gellone Sacramentary, *In honorem* provides additional evidence of how Theodulf's doctrines belonged to and possibly influenced the particular climate of thought about Christ and images that prevailed in the early Carolingian period. Hrabanus did not necessarily get any ideas directly from the *Opus*, but in certain respects his thinking moves in remarkably similar directions. One is his expressed antipathy towards artistic imagery, in the verses for Hatto. A second parallel with Theodulf's treatise, as should already be obvious, is the significance that *In honorem* attributes to the cross as the sacred instrument of the crucified Christ's conquest and eternal rule. Here, however, a divergence with the *Opus Caroli regis* should also be noted, for it is fairly clear that Hrabanus ascribes sacral significance not only to the true cross but to its manufactured images, in spite of his evident disinterest in other types of artistic depiction. As does not appear true of the *Opus*, *In honorem* seems to associate all manner of cross images with the praise rendered both the cross and the poems' figures. Any such representation, not merely the figure of a *carmen figuratum*, is implied to be rightly the subject of contemplation and of the worship the poet bestows in Poem 28 (fig. 15). Repeatedly, through figures and words, *In honorem* urges readers to meditate on the cross's form, to look at and study its structure in order to enter into the sacred mysteries manifested there. That these comments apply to other depictions of the cross besides the treatise's figures seems confirmed by the *declaratio figurae* of Poem 1, which remarks that "as often as we behold the / a cross," we should be brought to remember Christ's suffering and victory and increase our devotion to him.[97]

While *In honorem* is not overtly polemical, Hrabanus may have been partly encouraged to affirm the value of both the cross and crosses by interference from Abbot Ratgar with processions of crosses at Fulda, in the decade prior to Ratgar's deposition in 817.[98] Along with the remarks con-

---

[96] Cf. Ferrari, *Liber s. crucis*, 314–319.

[97] Hrabanus, *In honorem*, CCCM 100, C 1, esp. lines 5–7. (Latin text below, n. 101)

[98] See Luke Wenger, "Hrabanus Maurus, Fulda, and Carolingian Spirituality" (Ph.D. diss., Harvard University, 1973), 228 and n. 5. The interference is reflected in a chapter of Fulda's *Supplex libellus*, presented to Charlemagne in 812 to win the emperor's support for the monks against their abbot:

cerning crosses in Book 1 Chapter 19 of the *Opus Caroli regis*,[99] Ratgar's actions and those of Bishop Claudius of Turin (817–827), to be discussed below, imply that the practice of using such objects in Carolingian devotional practises did not meet unanimous approval. But although Hrabanus seems to believe that crosses are worthy objects of reverence, whereas Theodulf and Claudius evidently deny this, it is striking how closely the reasons for Hrabanus' acceptance of their holiness correspond to the definition of *res sacratae* in the *Opus Caroli regis*. Essentially, the criteria remain the same, yet they are found to be fulfilled in a type of object to which Theodulf would appear to deny their applicability. *In honorem* insists that the crucified Christ blessed not merely the cross but its form, a blessing proclaimed in the Bible, as the *Opus* asserts is the case for all sacred things. Apparently, therefore, a visible repetition of the form of the cross may be considered sacred.[100] A primary function of Poem 1 (fig. 11) is to identify Christ, the crucified savior and universal lord, as this blessing's source. That is why no cross appears behind him, as becomes apparent from the opening of the poem's *declaratio figurae*, where occurs the reference to beholding the / a cross noted above:

> Look, the image of our lord, by the position of his limbs, consecrates for us
> the most saving, sweetest, and most lovable form of the holy cross, in order

"Ut crucis gloriatio in singulis diebus dominicis fiat ante missam fratribus omnibus circa vicina quaeque loca monasterii crucem sequentibus hymnos et antiphonas cantantibus sicut apud maiores nostros usus erat in diebus dominicis passionis et resurrectionis domini gloriam celebrari. Et quod in diebus ieiuniorum ab episcopo decretis crucem portare et litanias facere liceat." CCM 1.319–327, at 326. I mentioned the possibility of a connection with Hrabanus' treatise in my dissertation, "The Cross, the Image, and the Passion in Carolingian Thought and Art" (Ph.D. diss., Yale University, 1985), 192–193. This idea was expanded by Johannes Fried, "Fulda in der Bildungs- und Geistesgeschichte des früheren Mittelalters," in *Kloster Fulda in der Welt der Karolinger* (1996), 3–38, at 23–26; further discussion in Ferrari, *Liber s. crucis*, 386–388.

[99] Theodulf, *Opus Caroli regis* 1.19.192–193. See chapter 2, at n. 128.

[100] The doctrine is clearly influenced by the traditional belief that the crucified Christ's posture, and hence his cross's four arms, signify his universal dominion. It is also connected with the notion that the sign of the cross is holy, whether traced by hand, written as a sacred letter, or carried spiritually within the faithful soul. The verses of Sedulius' *Carmen paschale* praising the four-part cross as symbol of Christ's rule over the cosmos, for instance, are quoted in C 12, lines 21–26 (Sedulius, *Carmen paschale* 5, lines 190–195). Cf. Dölger, "Beiträge zur Geschichte des Kreuzzeichens, I–IX"; Ferrari, *Liber s. crucis*, 408–409. An interesting parallel to Hrabanus' doctrine is hinted in a letter of Pope Nicholas I, referring either to a cross or to a crucifix; see Jean-Marie Sansterre, "Entre *Koinè méditerranéenne*, influences byzantines et particularités locales: le culte des images et ses limites à Rome dans le haut Moyen Age," in *Europa medievale e mondo bizantino: contatti effettivi e possibilità di studi comparati*, ed. G. Arnaldi and G. Cavallo (Rome, 1997), 109–124, at 119.

that as we believe in his name and obey his mandates, we have hope of eternal life because of his passion. Hence as often as we behold the/a cross, we remember him who suffered on it for us in order to snatch us from the power of darkness, indeed abolishing death so that, now that he has departed into heaven with the angels and powers and virtues subjected to himself, we might be heirs to eternal life. Let us thus recognize that we are not redeemed by corruptible silver and gold, following the vanity of ancient tradition, but by Christ's precious blood, like that of a pure and spotless lamb, so that we may be holy [and] immaculate in his sight, in [his] love, and through this may become consorts of the divine nature, fleeing the corruption of worldly greed.[101]

The form of the cross and consequently any representation of its structure, it seems, mirror the position of Christ's body in the crucifixion. There is no cross in the poem's figure, since the purpose is not only to recall that he was crucified, but to teach viewers that the crucified humanity exemplified the cross's shape and thereby sanctified it. In Poem 1, Christ's body *is* the cross, the supreme manifestation of the glory that its form radiates because of his blessing, and that is depicted and lauded in the remaining poems of *In honorem sanctae crucis*. In gazing at a cross, the Christian is made mindful of the miracle of redemption that is the source of its consecration and revelation of sacred wisdom, as recorded in scripture. By this means, he or she is inspired to turn from this world, in which human flesh is imprisoned in sin, to the divinity that belongs to the same Christ and the divine secrets revealed in the cross's form.[102]

Finally, *In honorem sanctae crucis* is reminiscent of the *Opus Caroli regis* and, more generally, of the theological concerns of Charlemagne's court in the centrality of Christological doctrine to its teachings. Like the

---

[101] Hrabanus, *In honorem*, CCCM 100, C 1 lines 1–15: "Ecce imago Saluatoris membrorum suorum positione consecrat nobis saluberrimam, dulcissimam et amantissimam sanctae crucis formam, ut in eius nomine credentes et eius mandatis oboedientes, per eius passionem spem uitae aeternae habeamus; ut quotiescumque crucem aspiciamus, ipsius recordemur, qui pro nobis in ea passus est, ut eriperet nos de potestate tenebrarum, 'deglutiens quidem mortem, ut uitae aeternae heredes efficeremur,' profectus in caelum subiectis sibi angelis et potestatibus et uirtutibus; utque recogitemus, 'quod non corruptibili argento uel auro redempti [sumus] de uana [nostra] conuersatione paternae traditionis, sed pretioso sanguine quasi agni incontaminati et inmaculati Christi,' ut simus sancti et inmaculati in conspectu eius, in caritate, ut per haec efficiamur diuinae consortes naturae, fugientes eius quae in mundo est concupiscentiae corruptionem." See 1 Peter 1.18, 3.22.

[102] Cf. Hrabanus, *In honorem*, CCCM 100, A 7 lines 20–28.

Gellone Sacramentary and several of Alcuin's writings that touch on Christological issues, Hrabanus' treatise did not overtly contribute to the inquiries regarding Adoptionism or Byzantine image worship. In its exploration of why the crucifixion is salvific and the cross holy, though, the treatise shows an attentiveness to the passion's role as proof of Christ's mediatorship that must reflect Hrabanus' years at the court or his closeness with Alcuin. The theme of the divine incarnation and the relation between divinity and humanity in Christ regularly arises in the prose and poetical texts of *In honorem*; but it is especially Poem 1 and its *declaratio figurae* that show the two natures' union to be the basis of the passion's efficacy and its manifestation of the cross's role as the redeemed universe's sacred symbol: the poem through its list of Christ's names, where the humanity's union with divinity is clearly asserted but references to the former nature are permeated by reminders of the latter, the *declaratio figurae* through its explanation of the source of the cross's blessing. As these texts indicate, the incarnation provided a body that, for all its humanity, possessed the power to consecrate the form of the cross by the very position of its crucified limbs. It is because Christ is not only divine but God-made-man, with arms and legs indeed belonging to God, that he was able to establish the cross's visible form as a symbol of the whole creation governed in his invisible divinity. The *declaratio figurae* of Poem 1 develops this theme in the lines following the passage just quoted. Some of the names of Christ listed in the verses designate the "substance of his divinity," it remarks, while others are drawn "from the assumed dispensation of the received humanity." Thus it is shown that "the same is the mediator of God and men, in deity consubstantial and coequal to the father, and in the received humanity co-similar and co-natural with the mother, since he assumed our entire nature perfectly, without sin."[103] Which names refer to the human and which to the divine nature is easily recognized through the use of reason. Christ is called anointed because he is both king and priest, Emmanuel because he is "God with us," since "born through the virgin he appeared to men as God in mortal flesh." He is God since one substance with the father, and figure, "since receiving the form of servant, through the likeness of works and virtues, he designated in himself the father's image and immense greatness."[104]

---

[103] Ibid., *CCCM* 100, C 1 lines 16–23.   [104] Ibid. *CCCM* 100, C 1, esp. lines 24–26, 29, 35–38, 57–60.

The conviction that Christ's mediatorship lies behind the passion's ability to redeem and the cross's holiness, though, is less forcefully announced in the texts of Poem 1 than it is visually. Once again, the interweaving of text and figure in the *carmen figuratum* was ideal for Hrabanus' purpose. Reaching over the length of the poem, with arms stretched to either side of the page to signify both his rule of the cosmos and his consecration of the cross's form, Christ embraces the entire list of divine and human names that runs through his body. His posture alone reveals that all these titles refer to the one figure, which literally contains the divinity as well as the humanity praised in the verses. The body imitated in the form of the cross, whose limbs, because perfectly human, could be covered with a "small garment," according to the verses in the perizoma, belongs to the God who "encloses the earth in his hand."[105] The absence of a cross, the cruciform halo marked by the *alpha*, "*M*" [for "middle"], and *omega*, the erect body, open eyes, and lack of signs of suffering underscore Christ's divinity. Even more than the Gellone images of the crucified Jesus, this figure seems divorced from temporal considerations, whether the historical circumstances of the crucifixion or the return at the end of time. On the other hand, the depiction is of a human body. Although in a work that draws on a classical literary genre, Christ's loincloth was conceivably intended to recall a late antique crucifixion image like the fifth-century London ivory,[106] his semi-nudity was probably also understood to emphasize his true humanity. No single aspect of the figure in Poem 1, however, symbolizes the union of divine with human better than the three letters of the word *Deo* designating Jesus' nipples and navel, the last-named attribute one of the strongest imaginable proofs of his human birth.[107]

The adoration of the cross

In their efforts to find artistic means to express the presence of two natures in one crucified person, both the Gellone Sacramentary and *In honorem sanctae crucis* are reminiscent of the crucifixion theologies articulated in the early Carolingian court's defenses of orthodox doctrine of Christ. Of the two works, the sacramentary, probably made between 790 and c. 804, was perhaps more directly affected by the doctrinal discussions of the 790s.

---

[105] Ibid., *CCCM* 100, B 1 lines 23, 28–29; D 1 lines 32–37.   [106] See above, n. 38.

[107] See Hrabanus, *In honorem, CCCM* 100, C 1 lines 135–136.

While much of its painting likely serves other purposes, such as simply decoration, its iconographic references to the Virgin's power, prestige, and royalty, to the joining of divinity with humanity in the crucified body received in the eucharist and commemorated in Holy Week, and to Jesus' status as adopter seem to reveal a direct sensitivity to the Christology that took shape as Charlemagne's scholars attacked Greek and Hispanic teachings. The image (possibly) of *Ecclesia* opposite the *Te igitur* illumination and, possibly, Mary's identification with the church link catholic belief with ecclesiastical authority, further evidence that the church is the representative and defender of the true faith.

In honorem sanctae crucis, in which Hrabanus' poetry and prose shed greater light on the imagery's signification than do the sacramentary's texts, was completed a decade after Alcuin's death and after the court circle's discussions of Nicea II and Adoptionism had largely concluded. It is conceivable that Hrabanus was interested in the deliberations over the *filioque* at Aachen in 809, and in the challenge to Christ's full divinity that Greek opposition to this insertion to the creed supposedly presented.[108] There is no evidence that the *filioque* debate influenced *In honorem sanctae crucis*, though, or that this treatise has a polemical purpose, despite the possibility that one motivation for its composition came from the actions of Abbot Ratgar. Overall, *In honorem* is a didactic work whose encomia of the cross, the passion, and Christ provide a wide-reaching display of Hrabanus' poetical talents and learning. Yet still, here as in the Gellone Sacramentary, the perception of the cross and the crucified Christ appears informed by concerns similar to those of the first generation of Carolingian theologians – possibly concerns over the function of images and the relative value of imagery and the written word, such as are discussed in the *Opus Caroli regis*, but also, again, over Christological belief. Perhaps inspired by Alcuin, Hrabanus used the genre of the *carmen figuratum* – a much more thorough amalgam of text and image than liturgical prayers made possible in the Gellone Sacramentary – to demonstrate through both media the conjunction of two natures in Christ, and to suggest their union's significance to the passion's saving power and to the sanctity of the cross and its form.

Given what has been said so far about *In honorem sanctae crucis*, it is helpful to give some attention to the Carolingian tracts of the 820s to 840s

---

[108] David Ganz, "Theology," *NCMH* 2.766.

that defend the holiness of the cross and crosses and their worship, particularly their "adoration." Most of these writings were directed against Bishop Claudius of Turin or meant to respond to the iconoclastic quarrels that resurged in Byzantium in the first quarter of the ninth century. While certain differences between them and Hrabanus' treatise are obvious – that of literary genre, for one, and the more clearly polemical function of the majority of the later texts – an examination of their thought will assist in clarifying what is distinctive about his approach.

Probably soon after election to the see of Turin in 817, Claudius decided to remove crosses and artistic images from his diocesan churches because he disapproved of the reverence the public paid them.[109] Abbot Theutmir of Psalmody (Nîmes) had written to Claudius that complaints about the bishop's beliefs and actions were being heard "throughout the entirety of Gaul up to the borders of Spain."[110] Claudius' letter-book responding to Theutmir situates his attack on images alongside his opposition to worship and adoration of crosses, including possibly crucifixes, his campaign against pilgrimages to St. Peter's shrine in Rome, and his doubts about papal supremacy. Two treatises challenging Claudius have survived, one by Dungal, written before the bishop of Turin's death in 827 but probably after the synod of Paris (825), which Claudius evidently was asked but refused to attend,[111] the other by Jonas, Theodulf's successor at Orléans. Jonas abandoned his work in 827 but returned to it in the early 840s, because, its introduction claims, allies of the late bishop of Turin had emerged whom, together with Claudius, Jonas accuses of supporting Adoptionism, a heresy he links with Arianism. The charge, the bishop of Orléans asserts, is partly based on papers left among Claudius' affairs after his death;[112] it is apparently also connected with Claudius' earlier association with Felix of Urgel, and conceivably, too, with the rationale he offered for his opposition to crosses as well as perhaps crucifixes. People "of false religion and super-

---

[109] See Wirth, *Image médiévale*, 155–162.

[110] Claudius, *Ep.* 12, *MGH Epp.* 4, ed. E. Dümmler (Berlin, 1895), 610–613, at 610 lines 20–21. See Chazelle, "Memory, Instruction, Worship," 196–197; Ferrari, *Liber s. crucis*, 311–314. On the relationship between Claudius and Theutmir: Gorman, "Commentary on Genesis of Claudius of Turin," 282–283.

[111] Dungal, *Ep.* 9, *MGH Epp.* 4.583–585, at 585 lines 17–18 (recalling that Claudius had referred to the synod as a "congregationem asinorum"). Dungal's full treatise, *Liber Adversus Claudium Taurinensem*, is published in *PL* 105.457–530, see 529A.

[112] Jonas, *De cultu imaginum* 1, *PL* 106.305–388, see 307–311B. Cf. Dungal, *Adv. Claudium*, *PL* 105.466B/C.

stition," he argues to Theutmir, wrongly justify the "worship, veneration, or adoration" of a cross (crucifix?) by declaring that the reverence is directed to Christ, in whose memory and honor the object is "depicted and imaged" (*ob recordationem salvatoris nostri crucem pictam atque in eius honore imaginatam*). What such persons actually honor is Christ's mortal humanity alone and, therefore, the "shame of [his] passion and ridicule of [his] death," the focus of Jews and pagans who deny the resurrection. They forget the words of St. Paul: "And if we have known Christ according to the flesh; but now we know him so no longer" (2 Cor. 5.16).[113] Claudius' comments might be read differently if we knew the larger context in which they were made; only fragments from his treatise are extant. But taken on their own they suggest a tendency, to which his followers may also have subscribed, to separate Christ's humanity radically from his divinity and to associate the passion solely with the former nature, as though the man was crucified without the God. Such a perspective on the crucifixion recalls some of the accusations made by Alcuin, Paulinus, and Benedict against Felix and Elipandus.

The bishop of Turin's ideas had most likely caused worry at Louis the Pious' court before he received a letter in November 824 from the Greek emperors, Michael II and Theophilus. This outlines the moderate form of iconoclasm the Byzantine government had reinstituted and expected the Carolingian emperor to support. The churchmen meeting at Paris in 825 to consider the eastern position were clearly concerned about Claudius, as well, even though their documents do not expressly mention him. Their opinions are outlined in a *libellus* prepared for Louis; from this, Jonas of Orléans and Jeremiah of Sens made an *epitome* for Pope Eugenius II, who had authorized the synod to examine the issues of the Greek controversy.[114]

---

[113] Claudius, *Ep.* 12, *MGH Epp.* 4.611. If "omne lignum scemate crucis factum" should be adored because Christ was crucified, the bishop continues, then so should other objects representing things he did "through the flesh." To worship a cross is to crucify the son of God again and through the "execrable sacrileges of idols" to bring one's soul to everlasting damnation. Here the reference seems clearly to crosses. On Claudius' early years and education under Felix, see the clear overview by Joop van Banning, SJ, "Claudius von Turin als eine extreme Konsequenz des Konzils von Frankfurt," in *Das frankfurter Konzil von 794*, ed. Berndt, 2.731–749, esp. 733–734. I cannot accept, however, van Banning's assertion that the treatise *De picturis et imaginibus* attributed to Agobard (*CCCM* 52. 149–181) is actually by Claudius, for one reason that it implies that representations of the cross are holy and deserve respect, a position at odds with the disparaging comments in Claudius' letter. See below, n. 126.

[114] *Libellus synodalis parisiensis, Concilium Parisiense A. 825, MGH Conc.* 2.480–532; *Epitome libelli synodalis parisiensis,* ibid. 535–551. See Hartmann, *Synoden,* 168–171.

Along with the documents of the council of Paris and the anti-Claudian treatises by Dungal and Jonas, several other Carolingian writings from the 820s to 840s also discuss artistic images and / or crosses. One is the *Liber officialis* of Amalarius of Metz, initially published in 823 and twice revised before 835; the chapter on the *Adoratio crucis* defends that ritual and possibly refers to the controversy Claudius stirred about crosses.[115] Further tracts to note are *De picturis et imaginibus* by Agobard of Lyons, probably written for or in reaction to the synod of 825;[116] Einhard's *Quaestio de adoranda cruce*, composed in spring 836 to answer a request from Lupus of Ferrières for an explanation of why the cross merits adoration;[117] and Walafrid Strabo's *De exordiis et incrementis*, dating to the decade before his death in 849, which contains a chapter on the role of images.[118] Like the *Opus Caroli regis*, the writings of this group that comment on artistic representations, by which I mean images other than crosses (therefore excluding Amalarius' *Liber officialis* and Einhard's letter to Lupus), present positions that their authors see as falling between the two "extremes" of iconoclasm and iconodulism; the latter error is defined as the bestowal on images of the adoration owed to God. Dungal, Jonas, Agobard, and the Paris synod mainly develop their arguments through pastiches of patristic texts; one of the sources they all cite is the correspondence of Gregory I.[119] Aside from Dungal's treatise, neither these writings nor Walafrid's discussion of images attributes to artistic productions a religious significance comparable to that which ninth-century Carolingian writings generally assign to crosses and relics, yet images are understood to perform certain important functions. Most often mentioned are decoration, the commemoration of

---

[115] Amalarius, *Liber officialis* 1.14, *ST* 139.99–107, see esp. 104, cf. above, n. 113.

[116] Agobard, *De picturis et imaginibus*, *CCCM* 52.149–181. Freeman, ed., *Opus Caroli regis*, 11–12 and n. 69, suggests that Agobard was reacting to the letter of Michael II to Louis' court that led to the Paris synod of 825.

[117] Einhard, *Quaestio de adoranda cruce*, ed. K. Hampe, *MGH Epp.* 5 (Berlin, 1899), 146–149.

[118] Walafrid, *De exordiis et incrementis quarundam in observationibus ecclesiasticis rerum* 8, *MGH Capit.* 2, ed. V. Krause (Hanover, 1897), 473–516, at 482–484. Lucid translation with commentary in Alice Harting-Corrêa, *Walafrid Strabo's Libellus de exordiis et incrementis quarundam in observationibus ecclesiasticis rerum: a Translation and Liturgical Commentary* (Leiden, 1996).

[119] *Libellus* 11–14, *MGH Conc.* 2.487–489, 507–508, 527–528 (including the ps-Gregorian letter to Secundinus; see 489 n. 1); *Epitome* 12–13, ibid., 539–540, see 547; Jonas, *De cultu imaginum* 1, *PL* 106.310–311, see 332; Dungal, *Adv. Claudium*, *PL* 105.468–469; cf. Agobard, *De picturis* 22, *CCCM* 52.171–172. Gregory's correspondence is used to support different viewpoints, however. The teachings of these tractates and their relation to Gregory's own thought are discussed in Chazelle, "Memory, Instruction, Worship," see esp. 192–201.

past events and holy persons, the demonstration or encouragement of love for Christ and the saints, and the assistance of the ignorant or illiterate to knowledge of the persons and deeds depicted. Every Carolingian treatise on images mentioned except Claudius' tract opposes iconoclasm, though Agobard is so worried about the inappropriate worship of images that he suggests they should not be allowed in churches if such behavior occurs.[120] All of them reject the notion that images should receive the adoration God alone deserves; but certain of them, in particular the Paris synod's *libellus* and Walafrid's treatise, seem to leave open the possibility that some acts of reverence might be tolerable, and Dungal clearly accepts this viewpoint.

Lupus' request to Einhard, Einhard's reply, and Jonas' decision to complete his treatise in the early 840s suggest that worries about the worship or adoration of the cross and crosses, perhaps even outright attempts to halt acts of reverence, continued after Claudius' death in 827. Two basic teachings about the cross in these tracts and in the writings of Amalarius, Dungal, and the Paris synod show similarities to, though also significant differences from, the perspective in Hrabanus' work. In some ways, it can therefore be seen, *In honorem* represents a transition from the concerns of Charlemagne's court to those that predominated in the second quarter of the ninth century. The first doctrine has to do with cross worship. In line with the contrast drawn between bodily vision and true worship of God through the eyes of the soul, the *Opus Caroli regis* does not praise crosses or defend their veneration. Indeed, it has nothing explicitly positive to say about physical acts of worship performed toward any inanimate material things except relics, even other *res sacratae*.[121] A different attitude is suggested in Hrabanus' treatise; but although the cross and crosses are shown to deserve reverence as well as praise, especially in Poem 28, the precise liturgical contexts in which crosses should be revered, the conduct, and the nature of the reverence to be accorded are not major issues. Moreover, the "crosses" of Hrabanus' poems, forms that float in a cosmic realm created of words, differ noticeably from the manufactured representations and relics worshiped in churches. In general, however, the later writings by Einhard, Jonas, and others on crosses and images show greater interest in distinguishing the possible modes of physical worship of visible things and the meanings of those acts, including the veneration given to relics of the

---

[120] Agobard, *De picturis* 33, CCCM 52.180.   [121] Cf. chapter 2, at nn. 92, 127.

saints, where they are discussed.[122] This effort to define the various types of
worship corresponds to the relative openness some of the same ecclesiastics demonstrate (Dungal, the Paris synod, Walafrid) to the veneration of
artistic representations. Given that multiple "degrees" of reverential practice exist, not all such behavior involving images is necessarily idol-
atrous.[123] Similarly, where Dungal, Jonas, the synod of Paris, Einhard, and
Amalarius comment on the cross, many reasons for its greatness are proposed, but the basic consideration guiding the discussion is its place in the
liturgy and the right of its relics and images to liturgical worship, especially
adoration on Good Friday. As Hrabanus also implies in Poem 28 yet does
not discuss as directly, both images and relics of the cross are to be worshiped or adored on these occasions not for their own sakes, but in
memory and honor of the unseen, crucified savior and God. [124] According
to Einhard and Amalarius commenting on Jerome – Jonas makes a similar
remark – the worshiper prostrates himself before the cross or its relic, "as if
he saw the lord hanging there."[125] Christ is the sight the worshiper most
desires and who deserves this respect, yet the material, visible cross is an
acceptable substitute.

[122]   On saints and their relics, Jonas, *De cultu imaginum* 3, PL 106.365–388; Dungal, *Adv. Claudium*,
esp. PL 105.496–518. Several of the treatises quote from Augustine's analysis of the different
forms of worship in *De civitate Dei* 10.1: e.g. Dungal, *Adv. Claudium*, esp. PL 105.484–485; Jonas,
De cultu imaginum 1, PL 106.319–320; *Libellus* 63, MGH *Conc.* 2.501–502. Cf. (not using Augustine)
Walafrid, *De exord. et increment.* 8, MGH *Capit.* 2.482.

[123]   Their tolerance of such practices relative to what is found in the *Opus Caroli regis* may reflect
the gradual increase of influence north of the Alps, during the Carolingian period, of attitudes earlier well established in the Italian peninsula. Not only the veneration/adoration of
images but even stories of miracle-working images have been traced in Italy to before the
ninth century. These have been the subjects of several careful studies by Jean-Marie Sansterre;
see in particular, "La vénération des images à Ravenne dans le haut moyen âge: notes sur une
forme de dévotion peu connue," *Revue Mabillon*, n.s. 7 (= t. 68) (1996), 5–21; idem, "L'image
blessée, l'image souffrante: quelques récits de miracles entre Orient et Occident (vie–xiie
siècle)," *Bulletin de l'Institut historique belge de Rome* 69 (1999), 113–130.

[124]   See Amalarius, *Liber officialis* 1.14, ST 139.101–102; *Libellus* 65–76, MGH *Conc.* 2.502–506, esp. 506,
see *Epitome*, ibid., 549–551, where liturgical concerns are not paramount; Dungal, *Adv.
Claudium*, PL 105.477–496, esp. 481–485, see 527D–528; Einhard, *Quaestio*, MGH *Epp.* 5.146–149;
Jonas, *De cultu imaginum* 1, 2, PL 106.331–366, esp. 331–333, 342–343. Cf. Agobard, *De picturis* 19,
CCCM 52.168. As Wenger noted, Hrabanus does not directly connect the choice of subject for
In honorem with liturgical practice, despite the possible influence of Ratgar's objections to
cross processions: Wenger, "Hrabanus Maurus," 228. Still, the figure as well as the verses of
Poem 28 suggest that, in defending the cross and its form, he is mindful of the devotion
Christians pay to it through ecclesiastical ritual: *In honorem*, CCCM 100, B 28, C 28, D 28.

[125]   Einhard, *Quaestio*, MGH *Epp.* 5.149; Amalarius, *Liber officialis* 1.14, ST 139.101 (Jerome, *Ep.* 108).
See Jonas, *De cultu imaginum* 2, *Praef.*, PL 106.342.

Second, like Hrabanus in *In honorem sanctae crucis*, all these theologians accept that the cross is holy and, although the rationale for this belief is not clarified, that this sanctity is somehow reflected in or shared by its manufactured representations. Dungal, Jonas, the Paris synod, and to a lesser degree Amalarius uphold the concept that the crucified savior's blessing made the cross into the heavenly sign of his divine omnipotence and majesty, an idea to which Agobard also alludes.[126] In support, they quote and cite passages from scripture, poetry, liturgical texts, and patristic treatises that remember and praise the crucifixion, the cross, and the "sign" of the cross, describe the manifestations of its glory in visions, miracles worked through its relics, and the sign made by hand or worn inwardly, point to the use of signing in Christian devotion, and look forward to the cross's return with Christ at the end of time. Underlying these arguments, as is true with *In honorem sanctae crucis*, is the cult of the holy cross whose strength is evident from abundant eighth- and ninth-century sources, and the widely held doctrine of the passion as Christ's victory and revelation of divinity. The event that sanctified the cross was the conquest of sin/death/Satan by the son of God, the celestial lord.[127] Attacking Claudius' association of crosses with Jesus' torments and "shameful" death, Dungal stresses the power present even in the redeemer's humility, as revealed in the devil's defeat. For him, the crucifixion's glory is proven by Christ's command that the event be commemorated in the mass and by the disciples' imitation of his sufferings.[128] While Einhard does not discuss the origins of the cross's holiness in his *Quaestio de adoranda cruce*, he connected its glorification with Christ's conquest on his triumphal arch (fig. 17).[129] This silver structure, which may have been originally surmounted by a cross, was decorated with images of warrior saints or *milites Christi*, two on horseback treading on serpents to symbolize the victory over evil. Above were depicted the annunciation and John the Baptist pointing to Christ as the lamb of God, evangelist portraits, and an enthroned Christ with the apostles. The arch's inscription refers to the cross relic, the

---

[126] Agobard, *De picturis* 19, *CCCM* 52.168.

[127] As Jonas, for example, explains, "nec tamen ideo crucem ut Dominum adoramus, sed magis eum qui per crucem mortis destruxit imperium, atque chyrographum peccati nostri affixit, pacificans in ea sanguine suo sive quae in terris, sive quae in coelis sunt": *De cultu imaginum*, 2, *Praef.*, *PL* 106.342D. See Col. 2.14.   [128] Dungal, *Adv. Claudium*, *PL* 105.478–479B.

[129] Paris, BNF, cod. fr. 10440, fol. 45r.

Figure 17. Drawing of the lost Arch of Einhard, Paris, Bibliothèque Nationale de France, cod. fr. 10440, fol. 45 recto

"trophy of the eternal victory," contained either in it or in the reliquary cross it bore.[130]

Insofar as Hrabanus in his *In honorem*, Einhard, and the other scholars mentioned ascribe sanctity not only to the true cross but its representations and stress their value to Christian devotion, they reflect the new interest, among Carolingian ecclesiastics, in the role of corporeal sight in the exercise of faith.[131] The *Opus Caroli regis* defends the spirituality of true worship of God and sharply distinguishes this from contact with the material, visible world, in spite of the link the treatise posits between meditation on the divine and Bible study. In contrast, even though the crosses of *In honorem* are embedded in texts (perhaps reflecting the impact of discussions of art's function at Charlemagne's court) and the responses to Claudius and the Byzantine iconoclastic controversy reject the "excessive" veneration of artistic images, these treatises all recognize that religious devotion suitably involves the body's eyes. This idea is suggested by other features of Carolingian piety, too, that gain prominence in the ninth century, some of which I will return to in the following chapters: the expansion of the cult of relics, visible reminders of the departed saints; discussions of the liturgy's visual representation of holy events and their actors; the increase in vision literature; the debates over the relationship between what is seen in the eucharist (bread and wine) and the sacral reality it contains; the analyses of the final vision of God that occurred partly within the context of the quarrel over divine predestination. But most of the later Carolingian writings (by Einhard, Dungal, etc.) that defend crosses, their sanctity, and their worship do not place their arguments within a Christological framework of thought such as *In honorem sanctae crucis* presents. Despite their association of the cross and crosses with Christ's power and, on the other hand, occasional allusions to his suffering, they do not give significant attention to the union between immortal divinity and mortal humanity as the basis of the holiness of the cross or crosses, or of the passion's ability to save. Only in Jonas' *De cultu imaginum* do similar issues clearly arise, as a result of his concern that

---

[130] See Lawrence Nees, "Art and Architecture," *NCMH* 2.834, with reference to earlier literature. David Ganz (oral communication, September 1999) suggested that it is not absolutely certain the arch was surmounted by a manufactured cross.

[131] E.g. concerning relics of the saints and pilgrimages to their shrines, Jonas states, "Sane est etiam proprium humanae menti non adeo compungi ex auditis sicut ex visis": *De cultu imaginum* 3, *PL* 106.368C.

Claudius and his followers showed Adoptionist and Arian tendencies. Evidently because Claudius seemed to divide the divine from the human in the crucified Christ, Jonas more noticeably than Dungal stresses their union, though the theme is not, by any means, as consistently or fully developed as in the anti-Adoptionist tracts or *In honorem sanctae crucis*. Jesus' death did not constitute a source of "shame" and the cross was no mere instrument of humiliation, Jonas declares, for then the crucifixion would not have been salvific. The passion's sufferings do not displease Christians as they do Claudius, since the faithful know them to have been redemptive and that death was followed by resurrection. The man who died is the same one who rose from the tomb. The cross's torments along with the victory, the crucifixion together with the resurrection are the foundation of the hope for redemption and of reverence for the cross.[132]

As will be discussed further in chapter 4, the emphasis on liturgical devotion and the cross's liturgical significance in the writings of the 820s to 840s is indicative of the Carolingian church's growing attentiveness, after Charlemagne's death, to the signification and proper conduct of ecclesiastical ritual. This is an important element of the background to the mid-ninth-century quarrels over divine predestination and the nature of the eucharistic presence that will be investigated in chapters 5 and 6. The less interest that *In honorem s. crucis* shows in liturgical worship, and the far greater effort to establish a Christological basis for belief in the cross's sanctity, distinguish Hrabanus' treatise from the later tractates. In spite of the other characteristics of thought they share in common, these features, particularly the second-mentioned, tie *In honorem* instead to the intellectual preoccupations of Alcuin and Charlemagne's court. In its Christology as perhaps in the attitudes it implies towards the artistic image and the definition of a sacred thing, *In honorem sanctae crucis*, like the Gellone Sacramentary, testifies to the impact of the doctrines formulated against Nicea II and Adoptionism on Carolingian churchmen beyond the scholars involved in those affairs.

Nevertheless, during the 820s to 840s, Hrabanus' work was most likely regarded by him and fellow scholars as a major precedent for the efforts to defend the cross and manufactured crosses as legitimate subjects of praise, meditation, and liturgical reverence. Possibly this sheds light on some of

---

[132] Jonas, *De cultu imaginum* 1, PL 106.334–336. Cf. Dungal, *Adv. Claudium*, PL 105.466, 528A.

the early copies of *In honorem*, since the first important period of its diffusion outside Fulda was the second quarter of the ninth century.[133] Four of
its extant manuscripts were probably produced at Fulda while Hrabanus
was abbot and two were completed under him at Mainz; others from the
same period, now lost, are known from dedications.[134] The dedicatory
verses do not mention the debates over artistic images, crosses, and their
worship, and it is significant that these are the years in which Hrabanus had
greatest access to the resources necessary for the production of copies; yet
the energy put into the task was conceivably motivated by contemporary
issues. That may be especially true with the presentation copy made for
Louis the Pious. The dedication figure poem for Louis (fig. 18), presented in
subsequent copies as an integral part of the treatise,[135] depicts the emperor
as a *miles Christi*. Dressed in armor, holding a shield and cross staff, he
stands ready to fight his savior's battles on earth with both material and
spiritual weapons, but above all the cross lauded in the remaining pages of
In honorem sanctae crucis.[136] Like Charlemagne in the *carmina figurata* by
Alcuin, Joseph, and Theodulf (figs. 1, 2), Louis is implicitly compared to
Constantine, who was honored in the collection of figure poetry by
Porphyry that influenced Hrabanus as well as, probably, Alcuin and Joseph.
A clear parallel is also drawn with Christ, that is, between the victorious
redeemer and the earthly ruler who conquers in his name. The cross is the
sign of *imperium* by which the Frankish emperor defends Christianity in his
lands, the weapon that allows justice to triumph in him, just as through the
cross Christ, the heavenly king, overcame sin and death.[137] Christ's blessing
and protection of Louis' rule are sought, assistance that is merited because
of the latter's justice and propagation of the faith.[138] Michel Perrin has

---

[133] Perrin, ed., *In honorem*, CCCM 100.xv–xvii, xx–xxvi; Ferrari, *Liber s. crucis*, 23–25.

[134] Biblioteca Apostolica Vaticana, Reginensis Latinus 124 (Fulda, second quarter ninth century);
Paris, BNF, lat. 2423 (Fulda, second quarter ninth century); Amiens, BM 223 (Fulda, second
quarter ninth century); Turin, Biblioteca Nazionale Universitaria K. II. 20 (Fulda, second
quarter ninth century); Paris, BNF, lat. 2422 (Mainz and Fulda, mid-ninth century); Vienna,
Österreichische Nationalbibliothek 652 (Mainz and Fulda, mid-ninth century). See Perrin,
ed., *In honorem*, CCCM 100. xx–xxvi, xxx–xxxii.

[135] Ferrari, *Liber s. crucis*, 216; on the poem and its figure, see Sears, "Louis the Pious," in
Charlemagne's Heir, ed. Godman and Collins, 605–628.

[136] Hrabanus, *In honorem*, CCCM 100, A 5. Ferrari, *Liber s. crucis*, 216–217, 338–339; Ernst, *Carmen figuratum*, 292–297; Sears, "Louis the Pious," 610–620.

[137] Hrabanus, *In honorem*, CCCM 100, A5, lines 1–4, 8–10, 12, 31–35.

[138] Ibid., CCCM 100, A 5, lines 9–23, 31–38.

Figure 18. Dedication to Louis the Pious, *In honorem sanctae crucis*, Vatican, Biblioteca Apostolica Vaticana, cod. Reg. lat. 124, fol. 4 verso

suggested that the copy of the treatise for which the dedication poem was composed was intended to honor Louis' recoronation at Metz in February 835. The figural verse forming the halo around Louis' head – "You Christ, crown Louis" – perhaps refers to the crown returned to him on this occasion, an emblem of his office that had supposedly belonged to Constantine, contained a relic of the true cross, and had been given to

Louis at his coronation by Pope Stephen III in 816.[139] Whether written in 835 or earlier in the 830s, as Elizabeth Sears has proposed, the dedication poem may have reminded Louis that he deserved the imperial throne and reliquary crown because, like Charlemagne and Constantine before him but unlike the iconoclasts who in the 830s controlled the eastern empire, he defended orthodoxy, including true belief regarding the cross and artistic images.[140]

[139] "Tu, Hludouuicum, Criste, corona"; see ibid., *CCCM* 100, A 6 (*declaratio figurae*) lines 92–93; Perrin, ed., ibid., *CCCM* 100.xxii and n. 33. Perrin argues (xlviii-lv) that Biblioteca Apostolica Vaticana, Reginensis Latinus 124 was probably not the copy intended for Louis. Cf. Sears, "Louis the Pious," 624–627. On Constantine's crown given to Louis see Elbern, "Liturgisches Gerät," 137–138; Anatole Frolow, *La Relique de la vraie croix: recherches sur le développement d'un culte* (Paris, 1961), 217, no. 91; Ermoldus Nigellus, *In honorem Hludowici, MGH PLAC* 2.5–79, esp. 36–37, lines 425–426, 447–450.

[140] The Synod of Paris convened at the behest of Louis and Lothar (*Libellus, MGH Conc.* 2.481 lines 1–6), and Dungal dedicated his treatise to the same rulers (*Ep. 9, MGH Epp.* 4.583 lines 20–23; *Adv. Claudium, PL* 105.465A). Jonas began his treatise for Louis but finished it for Charles the Bald: *De cultu imaginum, Praef., PL* 106.305–307.

CHAPTER 4

The crucified Christ in later Carolingian literature

As attested by the popularity of *In honorem s. crucis* and the energetic defenses of crosses from the 820s to 840s, monks and clergy under Charlemagne's heirs continued to immerse themselves and the laity in a devotional life marked by the cult of the divine savior and his cross, weapon of his defeat of sin / death / Satan and emblem of cosmic dominion.

The evidence for ninth-century devotion to the omnipotent, triumphant crucified Christ is as varied as it is for Charlemagne's court, but the volume markedly increases. As in earlier years, among the clearest, most consistent literary proclamations of such thought occur in the abundant poetry, works now composed by the second and third generations of Carolingian poet-scholars. Brief verse inscriptions by Hrabanus and other writers for crosses, crucifixes, and altars dedicated to the cross strenuously praise the lord who in the passion revealed his divinity, blessed the cosmos, embraced the world in his outstretched hands, and threw the devil into hell. For Mico of St.-Riquier, Jesus suspended on the cross "snatched" Adam "from the jaws of the hungry wolf" and "with his hands extended" gave life and salvation to men.[1] Fixed on the cross, Hrabanus declares, "God, Christ, the lord rules everywhere" and "broke the evil chains." The cross eternally shines in heaven, a perpetual symbol of salvation and celestial rule.[2] For Sedulius

---

[1] Mico, *Carm.* 8–12, 14, 152, *Carmina Centulensia, MGH PLAC* 3, ed. L. Traube (Berlin, 1896), 296–297, 358. Traube dates Mico's poetical works to 825–853 (pp. 265–274); but cf. Ferrari, *Liber s. crucis,* 186–191.

[2] Hrabanus, *Carm.* 55.5, *MGH PLAC* 2, ed. E. Dümmler (Berlin, 1884), 220. See also *Carm.* 49.6, 64,

Scottus, an altar holds a piece of the cross that "harrowed hell and opened the heavens."[3]

Longer verse compositions from the ninth century offer more sustained meditations on the powerful, crucified divinity, often within narratives of Christ's earthly life as a whole or alongside other themes. Audradus' *De fonte vitae*, the fifth book of the collection of poetry and prose that he gave to Pope Leo IV in 849, presents a dialogue with Hincmar of Rheims that describes the creation, the fall, and the birth of Christ, the "fountain of life," and then provides a theatrical retelling of his triumphant passion, harrowing of hell, and resurrection.[4] Christ is the merciful creator who grieves over the fallen human race; death and the devil plot against him, thinking him a mere mortal, to force him to cease disrupting their plans and entomb his body in "undesired death." The suffering lord counters his enemies, and in the end, death and the serpent would have fled the site of the cross, "had not the nearby strength of Christ and majesty of God, born of man, caught the leviathan on the fish-hook and slain death by dying."[5] Notker the Stammerer refers to the same popular image in his sequence for the feasts of holy women, pointing out to the serpent-devil the uselessness of its capture of the human race; for Jesus "took away your spoils and pierced your jaw with a hook, to afford an escape for Eve's children whom you wish to hold."[6] Still more vibrant imagery occurs in the series of poems honoring the cross and crucifixion, descent into hell, and resurrection that John Scottus Eriugena wrote between 858 and the early 870s. As will be considered further in chapter 5, the doctrine of these verses agrees with the distinctive theological system that John Scottus elaborated in prose writings of his later years, influenced by his translations and study of the works of the Greek theologians, Pseudo-Dionysius and Maximus the Confessor.[7]

65, 69, 77.8, 78.4, 79.2, 80.4, 11, *MGH PLAC* 2.215, 223–224, 230–232, 234. Cf. Ferrari, *Liber s. crucis*, 179–185, 423–432; Arnulf, *Versus ad picturas*, 151–152.

[3] Sedulius Scottus, *Carm.* 2.47, *MGH PLAC* 3.209–210; trans. E. G. Doyle, *Sedulius Scottus: On Christian Rulers and the Poems* (Binghamton, 1983), 147. Cf. (on a fresco of the passion) *Carm.* 7.5, *Carmina Sangallensia, MGH PLAC* 2.482; Arnulf, *Versus ad picturas*, 163.

[4] Audradus, *Carm.* 1, *MGH PLAC* 3.73–84. Other portions of the collection in *Audradi carminum supplementum, MGH PLAC* 3.740–745. See Paul Dutton, *The Politics of Dreaming in the Carolingian Empire* (Lincoln, NE, 1994), 129–156.

[5] Audradus, *Carm.* 1, *MGH PLAC* 3.80–81 lines 260–311.

[6] Notker, *In natale sanctarum feminarum*, trans. Godman, *Poetry*, 318–321, stanzas 7–10.

[7] *Iohannis Scotti Eriugenae Carmina*, ed. and trans. M. W. Herren (Dublin, 1993), see 6–7.

Within this framework, an understanding of the crucifixion as Christ's victory and the cross as symbol of his universal governance prevails. Encomias are rendered to the warrior-savior and cosmic ruler who overcame the "prince of the world," then entered hell to free its prisoners and "by your single death . . . dared to destroy our double death." The sign by which he conquered, which itself summoned the human race from hell, now embraces "earth, sea, winds, sky, and all else."[8]

The divine victory over sin/death/Satan is also remembered in the poetical *Liber evangeliorum* by Otfrid of Weissenburg, a pupil of Hrabanus Maurus, and in the extant lines of the anonymous *Heliand*. Both works count among the earliest evidence of the development of original vernacular literature in the Carolingian territories. In these compositions, a distinctively Germanic atmosphere is lent to the narratives of triumph that may well have made them more accessible to local populations, whether that was a deliberate aim of the authors or a less conscious result of the languages in which the verses were composed.[9] The Old Saxon *Heliand*, written under either Louis the Pious (814–840) or Louis the German (843–876) and probably the best known of all ninth-century Carolingian vernacular texts, describes Christ as the warlord of a faithful retinue of disciple-thanes. He alone operates above the workings of fate, though he voluntarily submits to its determination of his life's length. His warrior-companions wish to die with their lord, in accordance with the Germanic ideal for the loyal follower of a chieftain, but in the end he must suffer alone in order to overcome the enemy. The outward impassivity with which he endures the torments of the Jews demonstrates his greatness, even while inside he seethes with virile rage. Despite the physical pain of the cross, his acceptance of "the gallows" for humanity's sake proves his courage. His spirit escapes his adversaries as it leaves his body, and his kingship is revealed through the miracles accompanying his death and resurrection.[10]

---

[8] John Scottus, Poems 1, 2, ibid., 58–63 line 8, 64–67 lines 3–5, 19–21.

[9] Cyril Edwards, "Germanic Vernacular Literature," in *Carolingian Culture: Emulation and Innovation*, 152–157, dating the completion of the *Liber evangeliorum* to 863–871. See O. Erdmann, ed., *Otfrids Evangelienbuch* (Tübingen 1962); Wolfgang Kleiber, ed., *Otfrid von Weissenburg* (Darmstadt, 1978); Hulda Göhler, "Das Christusbild in Otfrids Evangelienbuch und im *Heliand*," *Zeitschrift für deutsche Philologie* 59 (1935), 1–52. Also Ferrari, *Liber s. crucis*, 240–242.

[10] G. Ronald Murphy, trans., *The Heliand: the Saxon Gospel*, Songs 60–68 (Oxford, 1992), 166–192; Burkhard Taeger, ed., *Der Heliand: Studiusgabe in Auswahl* (Tübingen, 1984). Edwards,

Although the practice of adorning books and bookcovers with crosses seems to decline after Hrabanus completed *In honorem sanctae crucis*, a wealth of other cross imagery extant and recorded in documents – wall paintings, processional, reliquary, and altar crosses – continued to present the message that the passion vanquished the forces of evil. Crucifixion images, formerly rare in the west, surge in number in manuscripts, on ivories, metalwork objects, and in other artistic media, with many showing the savior alive, impassible, undefeated by death.[11] An increasing volume of scriptural exegesis draws from a widening array of patristic authorities in order to interpret verses in the Old Testament, the New Testament letters, Acts of the Apostles, and Book of the Apocalypse that are linked to the passion. Sometimes the interpretations recall Jesus' redemptive torments, death, and sacrifice, but often allusions are made to his victory and the cross as its symbol. Leaving aside commentaries on the gospels and the letter to the Hebrews, to which I will turn shortly, the biblical texts that most often invite exegesis of the crucifixion are the other epistles. Certain passages in the letters typically lead Carolingian scholars to reflect on Christ's mortal humanity, oblation, and model of humility and suffering. For Claudius of Turin and Haimo of Auxerre, Galatians 6.14 is reminiscent of his paradigmatic, voluntary tolerance of hardship,[12] and Haimo notes that Romans 3.14 is a reminder of the Jews' cursing of Jesus and his followers and the "bitterness" of his passion.[13] Other verses, though, are more likely to elicit remarks about his divine power. Commenting on the discussion of baptism in Romans 6, for example, Sedulius Scottus interprets verse 6 to mean that, in the sacrament, the faithful crucify themselves with Christ in order to rid the body of vices; for the "body of sin" refers to the devil who was "destroyed on

"Germanic Vernacular Literature," 152–153, notes Fulda and Werden as possible places of origin, while Murphy tentatively suggests Corvey as another possibility, in *The Saxon Savior: the Germanic Transformation of the Gospel in the Ninth-Century Heliand* (New York, 1989), 12. See also Johannes Rathofer, *Der Heliand: theologischer Sinn als tektonische Form: Vorbereitung und Grundlegung der Interpretation* (Cologne, 1962).

[11] This material is surveyed in my dissertation, "The Cross, the Image, and the Passion," esp. 319–327, 342–354. See also Schiller, *Iconography* 2.99–102, 103–117; Haussherr, *Der tote Christus*, 108–111. A sense of the richness of the artistic remains is given by the reproductions published in the catalogue and with the articles of the recent Paderborn exhibition. For liturgical objects, see esp. Victor H. Elbern, "Liturgisches Gerät und Reliquiare," in *799: Kunst und Kultur, Beiträge*, ed. Steigemann and Wemhoff, 694–710.

[12] Haimo, *In Divi Pauli epistolas expositio, in epist. ad Galatas* 6, PL 117.698C; Claudius, *Enarratio in Epistolam D. Pauli ad Galatas* 6, PL 104.909C/D.

[13] Haimo, *Expositio, in epist. ad Romanos* 3, PL 117.388A/B.

the cross."[14] For Haimo, Romans 6.10 brings to mind the devil's defeat in the harrowing of hell, when Christ powerfully bore away from the underworld those mortals elected for salvation.[15] For both Hrabanus and Sedulius Scottus, 1 Corinthians 1 and especially verses 23–24[16] affirm Jesus' conquest of Satan and death through the cross; according to Hrabanus, combining references to 2 Corinthians 13.4[17] and Colossians 2.14–15,[18] Christ was crucified for sin, "so that destroying death, he might liberate from it those who believe in him," and erase the handwriting against Adam.[19]

Such perspectives on the crucifixion were reinforced in the ninth century by the expanding volume of prose and poetical hagiography, lives of the saints that, like the stories told by Alcuin and his contemporaries, follow well-established patterns of sanctity for which one biblical model was Jesus' own life, death, and resurrection. Through their miracles and virtue the saints of later Carolingian *vitae*, too, at least indirectly emulate their savior's struggle against evil that culminated in his crucifixion and resurrection, even while their humility, self-denial, and sufferings imitate his lowliness, pain, and sacrifice. Demons are repeatedly overcome through cross relics and the sign made by hand or worn spiritually, such as in the case of the deacon Sabinianus, in the *Vita sancti Romani*, who arms his heart "with the banner of the lord's passion" when the devil accosts him in the guise of two girls. In the *Vita Dalmatii*, the abbot Venerianus exorcizes a possessed girl by making the sign of the cross over her ears; Odo of Cluny, writing in the early tenth century, notes that through the same sign Gerald of Aurillac ended a magician's power and caused a mad woman to vomit the cause of her affliction. Occasionally Christ's power is manifested by

---

[14] "Knowing this, that our old man is crucified with him, that the body of sin may be destroyed, to the end that we may serve sin no longer"; Sedulius Scottus, *Collectanea in omnes B. Pauli epistolas* 1.6, PL 103.60.

[15] "For in that he died to sin, he died once; but in that he liveth, he liveth unto God"; Haimo, *Expositio, in epist. ad Romanos* 6, PL 117.415A.

[16] "But we preach Christ crucified, unto the Jews indeed a stumblingblock, and unto the Gentiles foolishness: But unto them that are called, both Jews and Greeks, Christ the power of God, and the wisdom of God."

[17] "For although he was crucified through weakness, yet he liveth by the power of God. For we also are weak in him: but we shall live with him by the power of God towards you."

[18] "Blotting out the handwriting of the decree that was against us, which was contrary to us. And he hath taken the same out of the way, fastening it to the cross. And despoiling the principalities and powers, he hath exposed them confidently in open shew, triumphing over them in himself."

[19] Hrabanus, *Enarrationes in Epistolas Pauli* 9.1, 13.13, PL 112.16, 242A/B; Sedulius Scottus, *Collectanea* 2.1, PL 103.130B, 131A.

means of a manufactured cross, as when St. Leoba successfully prays before one that God reveal the perpetrator of a crime.[20]

The sign of the cross and the protection of the conquering savior also possess special meaning for ninth-century princes besides Louis the Pious. In a few *carmina figurata*, possibly inspired by Hrabanus' dedication poem for Louis but with simpler, geometric designs closer to those of the figure poems by Alcuin, Joseph the Scot, and Theodulf and the earlier works by Venantius and Boniface, the cross and its sign are the glorified symbol of the son of God who blesses and guards the earthly lord, the main subject of praise.[21] Ninth-century sacramentaries continue to record prayers, litanies, and increasingly elaborate services for the welfare of rulers and their armies' success in warfare, placing them under the protection of the king who eternally vanquishes and rules.[22] A growing number of non-figural poems as well as prose *Fürstenspiegel* ("mirrors of princes") emphasize Old Testament models of good kingship and those presented by the early Christian emperors – David, Solomon, and the Roman emperor Theodosius are among the virtuous rulers most often noted. Direct connections with Christ are rarely drawn, yet like Charlemagne when presented with the *carmina figurata* of Alcuin and Joseph, or Henry of Friuli when he read Paulinus' *Liber exhortationis*, the nobles to whom these texts are directed would certainly have known that Jesus presented the supreme model of the behavior in which they are asked to engage: humility, a quality that the authors of the ninth-century tracts increasingly urge on their rulers, fasting, prayer, penitence, and participation in the church's sacramental life, but also perfect justice and vigorous struggle against vice and the enemies of the Christian faith.[23] This must have been true of Count Eberhard of Friuli when he received Sedulius Scottus' poetry acclaiming his magnificence in battle, faith, justice, and goodness, and declaring that

---

[20] *Vita sancti Romani* 17, MGH SRM 3, ed. B. Krusch (Hanover, 1896), 142; *Vita Dalmatii* 6, MGH SRM 3.546–547; Odo of Cluny, "The Life of Saint Gerald of Aurillac," ch. 32, trans. G. Sitwell, *Soldiers of Christ*, ed. Noble and Head, 293–362, at 345–346; Rudolf, "Vita Leobae 12, MGH SS 15.118–131, at 126–127. See Wallace-Hadrill, *Frankish Church*, 75–93; Flint, *Rise of Magic*, 173–185.

[21] Gosbert, *Carmen acrostichum* (for Count William of Blois), MGH PLAC 1.620–622; Milo, *Carm.* 1.1–3 (for Charles the Bald), MGH PLAC 3.561–565; cf. (not explicitly mentioning the cross, though the X figure was probably intended to evoke it) *Carm.* 5 (honoring St. Gall), *Carmina Sangallensia*, MGH PLAC 2.478–479. See Ernst, *Carmen figuratum*, 333–340; on Milo's poetry, Godman, *Poets and Emperors*, 176–179.

[22] McCormick, *Eternal Victory*, 342–384; Kantorowicz, *Laudes Regiae*, 65–111.

[23] Cf. Anton, *Fürstenspiegel*, 376–377, 419–446.

Christ provides him with the "sword and shield of salvation," the "lorica of faith and helmet of hope."[24] Writing to Pepin of Aquitaine in the early 830s, Jonas of Orléans most likely thought not only of Old Testament monarchs such as David but of his crucified redeemer's glorious death and resurrection when he told the Carolingian king to ignore "the ancient enemy, scorning the world which is so sunk in wickedness, scorning and trampling upon its riches." Thus Pepin should "make the saving change from vice to virtue, from the visible to the invisible, from the transient to the eternal."[25] In *De regis persona et regio ministerio*, composed for Charles the Bald, Hincmar of Rheims follows Augustine's *De civitate Dei* in outlining the reasons for which a good king may properly wage war and bear arms. These activities are acceptable when the battle has God as author and the king fights on God's behalf. David is the cited model, though comparison is also made to the clergy who fight invisible enemies through their prayers. Both the Old Testament ruler and the church's leaders strive to overcome the devil with his legions, and while Christ is again not directly mentioned as a paradigm, the relationship with his own battle against sin/death/Satan was doubtless recognized.[26] A connection between the mortal monarch and the victorious Christ is also implied on the ivory-decorated *Cathedra Petri*, made for Charles the Bald (figs. 19, 20 and 32).[27] The ivories of the backrest are carved with a portrait of Charles and other motifs that, as will be seen in chapter 7, have parallels on ninth-century crucifixion ivories. Among these reliefs, some depict armed combat signifying the conflict between vice and virtue in which the king was expected to participate. Thus the imagery associates him with David's successful struggles against his enemies, the major theme of the Utrecht Psalter illustrations that evidently provided models for many of the throne's figures;[28] but it also connects Charles with Christ, his heavenly lord, who was probably originally depicted in the central oval of the triangular pediment above his head (fig. 19).[29]

[24] Sedulius Scottus, *Carm.*2.67, MGH PLAC 3.220–221; trans. Doyle, *Sedulius Scottus*, 162.

[25] Jonas, *De institutione regia, Ep. ad Pippinem regem*, PL 106.279–306, at 282C; trans. R.W. Dyson, *A Ninth-Century Political Tract: the De Institutione Regia of Jonas of Orleans* (Smithtown, NY, 1983), 4.   [26] See Hincmar, *De regis persona et regio ministerio* 9–11, PL 125.833–856, esp. 841–842.

[27] Basilica di San Pietro in Vaticano; see Nees, *Tainted Mantle*, 147–177.

[28] Utrecht, Bibliotheek der Rijksuniversiteit, MS 32; see Nees, *Tainted Mantle*, 154–155.

[29] Nees, *Tainted Mantle*, 154–155; cf. (suggesting a different relation to David) Nikolaus Staubach, *Rex Christianus: Hofkultur und Herrschaftspropaganda im Reich Karls des Kahlen* (Cologne, 1993), 299–307.

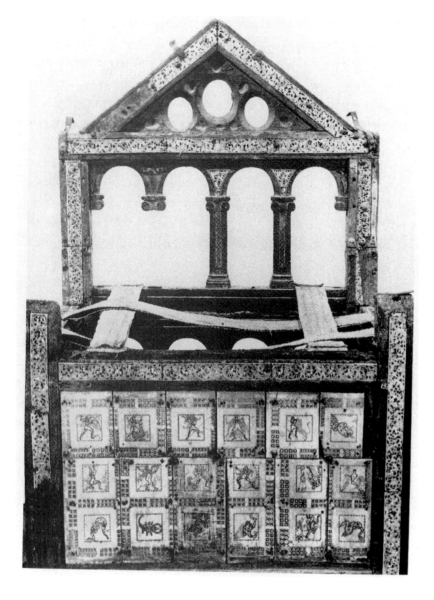

Figure 19. *Cathedra Petri*, general view before restoration, Basilica di San Pietro in Vaticano

Within the liturgy, the divine defeat of Satan and the crucified Jesus' omnipotence were still celebrated in the rites of Easter, baptism, and, as should be evident from the treatises defending cross-worship, in the ceremonies in its honor: the Good Friday *Adoratio crucis*, the Roman *Exaltatio crucis*, and the Gallican *Inventio crucis*. Both feasts (the *Exaltatio* and *Inventio crucis*) are recorded in the supplemented Gregorian sacramentaries that

Figure 20. *Cathedra Petri,*
portrait of Charles the Bald

gained popularity during the ninth century.[30] New orations venerating the
cross were composed for recitation *ad crucem* and in private prayer.
Dhuoda's manual for her son William, written in the early 840s, directs him
to end his devotions by tracing the sign of the cross and expressing his adoration of it as his salvation, defense, protection, refuge, his life and the
death of the devil.[31] Alcuin's votive masses were widely disseminated in the
ninth century, among them his mass for the cross that combines remembrance of the sacrifice for sin with praise of the "life-giving" cross that
guards believers.[32]

  The crucifixion and resurrection as together the victory over death and
Satan are stressed, as well, in later Carolingian exegesis of baptism and
Easter, in both poetry and prose. Like the responses to Charlemagne's ques-
tionnaire on baptism and ninth-century exegesis of Romans 6, such as
Sedulius Scottus', the comprehensive studies of liturgical ritual by
Hrabanus, Amalarius, and Walafrid Strabo view baptism as a purging of sin

[30] *Sacramentaire grégorien* 3, ed. Deshusses, esp. nos. 4326, 4418–4421, 4423–4427.
[31] "Cum hoc compleveris, fac crucem in fronte et super lectum tuum in similitudinem crucis
     illius a quo redemptus es, hoc modo: +, ita dicendo: 'Crucem tuam adoro, Domine, et
     sanctam resurrectionem tuam credo. Crux tua sancta mecum. Crux est quam cognovi,
     semper amavi, semperque adoro. Crux mihi salus, crux mihi defensio, crux mihi protectio
     semperque refugium. Crux mihi vita, mors tibi, diabole, inimice veritatis, cultor vanitatis;
     crux mihi vita, mors tibi semper'. Et item: 'Tuam, Domine, + crucem adoro tuamque glorio-
     sam passionem recolo qui dignatus es nasi, pati, mori ac resurgere a mortuis, qui cum Patre et
     Spiritu Sancto, + benedictio Dei Patris et Filii et Spiritus Sancti descendat et maneat super me
     servum tuum minimum. Amen'": Dhuoda, *Liber manualis* 2.3; quoted in Ferrari, *Liber s. crucis,*
     385–386. See also *Sacramentaire grégorien* 3, ed. Deshusses, nos. 4410–4427.
[32] Deshusses, ed., "Messes d'Alcuin," nos. 15–19; *Sacramentaire grégorien* 2, ed. Deshusses, nos.
     1835–1840, cf. pp. 25–27.

through which the faithful reject the devil, overcome his power, and ally themselves with Christ. According to Hrabanus' *De sacris ordinibus*, written after 822 when he was abbot of Fulda, the baptized Christian abandons the army of the devil, who had subjected mortals with the "arms" of vice, in order to join the army of Christ, who fought Satan with the weapon of virtue.[33] Prefigured in the crossing of the Red Sea, the recipient of baptism moves from memory and imitation of Jesus' death to the rebirth and new life proclaimed in his victory over sin, resurrection, and ascension.[34] According to Amalarius' *Liber officialis*, the Easter ceremonial links the crucifixion and resurrection together as the destruction of death's bonds, the illumination of the night of sin, the revelation of divine immortality.[35] The sermons for Easter in Hrabanus' collection for Haistulf (d. 826), original works composed by him using patristic sources, are representative of the significant development of this literary genre since the homiliary of Paul the Deacon. They hail the power revealed in the crucified Christ when he defeated the devil, tore down hell's doors, and ascended from the underworld.[36] "With the prince of darkness enchained and the gates of death broken, and the prize of the souls of the saints carried away, triumphant, he rose from hell in glory."[37] The death that was the destruction of death and the resurrection are together the source of mortals' rebirth in baptism.[38] Sermons for the feasts of the cross that circulated in the ninth century, including one for the *Inventio crucis* attributed to Hrabanus, tell the story of the finding of the true

---

[33] Hrabanus, *De sacris ordinibus* 12, PL 112.1173A; see Brunhölzl, *Histoire* 1.2.87–88. Such ideas parallel contemporary social relations: Smith, "Religion and Lay Society," 659.

[34] Hrabanus, *De institutione clericorum* 1.27–30, ed. Aloisius Knoepfler (Munich, 1900/1901), 46–58; also published in PL 107.293–420. See also idem, *De sacris ordinibus* (repeating portions of *De institutione clericorum*) 5–17, PL 112.1169–1177; Amalarius, *Liber officialis* 1.23–29, esp. 24, 27, ST 139.125–156; Walafrid, *De exord. et increment.* 27, MGH Capit. 2.510–511. Cf. *Ord.* 23, 24, 27–32, *Ordines romani* 3.273–523; Cramer, *Baptism and Change*, 137–138.

[35] See Amalarius, esp. *Liber officialis* 1.16–18, 31, ST 139.108–113, 157–161.

[36] Hrabanus, *Homiliae* I, PL 110.9–134, esp. *Hom.* 16–18, PL 110.33–37. On the two collections of sermons and homilies attributed to Hrabanus [= *Homiliae* I and II], R. Etaix, "L'homéliaire composé par Raban Maur pour l'empereur Lothaire," *Recherches augustiniennes* 19 (1984), 211–240; idem, "Le receuil de sermons composé par Raban Maur pour Haistulfe de Mayence," *Revue des études augustiniennes* 32 (1986), 124–137, dating the latter collection to 822–826. See also Barré, *Homéliaires carolingiens*, 13–16.   [37] Hrabanus, *Hom.* 16, *Homiliae* I, PL 110.33.

[38] See Hrabanus, *Hom.* 16–17, *Homiliae* I, PL 110.33–35. Striking a different tone, though, *Hom.* 18 begins by observing that the period of Lent, which "cum jejuniis et afflictione carnis nostrae habuimus, praesentis saeculi typum tenet, in quo per mortificationem corporis nostri passionibus Christi communicare debemus." Hrabanus closes by exhorting his listeners to turn away from the sin that leads to eternal death and listen to the redeeming precepts of Christ: *Homiliae* I, PL 110.36–37, esp. 36A/B, 37B/C.

cross, its loss to and recovery from the Persians. The account of these events is interwoven with praise of Christ as the triumphant hero and of the "admirable sign, on which our lord Jesus Christ the son of God, suspended, damned the punishment of death for the weight of our sins, and poured out his blood that is adored by the thrones and angels."[39]

Innumerable other examples could be given of ninth-century compilations of older works, original treatises, prayers, hymns, and other poetical and prose texts that, in a huge variety of different situations, recall, acclaim, and invite contemplation of Christ as the divine savior king who destroyed sin/death/Satan through his power-filled blood and cross, or that elaborate on the other ideas noted in the last chapters centering on his powerful divinity. Rather than multiply illustrations of these currents of thought, clearly significant in both the early and later Carolingian periods, though, the remainder of this chapter will focus on developments in the ninth century that were especially important in encouraging a shift away from this outlook: the growth of biblical and liturgical exegesis, and certain aspects of the liturgy's evolution.

It has already been seen that ninth-century commentaries on the Bible and church ritual provide evidence of the energy at this time of the cult of the immortal son of God. When ninth-century Carolingians prayed and meditated on the meaning of a scriptural or liturgical passage, it was often with such a vision of Jesus and his passion in mind. The same sources, however, also reveal two tendencies that ultimately direct thinking in quite different directions: the strengthening of interest, first, in mapping out the historical details of the crucifixion – the circumstances in which Jesus was nailed to the cross, who was there, what was done to him, when he died, etc. – and, second, in explaining the purpose of the crucified humanity and its death in the accomplishment of redemption. Such concerns were not absent from Charlemagne's court circle, as is evident from some literature, particularly by Alcuin, and from a few non-literary sources such as, possibly, the list of relics of Christ at St.-Riquier.[40] Nevertheless, in the decades

---

[39] Hrabanus, *Hom.*70, *Homiliae* I, *PL* 110.131D-134. The problems it raises are discussed in Etaix, "Recueil de sermons," 126. *Hom.* 36 (*In inventione sanctae crucis*), *Homiliae* II (Hrabanus' collection of exegetical homilies for Lothar, dating to 854–855), *PL* 110.213–214, is drawn from Ambrosiaster: Etaix, "L'homéliaire," 231. Ann Matter has informed me that further holy cross sermons are found in Rheims, BM 1395, fols. 48–56; Orléans, BM 342 (290), pp. 183–202; Paris, BNF lat. 5327a, fols. 80–80v; Paris, BNF lat. 5327b, fols. 198–201; London, BL Add. 11880, fols. 111–119.   [40] See chapter 2, at n. 70.

following Charlemagne's death, these perspectives gain a new prominence and are expressed with a clarity not seen previously in the medieval west.

In respect to the first-named tendency, one especially significant feature of Bible study in the ninth century is the expansion of gospel exegesis: formal tractates that, through original interpretations or, more often, *florilegia* of patristic sources selected, edited, arranged, and sometimes annotated by the Carolingian authors, map out the meaning of a gospel account even to the point of verse-by-verse and sometimes word-by-word analysis; exegetical homilies that comment in a similar manner on the lections used in liturgical observances; and verse compositions that rehearse the details of Jesus' life, death, and resurrection, sometimes exploring the different episodes' typological and mystical significance.[41] Most noticeably in the homilies and formal treatises, careful, sustained efforts are made to read discrete speeches and actions recounted in the gospel narratives at the literal and historical, as well as allegorical, levels of interpretation. In the most ambitious of these works, every individual moment in the unfolding story receives close attention as filled with sacred significance in its own right. The impact of this on how the passion is interpreted can be best appreciated if we compare the commentaries of three ninth-century scholars – Hrabanus, Christian of Stavelot, and an anonymous scholar whose work was interpolated into the collection of exegetical homilies by Haimo of Auxerre – on two of the episodes preceding the crucifixion and then on the crucifixion itself, as told in the gospel of Matthew.[42] Like Alcuin's commentary on John, in which the discussion of the crucifixion is an abbreviated version of Augustine's exegesis, the ninth-century tracts discuss the revelation of God's ordering of sacred events and of Christ's true divinity as well as humanity through the different levels of signification that, the exegetes demonstrate, the actors and actions in the drama possess. To some extent as in the *Heliand*, Otfrid's *Liber evangeliorum*, and Audradus' *De*

---

[41] More than 150 scriptural commentaries are recorded from Alcuin to Remigius of Auxerre: John Contreni, "The Carolingian Renaissance: Education and Literary Culture," in *NCMH* 2.734. On the general growth of exegetical studies in the ninth century, ibid., 733–734. See also idem, "Carolingian Biblical Studies," repr. in *Carolingian Learning, Masters and Manuscripts*, Variorum Collected Studies series 363 (London, 1992), v.

[42] The largest proportion of Carolingian gospel commentaries are on Matthew: Petrus W. Tax, "Remigius of Auxerre's Psalm Commentary and the Matthew Commentary Attributed to Him," in Dominique Iogna-Prat et al., eds., *L'Ecole carolingienne d'Auxerre: de Murethach à Remi, 830–908, Entretiens d'Auxerre 1989* (Paris, 1991), 413–424, at 424, citing the commentaries of Hrabanus Maurus, Claudius of Turin, Christian of Stavelot, Pascasius, and Sedulius Scottus.

fonte vitae, this means praise of the son of God's triumph over evil, a victory presaged in the miraculous events that surrounded the suffering on the cross. But no two exegetes develop precisely the same ramifications of this doctrinal theme. Furthermore, fidelity to the gospel sequence of episodes promotes other lines of thought, as well, as the writers draw on a range of patristic sources (usually unidentified) in order to present varying combinations of literal, allegorical, and moral exegesis, references to grammatical and etymological issues, other gospels, and Old Testament prefigurations.

Consider, first, the interpretations that Christian, Hrabanus, and the anonymous exegete propose of the Barabbas episode (Matthew 27.17–26), which express in some ways similar ideas while highlighting different portions of the story. The anonymous commentary informs us that Barabbas means either "son of the teacher" if it is read with two r's, or "their father" with one r and two b's, based on the Hebrew *abba*. In both cases, the name signifies the Antichrist to whom the Jews conform. Pilate's washing of his hands in Matthew 27.24 was prefigured in Psalm 25.6 ("I will wash my hands among the innocent; and will compass thy altar, O Lord"); Matthew 27.25 ("His blood be upon us and upon our children") refers to the curse on the Jews that will persevere until the final judgment; the scourging of Jesus either was done to fulfill Roman law or to encourage the Jews to cease to seek his death, since their hostility should have been satiated by his flogging.[43] Hrabanus' commentary, probably written in 821–822 and consisting chiefly of block excerpts from patristic sources,[44] stresses Old Testament prophecies of the passion and its divine ordination; the crowd's call to Pilate for Jesus' crucifixion (Matthew 27.23), for instance, is tied to Psalm 21, Jeremiah 12, and Isaiah 5. An excerpt from Augustine then refers to the crucifixion's cruelty, Jesus' innocence, and his desire that the cross be a sign of victory against the devil for his faithful to carry on their foreheads.[45] Christian of Stavelot, writing c. 865 for younger monks at his monastery (Stavelot-Malmédy), weaves his own analysis together with material from

---

[43] Ps.-Haimo, *Hom.* 64, *Homiliae de tempore*, PL 118.358–381, at 373D-374C.

[44] Hrabanus, *Commentarium in Matthaeum*, PL 107.727–1156. Identified sources include Cyprian, Eusebius, Hilary, Ambrose, Jerome, Augustine, Fulgentius, Victorinus, Fortunatianus, Leo I, Gregory I, among others. In the dedication to Haistulf, Hrabanus notes that his aim was to compile patristic teachings into one volume to assist readers who lack good libraries: PL 107.727–729. On the treatise's date, Etaix, "Recueil de sermons," 137.

[45] Hrabanus, *In Matth.* 8.27, PL 107.1132.

Jerome, other patristic sources, and Pascasius Radbertus' commentary on Matthew.[46] He declares that the *bar* in Barabbas means son, the *rabbi* (*rabbas*) means "of the teacher"; and he stresses the Jews' hatred of Jesus, despite the good things he had done for them, their desertion of the truth when they demanded Barabbas, and the contrast between their desire for Jesus' crucifixion and the crowds' welcoming of him into Jerusalem on Palm Sunday. Pilate's washing of his hands signifies the difference between him and the Jews who claimed to follow the law of God, yet wanted to kill an innocent man.[47]

For Christian and Hrabanus, the subsequent account of Jesus' flogging and humiliation (Matthew 27.26) is evidence of Pilate's adherence to Roman law. Hrabanus notes that Jesus was whipped by Pilate himself. Christian, who is particularly interested in the historical context of the narrative and in philological questions, observes that the column to which Christ was tied still stands in Jerusalem;[48] Matthew's statement that the soldiers received Jesus in a hall (*praetorium*) (Matthew 27.27) brings an exposition of that term and (referring to the Greek) *lithostratos*.[49] Christian, Hrabanus, and the anonymous commentary all pay careful attention to the mocking's mystical significance, with Hrabanus noting the variants among the four gospel accounts. The scarlet cloak symbolizes the royal purple, the crown of thorns and the reed were substitutes for a golden crown and scepter, the reed designates the sacrilege of the Jews and, for Christian, that Jesus deleted all magic. Each commentary also refers to the same objects' moral significance: the thorns denote the sins that Christ accepted in his body, "so that he might die on the cross for our sins," though himself innocent; for the anonymous commentator and Hrabanus, the cloak's color indicates the tortures he sustained in the flesh for the same purpose; for Hrabanus, the crown of thorns refers to the "ancient curse" thereby dissolved. Again, Hrabanus evokes Old Testament prophecy, and

[46] Published under Christianus Druthmarus, *Expositio in Matthaeum evangelistam*, PL 106.1261–1504. See John J. Contreni, "The Pursuit of Knowledge," in *The Gentle Voices of Teachers: Aspects of Learning in the Carolingian Age*, ed. Richard E. Sullivan (Columbus, OH, 1995), 106–41, at 121; F. G. Cremer, "Christian von Stablo als Exeget: Beobachtungen zur Auslegung von Mt. 9, 14–17," *Revue Bénédictine* 77 (1967), 328–341.

[47] Christian, *In Matth.*, PL 106.1486D-1488B.

[48] See Contreni, "Carolingian Renaissance," 734, noting Christian's opening comment (*PL* 106.1264), "In omnium principiis librorum tria quaerenda sunt, tempus, locus, persona. Similiter de isto evangelio haec tria tenenda sunt."

[49] Hrabanus, *In Matth.* 8.27, PL 107.1133; Christian, *In Matth.*, PL 106.1488D-1489A.

Christian comments on the differences among Greek, Latin, and Hebrew terms in discussing the soldiers' salutation of Jesus as "king of the Jews." The anonymous commentator stresses the same episode's signification of Jesus' divinity, and its distinction from the suffering humanity.[50]

When the same commentaries turn to the crucifixion itself, we see further divergences among them that reflect some of the different, intellectual tendencies already noted, together with the several points at which their exegesis coincides. Christian gives an exposition of the names, Golgotha and Calvary; he then underscores Christ's divinity by remarking that the crucifixion occurred where criminals were punished in order to erect there a "banner of powers," and by quoting the verses from Sedulius' *Carmen paschale* that proclaim the crucifix a symbol of Christ's dominion. The anonymous commentator asserts that it is false to link the name Calvary with the tomb of Adam and Eve, since the first parents were known to have been buried elsewhere. He suggests that the name actually denotes the tradition of beheading criminals on the site; and he declares the lord crucified on this location in order to establish there a "banner of martyrdom," signifying that "where sin abounded, grace did more abound" (Romans 5.20). Hrabanus' interpretation of the cross as a banner agrees with the anonymous exegete, but he also refers to Augustine's moral exegesis of the cross's dimensions, based on Ephesians 3.18.[51] The anonymous commentary and Hrabanus discuss the differences among the gospels in the timing of the crucifixion; Christian compares the three hours on the cross with the three days in the tomb. All three tracts affirm that Christ hung on the cross on the same hour in which Adam sinned in paradise, recalling Jesus' role as the second, victorious Adam. While all three stress the miraculous nature of the darkening, Christian and the anonymous commentary note the consequent need to reject the belief – which Christian attributes to the Jews – that this was caused by a naturally occurring eclipse. The anonymous commentator associates the darkness with the prophecy of Joel 2.31, and Hrabanus asserts that it fulfilled the prophecy of Amos 8. All three exegetes carefully analyze Christ's lament

---

[50] Hrabanus, *In Matth.* 8.27, PL 107.1133D-1134; Christian, *In Matth.*, PL 106.1489; Ps.-Haimo, *Hom.* 64, PL 118.374–375.

[51] Hrabanus, *In Matth.* 8.27, PL 107.1136; Christian, *In Matth.*, PL 106.1489–1490; Ps.-Haimo, *Hom.* 64, PL 118.375D-376. See Augustine, *De doctrina Christiana* 2.41; Sedulius, *Carmen paschale* 5 lines 188–195.

from the cross, with Christian, especially, attending to the philological
issues it raises. Hrabanus and the anonymous commentary observe that
the cry of dereliction designated only the condition of Jesus' humanity, not
the divinity that was inseparable from the father. Hrabanus points to the
cry's foreshadowing in Psalm 21, stresses the corporeal fragility it denoted,
and its moral significance as an example followed when the faithful weep
for their sins.[52]

Alongside these three tractates, it is useful to look at some sections of
the commentary on Matthew's passion that Pascasius Radbertus completed shortly before he died c. 859,[53] a work exceptional in later
Carolingian exegesis for its intricate synthesis of original commentary and
quotations from, paraphrases of, and allusions to earlier sources. Although
Pascasius, too, highlights the divine ordering of sacred events evident in
Matthew's passion narrative, two distinctive characteristics of his treatise
should be remarked. One, partly a reflection of the work's unusual length
and hence the exhaustive analysis of each gospel verse, is the extent to
which the moral signification of individual episodes is analyzed. An eloquent development of this interpretative line occurs in the exegesis of the
vinegar-filled sponge in Matthew 27.48. While the basic elements of
Pascasius' interpretation also appear in the commentaries just studied, as
well as in Alcuin's treatise on John,[54] this analysis is unusual in the extent to
which meaning is extracted from that one gospel verse. Using passages
from Jerome, Hilary, and Ambrose, Pascasius identifies the vinegar and gall
as symbols of the vice and faithlessness in Jews and unbelievers, since while
new wine is a sign of immortality, vinegar denotes the "corruption of
vices" and of human nature that "soured" in Adam. We give Christ wine
mixed with myrrh and vinegar mixed with gall when we believe him to
sleep and not see our evil deeds. The "wine of gladness" is defiled in us by
the bitterness of sin. But taking up a sinless human nature, he revealed that

---

[52] Hrabanus, *In Matth.* 8.27, *PL* 107.1140D-1142; Christian, *In Matth.*, *PL* 106.1491D-1492; Ps.-Haimo,
Hom. 64, *PL* 118.377C-378.

[53] Pascasius, *Expositio in Matheo Libri XII*, *CCCM* 56–56B, ed. B. Paulus (Turnhout, 1984), passion
exegesis in *CCCM* 56B.1343–1404. Although the treatise in its entirety was written over twenty
years, based on Pascasius' Corbie lectures on the gospel, he completed the final books —
including the passion exegesis — only near the end of his life, after his resignation as abbot of
Corbie: Paulus, ed., *In Matheo, CCCM* 56.viii-ix; David Ganz, *Corbie in the Carolingian
Renaissance* (Sigmaringen, 1990), 31–32.

[54] Hrabanus, *In Matth.* 8.27, *PL* 107.1143A; Christian, *In Matth.*, *PL* 106.1492C/D; Ps.-Haimo, *Hom.*
64, *PL* 118.378B/C; Alcuin, *Comm. in Joann.* 7.40, *PL* 100.985A.

he would restore the sinless immortality that had soured "in the vessels of the human race." Hence the sponge is a figure of the Jews, who are "puffed up" because they contain nothing but the "vinegar of sin and corruption, drawing all the dregs of shameful things into themselves." Christ drinks from the cup of death in order to absorb our vices; for we should transfuse our sins to him through baptism and then daily through penance, "in order that our sins may be deleted on his cross and, through him, death may be absorbed in victory." In the crucified redeemer, all the bitterness and corruption in the human race were emptied out. Transferred into his body, they became a "new wine, the wine of delight because it flowed from the vine-sprig that is the true vine," the drink of the lord and his followers in paradise.[55]

Second, Pascasius' commentary is striking for its insistence on the suffering's revelation of divinity in Christ and, a concept also suggested in other of Pascasius' exegetical and doctrinal writings, on the ability of Jesus' human nature to operate outside the boundaries of ordinary, physical existence.[56] The emphasis is thus on Christ's divine omnipotence and immortality, yet a notably careful analysis of each feature of his humanity's torment serves to demonstrate that, even in the seemingly most "human" occurrences, this was no mere man. The exegesis of the crucifixion, for example, borrows from Jerome, Origen, and an anonymous gospel commentary from Orléans to affirm, first of all, the proof in Jesus' refusal to descend from the cross that he was indeed God. The Christ who foreknew everything that would happen to him demonstrated greater power by rising from the dead. Although the priests wanted him to descend before he triumphed, knowing their deceits he remained on the scaffold, "so that he would conquer all the legions of hell and return victorious from the

---

[55] Pascasius, *In Matheo* 27.48, CCCM 56B.1388–1390; cf. the exegesis of the first drinking episode, *In Matheo* 27.34, CCCM 56B.1366–1367.

[56] The concept that God can and chooses to override the laws of physical nature is also strong in Pascasius' writings on the eucharist and Jesus' birth. Pascasius' doctrine of the eucharist is discussed in chapter 6; on the virgin birth see Pascasius, *De partu Virginis*, ed. E. A. Matter, CCCM 56C (Turnhout, 1985), 47–89; Pelikan, *Christian Tradition*, 3.72–74. Indicative of Pascasius' outlook is also the pseudo-Hieronymian *Epistola ad Paulam et Eustochium*, probably composed by Pascasius c. 820–830: ed. A. Ripberger, CCCM 56C (Turnhout, 1985), 109–162, see 111–115, defending the doctrine of Mary's bodily assumption. Cf. Henri Barré, "La lettre du pseudo-Jérôme sur l'assomption est-elle antérieure à Pascase Radbert?" *Revue Bénédictine* 68 (1958), 203–225; D. C. Lambot, "L'homélie du Ps.-Jérôme sur l'assomption et l'évangile de la nativité de Marie d'après une lettre inédite d'Hincmar," *Revue Bénédictine* 46 (1934), 265–282.

lower regions."[57] The exegesis of the cry of dereliction (Matthew 27.46) dwells on Matthew's description of the voice's "greatness" (*vox magna*). The same voice was heard when God called to Adam after he sinned, Pascasius declares, but so "great" a cry at the moment of human death went against nature. Whether or not it was great in the sound made, it must be recognized as such in the mystery represented. Consequently, anywhere in scripture that we read of a cry of Jesus, God, or of wisdom, we should know this to refer to a "great and ineffable sacrament."[58] A similar significance is attributed to the blood and water that flowed from Christ's side wound, which Pascasius observes occurred only after Jesus was dead. For these liquids to come from a dead man again goes "against human nature." His emission of the spirit was equally miraculous because it happened only when he willed it, provoking the centurion to pronounce him the son of God.[59]

These are only a few examples of the painstaking manner in which so many later Carolingian scholars sought to ferret out the meaning of the gospel passion narratives. Over and over in their commentaries, exegetical homilies, and in poetry, ninth-century churchmen meditated on the accounts of Jesus' sufferings as well as on the same episodes' adumbrations of his power. Such study of the Bible and the patristic writings from which the exegetes borrowed as they interpreted Matthew and the other evangelists, verse by verse, brought them and their readers to think carefully about the progression of Christ's life on earth and thus – despite the signs of divine omnipotence recognized in the narratives – about the significance of his dying as chronologically distinct from the triumph of his resurrection.

Yet while the development of gospel exegesis encouraged greater attentiveness to the historical reality of the passion and death on the cross, the fullest discussions of the redemptive significance of Jesus' human mortality in later Carolingian scriptural exegesis appear in relation not to the gospels, but to the epistle to the Hebrews. Hrabanus, Claudius of Turin, Sedulius Scottus, and Haimo of Auxerre, the principal ninth-century commentators on the epistle, used their knowledge of earlier exegetical writings, among them Alcuin's treatise on the letter, to elucidate the relationship presented in Hebrews between Christ's divine, heavenly kingship

---

[57] Pascasius, *In Matheo* 27.42, *CCCM* 56B.1372–1373, esp. lines 3446–3448.
[58] See ibid. 27.46, *CCCM* 56B.1383–1386.
[59] Ibid. 27.54, *CCCM* 56B.1398–1400, esp. lines 4281–4284, 4312–4315.

and his innocent blood sacrifice.[60] To offer just one example we may consider Haimo's tract, whose sources include Gregory I, Claudius, Jerome, Augustine, Cassiodorus, and Prosper of Aquitaine as well as Alcuin.[61] As in Alcuin's commentary, the exegesis and hence the theology of the crucifixion reflect the epistle's structure. The analysis of the first three chapters of Hebrews mirrors their proclamations of Jesus' sonship, equality with God the father, and the union of two natures through the incarnation. "Through corporeal death and the passion's shame, God the father made his son less than the angels, who are immortal and impassible, while according to the divinity he was [the father's] equal in omnipotent deity"; this comment on Hebrews 2.7 leads to comparative exegesis of Philippians 2.6–11.[62] Hebrews 2.9 brings a reference to the cross's "glory and honor," to the mortal's need to imitate Jesus's sufferings in order to reach heaven, and to his "ineffable grace" that tasted death for us. It also incites Haimo to allude to the predestination quarrel, as he does in other of his Pauline commentaries, over whether Christ died for all mortals or only "for the elect predestined to eternal life"; for this purpose he turns to Prosper of Aquitaine.[63]

With Hebrews 5–10, the focus shifts to the juxtaposition in Christ of eternal priesthood to the one-time oblation of humanity. The son of God, king and high priest as well as innocent man, ended the former testament by the sacrifice of his perfectly sinless flesh to the father in recompense for human sin, a blood offering that surpassed those of the ancient Jews. Regularly throughout this portion of the commentary, Jesus' blood oblation is linked with the church's mediation of redemption to the faithful, the responsibilities of the sacerdotal office, penance, and the sacraments. Hebrews 5.1–3, for instance, is interpreted as a teaching on the priestly ministry to offer sacrifices for sin.[64] The animal oblations of the old law are asserted to constitute the likeness of the eucharistic bread and wine, "namely [Christ's] flesh and blood" prefigured in Melchisedech's offering. That oblation was preferable to Aaron's because of the uniqueness of

---

[60] Riggenbach, *Historische Studien zum Hebräerbrief*, esp. 41–56.

[61] Haimo, *In epistolam ad Hebraeos*, PL 117.819–938. On Haimo's exegetical methods, see John J. Contreni, "Haimo of Auxerre's Commentary on Ezechiel," in *L'Ecole carolingienne d'Auxerre*, ed. Iogna-Prat et al., 229–242. See also Brunhölzl, *Histoire* I.2.233–234, 316–317.

[62] Haimo, *Ad Hebr.* 2, PL 117.835B.

[63] Ibid. 2, PL 117.836–837. Prosper's writings were among the most important sources used by Gottschalk's opponents in the predestination controversy. [64] Ibid. 5, PL 117.853–854A.

Melchisedech's priesthood, his position as king as well as priest, and, it is stressed, because his offering happened only once, in contrast to the repeated animal sacrifices of Aaron's office.[65] Hebrews 6 leads to a long commentary on the relation between Christian instruction, penance, and the sacraments. Observations are made concerning the catechumen's need to learn orthodox doctrine, confess his sins, and undertake a penance of forty, twenty, or seven days before receiving the sacraments, and concerning the importance of penitence after baptism as a purgation of subsequent sins – since "just as Christ died once in the flesh on the cross, thus we can also die once to sin in baptism."[66] Like Hebrews 9 itself, its exegesis shows particular interest in the sacrificial blood. The tabernacle and vessels of verse 21, the latter representing the different ecclesiastical offices, Haimo notes, are asperged with blood "because the universal church with all those ministering to her is cleansed by the blood of Christ's passion"; for only through that blood comes perfect cleansing and remission of sins. Unlike the ancient sacrifices in the Holy of Holies, that of Christ who is both priest and sacrifice was made only once with his own, not alien, blood. He offered himself once on the altar of the cross, a sacrifice that nonetheless sufficed for all believers.[67] The oblations of the law were the figure and likeness of the "heavenly" and "spiritual" oblations that the church celebrates "in truth," whereby Christians are cleansed of sin by "better sacrifices, namely by the blood of Christ's passion."[68]

More than the gospels, the letter to the Hebrews prompted ninth-century commentators and their readers to reflect on the meaning of Jesus' innocent, atoning oblation and purging blood, and on the connection of that offering on the cross to penance and the sacraments, especially the eucharist. The importance of these ideas in exegesis of the epistle, other ninth-century tracts as well as Haimo's, suggests that the increased interest in the letter among scholars was influenced not only by the general growth of biblical studies, but also by the final group of developments examined in this chapter. All of these, directly or indirectly, attest the momentum of liturgical and ecclesiastical reform under Charlemagne's successors; in different ways, all seem to have provided additional encouragement to churchmen to think about the passion's temporal progression and Jesus' human suffering and blood sacrifice.

---

[65] Ibid. 5, *PL* 117.855–856.   [66] Ibid. 6, *PL* 117.858–861, esp. 861A.
[67] Ibid. 9, *PL* 117.886A/B, 887A/B.   [68] Ibid. 9, *PL* 117.886C/D.

One development is the diffusion of the Gregorian sacramentary known as the *Hadrianum*, in copies that were almost invariably interpolated or had appended supplements: the *Hucusque* of Benedict of Aniane, the votive masses of Alcuin, and other additions. Such supplementary materials incorporated liturgical forms not found in the *Hadrianum*, which were often taken from the eighth-century Gelasian sacramentaries.[69] With the new liturgical books spread the notion, rooted in the Gallican liturgy and discernible in some eighth-century Frankish liturgical texts but more widely evident in the ninth, that the *Te igitur* constitutes the beginning of the canon of the mass. The remembrance of Christ's offering on the cross, in the portion of the mass that recalls the eucharist's institution at the last supper and crucifixion and its own function as a sacrifice, became more decisively separated from the *Vere dignum* and *Sanctus* acclaiming the eternal divine majesty – by a shift of the celebrant to silent prayer at the *Te igitur*; directives about making the sign of the cross specifically at this point in the mass; and, in some sacramentaries, by special decoration of the T that underscores its role as the commencement of the eucharistic oblation, without, as in the Gellone Sacramentary, linking the prayer with the preceding orations.[70] A comparable effect may have been had by the development of new ritual and prayers for the Good Friday *Adoratio crucis*.[71] Like the older prayers and other texts also used, these focus on Christ in both his suffering and his triumph. Yet the general elaboration of the *Adoratio crucis*, so that it became a longer, more complex ceremony, accentuated the importance of Good Friday as the anniversary of his death, a commemoration set apart from his victory's celebration in the Easter mass.

Most directly and obviously, though, Jesus' death and its redemptive value move into the intellectual foreground with the expansion of

---

[69] *Sacramentaire grégorien* 1, ed. Deshusses, 62–74; ibid. 2.20–30; ibid. 3.66–78; cf. Deshusses, "Les sacramentaires," 19–46.

[70] Jungmann, *Missarum Sollemnia* 2.130–133, 173–174, 179–180; McKitterick, *Frankish Church and Carolingian Reforms*, 141–142. For directives regarding the sign of the cross, *Ord.* 7 (end ninth century), *Ordines romani* 2.295–305. Decorated T's of the *Te igitur* in, e.g., the Drogo Sacramentary, Paris, BNF, lat. 9428, fol. 15v and the Coronation Sacramentary, Paris, BNF, lat. 1141, fol. 6v; Hubert et al., *L'Empire carolingien*, 285, fig. 298; Carl Nordenfalk, *L'Enluminure au Moyen Age* (Geneva, 1995), 67, 73. See (on this iconography throughout medieval art), Suntrup, "*Te Igitur*-Initialen," 278–366.

[71] A. Wilmart, "Prières médiévales pour l'adoration de la croix," *Ephemerides liturgicae* 46 (1932), 22–65, esp. 22–30; idem, *Precum libelli quattuor aevi karolini* (Rome, 1940), esp. 13–14, 105–106, 142; Lilli Gjerlow, *Adoratio crucis: the Regularis Concordia and the Decreta Lanfranci* (Oslo, 1961), 15.

Carolingian commentary on the ecclesiastical practices that, with greatest clarity, invite meditation on these facets of the crucifixion and on the church's role as mediatress of redemption: the mass, Holy Week, confession and penance, and the sacraments, especially the eucharist. A large amount of the ninth-century literature that dwells on the crucified Christ's torments or sacrifice ties them to penance, the mass, or the eucharist, as does Haimo's commentary on Hebrews. Or the primary subject is Holy Week, the mass, the eucharist, or confession and penance, and the passion is remembered in these contexts. As in Alcuin's *De virtutibus et vitiis* and some later Carolingian *Fürstenspiegel* literature, the crucifixion may be only implicitly recalled – through exhortations, for instance, that readers be washed of their sins by penance and the eucharist (or sometimes baptism), practise humility, and thus offer "sacrifices of tears," or through other allusions without overt reference to parallel qualities in the crucified redeemer.[72] In countless original writings and collections of older materials, however, a concern with the same rites and ceremonies leads to direct discussion, sometimes at length, of the passion's sorrows. Jesus' status as God is never ignored, and remembrance of his death is often balanced by equally strong affirmation of his divine nature, so that both natures are shown to be integral to the accomplishment of salvation. Yet even then, a pronounced interest is apparent in the historical event of his human death and its exact, redemptive meaning. In a sermon on Palm Sunday in Hrabanus' collection for Haistulf, the memory of Jesus' entry into Jerusalem and of the last supper, crucifixion, and burial stirred by the liturgy of Holy Week is seen as central to the Christian's struggle to purge the soul and earn Christ's mercy before Easter, "through fasting and generous alms, vigils and prayer, tears and compunction of the heart."[73] A sermon for Holy Thursday, based on John 13, encourages the congregation to think about Jesus' foreknowledge at the last supper that he was about to die, a demonstration of love for his friends (John 15.13), his paradigmatic humility in the foot washing, imitated in baptism and penance, and the redemption as well as the model of ethical behavior he provided in the scourging, spitting, and wearing of the crown

---

[72] Hincmar, *De cavendis vitiis et virtutibus exercendis* 2.10, MGH Quellen zur Geistesgeschichte des Mittelalters 16, ed. D. Nachtmann (Munich, 1998), 225 line 13 (Gregory I). Cf. Wilmart, *Precum libelli*, 27–30; Hrabanus, *De puritate cordis, De modo poenitentiae*, PL 112.1282–1332; *Poenitentium liber ad Otgarium*, PL 112.1397–1424; Anton, *Fürstenspiegel*, 426–429, on David as a model of humility.   [73] Hrabanus, *Hom.* 14 (*In die Palmarum*), Homiliae I, PL 110.29–30, esp. 30C.

of thorns, dying on the cross and then rising from the dead.[74] In a series of anonymous late-ninth-century sermons, one for Palm Sunday refers to the mortal's need to imitate the crucified Christ through the battle against vice modeled on his conquest of Satan; but that for Good Friday insists on the grief and "compassion" the passion should arouse, the oblation of Christ the immaculate lamb who spilled his "most precious blood" to wash away sin, and the importance of imitation of his humanity – by suffering for him, avoiding vice, fasting, and cleansing the soul through penitence – in order to avoid his wrath on the last day.[75]

These themes recur in contemporary poetry. Verses by Mico of St.-Riquier for Holy Thursday and Good Friday, for example, reflect on Jesus' demonstration of humility in the footwashing, Judas' desire to betray him "lest he [Judas] be repaired by the blood that Christ strove to pour out for us unhappy mortals," the divine descent to earth to become a humble oblation, and, in careful detail, Christ's innocent acceptance, for humanity's sake, of the torture, blows, and other sufferings of the passion, before rising victorious from the dead.[76] A hymn for matins by Gottschalk of Orbais expresses his unique sense of the dreadful conjunction of power and mercy – for the elect – in the omnipotent deity, as manifested in the agony and sacrifice of a crucifixion that foreshadows the eschaton:

> Pleasing yet fearsome, gentle yet terrible,
> Who was on the altar of the cross; he piously wept in the evening,
> And reconciled us to the father, his entire body cleaved,
> By offering himself, an acceptable sacrifice on our behalf.
> The unique holocaust, the wondrous victim,
> Marvelously great recompense, undertaking, sweet sacrifice.[77]

[74] Hrabanus, *Hom.* 15 (*In coena Domini*), *Homiliae* I, PL 110.30D-33, esp. 32D-33B. *Hom.* 13 (*In Feria VI*) (Good Friday), *Homiliae* II, PL 110.163–166 is by Smaragdus of St.-Mihiel; see Etaix, "L'homéliaire," 231. It opens by noting that imitation of Christ consists of suffering for sin, in commemoration of his one time death for sin, and continues with discussion of baptism and its prefiguration in Noah's ark as the avenue to the heavenly kingdom.

[75] Riccardo Quadri, "L'omeliario di Eirico di Auxerre," in *L'École carolingienne d'Auxerre*, ed. Iogna-Prat et al., 275–295, at 290–295.

[76] Mico, *Carm.* 21, 22, *Carmina Centulensia*, MGH PLAC 3.303–305.

[77] Ille blandus et tremendus, mitis et terribilis,
  Qui crucis in ara pie nostrum flevit vespere
  Et patri conciliavit toto fissus corpore,
  Se pro nobis offerendo hostiam placabilem,
  Holocaustum singulare, victimam mirabilem,
  Mire multum libra pensum, dulce sacrificium.
 F.III.10.4, *Die Gedichte des Gottschalk von Orbais*, ed. M.-L. Weber (Frankfurt am Main, 1992),

In a poem on the Virgin Mary probably composed in 845–849 and in the surviving verses of the *Ferculum Salomonis*, written c. 853–856, the latter work possibly a figure poem, Gottschalk's archenemy, Hincmar of Rheims, identifies the crucifixion as the source of the consecrated bread and wine of the mass. Christ is the lamb and fountain of life who eternally reigns in heaven, yet cleanses mortals of sin in the passion replicated at the altar, giving them his own blood to drink and feeding them from the body fixed to the cross.[78] Mortals are redeemed through the passion of their creator and redemption comes from the omnipotent God, Hincmar makes clear in his prose *explanatio* of the *Ferculum Salomonis*; but it is a gift requiring Jesus' human oblation, the source of baptism and the healing food and drink of the mass. Particular emphasis is placed on the sacrificial blood, which purges of sin all who undergo penance and receive the eucharist in faith.[79] As Robert Deshman showed, the concept of the dying Jesus as a model of patience and self-denial imitated on Good Friday, and the connection drawn in contemporary *Fürstenspiegel* between that doctrine and the royal virtue of humility, find a visual counterpart in the miniature of the Carolingian monarch adoring a crucifix in the Prayerbook of Charles the Bald, completed in 846–869 (Munich, Residenz, Schatzkammer, fols. 38v–39r; fig. 21). Prefacing prayers for worship of the cross, the two-page illumination depicts Christ dying on the cross before the kneeling, crowned Charles; on Good Friday, the monarch imitates both the savior's humility and his majesty. The title above Charles' head asks the Christ who absolves the sins of the world to absolve the Carolingian king of all his "wounds." The earthly ruler's imitation of the crucified redeemer through both the Friday liturgy and his humble repentance of sin makes it possible for the redeemer's pain – the wounds of his own crucified body – to heal the injuries of the king's soul.[80]

179–181, at 179–180 lines 3–8, see discussion, pp. 316–320; Szövérffy, *Annalen* 1.239, see 240. I am grateful to David Ganz for his advice on the translation.

[78] Hincmar, *Carm.* 2 (on the Virgin), MGH PLAC 3.410–412, *Carm.* 4.1 (portion of *Ferculum Salomonis*), MGH PLAC 3.414–415. Additional verses of the latter discovered by Bernhard Bischoff are published in Taeger, *Zahlensymbolik*, 144–147, with discussion 148–192; see *Deutsches Archiv* 17 (1961), 7. Part of the *Explanatio in ferculum Salomonis* is printed in PL 125.817–834. See Ernst, *Carmen figuratum*, 342–355, esp. 350–351 on the issue of whether the poem was a *carmen figuratum*. Also Jean Devisse, *Hincmar, archevêque de Reims, 845–882,* 3 vols. (Geneva, 1975), 1.54–59; André Wilmart, "Distiques d'Hincmar sur l'eucharistie? Un sermon oublié de S. Augustin sur le même sujet," *Revue Bénédictine* 40 (1928), 87–98.

[79] See Hincmar, *Explan. in ferc. Salom.*, PL 125, esp. 817–818, 826C/D, 827, 828A, 830–832.

[80] "In cruce qui mundi soluisti crimina Christe / Orando mihimet tu uulnera cuncta resolue." Robert Deshman, "The Exalted Servant: the Ruler Theology of the Prayerbook of Charles the Bald," *Viator* 11 (1980), 385–417, 390–391 on the *titulus*.

Figure 21. Charles the Bald before the crucified Christ, Munich, Residenz, Schatzkammer, Prayerbook, fols. 38 verso-39 recto

Once more examples could be multiplied of writings – poetry, passages in doctrinal treatises, homilies, sermons, and others – and artistic images that, in different ways, link the dying, bleeding Jesus with penance, the liturgy, and the sacraments, above all the eucharist. The works of art studied in chapter 7 clearly fall in this category. Rather than piling up diverse literary or artistic sources relevant to this point, though, it is best to conclude this chapter by examining a number of ninth-century expositions of the mass and Holy Week; for these offer some of its most elaborate analyses from this period of the historical circumstances of Jesus'

death, his sacrifice's redemptive function, and its connection with the liturgy.[81] Like the exegesis of the liturgy discussed in chapter 2 and the commentaries on baptism and Easter by Amalarius, Hrabanus, and Walafrid noted at the start of this chapter, the later Carolingian tracts on Holy

---

[81] Numerous such works survive from the ninth century: see Jean-Paul Bouhot, "Pour une édition critique de *l'Expositio missae* de Remi d'Auxerre," in *L'Ecole carolingienne d'Auxerre*, ed. Iogna-Prat et al., 425–434, esp. 425, 432; Jungmann, *Missarum Sollemnia* I.114–120.

Week and the mass generally view the rites as in some measure representations, especially visual, of the events commemorated. Hence the mass, it is generally agreed – here I leave to one side the writings studied in chapter 6, relating to the controversy over the eucharistic presence – recalls and presents a likeness of the last supper and crucifixion, while it also provides the sacrament that actually consists of Christ's body and blood; those entities make possible the recipients' union with God and with one another in the church. As Amalarius states in the preface to his *Liber officialis*, drawing on Augustine, the "sacraments should have a certain similitude to the things of which they are sacraments." The priest of the mass is similar to Christ, the bread and wine to his body and blood, and the sacrifice on the altar to his sacrifice on the cross, while the Christian eats and drinks Christ's flesh and blood, "in a manner of speaking," in order to resemble Christ at the resurrection.[82] The resemblance is crucial to the union achieved through the mass; when the faithful eat and drink the eucharist, "by virtue of the assumed humanity, Christ remains in us and we in him."[83] Yet while such ideas have precedents in earlier literature, some ninth-century scholars develop them much further than did their predecessors. In doing so, they bring a sharper focus on the crucifixion's role as a blood sacrifice, despite the importance they also attribute to the son of God's divinity in assuring that the oblation on the cross and in the eucharist is salvific.

Most noticeably, this is true of Amalarius' discussion of the mass in the *Liber officialis*, in particular the chapters beginning with commentary on the offertory, "the sacrifice of those who render their prayers to the lord."[84] This portion of the treatise assigns to virtually every actor, instrument, prayer, reading, chant, and other action of the mass an allegorical meaning that emphasizes its reenactment of the crucified Jesus' human mortality and sacrifice, the union of God with humanity, and the liturgy's role, together with the crucifixion, as a paradigm that the Christian imitates by means of faith and virtue. The exegesis of the *Te igitur*, for example, which

---

[82] Amalarius, *Liber officialis Prooem.*, *ST* 139.14 (Augustine, *Ep.* 98). Most of *Liber officialis* 3 (chaps. 1–38) is an exposition of the mass: *ST* 139.255–372. Other works by Amalarius present similar exegesis of the mass though generally more abbreviated. See chapter 2 n. 65, and *Canonis missae interpretatio* (*ST* 138.284–338), possibly the *Eclogae de ordine Romano* (*ST* 140.225–265, see Hanssens, ed., *ST* 138.213–214 regarding doubts about Amalarius' authorship), and the two commentaries entitled, *Ordinis totius missae expositio* (*ST* 140.296–321).

[83] Amalarius, *Liber officialis* 3.34, *ST* 139.365.   [84] Ibid. 3.19, *ST* 139.311.

Amalarius interprets as a prayer in the middle of the mass canon,[85] distinguishes between two sacrifices "of the elect" and "for sinners."[86] At the institution, with its echo of Christ's words at the last supper, the faithful "descend" from the first of these two oblations, which is joined with the angels' heavenly offering, to the universal sacrifice of Jesus for sinners; for the lord of all descended to be immolated for those unable to offer a sacrifice that would reconcile them to God.[87] Although the bread and wine constitute one oblation of Christ's body and blood, the true sacrifice is that of the heart, which God seeks from every priest. Anyone who wishes to give presents to God should offer himself. To bestow gifts inwardly is to be mindful of one's blessings, and the phrase "inviolate sacrifices" in the *Te igitur* designates the offerings of humility, praise, and charity. By eating and drinking the sacrifice of the mass, the *Liber officialis* later states, Christians are united with their crucified and resurrected savior and made members of the one body of the church. The claim that the eucharistic bread represents the "triform" nature of Christ's body, an element of Amalarius' exegesis denounced by his opponents who interpreted him to mean that Jesus had three bodies, was probably intended to reinforce this notion of ecclesiastical unity and joining to Christ.[88]

Although attacks by Agobard and Florus of Lyons on the *Liber officialis*' allegorization of the mass led to its condemnation at Quierzy in 838, the

---

[85] Ibid. 3.27, *ST* 139.351 line 12.

[86] See esp. ibid. 3.23, 24, *ST* 139.331, 337; Allan Cabaniss, *Amalarius of Metz* (Amsterdam, 1954), 61, and Agobard's charge that Amalarius therefore claims many people are sinless, a heresy worse than that of Pelagius: Agobard, *Contra libros quattuor Amalarii*, *CCCM* 52.353–367, at 363, cf. 362–365.   [87] Amalarius, *Liber officialis* 3.24, *ST* 139.337 lines 24–26.

[88] See ibid. 3.23, 34, 35, *ST* 139.333–334, 365, 367–368. Amalarius comments that the faithful, both the dead and the living, belong to Christ's body in what are evidently understood as three periods of its existence: the humanity assumed from Mary, the incarnate life, and death, when he lay in the sepulchre. The eucharistic bread shows the triform nature of Christ's body in the three particles into which it is broken after consecration: the particle mixed into the chalice signifies the body that rose from the dead; the eaten portion designates it walking on the earth; and the particle left on the altar designates it lying in the tomb. Thus Amalarius probably meant to affirm that the body of the church is one with the body of Christ in every stage, and this oneness is shown in the eucharistic bread, despite its fraction into three parts. The church is composed of all believers, living and dead, who through the consecrated bread and wine have become members of a single body of Christ who was born of Mary, walked on earth, lay in the tomb, and rose from the dead. See Cabaniss, *Amalarius of Metz*, 86–89; Henri de Lubac, *Corpus mysticum: l'eucharistie et l'église au moyen âge* (Paris, 2nd. rev. edn., 1948), esp. 297–339; Florus, *Opuscula adversus Amalarium*, *PL* 119.71–96, *Opusc.* 1, *PL* 119.74–77, *Opusc.* 2, *PL* 119.81–92. Florus, *Opusc.* 1 is also published with Amalarius' letters, as *Ep.* 13, ed. E. Dümmler, *MGH Epp.* 5 (Berlin, 1899), 267–273.

work remained popular.[89] Moreover, Amalarius' enemies as well as other
ninth-century commentators agreed with his basic principle that the mass
is a representative commemoration of the offering on the cross, one that
lays the foundation for ecclesiastical unity. Florus of Lyons' *De expositione
missae* presents a catena of patristic sources exploring this theme. Jesus was
the innocent victim who spilled the blood that washes away sins; the mass
is a reminder of his lowliness, since "unless he were humble, he would not
be eaten or drunk," and it recalls his model of humility and patience in the
prayer, *Sursum corda*.[90] The commentary on a synopsis of the four gospels,
De passione Domini, by Hrabanus' contemporary at Fulda, Candidus
Bruun, was intended to assist the Fulda monks to "follow the footsteps of
[Christ's] death" in their Holy Week devotions.[91] According to the discussion of Holy Thursday and the last supper, bread is used for the eucharist
both because its many grains resemble the church, formed "from many
saints," and because it corresponds to the earth from which Christ assumed
his body, breaking it on the cross "when he permitted it to die" and then
giving it to his disciples.[92] For Hrabanus in *De institutione clericorum*, the
mass is a "time of sacrifice" in memory of the oblation of the "mediator of

[89] See Agobard, *Contra libros quatuor Amalarii*, CCCM 52.353–367. On the continued popularity of
the *Liber officialis*, especially the first and second editions, despite the decision of Quierzy, see
Hanssens, ed., *ST* 138.79. (Relatively few copies of the third edition survive.) Florus (*Ep.* 13,
MGH *Epp.* 5.268; *Opusc.* 1, PL 119.74A, *Opusc.* 2, PL 119.80) complains about the diffusion of
Amalarius' ideas. Passages from Amalarius were sometimes added to *ordines*: Roger E.
Reynolds, "Image and Text: a Carolingian Illustration of Modifications in the Early Roman
Eucharistic *Ordines*," *Viator* 14 (1983), 59–75, at 64.

[90] Florus, *De expos. missae* 3, 4, 15, PL 119.17B (Augustine), 18B/C, 28–29 (Cyprian). Cf. Agobard,
Contra libros 13–15, CCCM 52.363–365. On Florus' *expositio*, see Jean-Paul Bouhot, "Fragments
attribués à Virgile de Thapse dans l'*Expositio missae* de Florus de Lyons," *Revue des études augustiniennes* 21 (1975), 302–316. Florus' work is available in a critical edition by Paul Duc ("Etude sur
l'*Expositio missae* de Florus de Lyon suivie d'une édition critique du texte" [Thèse de doctorat
présentée à la Faculté de Théologie de Lyon, Belley, 1937]), which I have unfortunately been
unable to consult, though Bouhot's article provides guidance to some of its contents.

[91] Candidus Bruun, *Opusculum de passione Domini Praef.*, PL 106.57–104, see 59C-60A. The treatise
seems to me more likely to have been written by the Fulda monk and priest, Candidus Bruun,
than Candidus Wizo, Alcuin's pupil. See Brunhölzl, *Histoire* 1.2.99–100; cf. Christine E.
Ineichen-Eder, "Candidus-Brun von Fulda: Maler, Lehrer und Schriftsteller," in *Hrabanus
Maurus und seine Schule*, ed. W. Böhne (Fulda, 1980), 182–192, esp. 187–190, arguing unconvinc-
ingly (to my mind) for Wizo's authorship and thus an earlier dating. For one reason, the text
bears a thematically strong resemblance to other writings of the second and third quarters of
the ninth century, including works composed by Hrabanus at Fulda, as my discussion here
should partially indicate. On Candidus Wizo, see Bullough, "Alcuin and the Kingdom of
Heaven," 176–181; Marenbon, *From the Circle of Alcuin*, 30–43, 144–170.

[92] See Candidus, *De pass. Domini* 5, PL 106.68–70, esp. 68C/D.

God and men" and a "bringing together of God with men," in which the
"office of binding" belongs to the priest who offers the people's prayers to
God. These ideas are expanded in his later treatise, *De sacris ordinibus*.[93]
Frequently, the notion of the eucharist as a sacrifice that unites its recipients with their creator inspires references to Jesus' speech in John 6, in
which he identifies himself as the bread of eternal life descended from
heaven. The traditional analogies between the joining of Christ with his
people and the eucharist's ingredients are regularly recalled: water mixed
with wine, the water used in fabrication of the bread, or the many grains
and grapes all symbolize Christ's union with his church and its members
with one another.[94] Frequently, too, it is noted, echoing 1 Corinthians
11.28–29, that participants in the mass should repent their sins and receive
the eucharist in faith in order to be joined to God, rather than risk separation from Christ's body by consuming it in a state of sin.[95]

Finally, the analyses of the Holy Week liturgy in *De institutione clericorum*,
the *Liber officialis*, and *De passione Domini* carefully attend to the chronology
of events in the passion and its correspondence to the progression of the
church's rites. Hrabanus, Amalarius, and Candidus agree that certain aspects
of the week's ceremonies recall and represent the crucified Christ in his
immortal divinity and victory over death. In the opening and concluding sections of the chapter on the *Adoratio crucis* in the *Liber officialis*, the dominant
idea is the triumph of the new Adam revealed in the cross, the tree of life,
which joined in his conquest and eternally proclaims his power.[96] Hrabanus'
exegesis of Palm Sunday and half his discussion of Good Friday follow Isidor

[93] Hrabanus, *De instit. cleric.* 1.32, ed. Knoepfler, 70–71; idem, *De sacris ordinibus* 19, PL
112.1177–1192, where the exposition of the mass is from *De institutione clericorum* (the exegesis
there is based on Isidor) and the tract, *Dominus vobiscum*; Brunhölzl, *Histoire* 1.2.88.

[94] E.g. Smaragdus, *Collectiones in epistolas et evangelias, Passio Domini*, PL 102.179A; Hrabanus, *De
instit. cleric.* 1.31, ed. Knoepfler, 63–67 (Augustine, Cyprian); Amalarius, *Liber officialis* 3.19, 34, ST
139.319–320, 365; Ps.-Haimo, *Hom.* 64, PL 118.363D-364A; Walafrid, *De exord. et increment.* 16, MGH
Capit. 2.489–490, cf. 490–491. See Heiric of Auxerre, *Augustini de eucharistia, Scolia Quaestionum*,
in *I Collectanea di Eirico di Auxerre*, ed. R. Quadri (Fribourg, 1966), 133–134 (Augustine, *Serm.* 272),
cf. idem, *Hom.* 1.64, *Homiliae per circulum anni*, CCCM 116A, ed. R. Quadri (Turnhout, 1992),
612–641, at 640. Also Remigius of Auxerre, *Expositio missae*, PL 101.1251D-1252A, see 1260D
(= part of Ps.-Alcuin, *De divinis officiis* 40, PL 101.1246–1271); and the discussion of Remigius'
work in Bouhot, "Edition critique," 425–434; idem, "Fragments attribués," 306–308.

[95] E.g. Hrabanus, *De instit. cleric.* 1.31, ed. Knoepfler, 68–69; Walafrid, *De exord. et increment.* 18,
MGH *Capit.* 2.491; Candidus, *De pass. Domini* 5, PL 106.70A/B; cf. Amalarius, *Liber officialis* 3.34,
ST 139.366.

[96] Amalarius, *Liber officialis* 1.14, ST 139.99–100, 102–107. The chapter concludes with Sedulius,
Carmen paschale 5 lines 190–194.

of Seville's *De ecclesiasticis officiis*; reflections on the week's rehearsal of the passion are interwoven with praise of the divine king and second Adam, who "through the cross, with death vanquished, absolved the sin of the world."[97]

Yet Hrabanus and, even more, Amalarius and Candidus also interpret Holy Week, especially Good Friday, as the solemn remembrance of Jesus' self-abnegation, suffering, and dying. Departing from Isidor, Hrabanus attributes an allegorical significance to the different elements of the Friday ceremonial that highlights their representation of the passion's temporal progression: the stripping of the altar symbolizes the stripping of garments and rending of the temple veil; the darkness of the church recalls that as Christ died the stars were obscured; the prayers said for the church, unbelievers, and others are reminders that he spilled his blood for the redemption of all; the Mass of the Presanctified Elements commemorates the disciples' fasting from the crucifixion to the resurrection; and vespers are celebrated in silence, in veneration of the silence of the lord's sepulchre.[98] Amalarius' detailed exegesis of the week gives particular notice to the example of tolerance and ethical behavior set in the crucifixion. Jesus' paradigm is emulated through participation in the liturgy and, inspired by its ceremonies, through faith, humility, obedience to God, the suffering and self-oblation of repentance and good works. These are already refrains of the exegesis of Palm Sunday, Wednesday, and Holy Thursday, though not surprisingly they are most developed in the commentary on Good Friday.[99] The Friday reading from Exodus, it is noted, incites the faithful to remember that Christ was the passover lamb whose sacrifice is imitated by repentance of sin. The verses from Osee indicate that God chastises sinners in preparation for the resurrection, because "if we suffer [with Christ] we will also reign with him." Following Augustine, Psalm 90 recalls that Christ should be imitated not in his divinity and miracles but in his exhortation, "Learn of me, because I am meek, and humble of heart" (Matthew 11.29). When the passion narrative is read, it is "as if we see Christ on the cross"; and the prayer, *Deus, a quo et Iudas*, designates both the sinners whom suffering cannot correct and those who, like the good thief, fruitfully

---

[97] Hrabanus, *De instit. cleric.* 2.35, 37, ed. Knoepfler, 125–131; Isidor, *De eccl. off.* 1.28 (27), 30 (29), *CCSL* 113.31–34. Cf. Candidus, *De pass. Domini* 16–19, *PL* 106.90D-101.

[98] Hrabanus, *De instit. cleric.* 2.37, ed. Knoepfler, 129–131.

[99] Amalarius, *Liber officialis* 1.10–12, *ST* 139.58–90 (= Palm Sunday, Holy Wednesday and Thursday); ibid. 1.13–15, *ST.* 139. 90–108 (= Good Friday).

undertake penance.[100] While the justification for worshiping the cross presented in the chapter on the *Adoratio crucis* stresses the divine victory, the act itself of adoration is linked with the crucified Jesus' exemplary humiliation and death for sin. The worshiper imitates Christ through humble prostration before the cross, the inner "humility of mind," empathy for his sufferings, and the contrition that should accompany the veneration.[101]

In Candidus' *De passione Domini*, the crucifixion's exemplary function is more closely tied to the washing of sins in Jesus' blood and to the clerical office. The faithful who imitate their redeemer's example of love, obedience, and humility, and during Holy Week are purged by his blood through good works, the sacraments, and penance, are bound with one another in Christ's body the church.[102] "Whatever was done in the lord's passion, my brothers, was for the sake of our salvation and a saving example," it is announced towards the treatise's conclusion.[103] Sacrificed for the world, Christ enabled the old law to be replaced by grace and sins deleted "by the sweet medicine of repentance." Evoking Augustine's exegesis of Ephesians 3.18 and John 19, but also perhaps Poem 1 of Hrabanus' *In honorem sanctae crucis*, Candidus encourages his brothers to contemplate the position of Christ's body on the cross. The faithful must follow the model presented there, through baptism, the preaching of love of neighbor and God, and patience in adversity. Jesus' hands outstretched on the cross signify the "double charity"; his unbroken legs are the "columns of Christ's body, that is the pastors of the church," who like him should not be broken by threats or softened by flattery. "Set before the eyes of the heart," the death Christ accepted in order to leave an example, "strengthens the hearts of the faithful, so that they do not fear to suffer for him."[104]

The varied meditations on the historical reality and redemptive significance of Jesus' death, in the later Carolingian poetical and prose writings just discussed, reflect the growth of biblical studies and study of the liturgy

---

[100] Ibid. 1.13, *ST* 139.91–98.

[101] Ibid. 1.14, *ST* 139.101. In *Liber de ordine antiphonarii*, regarding some of the responsories for Good Friday, Amalarius asserts, "in quibus compunctio traditionis eius [i.e. Christ's] frequentatur, et dolor crucifixionis eius stimulat corda fidelium." On Holy Saturday, "recolitur sepultura eius in aliquibus responsoriis, in aliquibus vero planctus et fletus dolentium de nece iniusta": *ST* 140.79 lines 32–34, 37–39.

[102] Candidus, *De pass. Domini Praef.*, 3, 5, *PL* 106.59, 64–66, 68C-70.

[103] Ibid. 19, *PL* 106.101A.

[104] Ibid. 19, *PL* 106.98D, 101. Cf. Augustine, *De doctrina Christiana* 2.41, idem, *Tract.* 118.5.

in the years after Charlemagne's reign. Developing refrains found in church ritual, scripture, and the patristic sources that guided Carolingian exegesis of both, these texts recognize the son's omnipotent divinity as crucial to his human nature's ability to save. But the primary issue is not the crucified lord's victory over sin/death/Satan or the passion's revelation of his universal governance, ideas that blend its meaning into that of the resurrection and the subsequent demonstrations of his power. Rather, it is the significance of his death on the cross, isolated from his victory, in the divine remission of sins and reunion of the faithful with God. In general, though emphases differ, sin is regarded less as an external force synonymous with the devil, in spite of numerous references to Satan's role, than as a personal burden within the soul that distances the individual from his creator. Release from sin's oppression is based on the crucified Christ's example of humility and virtuous suffering, his atoning sacrifice, its cleansing blood, and, as is often stressed, on the transmission of the benefits of his death and oblation through penance, the liturgy, and the sacraments, especially Holy Week, the mass, and the eucharist. Through these forms of devotion, Christians are reminded of their suffering savior in a manner that, on Good Friday, corresponds to an inner vision; for Amalarius, when the Friday's gospel lection is heard it is as if the crucified Jesus is seen, for Candidus, his death is set "before the eyes of the heart." Where the mass and the eucharist are discussed, the concept of the liturgy as the commemorative representation of the crucifixion and last supper is framed by considerations of Christ's sacrifice as the source of healing food and drink. The divinely empowered body and blood of the mass purge those who eat and drink in faith, offering others only judgment. Proper, repeated consumption of the eucharistic blood and body confirms and strengthens the union created at baptism among the members of the ecclesiastical body, and between them and their head, assuring the church's unity with the crucified and heavenly Christ and its separation from sinners and unbelievers.

A notable indication of the importance that later Carolingian thinkers attached to biblical and liturgical exegesis and to these ways of thinking about the crucifixion is their importance in the quarrels over divine predestination and the eucharistic presence. It is in light of the doctrinal developments surveyed in this chapter, therefore, that two of the most heated ninth-century controversies and the theologies of the crucifixion defended in them now need to be examined.

CHAPTER 5

For whom did Christ die?: the controversy over divine predestination

Like the deliberations that Nicea II and Adoptionism occasioned in Charlemagne's entourage, the Carolingian church's quarrels over divine predestination and the eucharistic presence required that participants – this time ecclesiastics all living in Carolingian territories – elucidate their interpretations of some of the fundamental teachings of Christian theology. In the *Opus Caroli regis* and the anti-Adoptionist tracts, the first generation of Carolingian scholars saw the ecumenical councils of the early church as the preeminent models of opposition to heresy. While their attentiveness to Christ's status as God is in line with the general early Carolingian preoccupation with his divinity, they interpreted their opponents' doctrines as deviations from the orthodoxy defined by the early synods and, working from this perspective, taught that the crucifixion was a critical revelation of Jesus' union of two natures in one person. The Christological orientation of thought apparent in the treatises against Nicea II and Adoptionism also influenced other writings from the court circle, as is clearest with those of Alcuin. It is likely that it had an impact, too, on the illuminations of the Gellone Sacramentary and the poems and figures of Hrabanus Maurus' *In honorem s. crucis*.

The two quarrels to which we now turn also necessitated reexamination of the union of divinity and humanity in Christ, and the participants in the predestination controversy again looked back to earlier theological conflicts to guide their argumentation. In particular, they were aware of Augustine's quarrel with Pelagius and the fifth- and sixth-century discussions of so-called "semi-Pelagianism" that culminated with the council of

Orange in 529; there, Prosper of Aquitaine's interpretation of Augustine had been crucial to the definition of doctrine.[1] Hincmar of Rheims compared his opponents in the ninth-century predestination controversy to the "old predestinarians," essentially fabricating an earlier heresy against which he claimed that Augustine had written the (pseudo-Augustinian) *Hypomnesticon*.[2] But unlike Theodulf in his attack on Nicea II and Paulinus and Alcuin opposing the Hispanic Adoptionists, the participants in the ninth-century debates were all educated in basically the same cultural and intellectual milieu. At least partly for this reason, they are closer to one another in the starting points and directions of their arguments than are Theodulf and his colleagues to their opponents. Although misinterpretations of each other's views occur, the later Carolingian quarrels constitute real debates in a sense that is not true of the earlier conflicts.

Furthermore, both ninth-century disputes show the affect on theological discussion, by the middle of the century, of the primary importance of the liturgy and sacraments to Carolingian devotion, the growing intensity of biblical and liturgical studies, and scholars' increased access to and familiarity with patristic writings. One consequence is that the ninth-century conflicts involve clear differences of opinion about the proper interpretation of specific passages in scripture and about the role and nature of the sacraments, with the divergent opinions fueled by readings in patristic sources, especially though not exclusively Augustine. Thus a pivotal issue that arose within the context of the predestination controversy was the function of penance and the sacraments, both baptism and the eucharist, in light of the church's belief in divine predestination. A second issue, as in the fifth- and sixth-century discussions,[3] was the need to reconcile those biblical verses that seem to describe a divine will for universal salvation, such as 1 Timothy 2.4, or that like Romans 8.32 suggest Christ died for all mortals,[4] with the scripturally grounded belief that the same omnipotent God, clearly capable of doing what he wills, decrees the damnation of the wicked at the end of time.

The complexity of the predestination quarrel makes it best to begin

---

[1] Pelikan, *Christian Tradition* 1.318–331, 327 on Prosper and the council of Orange.

[2] Hincmar, *De praedestinatione Dei et libero arbitrio*, PL 125.65–474, at 298A/B.

[3] Pelikan, *Christian Tradition* 1.321–329.

[4] 1 Timothy 2.4: "Who will have all men to be saved, and to come to the knowledge of the truth." Romans 8.32: "He that spared not even his own Son, but delivered him up for us all, how hath he not also, with him, given us all things?"

with an overview of its evolution, before turning to a closer investigation of the arguments it engendered. A relatively early reference to a doctrine possibly connected with predestination occurs in the records of the council of Paris (829), which, in urging obedience to divine precepts, expressed opposition to the idea that baptism alone without subsequent penance and good works would save the recipient from eternal damnation. On the contrary, the council asserted, the future torments of sinful Christians would be worse than those of good pagans.[5] More generally, as is indicated by some of the sources discussed in the last chapter, the concepts of election, predestination, and damnation regularly arose in ninth-century biblical exegesis, especially of the Pauline epistles, and in liturgical discussions such as those at Quierzy in 838, regarding Amalarius' claim that the canon of the mass symbolizes two sacrifices, one for the elect and another for sinners. The deliberations inspired by these scholarly activities broadly helped create an intellectual climate in which a controversy over predestination might ignite. The first surviving notices of a dispute that without doubt centers specifically on a doctrine of predestination, however, are preserved in a letter and *opusculum* sent by Hrabanus Maurus to Bishop Noting of Verona c. 840. Hrabanus' letter mentions that Noting complained to him about certain heretics who asserted that the "good and just God" predestined all humanity; "the man predestined to life cannot fall into death, and the man predestined to death is completely unable to restore himself to life."[6] While Hrabanus does not name the advocates of this view, a subsequent letter to Hincmar reveals that one person he had in mind in writing to Noting was the former monk of Fulda, Gottschalk of Orbais. We know from another letter by Hrabanus to Count Eberhard of Friuli that, by c. 846, Gottschalk was preaching similar doctrines at Eberhard's court.[7]

Despite these hints of disagreement stirred by Gottschalk's views during the 840s, a full-scale quarrel over divine predestination did not erupt in the

---

[5] *Concilium Parisiense A. 829, MGH Conc.* 2.661–663.

[6] Hrabanus, *Ep.* 22, *MGH Epp.* 5.428.

[7] Hrabanus, *Ep.* 42, *MGH Epp.* 5.481–487, esp. 481. See *Ep.* 44, *MGH Epp.* 5.490 lines 32–35; *Ep.* 5, *PL* 112.1530–1553; and John Marenbon, "Carolingian Thought," in *Carolingian Culture,* ed. McKitterick, 171–192, at 180–181 on Carolingian questions about grace prior to the predestination controversy. On correspondence with Hincmar relating to the quarrel, including Hrabanus', see Martina Stratman, "Briefe an Hinkmar von Reims," *Deutsches Archiv* 48 (1992), 37–81; on Gottschalk's life, see Weber, ed., *Gedichte,* esp. 7–23.

Carolingian empire until the end of the decade, when Gottschalk was active in Mainz, where Hrabanus was the new archbishop.[8] A synod convened there under Hrabanus in 848 condemned the monk of Orbais and sent him to Hincmar, archbishop of Rheims and Gottschalk's metropolitan. He was denounced again at the synod of Quierzy, over which Hincmar presided, early in 849. On the synod's command he was divested of the priesthood and flogged, texts he had prepared in his defense were burned, and he was confined to the abbey of Hautvillers, partly, it seems, so that he would not harm others with his teachings, partly on the grounds that he was a wandering monk who had illegitimately abandoned monastic life. He remained at the monastery until his death in 868 or 869.[9] Throughout the years spent at Hautvillers, despite the order of the synod of Quierzy for his silence,[10] Gottschalk defended his beliefs about predestination as well as his doctrine of the trine deity (*trina deitas*), which Hincmar also condemned.[11] He wrote widely on other theological subjects, too, one being the eucharist, as well as poetry and tracts on dialectical and grammatical questions that attest his special interest in these issues. Much of what survives of his work probably dates to his years at Hautvillers.[12]

In 849 Hincmar produced his "first treatise" on predestination, framed as a letter to the *dilecti filii simplices* of his province – its priests and monks – that directed them to beware the "false prophet" Gottschalk and his pernicious ideas; and the archbishop of Rheims wrote to Hrabanus for advice on how to handle Gottschalk, as the latter continued to assert his

---

[8] The controversy's circumstances are also discussed in the following recent works: David Ganz, "Theology and the Organisation of Thought," *NCMH* 2.758–785, at 767–773; idem, "The Debate on Predestination," in *Charles the Bald: Court and Kingdom*, ed. M. T. Gibon and J. L. Nelson, rev. edn. (Aldershot, 1990), 283–302, with references to earlier literature; John Marenbon, "John Scottus and Carolingian Theology: from the *De Praedestinatione*, its Background and its Critics, to the *Periphyseon*," in ibid., 303–25; D. E. Nineham, "Gottschalk of Orbais: Reactionary or Precursor of the Reformation?" *Journal of Ecclesiastical History* 40 (1989), 1–18. See also Devisse, *Hincmar*, 1.115–153, 187–279; Pelikan, *Christian Tradition* 3. 80–95.

[9] Synodal records in no. 16. *Mainz (Oktober 848)*, no. 18. *Quierzy (Frühjahr 849)*, MGH *Conc.* 3, ed. Wilfried Hartmann (Hanover, 1984), 179–184, 194–199. Cf. Hincmar, *De praed.*, PL 125.84–85.

[10] No. 18. *Quierzy (Frühjahr 849)*, MGH *Conc.* 3.199.

[11] George H. Tavard, *Trina deitas: the Controversy Between Hincmar and Gottschalk* (Milwaukee, 1996).

[12] D. C. Lambot, ed., *Œuvres théologiques et grammaticales de Godescalc d'Orbais* (Louvain, 1945). Poetry edited by Weber, *Gedichte*; see also Fidel Rädle, "Gottschalks Gedicht an seinen letzten Freund," in *Scire Litteras: Forschungen zum mittelalterlichen Geistesleben*, ed. S. Krämer and M. Bernhard (Munich, 1988), 315–325. The writings on the eucharist are discussed in chapter 6.

position.[13] With Charles the Bald, Hincmar also asked for the assistance of other scholars, among them Amalarius, who was by then living in Metz (his response, if ever written, is lost), Lupus of Ferrières, and Ratramnus of Corbie. Another council of Quierzy, attended by bishops from Charles the Bald's realm of western Francia and led by Hincmar in 853, who formulated its *capitula* on predestination, confirmed the rejection of Gottschalk's doctrine.[14] A synod held at Valence in 855, though, attended by bishops from Lotharingia, presented decrees ostensibly supportive of Gottschalk. These reject the decisions of Quierzy (853) and the treatise attacking Gottschalk by John Scottus Eriugena, who wrote at Hincmar's request in autumn 850 or spring 851.[15] In 856, Prudentius of Troyes demanded that Aeneas sign *capitula* opposing Quierzy as a precondition to appointment to the see of Paris.[16] Hincmar wrote a second treatise in the mid 850s, no longer extant, against Gottschalk and his two allies, Prudentius and Ratramnus.[17] The quarrel started to cool off towards the end of the decade; a council of Lotharingian bishops at Langres in June 859 rescinded the condemnation of Quierzy, while affirming that of John Scottus' *De praedestinatione*, and in the same month a compromise settlement between Gottschalk's supporters and opponents was presented to the synod of Savonnières.[18] Hincmar's "third treatise" on predestination, his fullest extant discussion of the subject, written in 859–60,[19] responded to Langres, defended Quierzy, and attacked Valence and Prudentius' *capitula* for Aeneas. In October 860, a council at Tusey, with bishops from provinces representative of both sides, affirmed a position that emphasized the doctrines on which there was

---

[13] Hincmar, *Ad simplices*, ed. Wilhelm Gundlach, "Zwei Schriften des Erzbischofs Hinkmar von Reims, II," *Zeitschrift für Kirchengeschichte* 10 (1889), 258–309; idem, *Epp.* 37, 39, *MGH Epp.* 8 (Berlin, 1939), 12–23, 24; Flodoard, *Historia remensis ecclesiae* 3.21, *MGH SS* 36, ed. M. Stratmann (Hanover, 1998), 270.

[14] No. 28. *Quierzy (Frühjahr 853)*, *MGH Conc.* 3.294–297. See Hincmar, *De praed.*, PL 125.63–64 and esp. 16–30, PL 125.129–296; Devisse, *Hincmar*, 1.203–205.

[15] No. 33. *Valence (8. Januar 855)*, *MGH Conc.* 3.347–365; John Scottus Eriugena, *De divina praedestinatione*, CCCM 50, ed. G. Madec (Turnhout, 1978). On the date, John J. O'Meara, *Eriugena* (Oxford, 1988), 37.

[16] Prudentius, *Epistola tractoria*, PL 115.1365–68. See Hincmar, *De praed.* 21, PL 125.182C/D; Devisse, *Hincmar*, 1.221–222.

[17] The dedication letter to Charles the Bald has survived: Hincmar, *Ep.* 99, *MGH Epp.* 8.44–49. This was possibly his longest work on predestination: Ganz, "Debate," 298.

[18] No. 46. *Langres (1. Juni 859)*, *MGH Conc.* 3.445–446; No. 47. *Savonnières (14 Juni 859)*, *MGH Conc.* 3.447–489.

[19] On the treatise's preparation and probable date, see Devisse, *Hincmar* 1.224–243.

general agreement. Predestination to salvation, human free will, and the need for grace are all upheld, while no mention is made of predestination to damnation either to support or condemn the notion.[20] Yet although predestination thereafter ceased to be a major issue, reverberations of the dispute appear in writings by Hincmar and John Scottus from the 860s and 870s, and Gottschalk's teachings were evidently being discussed near the end of the century.[21]

On several grounds, the debate over predestination may be called the most important of the Carolingian doctrinal controversies. It was the longest, involved the most theologians and conciliar decisions in different ecclesiastical provinces and realms of the empire, inspired the most Carolingian letters and treatises on any single theological issue, and represented the only Carolingian theological dispute besides that over Adoptionism to result in a participant's confinement. Several recent studies have identified a number of factors behind its vigor.[22] One is the personal animosity towards Gottschalk felt by Hrabanus Maurus and Hincmar of Rheims, two of the most powerful ecclesiastics under the successors of Louis the Pious. The tension between Gottschalk and Hrabanus is already evident in 829, when the former, having been raised at Fulda as a child oblate, sought to leave the monastery against the will of the latter, its abbot.[23] Hincmar's hostility was influenced by the ties between Gottschalk and Ebo, the previously deposed archbishop of Rheims, whose supporters opposed Hincmar's appointment to the see in 845.[24] In the 850s, the quarrels over predestination were further colored by the difficulties that Hincmar's position created, as Gottschalk's strongest support emerged

---

[20] No. 3. *Tusey (22. Oktober–7. November 860)*, *MGH Conc.* 4, ed. W. Hartmann (Hanover, 1998), 12–45, esp. 22–34; P. R. McKeon, "The Carolingian Councils of Savonnières (859) and Tusey (860) and Their Background," *Revue Bénédictine* 84 (1974), 75–110. The council mentions the divine will for universal salvation announced in 1 Tim. 2.4, but without interpreting the verse. It declares Christ to have died for all believers (avoiding the issue of whether he died for all humanity or only the elect); and it stresses the need for baptism, reception of the eucharist, penitence, and ethical behavior in order to count among the saved.

[21] I am grateful to David Ganz (personal communication) for pointing this out. It is likely that Bern, MS 584, used by D. C. Lambot for his edition of Gottschalk's theological writings, was produced in Rheims at the end of the ninth century, which suggests continued concern with Gottschalk's doctrines. See Lambot, ed., *Œuvres*, xii.   [22] See above, n. 8.

[23] Mayke De Jong, *In Samuel's Image: Child Oblation in the Early Medieval West* (Leiden, 1996), 73–91.

[24] Celia Chazelle, "Archbishops Ebo and Hincmar of Reims and the Utrecht Psalter," *Speculum* (1997), 1055–1077, at 1069–1071; reprinted in *Approaches to Early-Medieval Art*, ed. Lawrence Nees, (Cambridge MA, 1998), 97–119.

south of the Loire, where the church hierarchy resented the growing power of the Rheims archbishop.[25]

Finally and most important, however, the dispute over divine predestination and the issues participants addressed concerning the sacraments and biblical exegesis, as noted at the beginning of this chapter, are testimony to the profound ethical questions that contemporary social upheavals had stirred. In the face of Viking incursions, false prophets to whose group Hincmar assigned Gottschalk, strife among Louis' successors, and natural disasters – all sources of disquiet that Carolingian churchmen themselves identified by the mid ninth century – Gottschalk seemed to some of them to explain why human wickedness existed and offer a rationale for moral behavior, including penitence and liturgical and sacramental devotion, that protected the concept of an omnipotent, perfectly good yet perfectly just creator. But to his opponents, his teachings contributed to the social turmoil and the destruction of the moral order. Not only did he appear to them to preach a "new" doctrine contradicting the teachings of Rome, as had been thought true of Nicea II, the Adoptionists, Claudius, and the different parties in the Byzantine image controversy. The proponents of those errors had strayed in the manner of their worship and the doctrines that underlay their devotion, while accepting the principle that Christians must pray, worship, and receive the sacraments. Gottschalk's ideas, though, seemed (to his opponents) utterly to negate hope that the sacraments or other virtuous behavior helped the sinner achieve salvation. His enemies may have overestimated the danger his ideas posed, and they clearly misrepresented elements of his thinking; but they were convinced that his teachings would cause other Christians to lose every incentive to pursue the avenues of virtue, devotion, and cleansing of sins that, by the middle of the ninth century, the church had worked so hard to make available throughout the empire. Hence his doctrines would totally undermine ecclesiastical authority in those territories.[26] As Hincmar observed, quoting Hrabanus, Gottschalk told his listeners that "God's predestination was to good and to evil; and thus there are some in this world who by God's predestination . . . are unable to turn themselves from error and sin, as if from the beginning God made them incorrigible."

[25] See Ganz, "Debate"; Janet L. Nelson, *Charles the Bald* (London, 1992), 168–169.
[26] Ganz, "Debate," 284–285; idem, "Theology," 767–768; G. Schrimpf, "Die ethische Auseinandersetzung zwischen Hraban und Gottschalk um die Prädestinationslehre," in *Hrabanus Maurus und seine Schule*, ed. W. Böhne (Fulda, 1980), 164–174.

These people now ask one another, "What advantage is it for me to work at serving God, since if I am predestined to death, I will never escape that, yet if I do evil and am predestined to life, there is no doubt that I will go to eternal rest?"[27]

Employing their improved libraries, their new expertise in biblical and patristic scholarship, and skills in doctrinal argumentation honed by the earlier Carolingian debates and readings in classical literature, Gottschalk's attackers and supporters were forced to reconsider, justify, and revise their beliefs respective to the semi-Pelagian traditions on which their church's system of penance, liturgy, and sacraments was based, partly by coming to terms with the radically Augustinian theology Gottschalk thrust before their eyes. The extant texts that reflect these efforts express a range of views; no two theologians say precisely the same thing, and it is impossible here to do justice to all the different ideas enunciated in the literature. While we will need to discuss some aspects of other Carolingian contributions to the dispute, therefore, my main concern is with those participants whose writings most decisively explore the relation between predestination and the crucifixion. Although every Carolingian treatise from the controversy at least implicitly views the crucifixion in light of the eschaton, the most thorough examinations of the issue of precisely which mortals God intended the passion to save are by Gottschalk, Hincmar, and John Scottus, the last-named theologian in poetry and prose not specifically concerned with the conflict but reflecting features of the doctrine he espoused against Gottschalk. Above all, it is Hincmar who most vociferously attacks the monk of Orbais on these grounds. Hincmar's "third treatise" on predestination, his longest surviving work from the quarrel, reveals that for him, in particular, his adversary's presumed failure to accept the Bible's teaching that Christ died for everyone was a crucial element of Gottschalk's error on predestination. A correct grasp of the relationship between the end of time and the crucifixion's place in the divine work of salvation, Hincmar was convinced, made his opponent's position untenable.

Gottschalk and his supporters

In spite of the fragmentary form in which some of Gottschalk's writings on predestination have survived, enough was preserved by his adversaries

---

[27] Hincmar, *De praed.* 2, PL 125.84C-85A. See Hrabanus, *Ep.* 42, *MGH Epp.* 5.481.

and allies, sometimes as quoted excerpts, to allow us to understand clearly the beliefs he articulated against his challengers and the consistency with which he adhered to them.[28] His unbending logic, frequently expressed through syllogisms and grammatical analysis, in certain respects recalls the driving prose of the *Opus Caroli regis*. In part, this attests Gottschalk's interest in grammar and dialectic; at the same time, it is a reminder of his personal certainty about his ideas and his own relation with God, as a mortal burdened with sin, yet convinced of his election and reception of the grace that alone can guarantee salvation.[29] The predestination theology behind this conviction was intended to be loyal to Augustine's anti-Pelagian writings, yet it goes well beyond the church father in working out the consequences of those ideas.[30] Even Gottschalk's advocates could not fully embrace his views. Despite the support he received from Lupus of Ferrières, Ratramnus of Corbie, Prudentius of Troyes, and other Carolingian theologians, on this issue, as in other domains of his life, he ultimately stood alone.

The structuring principle of Gottschalk's teachings on predestination is the concept of its "twinness" that he derives from both Augustine and Isidor, who provided its "classic statement": the one predestination of God, a predestination only of "good things," applies in different ways to the elect and the reprobate.[31] Every human being possesses what Gottschalk defines as free will, yet since Adam the will has been so corrupted by original sin that no mortal, on his own, can desire the good. Left to their own devices, all human beings remain mired in sin, both original sin and those wrongs they incessantly commit because they cannot do otherwise. No one in that condition can even experience true contrition for sin, and everyone, therefore, by nature deserves eternal damnation.[32] But God, in his infinite mercy, has not abandoned the entire human race to punishment. Before the beginning of time, he predestined a small, precisely established number of mortals to receive the gift of divine grace that makes

---

[28] Esp. Gottschalk, *Confessio, Confessio prolixior, Opuscula theologica* 7–18, 24, *Œuvres*, ed. Lambot, 52–78, 180–258, 338–346.

[29] See Peter von Moos, "Gottschalks Gedicht *O mi custos* – eine *confessio*," *Frühmittelalterliche Studien* 4 (1970), 201–230, ibid. 5 (1971), 317–358. Trans. Godman, *Poetry*, 232–247; new edition, F.III.9, *Gedichte*, ed. Weber, 160–175.   [30] See Pelikan, *Christian Tradition* 3.80–95.

[31] See Gottschalk, *Conf., Conf. prol., Opus. theol.* 24.1, *Œuvres*, ed. Lambot, 52–54, 55–56, 67–68, 339–342; Pelikan, *Christian Tradition* 3.88.

[32] E.g., quoting Augustine, "Nullum deus eligit dignum sed eligendo efficit dignum, nullum tamen punit indignum": Gottschalk, *Opus. theol.* 9.1, *Œuvres*, ed. Lambot, 202.

repentance possible and redeems sin, healing the free will so it turns to
virtue and God. Each elect is changed from a *vas irae* into a *vas misericordiae*
that merits eternal beatitude. Through this grace, "those who were by
nature sons of wrath [are] made sons of mercy"; they whom "corrupt
nature had submerged in the depths, now climb rejoicing to the heights."[33]

Freely given by God, grace is something no human being merits, since
sinful humanity only deserves damnation. Synonymous with God the son
and the holy spirit, it is a manifestation of divine omnipotence as well as
mercy, in marked contrast to the mortal's powerlessness to avoid evil. Just
as no one can say a creature is greater than its creator, Gottschalk asserts, it
is impossible to say that nature is greater than grace, for "grace is God and
hence eternally all powerful, while nature without grace is completely
impotent."[34] Thus although without grace no mortal can do what is good,
with it no one can truly withdraw from God. The elected individual may
sin, just as Gottschalk ardently proclaims his misdeeds in some of his
poetry. One of his poems warns a former friend that the heretical view of
predestination he has adopted will bring damnation. Yet evidently if the
friend can change his opinion, this will be a sign that he counts among the
elect, while, for himself, the poet is sure that grace is there to make the
tears of repentance flow and purge the soul.[35] It is a gift that cannot be
chosen, rejected, or ever abandoned.[36] Those mortals who do not receive
grace face the just, and in this regard good, punishment to which God
justly assigned them, in the same act of predestination by which he showed
mercy to the elect.[37] Bereft of grace, the reprobate lack the slightest
hope of redemption, just as nothing causes its recipients to lose their
place among the blessed, since for both groups, God's "predestination is
disposed incommutably by unretractable preordination."[38] Indeed, the distinction between the elect and the reprobate is so absolute and unchange-

---

[33] Gottschalk, *Opus. theol.* 7.2, ibid., 181; see *Opus. theol.* 15, 24.1, ibid., 240–242, 343–344.

[34] Gottschalk, *Opus. theol.* 7.8, ibid., 185.

[35] Rädle, "Gottschalks Gedicht," 315–325, esp. 316–318, 320–321. Cf. Gottschalk, F.III.1–5, *Gedichte*,
ed. Weber, 135–147; von Moos, "Gottschalks Gedicht," 201–230.

[36] See Gottschalk, *Opus. theol.* 7.8, *Œuvres*, ed. Lambot, 184–185, 187–188 (Augustine). Cf. Pelikan,
Christian Tradition 1.294–304 on Augustine's doctrine of grace.

[37] See Gottschalk, *Conf. prol.*, *Opus. theol.* 7.7, 9.1, 24.1, *Œuvres*, ed. Lambot, 55–56, 183, 202, 342.

[38] Gottschalk, *Conf. prol.*, ibid., 61–62. Gottschalk also expresses the immutability of predestination to damnation and its connection with God's eternity when he identifies the destination of
the reprobate with their predestination, e.g. *Opus. theol.* 9.5, ibid., 207: "si reprobi non sunt ad
mortem praedestinati, neque illic sunt destinandi. Destinandi sunt autem…"

able, according to Gottschalk, that they constitute separate worlds identifiable as separate bodies, one Christ's body the church, who is also his bride, the other the body of the Antichrist.[39]

For Gottschalk, this doctrine of divine predestination is the only one compatible with God's eternal omnipotence and immutability, attributes on which he vigorously insists.[40] Twin predestination, as he interprets it, constitutes a formidable demonstration of the complex interface between the timeless in God and the temporal realm of sinful humanity. Because of God's nature, it would be impossible for the wicked to receive punishment at the end of time unless they were predestined to it.[41] On the one hand, God's omnipotence means that what he wants to do he necessarily accomplishes; nothing he does conflicts with his will. On the other, if God is eternal and therefore immutable, every one of his acts is part of the unchangeable plan for the universe that he, as creator, eternally willed in his immutable wisdom.[42] God cannot do anything he has not predestined, neither the salvation of the blessed nor the damnation of the wicked, for to posit any change in God would make him subject to time and hence, Gottschalk argues, capable even of dying.[43] To predestine sinners to hell might seem incompatible with divine goodness inasmuch as, established before time began, the predestination could be understood to precede Adam's sin and the sins that mortals individually commit, making the judgment prior to the crime. But in Gottschalk's belief, the penalty is actually a "just evil" reflecting the good of God's justice – evil because it consists of punishment, yet good because it is the just response to the enormously "unjust evils" of human sins. It does not precede the wrongdoings, since God possesses eternal foreknowledge of these, as he does of all his own actions.[44] God predestines only the punishment and sinners to it, based on

---

[39] See Gottschalk, *Opus. theol.* 23, ibid., 328, 333, esp. lines 26–29 (lacuna in text); *Opus. theol.* 7.9, 9.3, 24.1, ibid., 188–189, 203–205, 344. When God gave his only son for the world, according to John 3.16, it was solely for that of the elect: *Opus. theol.* 9.3, ibid., 204 lines 21–22.

[40] Devisse, *Hincmar* 1.265–266, offers a psychological explanation of this aspect of Gottschalk's thought. Again, the sense of God's power and the utter difference between him and his creation comes through with particular force in the poetry; see above, nn. 29, 35.

[41] Gottschalk, *Conf. prol.*, *Œuvres*, ed. Lambot, 56.

[42] Gottschalk, *Opus. theol.* 9., ibid., 202.   [43] Gottschalk, *Conf. prol.*, ibid., 59–60.

[44] Gottschalk, *Conf., Conf. prol.*, ibid., 52, 55–56; see *Opus. theol.* 7.7, 9, ibid., 183 ("… talis est differentia inter iniusta mala quae homo quisque commisit committit committet iniustus et mala iusta quae deus per aduersa praesentia et tormenta perpetua reddidit reddit reddet….."), 189–190.

this foreknowledge, not the sins themselves that the wicked freely commit and that earn them damnation. And yet divine foreknowledge, will, and predestination are inseparable; there is no interval between them, because they are all eternal and immutable. What God wills is necessarily by that same act foreknown, predestined, and "foredone" (*praefinita*), or he would be subject to time.[45]

The mechanism by which omnipotent grace is bestowed on the elect is Christ's passion, death, and bloodshed. Gottschalk, like some of his opponents in the predestination controversy, especially Hincmar, frequently describes the crucifixion and its power to save in terms of Christ's blood. In his thought, that image fits well with his concept of grace as a special anointment offered to some individuals but not others, much as in Exodus 12 the blood of the passover lamb protected the Jews from the angel of death while the Egyptian children were slaughtered. God's predestination to damnation as well as to salvation, and the simple fact that the wicked face hell, are reconciled with the scriptural passages suggesting a divine will for universal salvation by interpreting those texts as references to the salvation uniquely of the elect. The world to whom Christ offered life through his flesh, holy bread, is the "world" only of the church.[46] God willed that the crucifixion, the one vehicle for the provision of the grace necessary for salvation, save only those predestined to be saved. For Gottschalk, this exegesis is supported by the claim in the epistle to the Hebrews that Christ suffered "to exhaust the sins of many"(Hebr. 9.28). The elect, not those predestined to hell, are the sheep redeemed by the spilling of Christ's blood, "through which they are fully liberated from all sins, past, present, and future, by the free grace of God."[47] In love of his church alone he "handed over and poured out" his body and blood, a church – a people – who can therefore never lose that promise of salvation.[48]

Only such an understanding of the crucifixion, in Gottschalk's view, accords with the doctrines of divine omnipotence and immutability that underlie the concept of twin predestination. That any element of Christ's torments and humiliation in the passion was not fully redemptive is

[45] Gottschalk, *Conf. prol.*, ibid., 59, see 56–60, 63–64.
[46] Gottschalk, *Opus. theol.* 7.9, ibid., 188–189; *Opus. theol.* 23, ibid., 328.
[47] Gottschalk, *Opus. theol.* 24.1, ibid., 343; see *Opus. theol.* 7.3, 12, ibid., 181–182, 224–231.
[48] Gottschalk, *Opus. theol.* 7.9, 10.1, ibid., 188–189, 216.

unthinkable. Given his sufferings, whomever Christ thereby redeemed clearly must be forever saved from eternal death.[49] Otherwise, the crucifixion and his redeeming blood are not omnipotent, God's grace is limited in its power, and the divine will is changeable. The damnation of the wicked would not be part of God's original plan, but became necessary when grace failed to effect the redemption of everyone.[50] Such scenarios that attribute weakness and mutability to God fail to do justice to so astounding an achievement as Christ's passion, an event so marvelous and powerful that it must have brought life to everyone meant to receive it.[51] A passage from Cassiodorus' commentary on Psalm 54 is interpreted as confirmation of this doctrine: the crucified Christ is the "inestimable price that redeemed the human race, the holocaust that helped us escape the eternal flames, he who dead bore away extinction, the end who gave good remaining without end."[52]

Like Gottschalk's theology of the eucharist, studied in the next chapter, his interpretation of baptism's function undergirds his belief that God willed that the passion bestow grace on only a predestined portion of humanity. What baptism offers the reprobate, he indicates, is different from what it gives the elect through Christ's passion, death, and bloodshed. Although the elect are recognized to include baptized Christians along with, it seems, certain Old Testament figures who foresaw the incarnation,[53] it is made clear that many who are baptized are nonetheless damned. The elect who have lived since the incarnation are all baptized, but not all the baptized are elect; not all of them number among those who have been redeemed by

---

[49] Gottschalk, *Opus. theol.* 10.1, ibid., 214. Note the emphasis on the passion's torments (lines 4–15): "Nam qui sicut expedit dei patris erga [hominem] beniuolentiam et dei filii oboedientiam humilitatem patientiam perpendit, qualiter scilicet pro electis ieiunauerit esurierit sitierit fatigatus fuerit blasphemias calumnias contumelias ignominias maledicta improperia obprobria conuicia ludibria uincula alapas colaphos sputa flagella sustinuerit spineam quoque coronam libenter imponi capiti suo permiserit crucem sibi portauerit eamque sponte subierit ibique tunc temporis turpissima morte suspensus et occisus fuerit, procul dubio fatetur incunctanter et laetus asserit quod omnes omnino quos tali pretio redemit a morte perpetua redemptor pius redemerit et eis omnibus uitam aeternam dederit."

[50] See Gottschalk, *Conf. prol.*, ibid., 59–60; Ganz, "Debate," 288.

[51] Gottschalk, *Conf. prol.*, *Opus. theol.* 10.1, 12, 14, *Œuvres*, ed. Lambot, 59–60, 212–213, 229, 239; see *Opus. theol.* 6, ibid., 158.

[52] Gottschalk, *Opus. theol.* 10.1, ibid., 212 (Cassiodorus, *In Ps. 54, concl.*) Similarly, Gottschalk's exegesis of the antiphon celebrating the power of the cross: "O crux admirabilis euacuatio uulneris restitio sanitatis," in *Opus. theol.* 7.3, ibid., 181–182.

[53] E.g. Job: Gottschalk, *Opus. theol.* 16, ibid., 243.

the crucifixion and its blood. "If by his blood Christ redeemed the reprobate baptized," Gottschalk remarks, "surely he transmitted them to the contemplation of his father. However he did not transmit them to contemplation of his father, [and] therefore he did not redeem them in his blood."[54] This means that while baptism remits original sin and any sins committed before the sacrament for the wicked as much as the elect,[55] only the elect also acquire that grace, brought in the crucifixion, by which present and future sins are remitted. This "special redemption," distinguished from the "common redemption" or "grace of baptism" given to reprobate and elect alike, alone constitutes redemption in Christ's blood.[56] Baptism is evidently the instrument by which, since the incarnation, special redemption is bestowed on the elect, including those who may appear reluctant to receive the sacrament, such as infants.[57] But God's decision as to who in baptism receives that gift occurs in his immutable and omnipotent predestination. The sacrament is at best a clue that the participant is *perhaps* one of the blessed. Whereas the benefits that baptism brings to the reprobate are temporal, then, those it grants to the elect are eternal. Recalling the decree of the council of Paris (829) noted earlier, but lending the concept a different significance by associating it with his doctrine of predestination, Gottschalk suggests that the reprobate baptized are worse off than unbaptized pagans who are ignorant of Christ, because the former knew Christ but rejected him (freely, though with corrupt free wills unhealed by grace). As a result, the punishments they will suffer in hell are greater than those of the pagans.[58]

Carolingian theologians who were more sympathetic to Gottschalk's teachings than to the positions that Hincmar, Hrabanus, and John Scottus Eriugena defended still questioned certain of his ideas, sometimes because they were misunderstood or, it is likely, were unknown even to his supporters. Lupus of Ferrières concludes his tract, *De tribus quaestionibus*, by disagreeing with the notion that the passion benefits only the elect. Although it does not save the reprobate, he holds, it may lessen their sufferings in

---

[54] Gottschalk, *Opus. theol.* 10.2, ibid., 217; see *Opus. theol.* 7.3, 12, ibid., 181, 226–230.

[55] See Gottschalk, *Fragmentum* 24, *Opus. theol.* 12, 24.1, ibid., 42–43, 226–227, 342–343.

[56] Gottschalk, *Opus. theol.* 11, 20, ibid., 221–222, 279–280. See Marta Cristiani, "La notion de loi dans le *de praedestinatione* de Jean Scot," *Studi medievali*, 3rd series, 17 (1976), 81–114, at 88–89.

[57] Thus God "saves infants when they are baptized" ("... saluat paruulos infantes quando baptizantur") despite their weeping and resistance: Gottschalk, *Opus. theol.* 14, *Œuvres*, ed. Lambot, 239. The concern is to demonstrate that grace is omnipotent, such that those who receive it cannot reject it. Mortals not baptized since Christ's incarnation are clearly damned: see *Opus. theol.* 16, ibid., 243–244.   [58] Gottschalk, *Opus. theol.* 12, ibid., 229–230.

hell, just as the sun comforts the blind even if it does not enable them to see. Similarly, "why should a more powerful son by means of such a price not punish the blinded and damned less, even if he did not save them by his own merit?" It is not necessarily wrong to believe Christ "tasted death for all," therefore, and in the end each person must decide for himself, aided by divine inspiration or scriptural study, which doctrine has greatest merit.[59] Florus of Lyons, who misconstrues Gottschalk's teachings on grace and free will,[60] rejects the doctrine that without grace human nature is completely unable to will the good. It is true, in his view, that the will is weakened by the fall and that the grace brought by Christ "liberates" and "renews" it, restoring its freedom to turn towards the good. Christ's blood is the key to redemption; through it, the saved mortal "is cleansed from dead works and revived to serve the living God" (see Hebrews 9.14). The reprobate lack the "redemption of Christ's blood," so that all their works are ultimately "dead." And yet they retain a "natural good" bestowed by God or they are sometimes moved "by a natural law," allowing them to appear to act virtuously without grace. God's punishment of them is just, though, since whatever virtuous behavior they display is not indicative of true virtue or faith, for it does not proceed from the "root of truth and goodness."[61] Both Lupus and Florus also suggest alternatives to Gottschalk's explanation that when the Bible refers to the salvation of "all men," it means only those whom God wills to save, i.e. the elect. For Lupus, the "all" of 1 Timothy 2.4 ("Who will have all men to be saved, and to come to the knowledge of the truth") can denote those whom God wishes to save, that is his elect, or it can indicate that he saves some members of all groups of humanity: Jews as well as gentiles, clergy as well as laity, lords as well as peasants.[62] Florus lists four possible readings of the passage in 1 Timothy; only the last of them, the notion that God wants to save all who will their own salvation, which he identifies as Pelagian, is declared incorrect.[63] Any of the other three proposed interpretations is

---

[59] Lupus, *Liber de tribus quaestionibus*, PL 119.619–648, at 646D-648.

[60] Florus (Pseudo-Remigius), *De tribus epistolis* 21, PL 121.985–1068, at 1023A/B. Florus maintains that for Gottschalk only divine grace without free will works in the elect towards the good, because with Adam's fall the will became incapable of virtue.

[61] Ibid., 22, PL 121.1025C; see Pelikan, *Christian Tradition* 3.83.

[62] Lupus, *De tribus quaest.*, PL 119.636–37, see 645–46.

[63] Florus, *De tribus epist.* 11–12, PL 121.1005–1009; cf. idem, *Libellus de tendenda immobiliter scripturae veritate* 12, 14, PL 121.1083–1134, at 1117, 1125.

potentially valid: the "all" may refer to all races of men; it may mean that God inspires in his saints a will to salvation, which would make it indeed true that all who will their own salvation are saved; or the passage in Paul's letter perhaps shows that God saves all whom he wishes to save.[64]

Moreover, several theologians open to Gottschalk's ideas made greater effort than do his doctrinal tractates to explain the benefits of prayer, penance, and the sacraments in a way compatible with God's eternal predestination.[65] Like Hrabanus, they were concerned about the danger that penance, the sacraments, and other forms of virtuous action might seem useless for entrance into heaven.[66] Ratramnus' treatise on predestination is largely a collection of patristic texts, with brief connecting remarks by its Carolingian author that firmly support Gottschalk's teachings on God's eternal disposition of all things and twin predestination;[67] but it suggests that there are different degrees of election. Some mortals who eventually fall away from God are at first "temporarily" elected, evidently through baptism. They do not receive the salvation reserved for the blessed who "remain to the end," persevering in good works, a perseverance that is itself a gift from God. Hence while the predestined blessed may sin, they do not continue in their wrongdoing but return to God, who mercifully grants that they live long enough to repent.[68] For Florus, the behavior by which the elect show themselves to be good, like the misdeeds of the wicked, provides evidence of their destiny; for both Florus and Ratramnus, following Gregory I, God predestines that he will answer the saints' prayers, bestowing on them the salvation they merit through their own labor.[69] According to Lupus, God removes the "insanity" from every Christian (i.e. the elect) of thinking he is one of the damned lest he believe that nothing can turn

---

[64] See Florus, *De tribus epist.* 13, *PL* 121.1010. Cf. Prudentius' *capitula* for Aeneas of Paris: no. 37. *Sens (856)*, *MGH Conc.* 3.379–382, at 380–81; and Haimo, *Expositio*, *PL* 117.437 (to Rom. 8.32), 789 (to 1 Tim. 2.4).On Augustine's teaching, Pelikan, *Christian Tradition* 1.321.

[65] While Gottschalk certainly does not think that faith, sacraments, or good works help the individual gain salvation, he never explicitly states that they even signify election, and he is clear that baptism, at least, does not automatically do so. His poetry, though, implies the importance of prayer for the elect; see above, at n. 35; and *Opus. theol.* 7.9, 9.9, *Œuvres*, ed. Lambot, 190, 211.

[66] E.g. according to Lupus, someone might say: "Et si mihi semel pereundum est, cur hujus vitae perdo compendia? cur cum mihi alibi semper futurum est male, non sit hic aliquandiu bene? quare non omnes voluptatis effundo habenas, totumque quod delectat perficio?" *De tribus quaest.*, *PL* 119.640A/B.　　　[67] Ratramnus, *De praedestinatione Dei*, *PL* 121.11–80.

[68] Ibid. 1, 2, *PL* 121, e.g. 26A, 35, 45C.

[69] Florus, *De tribus epist.* 6, *PL* 121.999–1000A; Ratramnus, *De praed.* 1, *PL* 121.27B/C.

him from evil, even though predestination cannot be altered. Repentance of sin and other virtuous behavior stems from the hope of divine mercy and salvation which God places in the elected soul. Thus the Christian should remember that "he is redeemed by such a price as Christ's blood" and not love sin too much or despair, but remain mindful of the saving benefits of baptism, penance, and prayer, and pursue these paths to God.[70]

The synod of Valence (855), like Gottschalk, emphasizes divine immutability; in God, "those things that will be are already done." God's foreknowledge of how the wicked will behave does not impose any necessity on them; based on his just judgment of the evil deeds that he foreknows they will freely commit, he predestines them to punishment. By those deeds, they evidently show their lack of faith in Christ. Free will, made infirm through Adam, is healed through grace only for the faithful; Christ did not pour out his blood for the impious damned, but only for those who believe in him, as indicated in John 3.14–16.[71] The power of grace is seen as limited, though, insofar as the human free will has an independent ability to choose evil even when grace has been bestowed. All baptized faithful are washed of sins, incorporated in the church, and made recipients of grace through that sacrament, but only those who spend the rest of their lives persevering "faithfully in their redemption," apparently meaning that they continue in faith and good works, are finally saved. Others fall away by their own will, because "they did not wish to remain in the salvation of faith, which they received in the beginning," and "chose to make void the grace of redemption."[72]

Hrabanus and Hincmar

These varied arguments provided the theological foundation for the resolution to the quarrel achieved at Langres, Savonnières, and Tusey in 859–860. While the councils' decisions had clear political dimensions, the two parties discernible in the controversy throughout the 850s advocated doctrines more easily bridged than if Gottschalk alone had been allowed to

---

[70] Lupus, *De tribus quaest.*, PL 119.640B-641.

[71] "And as Moses lifted up the serpent in the desert, so must the son of man be lifted up: That whosoever believeth in him, may not perish; but may have life everlasting. For God so loved the world, as to give his only begotten son; that whosoever believeth in him, may not perish, but may have life everlasting."

[72] No. 33: *Valence (8. Januar 855)*, MGH Conc. 3.353–356, esp. 355 line 28 to 356 line 1.

speak publicly. Yet despite the inability of his allies to affirm all his ideas, the real source of worry for them, at least until the controversy was resolved, was the teachings of his principal opponents: Hrabanus Maurus, until his death c. 856, Archbishop Hincmar of Rheims, and the brilliant scholar of Charles the Bald's court, John Scottus Eriugena.

It was Hrabanus who brought Gottschalk's predestination theology to Hincmar's attention. In its basic characteristics, the archbishop of Rheims' thinking falls within the framework of opposition set forth in the letters and *opusculum* that Hrabanus sent to Bishop Noting of Verona, Count Eberhard of Friuli, and Hincmar in the 840s. These texts, Hrabanus' principal statements on predestination, were the opening shots in the battle. From Hincmar, who was far more prolific on the issue, the most important extant works are the *capitula* of the synod of Quierzy, which he composed; the letter-treatise *Ad simplices*, completed in the fall of 849 and sent to Hrabanus in early 850; and the "third treatise" of 859–60. All three documents by Hincmar, reflecting doctrines that Hrabanus also enunciated though in general more briefly, view the meaning and purpose of Christ's passion as critical issues raised by Gottschalk's contentions that God did not will the salvation of all humanity and that Christ did not suffer or shed his blood to redeem the entire human race. It seems likely that the same issues also played an important role in the lost "second treatise" and the lost verses of the *Ferculum Salomonis*, written c. 853–856, judging by the extant verses of the latter work and the surviving portion of its prose *explanatio*. Using number symbolism, what is left of the *Ferculum Salomonis* combines meditation on the eucharist with commentary on the Trinity, salvation, predestination, and the final vision of God. The framework for all these topics is an allegorical exegesis of Solomon's litter (Canticle 3.9–10) as a type of the church.[73]

The most extensive exploration of the crucifixion's significance in surviving Carolingian predestination literature, though, as suggested earlier, occurs in the third treatise. Its loose organization and heavy reliance on block excerpts from patristic and early medieval sources to carry forward its teachings, among them writings by Augustine, Pseudo-Augustine, Chrysostom, Cyprian, Celestine, Hilary, Prosper of Aquitaine, and the

---

[73] Hincmar, *Explan. in ferc. Salom.*, PL 125.817–834; *Carm.* 4.1, MGH PLAC 3.414–415; Taeger, *Zahlensymbolik*, 89–192, esp. 144–147.

tract, *De obduratione cordis Pharaonis* erroneously attributed to Jerome,[74] frequently obscure the direction of Hincmar's thought.[75] Yet regardless of this difficulty, no other Carolingian treatise on predestination discusses in such depth and from so many angles the relation of the passion to the eschaton.

Let me begin by examining the teachings of Hrabanus that Hincmar essentially reiterates, before looking at the ways in which the archbishop of Rheims moves beyond his older colleague, especially in the third treatise. Simply the greater volume of Hincmar's writings on predestination means that they more clearly highlight the inconsistencies and logical weaknesses of the ideas that he and also Hrabanus uphold, especially when compared with the dialectical thrust of much of Gottschalk's work. To some degree, these failings grow out of the two archbishops' pastoral concerns; for them, the doctrine of twin predestination promoted fatalism before a deterministic God who left no room for human free will, by denying God's infinite mercy and willingness to forgive sinners.[76] Somewhat paradoxically, though, both Gottschalk's opponents agree with certain of the monk's ideas, at times because they misinterpret him. Both Hrabanus and Hincmar, for example, believe their primary patristic support lies in Augustine, though their sources include the pseudo-Augustinian *Hypomnesticon* and they interpret Augustine through Prosper of Aquitaine. Based on these texts, which are claimed to show that Gottschalk contradicts Augustine, his two adversaries confirm that no one can be saved without the grace brought through the blood of the crucified Christ. Only those who receive grace can live virtuously, while God will justly punish the wicked because, lacking this gift, they continue to sin. Baptism in a state of faith removes both original sin and the sins committed prior to the sacrament from all its recipients, even the damned; Hincmar and Hrabanus evidently believe that Gottschalk teaches it to do this only for the elect. The baptized faithful facing damnation deserve their penalty because of the

---

[74] D.G. Morin, "Un traité pélagien inédit du commencement du ve siècle," *Revue Bénédictine* 26 (1909), 163–88; G. de Plinval, *Essai sur le style et la langue de Pélage, suivi du traité inédit de induratione cordis pharaonis* (Fribourg, 1947).

[75] As observed by Leo Donald Davis, commenting on Hincmar's quarrel with Gottschalk over the Trinity, Hincmar was "a maddeningly untidy thinker and writer" who nonetheless had a sound grasp of the issues: "Hincmar of Rheims as a Theologian of the Trinity," *Traditio* 27 (1971), 455–468, at 456.

[76] See Devisse, *Hincmar* 1.256, 265–268; Ganz, "Theology," 772; Pelikan, *Christian Tradition* 3.81–95.

sins they commit after the sacrament, sins committed of their own free will. God is not the author of human wickedness, but only of goodness, as manifested in both his mercy and the justice by which he justly condemns the reprobate for the sins they freely undertake.[77]

But Hrabanus and Hincmar are convinced that the doctrine of predestination to damnation, which, reflecting their misunderstanding of Gottschalk, they effectively equate with predestination to sin,[78] means that the condemned individual has no control over and therefore no responsibility for his destiny. Hence they look to sources that they are convinced reflect Augustine's thought, often texts by Prosper, to argue that there is predestination to salvation but not to damnation. For Gottschalk, as we have seen, God's eternal immutability and omnipotence make it impossible to separate his foreknowledge of his acts from his predestination of them. Because God foreknows the sins of the wicked and that he will punish them, he necessarily predestines those mortals to damnation, an end in keeping with his justice and therefore his goodness. Hrabanus and Hincmar, on the other hand, supported by Prosper, accept that God eternally foreknows and predestines that the elect will receive grace and be saved, yet with the wicked a distinction is envisioned between divine foreknowledge and predestination. God foreknows their sins and that they will be punished, based on his just judgment, but he predestines neither. Setting divine action more firmly in the temporal realm than does Gottschalk, both archbishops hold that while God predestines the final tribunal and, therefore, the punishment of sinners, to speak of predestination to sin or to damnation attributes evil to him. If God predestines the wicked *to* punishment, his judgment unjustly occurs before, rather than in response to, their wrongdoings. On the contrary, as stated in Matthew 16.27, God "renders to every man according to his works." Divine condemnation of sin follows rather than precedes the sin itself, for God's predestination is only to the good, whether it pertains to the gift of grace or the retribution of justice.[79]

---

[77] Hrabanus, *Ep.* 42, *MGH Epp.* 5.483–486, primarily quoting Prosper; Hincmar, e.g. *Ep.* 37, *MGH Epp.* 8.14 lines 12–13 (on baptism) 17 (on divine goodness); *Ad simplices*, "Zwei Schriften," ed. Gundlach, 267–270.

[78] This is clearest with Hrabanus, e.g. *Ep.* 42, *MGH Epp.* 5.483, lines 28–30 (Prosper); *Ep.* 44 (to Hincmar), *MGH Epp.* 5.490. Cf. Hincmar, *De praed.* 24, *PL* 125.221A (Chrysostom): if God predestined the damnation of the wicked before time began, God would be responsible for their sin, making him the author of evil, and human free will would count for nothing.

[79] In general, Hrabanus, *Epp.* 42–44, *MGH Epp.* 5.481–499, and *Ep.* 5, *PL* 112, esp. 1531–1533, 1548–1553.

Three related concepts are critical to this position. One is that grace is not all-powerful in the sense Gottschalk believes. As Gottschalk recognizes, if grace has the omnipotence he ascribes to it, thinking his position consistent with Augustine's, God cannot offer it to all mortals or everyone will be saved. For Gottschalk, God offers his grace to, and Christ died for, the portion of the human race that alone is predestined to salvation. Hrabanus and Hincmar, though, no doubt influenced by their pastoral duties, which the ninth-century Carolingian church so tightly linked with penance, the sacraments, and the liturgy, and looking to different sources believed consistent with Augustinian thought, insist on the freedom of the human will even when endowed with grace. In passages reminiscent of the emphasis on repentance and ethical behavior in portions of Hrabanus' commentary on Matthew and Hincmar's *Ferculum Salomonis*, they defend the mortal's personal responsibility to deserve to be saved. While grace restores the ability to will the good, it cannot prevent some recipients from freely turning away from it and God so as to deserve damnation. Much as is true of the council of Valence,[80] both archbishops see membership in the elect as dependent not on the bestowal of grace on a passive recipient, such as Gottschalk seems to have in mind, but on the individual's voluntary acceptance of and perseverance in that gift. These qualities are demonstrated through faith, and thus through baptism, prayer, virtue, and repentance of any sins into which he or she nonetheless falls. The human being, despite grace, may fail to persevere in the good.[81] Second, even prior to its reception, the human free will has a certain capacity to act well, by desiring the faith that is itself a divine gift. This "wish to believe," Hrabanus indicates, foreknown by God and leading those who live since the incarnation to seek baptism, is a precondition to election.[82]

Third, that the power of grace is limited and that God elects those who possess a desire for faith, foreknowing but not predestining the damnation

---

Hincmar, e.g. *Ad simplices*, "Zwei Schriften," ed. Gundlach, 267–270, 298–309; see idem, *Ep. 37, MGH Epp.* 8.17–19; *De praed.* 9, 12, 17, *PL* 125.98C/D, 112–114, 117–122,166–168 (Augustine, Prosper, Cassiodorus).

[80] No. 33 *Valence (855)*, ch. 5, *MGH Conc.* 3.355–356.

[81] See Hrabanus, *Epp.* 42, 44, *MGH Epp.* 5.483–486, 491–492 (Prosper, Pseudo-Ambrose, Jerome, Bede); *Ep.* 5, *PL* 112.1544; Hincmar, e.g. *Ad simplices*, "Zwei Schriften," ed. Gundlach, 270, 285 (Prosper); *De praed.* 17, 26, 28, *PL* 125.166D, 269, 288 (Prosper).

[82] Hrabanus, *Ep.* 44, *MGH Epp.* 5.491, esp. lines 33–35: "Hoc autem predestinavit, ut haberet potestatem filius Dei fieri omnis, qui credere voluisset in ipsum; quia nemo filius Dei fieri poterit, nisi fidem et caritatem, quae per dilectionem operatur, habeat."

of the rest of humanity, are understood to accord with the divine will for universal salvation. The doctrine that the scriptural references to God's desire to save all humanity must be interpreted "literally," despite the reality of future damnation, is the one that most clearly highlights the differences between the positions of Hrabanus, Hincmar, and also John Scottus Eriugena, on the one hand, and Gottschalk and his allies on the other. For Hrabanus and Hincmar, the divine will for universal salvation is fulfilled by the universality of the offer made through the crucifixion. The crucified Christ and his blood make grace available to everyone, even though only some mortals are finally saved because they accept this gift and continue in it. In this regard, divine will and act are unified, as Gottschalk claimed they had to be: God acted to achieve the end he wanted, when he "spared not even his own Son, but delivered him up for us all" (Romans 8.32). It is the fault not of God but of mortals who lack faith and freely sin that they face hell, including evidently those who never hear the gospel. Only such a belief, in the archbishops' view, conforms with the doctrine of human free will and the dictates of divine mercy and charity as well as justice.[83]

Although they offer literal interpretations of those biblical verses that seem to express a divine will for universal salvation, both Hincmar and Hrabanus view baptism as crucial to the reception of grace by mortals living since Christ. This is, apparently, the act that demonstrates the desire to believe and constitutes acceptance of God's gift. For Gottschalk, in spite of the temporal cleansing that he believes baptism to provide everyone who receives the sacrament, not all the baptized gain divine grace and hence salvation. But Hrabanus and Hincmar, with support from Prosper, maintain that all participants in baptism – or at least all who approach the sacrament in faith, Hincmar implies – receive the grace offered to all human beings through Christ's blood. That grace, it appears, is synonymous with the "grace of baptism" that removes original and other sins from every recipient of the sacrament.[84] Prosper alludes to the problem of reconciling the concepts that God wants all mortals saved and that baptism

---

[83] E.g. Hrabanus, *Ep.* 42, *MGH Epp.* 5.482, 484, 485 (Prosper); *Ep.* 44, *MGH Epp.* 5.491, 496; *Ep.* 5, *PL* 112.1552–1553. For Hincmar, see below, at n. 90.

[84] See Hrabanus, *Ep.* 42, *MGH Epp.* 5.483–484 (Prosper), *Ep.* 5, *PL* 112.1532, 1542, 1549D-1550A; Hincmar, *De praed.* 22, 23, 26, 32, 35, *PL* 125.200C, 207D-208, 269C, 302C-303 (Bede), 371, 373–382; cf. idem, *Ad simplices*, "Zwei Schriften," ed. Gundlach, 261. On the baptism of infants, where the required faith is that of the parents, Hincmar, *De praed.* 29, 293D-294A (Augustine).

is necessary to salvation, but the issue is never fully resolved in the writings of the two Carolingian archbishops. Why God chooses to allow some to hear the gospel, and not others, remains a mystery with God.[85]

Although the doctrines just outlined represent the core arguments that both Hrabanus and Hincmar present against Gottschalk, it is impossible to see Hincmar's position as merely an outgrowth of the older scholar's, since it is so thoroughly moulded to fit his uniquely imposing personality. Above all in the third treatise – to some extent this is also true in *Ad simplices* and *Explanatio in ferculum Salomonis* – Hincmar's ardor and tenacity as he battles an adversary who chooses to persevere in heresy, in face of the opposition of his ecclesiastical superiors, result in a dramatic expansion of the teachings just noted. A new clarity is lent to some, and others are developed along new paths.

Even more than Hrabanus, first of all, Hincmar stresses the active participation of the elect in their own salvation. As he describes the situation, human beings, though corrupted by original sin, possess an ability and responsibility, preceding grace, to be open to its reception, "cooperate" with it, and "obey their creator and adhere to his mandates and draw themselves to his grace," holding onto it once received. Unless "preceded and aided" by grace, no human being since the fall has been able to adhere to the good.[86] "Whoever seeks shall find," a passage quoted from *De*

---

[85] See Hrabanus, *Ep.* 42, *MGH Epp.* 5.483–484. Amolo of Lyon, who also agreed with Hrabanus' interpretation of Gottschalk's doctrine, sent two *opuscula* and a letter to Gottschalk, accompanied by a collection of *sententiae* of Augustine, underscoring the sacramental concerns that Gottschalk's teachings seemed to him to raise: *Ep.* 2, *PL* 116.84–96; *Opuscula* 1–2, *PL* 116.97–106; *Sententiae*, *PL* 116.105–140. The five actions that Amolo identifies as sacramental — exorcism, laying on of hands, chrism, baptism, and the eucharist – are asserted to benefit those with faith. The "grace of baptism" washes those who approach the sacrament with true piety of their sins in Christ's blood. While Amolo seems to believe in predestination to damnation, stressing that it follows from divine foreknowledge of sin, he implies that this predestination is not immutable, and he distinguishes his position from the doctrine of predestination to sin that he ascribes to Gottschalk: *Ep.* 2, *PL* 116.91D–92A. In Amolo's belief, the mortal can lose grace and redemption after it is granted, so as to face eternal damnation, and have it restored by God. Those who are redeemed by baptism and other sacraments include mortals possessing a faith they will later lose: *Ep.* 2, *PL* 116.87D-88C. The grace given in baptism is also bestowed daily in every good thought, work, and speech. Through this grace, sins are remitted for those who humbly confess; true confession and penance may help sinners to the restoration of grace: *Opusc.* 2, *PL* 116.101, see *Ep.* 2, *PL* 116.92. On Florus' responsibility for the Augustinian *sententiae*, Ganz, "Debate," 294.

[86] Hincmar, e.g. *Ad simplices*, "Zwei Schriften," ed. Gundlach, 269, 293–294; no. 28 *Quierzy (853)*, ch. 3, *MGH Conc.* 3.297; idem, *De praed.* 12, 21, *Epil.* 5, *PL* 125.117D-118A, 185 (Augustine), 188D (*Hypomnesticon*), 190 (Gregory I), 449D-450A.

obduratione cordis Pharaonis in *Ad simplices* notes, but those who do not actually seek bring damnation on themselves.[87] An excerpt from John
Chrysostom in the third treatise describes the "inestimable" divine mercy
revealed in an imagined speech by God, who calls on the mortal to contribute something to his own salvation – to "lend a hand" – in order to alleviate
the burden of his sins.[88] As a consequence, based on passages from
Augustine and Prosper, Hincmar maintains that in the end not all people
who are elected are saved; the *electio salvandorum*, an initial call from God
that leads the faithful to baptism, is distinguished from the *salvatio electo-
rum*, which guards the soul's health so the mortal can continue to live
rightly, and which is bestowed according to divine predestination on the
smaller number of "elect" whom God foreknows will persevere in grace
until death. Anyone while alive may move between the group of the elect
and the *massa perditionis*. Indeed, at least some dead sinners continue to
have hope of salvation, since they are cleansed of their sins in the fires of
purgatory as they await judgment day. But knowledge of who will ultimately reach heaven rests with God.[89]

Second, some of the most passionate sections of Hincmar's writings on
predestination, especially the third treatise – again with no real parallel in
Hrabanus' work – defend his literal understanding of the divine will for
universal salvation and Christ's redemptive suffering and bloodshed for all
humanity. As the archbishop of Rheims, especially, urges his readers to recognize, in the decrees of Quierzy and other attacks on Gottschalk, these
two doctrines constitute the bedrock of the orthodoxy the monk of Orbais
refuses to accept. Here it is important that we attend with particular care to
some of the language used to defend this position, both Hincmar's own
words and those he takes from the scriptural texts and abundant patristic
literature that he interprets as agreeing with him. Biblical passages such as 1
Timothy 2.4 and 2 Peter 3.9,[90] the church fathers, and the church of Rome,
the "mother who gave birth to us in Christ," he insists, demand belief that
God wants to save everyone and sent Christ for this purpose.[91] It is as false

[87] Hincmar, *Ad simplices*, ed. Gundlach, "Zwei Schriften," 277, see Luke 11.9, 10.
[88] Hincmar, *De praed.* 24, PL 125.220A (Chrysostom, *Hom. de Ps.* 50).
[89] Hincmar, *De praed.* 11, 32, PL 125.109C-110 (Augustine, Prosper), cf. 303 (Bede); *Explan. in ferc. Salom.*, PL 125.820D-821A.
[90] "The Lord delayeth not his promise, as some imagine, but dealeth patiently for your sake, not willing that any should perish, but that all should return to penance."
[91] E.g. Hincmar, *De praed.* 22, 24, PL 125.203, 214 (Bede). See *Ad simplices*, "Zwei Schriften," ed. Gundlach, 287 (Prosper), 307; no. 28: *Quierzy (853)*, chs. 3–4, *MGH Conc.* 3.297.

to say that God does not call all mortals equally to salvation as it is to believe he grants perseverance and obedience only to some.[92] God's will for universal salvation is fulfilled insofar as Christ died for all, in spite of the future damnation of the wicked; again, divine will accords with divine act. References to the "copiousness" of Jesus' death, blood, and redemption confirm his ability to redeem every mortal who desires it. In the words of the *Ferculum Salomonis* commentary, they are washed of their sins in the "living blood of the copious redemption of the immaculate and uncontaminated lamb."[93] Because this is the second Adam who assumed human nature as such, in its entirety, his innocent blood and death offered the entirety of that nature liberation from the original sin imposed by the first Adam, and from every subsequent wrongdoing. There is no human being whose nature he did not assume. Thus the passion made redemption available to everyone of the past, present, and future, even Judas.[94] That in the end many mortals are damned is the result of God's additional desire to allow freedom of the human will, a will that must and can, on its own, accept and persevere in the grace offered to all.

Sometimes the authorities to whom Hincmar refers in support of redemption's universality, such as Prosper of Aquitaine, direct attention to the omnipotence demonstrated by Christ's triumph over death and Satan. As suggested by the fourth *capitulum* of Quierzy, written by Hincmar and paraphrasing Prosper, the "magnitude and copiousness of the price" of redemption stem from the power it involved.[95] An excerpt from Cyprian in

---

[92] Hincmar, *Ad simplices*, "Zwei Schriften," ed. Gundlach, 275, 286–287.

[93] Hincmar, *Explan. in ferc. Salom.*, PL 125.826D. See also *Ad simplices*, "Zwei Schriften," ed. Gundlach, 288–289; *De praed.* 29, PL 125.291A/B.

[94] See Hincmar, *Ad simplices*, "Zwei Schriften," ed. Gundlach, 278, 287–292; *De praed.* 17, 28–30, 32, cf. 33, 34, PL 125.166D, 283–295, 298–311, 311–349, 357A. Mortals alive before Christ are like the crowds who preceded Jesus at his entry into Jerusalem. Just as some of the throng went before Christ and some followed him, so people of both the Old and the New Testaments may merit salvation by faith in his incarnation. All faithful, since time began, are united in Christ's one body: ibid. 32, PL 125.298–299 (Augustine, Bede), 310B, see 305 (Leo I). Cf. Cristiani, "La notion de loi," 97.

[95] No. 28: *Quierzy (853)*, ch. 4, MGH Conc. 3.297: "Christus Iesus dominus noster, sicut nullus homo est, fuit vel erit, cuius natura in illo assumpta non fuerit, ita nullus est, fuit vel erit homo, pro quo passus non fuerit, licet non omnes passionis eius mysterio redimantur. Quia vero omnes passionis eius mysterio non redimuntur, non respicit ad magnitudinem et pretii copiositatem, sed ad infidelium et ad non credentium ea 'fide, quae per' dilectionem 'operatur', respicit partem; quia poculum humanae salutis, quod confectum est infirmitate nostra et virtute divina, habet quidem in se, ut omnibus prosit, sed si non bibitur, non medetur." See Gal. 5.6. Cf. Hincmar, *De praed.* 32, Epil. 6, PL 125.309B, 472D-474B (Prosper).

the third treatise affirms that "by the grace of God [Christ] tasted death for all, handing over his own body even though by nature he is life and the resurrection of the dead. For in order that he crush death by ineffable power, and become in his own flesh the first born from the dead,. . . . he tasted death for all and plundered hell, rising on the third day."[96] "By the blood of our mediator and redeemer," Hincmar declares at the conclusion of the same work, God "snatched us from the power of darkness and transported us into the kingdom of his beloved son."[97] Equally often, though, the universality of redemption is connected less with Christ's victory over death than with his suffering. Because the crucifixion's impact was so far-reaching, it is implied, the experience was uniquely intense. Christ's torments, death, and above all his bleeding had to be great enough to redeem not merely some but all humanity. Hence, they are the supreme manifestations of God's perfect love and mercy, a love and mercy so great that God "did not spare his own son, but handed him over for us all" (Rom. 8.32).[98] An excerpt from Bede, in the third treatise, serves there to emphasize the radical intersection of solitude, humility, and universality in the crucified Jesus: "He alone prays for all, just as he alone suffers for everyone; and just as he is made for us the curse of the cross, and scourged, and crucified, thus for the salvation of all he is crucified like a criminal."[99] For Gottschalk and his allies to claim that Christ died and bled only for the elect is to "diminish and narrow" his "copious" redemption and "empty out" his copious blood, by suggesting it was not sufficient for everyone. On the contrary, "so plentiful is Christ's death that it redeemed the entire world, as long as [the world] believes in him who loved us and washes us of sins in his blood."[100] Yet Hincmar also makes it clear that the magnitude of the new Adam's suffering, bleeding, and death is itself evidence of divine omnipotence. To deny

---

[96] Ibid. 33, *PL* 125.338C.

[97] Ibid. *Epil.* 6, *PL* 125.474B; also *Ad simplices*, "Zwei Schriften," ed. Gundlach, 269: "Et tam copiosa est generis humani redemptio ex sanguine redemptoris nostri, qui ad passionem redemptionis nostrae conflictans cum diabolo et triumphans eum in semetipso non veniret, nisi Adam primus, diabolo suadente, per arbitrii libertatem ab inmortalitate decideret."

[98] See Hincmar, *De praed.* 28, cf. 29, 32, 33, *Epil.* 6, *PL* 125.286C (Chrysostom); 286–288, 291D, 298C/D, 324C/D (Chrysostom), 342A (Leo I), 454 (Leo I, Augustine), *Ad simplices*, "Zwei Schriften," ed. Gundlach, 288.

[99] Hincmar, *De praed.* 28, 33, *PL* 125.288A, 347D. See *Ad simplices*, "Zwei Schriften," ed. Gundlach, 277; *De praed.* 28, *PL* 125.286–288.

[100] Hincmar, *Ad simplices*, "Zwei Schriften," ed. Gundlach, 288 (Apoc. 1.5), see 269; *De praed.* 29, *PL* 125.291A.

that he offers redemption to every human being, as Gottschalk and his allies do, is to fail to understand scripture and God's power. As declared by Prosper, it is to ignore that the "true and powerful and singular remedy" for original sin was the death of the son of God.[101]

A discussion towards the end of *Ad simplices* concerning the final vision of God deserves attention at this point, because of its thematic relationship with ideas about the crucifixion and the vision expressed in the *Ferculum Salmonis* and third treatise.[102] That both the wicked and the good will stand before Christ's tribunal, Hincmar argues in those two later works, is further evidence that the passion and resurrection were for everyone, for "it is certain that if the lord's passion brought anything to [the reprobate], then the lord also suffered for them."[103] While in Adam everyone dies, then, in Christ all are given life and resurrection, though after they rise from the dead the wicked face eternal punishment whereas the blessed will be glorified, since they are sanctified in Christ's blood.[104] The observations in *Ad simplices* concerning what the elect will behold after their glorification, composed almost entirely of excerpts from Gregory I and Bede, are echoed in the surviving verses of the *Ferculum Salmonis*. According to *Ad simplices*, these comments are again motivated by erroneous teachings of Gottschalk and his supporters, ones that Hincmar implies stand apart from their doctrines of predestination yet have an obvious relationship with them.[105] The heavenly vision of the blessed is a subject to which Hincmar elsewhere also gives consideration;[106] it accords with the broader interest

---

[101] Hincmar, *Ad simplices*, "Zwei Schriften," ed. Gundlach, 291; *De praed.* 32, see 24, 26, 27, PL 125.309B, 214–216, 272–273 (Bede, Augustine, Gregory I, Jerome), 276D.

[102] Hincmar, *Ad simplices*, "Zwei Schriften," ed. Gundlach, 295–297; see Taeger, *Zahlensymbolik*, 148–157.

[103] Hincmar, *De praed.* 28, PL 125.283D. See *Explan. in ferc. Salom.*, PL 125.826.

[104] Hincmar, *De praed.* 28, 34, PL 125.284, 358D-359 (Ambrose, Chrysostom, Hilary). Cf. Gottschalk (on the final resurrection), *Opusc. theol.* 24.1, *Œuvres*, ed. Lambot, 343.

[105] Hincmar, *Ad simplices*, "Zwei Schriften," ed. Gundlach, 263–264, 295–296; see Taeger, *Zahlensymbolik*, 149; D. M. Cappuyns, "Note sur le problème de la vision béatifique au ixe S.," *Recherches de théologies ancienne et médiévale* I (1929), 98–107, at 100–104.

[106] The vision of God is a theme of Hincmar's eucharist doctrine, too, discussed in chapter 6. In general, the concern with vision's role in Christian devotion and with how God will be seen in the second quarter of the ninth century seems to me to indicate the context for the short treatise, *Num Christus corporeis oculis Deum videre potuerit* (PL 106.103–108) by Candidus. Ineichen-Eder ("Candidus-Brun," 186–189) argues that the author was Candidus Wizo, not Bruun; this opinion is repeated by Brunhölzl (*Histoire* 1.2.287) on the grounds that the tract's subject fits better with Wizo. However, the issue that the work addresses was more widely discussed in the period I have just indicated; it is also one subject of a treatise by Hrabanus,

in vision and visions evident in the later Carolingian church and, particularly after c. 850, in the nature of the eschatological vision of God, a development with some connection to the predestination quarrels.

Conceivably, in *Ad simplices*, Hincmar sought to rebut a doctrine attributed to Gottschalk that the resurrected elect would see God with their physical eyes. A letter by Lupus of Ferrières implies that the monk of Orbais holds to this concept, based on his reading of *De civitate Dei* 22, an interpretation of the Augustinian text that Lupus opposes.[107] Against Gottschalk, Hincmar quotes passages from Gregory I's *Moralia in Job* and from Bede distinguishing between the corporeal vision of God given to the damned and the saved at the last judgment, and the experience subsequently prepared for the elect, which is suggested to differ from bodily sight. The emphasis in *Ad simplices*, though, is not on whether the new vision will be corporeal or incorporeal, but on its vast superiority to earthly vision and its reservation solely to the blessed. Thus an excerpt from Gregory states that while all mortals will see Christ's wounded humanity, through the "corruptible eyes of this flesh," the saved alone will contemplate the divine glory and the "light of eternity." A passage from a sermon by Bede compares the experience with the transfiguration, while acknowledging that event's inferiority, and Bede notes that the heavenly contemplation of God can only be enjoyed once the bodies of the elect have been made "incorruptible" and "like to the body of [Christ's] glory" (Philippians 3.21). Aided by grace, the same blessed, Hincmar adds, strive to be pure of heart in this life so that they now see him "with faith" whom they will later behold directly in heaven.[108]

In *Ad simplices* and especially in the third treatise, the concept that the final vision of God, reserved to the blessed, is adumbrated by faith as a form of seeing serves to reinforce the doctrines that salvation is offered to the entire human race and that Christ died for everyone, yet many are still damned. The difference between the blessed and the wicked, Hincmar indicates in his

footnote 106 (*cont.*)

Candidus Bruun's contemporary: *De videndo Deum, de puritate cordis et de modo poenitentiae*, PL 112.1216–1332. On Candidus Wizo vs. Candidus Bruun, see also chapter 4 n. 91.

[107] Lupus, *Ep.* 30, MGH Epp. 6, ed. E. Dümmler (Berlin, 1925), 36–39; Augustine, *De civitate Dei* 22.29; Taeger, *Zahlensymbolik*, 149, 154–155. Hrabanus' position is similar to Lupus', in his *De videndo Deum*, written 842–856: PL 112.1261–1282. See Cappuyns, "Vision béatifique," 100–101.

[108] Hincmar, *Ad simplices*, "Zwei Schriften," ed. Gundlach, 295–297 (Gregory I, *Moralia* 4.3; Bede, *Hom.* 1.24).

own words and through his authorities, is one between sight and blindness or, as a corollary, between light or revelation and darkness or shadows. Underlying these passages is again the conviction that grace is there for all mortals, but each person must turn to God or Christ in faith, as towards a vision or source of light that anyone may see who desires to do so, and remain turned towards that "sight" in order to receive this gift. As is asserted in *Ad simplices*, the person obedient to the command of Psalm 33.6 ("Come ye to him and be enlightened") is the "son of the promise." Whoever "averts his eyes from the light," however, "surely does no harm to the light but will condemn himself to the shadows" and be alienated from salvation.[109] "Behold the head, behold the light of the predestined, behold the example of predestination," Hincmar declares of Christ in the third treatise.[110] Christ was the light given to the peoples of both the Old and New Testaments; but while Israel had the greater glory, the revelation was to the gentiles, "whose eyes of the mind, submerged in profound blindness . . . he deigned to visit, likewise to open and illumine." Abraham, Isaiah, Micah, and other prophets all "saw the lord's glory, for which reason they are called the seeing ones [*videntes*]," and all faithful, before and after Christ, "share the most joyful promise: 'Blessed are the clean of heart: for they shall see God.'"[111]

Sometimes allusions to Christ's interview with Nicodemus in John 3 identify the source of light and the subject of contemplation for the blessed in this life specifically as the crucified Jesus, the new brazen serpent. In Hincmar's belief, this is a gospel text that Gottschalk and his associates misunderstand to support the erroneous doctrine of predestination to damnation. For Hincmar, there is no question John 3.14–16 means that "for all men the son of man was exalted on the cross, and the only begotten son of God was given for the world, so that in him salvation was prepared for all, yet everyone who believes in him shall not perish."[112] The bronze serpent that prefigured Christ's death healed those bitten by the snakes, a passage from Augustine's tractates on John notes, though only the individual who confesses his sins and does truth comes to the light.[113] Gottschalk's doctrine that Christ was not crucified for the whole world shows he does not love his

[109] Hincmar, *Ad simplices*, "Zwei Schriften," ed. Gundlach, 287–288; *De praed.* 28, PL 125.285C (Prosper).   [110] Hincmar, *De praed.* 12, PL 125.119B, see 120D.

[111] Ibid. 32, PL 125.299B/C (Bede); Matth. 5.8.

[112] See Hincmar, *De praed.* 28, PL 125.285D-286A. Cf. no. 33: *Valence (855)*, ch. 4, *MGH Conc.* 3.354–355.   [113] Hincmar, *De praed.* 24, PL 125.215A/B (Augustine, *Tract.*12.13).

redeemer, who said in John 3.16, "For God so loved the world, as to give his
only begotten son, that whosoever believeth in him, may not perish, but
may have life everlasting." Hence Hincmar explains, quoting Bede, "those
who look upon the mystery of the lord's passion by believing, confessing,
sincerely imitating are saved in eternity from every death contracted
through sins of the soul as much as of the flesh."[114]

Finally, more than any other Carolingian writer on predestination, and
again at greatest length in the third treatise, Hincmar stresses the role of
penance and the eucharist in the mortal's voluntary, active turning to God
or Christ in order to be redeemed, and thus their function as the channels
for the seeing of Christ in faith. Christ is inwardly contemplated through
the sacraments, especially the eucharist, which is properly consumed only
once the soul has been cleansed of sin through penitence. The elect, therefore, who first demonstrate their adherence to the crucified Christ through
baptism, continue to live rightly by prayer, penance, and participation in
the mass, acts that constitute the "preparation" of God's grace and the
means by which "the predestined come to the eternal life predestined for
them." Whereas Gottschalk believes he can only weep for his sins if God
wills it, through the grace bestowed on him as one of the elect, Hincmar
perceives the tears of repentance as a necessary precondition to the reception of grace.[115] Sinners living under the Old Testament also had to repent
and receive the sacraments, which were "spiritually" available to them.[116]
Pharaoh, like Judas, was eternally damned because he failed to be penitent
for his sins. "If Saul had joined his tears with the tears that Samuel poured
out for him, he would not have been forever cast from the lord"; and Adam
and Eve, "we believe from the sayings of the blessed Augustine and other
saints, shall return by God's grace through penance to salvation in Christ's
blood."[117]

Where Hincmar's focus is on baptism and penance, the crucifixion's
redemptive efficacy is usually understood to flow through washing in the

[114] Hincmar, *Ad simplices*, "Zwei Schriften," ed. Gundlach, 288; *De praed.* 29, see 26, *Epil.* 5, *PL*
125.291D-292A (Bede, *Hom.* 2.18), 269C/D, 450C/D.
[115] Hincmar, *De praed.* 22, see 23, 35, *PL* 125.197 (Celestine), 207D-208, 371 (Augustine, Bede); *Ad
simplices*, "Zwei Schriften," ed. Grundlach, 288–289, 300. Cf. Gottschalk, F.III.9, *Gedichte*, ed.
Weber, 160–175.
[116] E.g. Hincmar, *De praed.* 32, *Epil.* 6, *PL* 125.310D-311 (Augustine, Ambrose), 458–459.
[117] Hincmar, *Ad simplices*, "Zwei Schriften," ed. Gundlach, 278 (Pseudo-Jerome, Chrysostom); *De
praed.* 26, 32, *Epil.* 3, *PL* 125.271D-272A, 309D-311A (Chrysostom, Augustine, Leo I), 430C.

blood released by Christ's sacrifice. Where his two extant treatises on pre-destination draw attention to the eucharist, like his *Ferculum Salomonis* and also *De cavendis vitiis et virtutibus exercendis*, whose doctrine of the eucharis-tic presence is discussed in the next chapter, they recall the passion for its cleansing through the sacrificial blood and for the atoning oblation that provides divinely blessed, healing food and drink, the source of unity between recipients and God.[118] Emphasizing the divine empowerment of this food, a passage near the end of the third treatise identifies it with Christ, the living bread from heaven (John 6.52) and the fruit of the tree of life, a pleasure forbidden to mortals "until he should come who was fore-shadowed, of whom it is also said that he is the tree of life, namely Christ, the power and wisdom of God."[119] For Hincmar, as the *Ferculum Salomonis* and *De cavendis* indicate, the fruit of that tree is the body and blood of the crucified savior. In general, however, whether the subject is the eucharist, penance, or baptism, the emphasis is on Christ's blood. Spilled to offer redemption to all humanity, it finally saves those who faithfully turn to him to be purged in baptism and penance, and who daily drink the saving liquid.[120] In the third treatise, references to the fourth *capitulum* of Quierzy, developed from statements by Prosper, reiterate the importance of receiv-ing the eucharistic chalice and thus actively participating with God in one's own salvation: "The cup of human salvation, fashioned from our infirmity and divine power, certainly has in it what benefits all, but if it is not drunk it does not heal."[121]

John Scottus Eriugena

The most distinctive refutation of Gottschalk's predestination doctrine was proposed by John Scottus Eriugena in his *De praedestinatione*. It was challenged by Florus of Lyons and Prudentius of Troyes and condemned

[118] Hincmar, *Ad simplices*, "Zwei Schriften," ed. Gundlach, 288–289 (Bede); *De praed.* 32, *Epil.* 1, PL 125.304C/D (Bede), 419–420.

[119] Hincmar, *De praed. Epil.* 6, PL 125.459A (see Augustine, *De Genesi ad litteram* 8.5.9, 11.40.54; *De civ. Dei* 13.20–21). Cf. Pascasius, *De corpore et sanguine Domini* 7, CCCM 16, ed. B. Paulus (Turnhout, 1969), 39; Gottschalk, *Opusc. theol.* 23, *Œuvres*, ed. Lambot, 328.

[120] E.g. Hincmar, *Ad simplices*, "Zwei Schriften," ed. Gundlach, 288–289, 290–291; *De praed.* 26, 28, 32, 35, PL 125.271D, 288 (Bede, Prosper), 302D (Bede), 304C/D (Bede), 309B/C (Prosper), 311 (Augustine, Ambrose), 371C/D (Bede), 373D (Augustine), 375 (Chrysostom).

[121] See Hincmar, *De praed.* 27, 28, 30, 34, PL 125.282B/C, 288C, 295A/B, 368D-369A.

twice, at the synods of Valence (855) and Langres (859). John Scottus never directly answered the attacks, but John Marenbon has shown that parts of his great work, *Periphyseon*, completed c. 867, elaborate on ideas set forth in his earlier treatise in ways that suggest his consciousness of the opposition they raised.[122] In *De praedestinatione*, the chief patristic source for John Scottus' rebuttal of Gottschalk is Augustine, though his teachings emphasize dialectical reasoning alongside argumentation from scripture and patristic authority.[123] In *Periphyseon*, his views are additionally shaped by the familiarity he achieved with the Greek theologians, Pseudo-Dionysius, Maximus the Confessor, and Gregory of Nyssa by his translations of their works. Yet although obviously major differences exist between the two treatises by John Scottus, where they touch on the same issues their thought is compatible. *De praedestinatione* expresses beliefs that fit within the larger doctrinal framework set out in the later tractate.[124] The texts in which John Scottus explores the crucifixion's purpose at greatest length, the surviving fragments of his commentary on John[125] and, most important, his poems celebrating the cross and the crucified and resurrected Christ, seem to date from between 859 and John Scottus' death sometime after 870. They, too, reflect the theological system more clearly outlined in the two doctrinal treatises, and were possibly written with his opponents again in mind. It is in light of *De praedestinatione* and *Periphyseon*, therefore, that the commentary and poetry on the crucifixion are best examined.[126]

As Marenbon has noted, John Scottus shares some of the basic assumptions about Gottschalk's ideas found in the writings of Hrabanus and

[122] *Periphyseon*, Books 1–3, CCCM 161–163, ed. E. Jeauneau (Turnhout, 1996–1999); *Periphyseon (De diuisione naturae)* 4, ed. E. Jeauneau with the assistance of Mark Zier, trans. J. J. O'Meara and I. P. Sheldon-Williams, Scriptores Latini Hiberniae 13 (Dublin, 1995). The full treatise (including Book 5) is published in *PL* 122. Translation of the entirety by I. P. Sheldon-Williams, revised by John J. O'Meara, *Eriugena, Periphyseon (Division of Nature)* (Montreal, 1987).

[123] Prudentius attacked John Scottus for his emphasis on reason, yet ironically he himself turned to the *Categoriae decem* for assistance: Ganz, "Debate," 293.

[124] Marenbon, "John Scottus," 314–323; idem, "Carolingian Thought," 184–187.

[125] *In Iohannis Evangelium*, SC 180, ed. E. Jeauneau (Paris, 1972).

[126] My discussion of the thought set forth in these writings is indebted to the work of other historians who have unraveled its complexities. Especially helpful among recent studies are Marenbon, "John Scottus"; O'Meara, *Eriugena*; Gangolf Schrimpf, "Der Beitrag des Johann Scottus Eriugena zum Prädestinationsstreit," in *Die Iren und Europa im früheren Mittelalter*, 2 vols., ed. H. Löwe (Stuttgart, 1982), 2.819–865; idem, *Das Werk des Johannes Scottus Eriugena im Rahmen des Wissenschaftsverständnisses seiner Zeit* (Münster, 1982); Cristiani, "La notion de loi."

Hincmar, as well as some of their objections.[127] Like both contemporaries, for example, he believes that Gottschalk's concept of twin predestination erroneously attributes evil to God, against the doctrine of divine goodness, and that it denies God's infinite justice and human free will by asserting divine punishment of individuals for sins they are forced to commit. But while John Scottus had numerous contacts within later Carolingian intellectual circles and enjoyed the favor of Charles the Bald throughout his scholarly career in the Carolingian Empire,[128] the starting point of his refutation of Gottschalk and the methods by which he pursues this task are altogether different from those of either Hrabanus or Hincmar, not to mention the incomprehension and hostility they aroused among Gottschalk's supporters. At the core of John Scottus' teachings on predestination lie, first, the notion of God's perfect simplicity, and second a radical separation of creation from evil. Christian theology, John Scottus insists, teaches that God is one. God's being can possess no opposites, it cannot for instance be both good and evil, since this would ascribe duality to him. Therefore since God is perfect goodness, he cannot be the source of evil in any form, and the creation that comes from him can only be good. Similarly, all God's other qualities must be simple – possessing the attribute of oneness – including those that theologians refer to as foreknowledge and predestination. There can be only one divine predestination and one divine foreknowledge; to defend the concept of twin predestination stems from the same error as the notion that the divine substance is triple – John Scottus' understanding of Gottschalk's doctrine of the trine deity.[129] Indeed, divine predestination and foreknowledge are identical since they belong to the one God. Given God's unity, it is in fact wrong to say that he possesses different qualities at all. More correctly, God *is* his predestination and foreknowledge, just as he is goodness and truth.

The terms predestination and foreknowledge are also inadequate since they imply a temporal quality to divine operation, when instead God's eternity means that he operates entirely outside of time. Despite theologians' frequent usage of such terminology, God's predestination is already his act and his foreknowledge is his knowledge.[130] As a result, God's single predestination, which is identical with his foreknowledge and his act, must

---

[127] Marenbon, "John Scottus," 304–308.   [128] Herren, ed., *Carmina*, 2–5.
[129] See Ganz, "Theology," 770; Devisse, *Hincmar* I.154–186.
[130] See John Scottus, *De praed.* 2, 9, CCCM 50.9–18, 55–61.

be a predestination to salvation, both because it must concern his creation, which coming from him is necessarily good, and because whatever lies outside God's creation – that is, evil – lies outside his act and knowledge. Strictly speaking, God cannot know evil any more than he can perform a wicked act. It is critical to John Scottus' reasoning that evil, as something separate from creation, is not merely the absence of good but itself lacks essence, since it does not come from God who is the source of all being. Evil is not a substance, but only substances can be known. We are aware of evil only insofar as it is "known by not knowing," or "not known by being known." In the strict sense, therefore, God has nothing to do with wickedness, including sin and its punishment. He does not create, destine, or predestine evil, he does not know or foreknow it.[131]

These ideas provide the grounds for John Scottus' solution to one problem that the predestination controversy posed and to which we have seen Gottschalk, Hrabanus and Hincmar, and to some extent Gottschalk's allies offer different solutions: the apparent conflict between the doctrine of eternal damnation of the wicked and the scriptural passages that seem to describe a divine will for universal salvation. Like both archbishops, John Scottus argues against Gottschalk that God does desire the salvation of all humanity; the biblical verses suggesting this must be interpreted literally. But his reasoning in favor of the position is very different from that of his two associates. He, too, considers Gottschalk's teachings to destroy the divine gifts of both human free will and grace.[132] Like human nature, John Scottus maintains, the free will is a substance that is part of the divine creation and hence inherently good, a substance that man possesses as a rational creature because he is made to God's image and likeness. But when grace was lost in Adam's fall, the vigor and power it provided the will, by which it clings to the good of obedience to God, also disappeared.[133] Thus weakened, the will remains free, as shown by its continued "natural" desire to live in beatitude and escape misery, yet it now possesses an "irrational and perverse motion" away from its creator that is not a substance, not part of

---

[131] See ibid. 3.3, 15.8, 18.4, *CCCM* 50.21, 91–92, 112–113; O'Meara, *Eriugena*, 41, on John Scottus' interpretation of Augustine on this point; Cristiani, "La notion de loi," 107–108.

[132] John Scottus, *De praed.* 4.1–4, *CCCM* 50.26–30.

[133] In Adam, the free will, strengthened by grace, was able both to desire the good and pursue it, remaining obedient to the one God. What was lost when Adam chose evil was not free will *per se*, because no substance can perish, but grace and the vigor and power it provided: John Scottus, *De praed.* 4.6, *CCCM* 50.31–32.

God's creation, and is therefore evil. Mortals are fully responsible for their misdeeds, which are voluntary and so can be properly judged on the last day, but they cannot approach God and the good without grace, which "cooperates" with their own efforts.[134] Only the elect, the "saints" whom God chose before the beginning of time because he foresaw the faith that enables them to turn to Christ, receive the divine grace by which the free will is "prepared, aided, crowned."[135] Because of this gift, freely given and – for John Scottus as for his associates – freely accepted, the wills of the elect are liberated of sin's burden. Their vigor and power is restored, so that they desire the good and, through their own efforts with grace cooperating, persevere in it.[136]

For Hrabanus and Hincmar, that Christ died for the entire human race, offering grace to every individual who was free to accept and persevere in it, fulfills the dictates of God's will for universal salvation. God wants everyone to be saved, and in the sacrifice of his only son he established the mechanism for all to be redeemed of sin; but the free will he also provides means that some mortals choose sin over grace, as he foreknows they will, for which divine justice rightly condemns them. While God predestines the final torments of the wicked, he does not predestine anyone *to* hell or the sin that earns the penalty, actions that would conflict with the divine will for universal salvation. Christians should fully believe in the agony awaiting the damned, then, but they should also know that the crucified Christ made it possible for them to escape that destiny, if they continue in faith, follow the church's teachings, and seek remission of their sins in penance and the sacraments. John Scottus' *De praedestinatione*, though, his outlook evidently less in tune with pastoral responsibilities, stresses the evil of both sin and damnation because both consist of the absence of the divine. God is the creator of neither sin nor its penalty, and therefore he does not judge or punish the wicked any more than he predestines them to damnation. Rather, his law, which is itself a good, ensures that sinners are punished by their own wickedness.[137] God "predestines" them only in the sense that before the beginning of time he defined their precise number,

---

[134] Ibid. 2.3, 4–5, 7.4–5, *CCCM* 50.15, 32–41, 47–48. Cf. Cristiani, "La notion de loi," 104–105.

[135] John Scottus, *De praed.* 4.4, *CCCM* 50.30.

[136] Ibid. 4.2, *CCCM* 50.27–28; Cristiani, "La notion de loi," 105.

[137] John Scottus, *De praed.* 5.3, 10, 15.8, 18.5, *CCCM* 50.36, 62–66, 91, 113. The holy authors who refer to mortals predestined to death, hell, or punishment speak abusively: ibid. 5.3, *CCCM* 50.36. See Ganz, "Theology," 770–771; Marenbon, "John Scottus," 309–310.

based on his foreknowledge of their sinfulness. On that basis, he abandons them to the punishment of their evil wills that they deserve and that they create for themselves. For the fire they face at the end of time stems from eternal separation from God, the true light, the source of all being and goodness, a darkness that is apart from the divine and that they voluntarily choose. Furthermore, that which will be punished, indeed is already punished insofar as it already turns from God, is the sinful will as distinct from human nature, which God can never destroy since it is part of his own, good creation. While it is legitimate to speak of hell and damnation, therefore, though only in the sense just noted, and also of the grace with which the elect alone cooperate, human nature as such will have no part in the penalty faced by sin.[138]

The salvation of human nature, the highest order of creation because it is made to the image and likeness of God, is dependent on Christ the second Adam's assumption of humanity in the incarnation.[139] An important theme in both the extant fragments of the commentary on John, a work probably left incomplete at John Scottus' death in the early 870s,[140] and the poetry is the bestowal of illumination on earth by means of Jesus' birth. The light that lay hidden in the father became visible when Christ was born of the Virgin, whose "blessed belly" sustained "a flame divine."[141] Parts of the exegesis of John 3 and much of the poetry take a sweeping view of the son's descent from and reascent to the father, from the incarnation through the ascension, as the restoration of light to the darkened world. The shadows of evil were overcome and mortals gained the ability to contemplate or "see" celestial things. Thus the poem just quoted opens by inviting Charles the Bald to gaze on heaven through the "path of the mind," as he is able to do because of the incarnation.[142] Another describes the astonishment of the shades in hell at the light that appeared when Christ entered; yet another recalls that he vanquished the night and led

---

[138] See John Scottus, *De praed.* 18.5, 18.8–10, 19, *CCCM* 50.113–114, 116–120. For John Scottus, sin is punished in the very effort to surpass the limits established by eternal law, which assure the universe's perfect ordering: Cristiani, "La notion de loi," 110–113. John Scottus' discussion of the forms of future punishment in *Periphyseon* 5 was perhaps influenced by his opponents' criticisms. See O'Meara, *Eriugena*, 145; Marenbon, "John Scottus," 319.

[139] See John Scottus, *In Ioh.* 1.31, *SC* 180.172–177, 3.6, *SC* 180.230–235.

[140] Jeauneau, ed., ibid., *SC* 180.20–21, 78–80.

[141] John Scottus, Poem 8, *Carmina*, ed. Herren, 84–89 lines 45–50, 65.

[142] John Scottus, Poem 8, ibid., 84–89 lines 1–4.

mortals home, "wretched and withdrawn from the light of heaven."[143] According to the commentary on John 3, the baptized, who are "spiritual men," turn towards the light of truth manifested in the incarnate Christ and abandon the darkness of disbelief in which impious, "carnal men" try to hide, remaining in the shadows of their own sins. Members through grace of the one, reascended body of Christ, these blessed ascend with him now in faith and hope, at the end of time in reality, to the supernal vision.[144]

In both the commentary and the poetry, however, it is the passion, specifically, that bestows grace on the elect and makes possible human nature's initial separation from sin, so that the nature can be saved while the wickedness is overcome.[145] In the commentary on John 3, as is generally not true in the poems, the crucifixion's special significance to humanity's salvation has to do primarily with Jesus' death. The analysis of the speech about the brazen serpent in John 3.14–16 presents the death on the cross, the divine sacrifice of the unique son in love for the human race, as the pivotal moment in human redemption.[146] Those who do not believe in the crucified Christ whom the serpent prefigured will be judged and condemned for their lack of faith and sinfulness, even as human nature itself is saved; faithlessness is its own punishment. But all who have faith in him and in his death as the release from sin, showing their faith in baptism, receive the grace that his crucifixion brought. This heals them of sin and joins them to the company of the elect, whose faith constitutes a turning towards the light of the crucified savior.[147] In the poems, on the other hand, the focus is not Christ's oblation of humanity or the individual mortal's need to participate in salvation by accepting and cooperating with grace. Instead, it is the divine omnipotence and the crucifixion as a universal victory over sin/death/Satan that prepares for and blends with the harrowing of hell to which John Scottus devotes greater attention. The two perspectives are clearly different sides of the same equation, insofar as both examine the separation of human nature from evil achieved through the passion; but the difference in outlook is nonetheless

[143] John Scottus, Poem 9, ibid., 90–95 lines 7–8; Poem 25, ibid., 116–121 lines 23–28; cf. Poems 6, 7, ibid., 80–83.
[144] See John Scottus, *In Ioh.* 3.5, 6, SC 180.222–229, 234–237; cf. Poem 8, *Carmina*, ed. Herren, 84–89.
[145] A fine image expressive of this idea is used in Poem 2. Lines 33–42 describe the soul that, thanks to Christ and the cross, is liberated from Egypt and passes through the Red Sea to the "happy shore" while its sins, symbolized by Pharaoh, are "vanquished and drowned" in the same waters: ibid., 64–67.   [146] John Scottus, *In Ioh.* 3.5, 6, SC 180.222–33.
[147] Ibid., *In Ioh.* 3.6, SC 180.234–237.

striking. According to John Scottus' verses, the crucifixion and harrowing of hell together accomplished a victory through which there is no doubt that the totality of human nature has been, or will be, fully liberated from the forces of sin and death. Past, present, and future merge into a single moment of universal triumph. Hell itself has already, in a sense, ceased to exist. The crucified Christ "approached the walls of hell," vanquished the "prince of the abyss," casting him from his seat, emptied the underworld of its prisoners, and restored "what was lost in our nature" as he himself "leapt from hell."[148] Its captives ascend from darkness into the light, a foreshadowing of or preliminary stage to their future ascent to heaven.[149] Covered in blood, the lord unlocked the "fount of salvation" in his side, from which flowed the water that washes the entire world clean of the ancient sin. By his death in the flesh, he "ruined death, which had devoured the entire world."[150] In a complicated passage that works this theme into an analysis of Jesus' two natures, one poem describes the "flesh of life" that died on the cross yet "by living and dying consumed all death," since it was the flesh of the word.[151] As another poem reveals, the cross through which the church is redeemed is the weapon of conquest, opening a path into hell along which all prisoners might pass just as the same cross earlier divided the Red Sea. Now it embraces the "earth, sea, winds, sky, and all else," symbol of the savior's eternal dominion.[152] The blood, too, is filled with divine power, even more than the water that also came from Christ's side. It is the blood that transforms mortals into gods. Poured out as an offering, its wave flowing from the word of God, it bathes the altar of the cross and "purges, redeems, releases, leads us back to life." This is the "potent antidote" that protects its drinkers, while those who refuse it perish.[153]

The image of the omnipotent blood of the crucifixion is also developed in a passage of *Periphyseon* 5, one of the few places in John Scottus' doctrinal treatises that discuss the passion's significance at any length. In an analogy

---

[148] See John Scottus, Poem 2, *Carmina*, ed. Herren, 64–67 lines 5, 19–20, 35–36, 50; Poem 3, ibid., 68–71 lines 48, 59–60; Poem 6, ibid., 80–83 lines 11–13, 20; Poem 8, ibid., 84–89 line 75; Poem 9, ibid., 90–95 lines 30, 52.

[149] John Scottus, Poem 2, ibid., 64–67 lines 48–50; Poem 7, ibid., 82–83 lines 1–6, 17–18.

[150] John Scottus, Poem 1, ibid., 58–63 lines 8, 25–27; Poem 8, ibid., 84–89 lines 53–54, 60. See *De praed.* 18.5, *CCCM* 50.113.   [151] John Scottus, Poem 9, *Carmina*, ed. Herren, 90–95 lines 15–24.

[152] John Scottus, Poem 2, ibid., 64–67 lines 3, 6, 13, 23.

[153] John Scottus, Poem 1, ibid., 58–63 line 28; Poem 2, ibid., 64–67 lines 57–60; Poem 3, ibid., 68–71 lines 51–55; Poem 8, ibid., 84–89 lines 76–78; see Poem 25, ibid., 116–121 line 76.

between the last day and the crossing of the Red Sea, the crucifixion is envisioned as a triumph completed when the world ends. Christ's blood and the gift of grace resulting from it are the future cause of, simultaneously, humanity's total redemption and evil's final downfall. Just as the Red Sea rescued the ancient Israelites from slavery but drowned Pharaoh and his army, so the blood of the crucifixion will ultimately purge the entire human race while drowning "the wickedness of the devil in everlasting damnation." Humanity's salvation will be Satan's destruction, "for the pride of the devil can suffer no greater penalty or deeper affliction than his envy at man's salvation and the consequent despair." Christ's final victory is the "perfection" of the baptism received in this life. The sacrament will become universal, since it will affect the whole of human nature through the "infinite vastness and depth of the effusion of grace" poured forth "in payment" for his blood. Thus human nature in its entirety will regain the pristine simplicity of its prelapsarian existence, while sins are punished.[154]

Although the themes of the omnipotent victory and revelation of divine majesty in this passage and the poetry are thoroughly traditional and recur in innumerable other Carolingian writings, especially verse, the cosmic scale that John Scottus ascribes to these accomplishments seems unprecedented in early medieval Latin literature. As the portion of *Periphyseon* just noted indicates, the sundering of human nature from sin, which the poetry links with the crucifixion and harrowing of hell – the liberation of the underworld's prisoners while the prince of the abyss remains enchained[155] – will only be completed at the end of time. *Periphyseon* clearly shows that God's eternal retreat from evil, culminating in the eschaton when every wickedness will be punished by separation from the divine, is part of the same process by which the whole of creation is restored to him from whom it draws existence. The saved world will be identical with the nature that the new Adam assumed; the inferior orders of creation will be taken up into superior, until the entire created universe has participated in the restoration. Two types of return to God are distinguished in this process, however, one general and the other special.[156] Through the former, it seems, the "essence" of every sensible thing will live forever, in that every impurity

---

[154] John Scottus, *Periph.* 5, *PL* 122.1002, trans. O'Meara, *Periphyseon*, 690. Cf. Augustine, *Tract.* 11.4.

[155] Esp. John Scottus, Poem 6, *Carmina*, ed. Herren, 80–83.

[156] John Scottus, *Periph.* 5, *PL* 122.1001–1002, cf. 1005; trans. O'Meara, *Periphyseon*, 689, 690, 694–695.

added to nature will disappear, including the interior ugliness caused by sin.[157] The "special" return only applies to the elect, who, John Scottus asserts, eat the fruit of the tree of life that is Christ in contemplation of the word.[158] Theirs is the superessential level of existence described in *Periphyseon* 5 as deification and alluded to in the poems that refer to the transformation of mortals into gods.[159] "For being and living and immortality will be common to all, good and evil alike; but well-being and blessed being will be the special property of those only who are perfect in practice and theory."[160] They alone will enjoy theophanies, though of differing degrees based on the differences among their states of blessedness.[161] The divine will for universal salvation is realized not simply by an offer of redemption to all, as Hrabanus and Hincmar claim. For John Scottus, God through Christ provides for the salvation of everything he created and effects it in the final return. Divine will accords with divine act. The doctrine that God wants all humanity to be saved is reconciled with that of his damnation of the wicked insofar as eternal punishment is assigned to sin, whereas human nature along with the rest of creation will ultimately rejoin its creator.

Conclusion

For Gottschalk, John Scottus, Hrabanus, and Hincmar, as to some degree is true for the other scholars discussed in this chapter, the dispute over God's

---

[157] John Scottus, *Periph.* 5, PL 122.868, 871D-872A, trans. O'Meara, *Periphyseon,* 531, 536; see O'Meara, *Eriugena*, 137, 142–147.

[158] See John Scottus, *Periph.* 5, PL 122.859–863, trans. O'Meara, *Periphyseon*, 523–526; cf. *Periph.* 5, PL 122.1002–1003, 1011–1012, trans. O'Meara, *Periphyseon*, 691, 702. See Donald F. Duclow, "Denial or Promise of the Tree of Life? Eriugena, Augustine, and Genesis 3:22b," in *Iohannes Scottus Eriugena: the Bible and Hermeneutics*, ed. Gerd Van Riel et al. (Leuven, 1996), 221–238; John J. O'Meara, "Eriugena's Use of Augustine in His Teaching on the Return of the Soul and the Vision of God," and "Eriugena's Use of Augustine's *De Genesi ad litteram* in the *Periphyseon*," in idem, *Studies in Augustine and Eriugena*, ed. T. Halton (Washington, DC, 1992), 244–254, 269–283.

[159] See John Scottus, *Periph.* 5, PL 122.1011–1015, trans. O'Meara, *Periphyseon*, 701–706; idem, Poem 1, *Carmina*, ed. Herren, 58–63 line 28; Poem 2, ibid., 64–67 lines 57–60.

[160] John Scottus, *Periph.* 5, PL 122.868B, trans. O'Meara, *Periphyseon*, 532.

[161] See John Scottus, *Periph.* 5, PL 122.1012–1015, trans. O'Meara, *Periphyseon*, 703–706. Such apparitions do not constitute visions of the divine essence, an inaccessible light that no creature can grasp, but the theophanies still allow angels and the blessed to "see" God in ways conforming to corporeal or intellectual nature: *Periph.* 1, CCCM 161.9–16, trans. O'Meara, *Periphyseon*, 31–37. See also *Periph.* 5, PL 122.926C/D, trans. O'Meara, *Periphyseon*, 601–602; Cappuyns, "Vision béatifique," 105–106; Marenbon, "John Scottus," 320–322; O'Meara, *Eriugena*, 145; and on the notions of space and time at the world's end in *Periphyseon* 5, Marenbon, *From the School of Alcuin*, 85–86.

predestination was bound up with the problems of how to interpret scripture's teachings on the divine will for universal salvation and Christ's death for the world, given the biblical doctrine of the final judgment and punishment awaiting the reprobate. These questions were brought to the attention of Carolingian scholars by Gottschalk's claims that predestination to damnation meant God did not seek and Christ did not die to save everyone. If John Scottus' *Periphyseon*, commentary on John, and poems are included, the writings that explore these and related issues span more than twenty years, the most fertile period, intellectually and culturally, of the Carolingian *renovatio*. The ideas they express about the crucifixion's significance have clear similarities to lines of thought seen in other ninth-century Carolingian literature, but each of these theologians gives them new colors, by bringing them into the arsenal of doctrinal material used to argue different beliefs about God's intentions for the eschaton. The passion is one stage in the divine plan for salvation that will be finally accomplished on the last day. Its true meaning lies not simply in what Christians remember about the crucified Christ, but in what they hope or fear will happen when he returns.

Significant differences are evident between Gottschalk's views and those of his allies, and among the doctrines that Hrabanus, Hincmar, and John Scottus espouse on predestination, the crucifixion, and the eschaton. Given the tendency of some modern historians to perceive John Scottus as isolated from the thought of his contemporaries, however, it is useful to clarify the main points on which the elements of his theology just studied overlap, without coinciding completely, with the teachings of Gottschalk's most tenacious opponent, the archbishop of Rheims, and of Hrabanus as far as his letters on predestination reveal. More than John Scottus or Hrabanus, Hincmar stresses the importance of the church's systems of penance and the sacraments to redemption. As he in particular insists, the mortal's ability to hold onto divine grace demands not only baptism in faith but also repeated cleansing of sins in Christ's blood, imitation of his suffering in penance and the eucharist, and regular reception of the healing benefits of that food and drink. All three theologians, though, agree that the scriptural verses that seem to announce God's will for universal salvation have to be interpreted in a "literal" sense. Christ suffered and spilled his blood to offer redemption to every mortal, even if only those who actually turn to him in faith and receive baptism gain remission of sins, and even though human wickedness will be condemned at the final judgment. Second, all three scholars, though Hincmar and John Scottus give this doctrine the most consideration, view the blood as one of the chief instruments of God's fulfillment of his will for universal redemption and one of the supreme signs of salvation's universality. In John Scottus' *Periphyseon*, the "infinite vastness and depth of the effusion of grace" in payment for Christ's blood, capable of purging human nature and destroying Satan, recalls the surging waves of the Red Sea. His poetry celebrates the power of both the cross and the blood; washing the cross and drunk in the eucharist, the wave from Christ's side – water, too, though especially blood – is the key to the elect's deification. According to Hincmar's third treatise, the blood possesses a "copiousness" sufficient for every mortal from the first day to the last. Thus it testifies to both the intensity of Christ's experience in the passion and, again, his omnipotence.

Third, both the archbishop of Rheims and John Scottus follow Augustine in teaching that Jesus is the tree of life who feeds the elect with his fruit. John Scottus' *Periphyseon* links this with the blessed's contemplation of the word in paradise; Hincmar's third treatise turns to Augustine's identification of the fruit with the eucharist. In the archbishop's case, this accords with his emphasis on the sacraments and particularly the eucharist as the means by which the pious experience Christ in the present. Fourth, both Hincmar and John Scottus support their positions by recalling the crucified Christ's status as the new Adam who assumed the totality of human nature, past, present, and future. John Scottus, though, clearly aligns this doctrine and his belief in the blood's cosmic extent with his conviction that all human nature will be saved. The crucifixion and its blood, the harrowing of hell, and the other events in Christ's triumph provided for the separation of the whole of human nature from sin, a reversal of the fall that took place in the first Adam, because Jesus took on that nature in its entirety. The rest of creation will be absorbed into it when the world ends. Hincmar, instead, ties the doctrines of the second Adam and the infinitude of Christ's blood to the universality only of the *offer* of salvation, emphasizing the final punishment that awaits mortals who fail to repent, receive the sacraments, and persevere in grace. For the archbishop of Rheims, as is not true for John Scottus, humanity will be firmly divided into two groups of saved and damned, regardless of the universal reach of salvation's offer. God wills that the "cup of human salvation" be available to all – again, the eucharist is critical – but those who fail to drink are not by any means redeemed.

Fifth, in accordance with the doctrine that the crucifixion's impact was in some manner universal, both John Scottus and Hincmar recognize the passion as a triumph whose consequences reach from heaven down to earth and into hell, and from the beginning to the end of history. While Gottschalk sees the crucifixion as limited to the elect in its efficacy, he, Hincmar, and John Scottus agree in envisioning it as, in part, the shattering victory that overwhelmed the forces of evil. Thus Book 5 of *Periphyseon*, John Scottus' poetry, and portions of the archbishop of Rheims' third treatise proclaim the divine Christ and his conquest, a refrain also heard in Gottschalk's writings on predestination. In Hincmar's belief, Christ's blood defeated the forces of darkness and death, as manifested in his resurrection, the model for the future resurrection of the entire human race so that every mortal can face his judge. The cosmic triumph over sin / death / Satan receives even more spectacular treatment from John Scottus, especially in his poetry, which reflects his belief that the crucified Christ divided human nature from sin so as to lead the former from hell to heaven. Yet both John Scottus in his commentary on John 3 and Hincmar in his third treatise, as in other of his writings, also show concern with Jesus' human death for sin and the message of John 3.14–16 that God's willing sacrifice of his only son demonstrates divine love for sinful mortals. For Hincmar and John Scottus, Jesus' speech on the brazen serpent confirms that the true elect consist of those who turn in faith to the crucified lord, receiving in baptism the gift of divine grace. Of the two thinkers, however, as far as their extant writings reveal, it is Hincmar who most fully develops this last set of ideas. Christ's torments and bloodshed, the "living blood of the copious redemption of the immaculate and spotless lamb,"[162] are suggested to have been uniquely great and a sign of the infinitude of his love for mortals because they had to suffice for the entire world. The oblation made on the cross and the power of the son of God are inextricably connected. Jesus' dying, bleeding flesh is able to redeem sinners because it belongs to the one creator God, and his suffering and death for all humanity attest his glory.

Finally, John Scottus' analysis of the return to God in *Periphyseon* has no real equivalent in Carolingian literature, but Hincmar, too, is interested in

---

[162] Hincmar, *Explan. in ferc. Salom.*, PL 125.826D.

the nature of the final, heavenly vision, and both scholars note its granting to the blessed as the final outcome of God's will for universal salvation. Both writers refer to the experience in terms of the contrast between light, sight, the approach to God and darkness or shadows, blindness, withdrawal from God. Both assert a parallel between the exercise of faith by those who accept the grace rendered available in the crucifixion, and the contemplation of their creator awaiting the elect at the end of time. Faithful perseverance in grace during this life constitutes an inner turning towards or seeing of God, a form of sight that, following John 3, has as its primary subject the crucified Christ, the new brazen serpent, the light that dispels the darkness of sin and unbelief. It is Hincmar, though, who makes it clearest that the inner vision of faith in this life, the basis of the vision of God granted the elect in the next, depends on penance and reception of the eucharist.[163] The possibility that the ivory cover of the Pericopes of Henry II mirrors this and other facets of Hincmar's thought, both where his ideas intersect with those of John Scottus and points at which they diverge, will be explored in chapter 7. Yet before discussing the ivory and two other artistic images that help elucidate its signification, it is necessary to examine the controversy over the nature of the eucharistic presence.

[163] See Hincmar, *Ad simplices*, "Zwei Schriften," ed. Gundlach, 288–289; *De praed. Epil.* 1, *PL* 125.419–420.

CHAPTER 6

One-time sacrifice, daily food and drink: the controversy over the eucharist

Like the texts examined in chapter 4 that discuss the passion's connection with penance, the sacraments, and the liturgy, the writings from the ninth-century eucharist controversy recall Jesus' powerful yet human oblation, his gift through his death of healing food and drink, the unity this imparts, and the church's control of this avenue of redemption. As they were drawn into the conflict over the eucharist, however, theologians were compelled to formulate and defend more precise doctrines than appear in any other Carolingian literature of the crucified Christ's relation to the consecrated bread and wine. In accordance with Jesus' words at the last supper, recorded in the gospels and the canon of the mass, all the churchmen involved in the dispute generally accepted that God makes the body and blood of their savior available in the eucharistic oblation. They agreed, too, that the passion was a unique sacrifice of his body meant to serve once for all time, as declared in the epistle to the Hebrews. Both were well-established beliefs of Carolingian commentators on the liturgy and the New Testament and ones that western Christian theologians had never questioned, since they were soundly based on scripture and the church's prayers. A clear impetus to the quarrel, indeed, lay in the heightened inter-est of ninth-century scholars in exegesis of the liturgy of the mass and Holy Week (including Holy Thursday), the gospels, and the letter to the Hebrews. But in the tractates that analyze the nature of the eucharistic presence and in certain other texts that reflect thinking which evolved in light of the quarrel, as is not typically the case with the material discussed in chapter 4, a major issue is the potential contradiction between the

doctrines of the crucifixion's uniqueness and the mass as a sacrifice of
Christ. The need is recognized to interpret each in a way that would reconcile them; for if the passion happened only once for all salvation history,
how can the mass, too, constitute the oblation of Jesus' body and blood?[1]
As in the predestination debates, considerations of the church's sacramental system are joined to questions regarding the proper interpretation of
the Bible, with both sides finding ammunition in the writings of church
fathers who had not themselves engaged in precisely the same debates.

The critical document in the conflict was the tract *De corpore et sanguine
Domini* that Pascasius Radbertus, monk of Corbie in northern Francia and
its abbot from 843–849, composed in 831–833 for the brothers of Corvey, a
monastery in Saxony founded by Corbie monks. The request for the treatise came from Corvey's abbot, Warin. Pascasius gave a revised edition of
his work to Charles the Bald, probably at the time of the monarch's visit to
Corbie at Christmas 843 or Easter 844.[2] Like other Carolingian commentators on the mass – *De corpore*'s first edition was finished about the same
time as Amalarius' third edition of the *Liber officialis* [3] – he sought to
clarify the meaning of the primary, daily ceremony of the Christian
liturgy. Rather than focusing on the signification of the mass ceremonial,
though, as does Amalarius, Pascasius sent to Corvey an explanation of the
eucharist's sacramental nature and purpose that investigates its status as
both figure and Christ's body and blood. The eucharist, he asserts, contains
the incarnate and crucified, or "historical" blood and flesh, an opinion that
I will here refer to as the "Pascasian doctrine." While the treatise's lengthy
discussion covers other topics pertaining to the sacrament's celebration, it
was the identification of the eucharistic presence with the incarnate body
and blood, the very entities sacrificed on the cross, that seems to have con-

---

[1] The issue is adumbrated in Alcuin's commentary on Hebrews: *Ad Hebraeos* 10, *PL* 100.1077B-D
(Chrysostom).

[2] *De corpore et sanguine Domini cum appendice epistola ad Fredugardum*, CCCM 16, ed. B. Paulus
(Turnhout, 1969), 1–131, see ix–x; Ganz, *Corbie*, 31–32.

[3] See Hanssens, ed., *ST* 138.161–162. Although Pascasius' treatise is non-polemical, Giorgio
Picasso suggests that it may have been indirectly inspired by concern over Amalarius' notion of
the "triform" body of Christ in the eucharist: "Riti eucaristici nella società altomedievale. Sul
significato storico del trattato eucaristico di Pascasio Radberto," *Segni e riti* 2.505–532, at
512–514. However, while Pascasius did oppose this doctrine in writing to Fredugard in the 850s
(*Ep. ad Fredugardum*, CCCM 16.145–173, at 173), there is no evidence that it had stirred discussion
in 831–833, i.e. several years before the synod of Quierzy (838) that condemned it. See chapter 4
n. 88.

tributed most to the quarrel which emerged sometime after the tract's initial publication.[4]

It is uncertain when the Carolingian dispute over the eucharistic presence began. Conceivably, as some historians have argued, the earliest challenge to Pascasius' teachings occurred in *De corpore et sanguine Domini* by Ratramnus of Corbie, a much more tightly argued, analytical work.[5] Ratramnus does not offer any internal evidence as to when he completed his treatise beyond its dedication to Charles the Bald, who, it is claimed, had requested its writing. Based on the references to Charles, we know only that it must have been finished before the imperial coronation of 875. Some historians have suggested that the monarch asked Ratramnus to write in the late 830s or early 840s, perhaps because he and monks at Corbie or Corvey had doubts about the Pascasian doctrine. If so, their worries were possibly fostered by the discussions centering on Amalarius' *Liber officialis* at Quierzy in 838; the synod may have encouraged a sense that errors about the mass and the eucharist were widespread.[6]

No allusion to the charges against Amalarius occurs in Ratramnus' tractate, however, and I think that better reasons exist for associating Charles' request to Ratramnus with the dispute over the eucharistic presence attested in a number of texts from no earlier than the late 840s, a few clearly dating between the early and mid 850s: a tract, *De corpore et sanguine Domini*, and the shorter fragment of a second work by Gottschalk of Orbais, from the period of his confinement to Hautvillers (849–868 or 869), which oppose Pascasius' ideas;[7] a patristic *florilegium* assembled by Adrevald of Fleury against the *ineptias* of John Scottus Eriugena (therefore completed no earlier than John Scottus' arrival in Francia, c. 848), possibly

---

[4] The eucharist controversy has been the subject of considerable scholarship. Recent discussions include Picasso, "Riti eucaristici"; my article, "Figure, Character, and the Glorified Body in the Carolingian Eucharistic Controversy," *Traditio* 47 (1992), 1–36; Ganz, *Corbie*, esp. 83–86, 88–89; Maria Angeles Navarro Giron, *La carne de Cristo: el misterio eucharistico a la luz de la controversia entre Pascasio Radberto, Ratramno, Rabano Mauro y Godescalco* (Madrid, 1989). Still valuable are Marta Cristiani, "La controversia eucaristica nella cultura del secolo IX," *Studi medievali* 9 (1968), 167–233; Henri de Lubac, *Corpus mysticum*.

[5] *Ratramnus: De corpore et sanguine Domini, édition renouvelée*, ed. J. N. Bakhuizen Van Den Brink (Amsterdam 1974), 40–69; transl. (based on Van Den Brink's 1954 edition) in George E. McCracken, *Early Medieval Theology* (Philadelphia, 1957), 118–147.

[6] See J. P. Bouhot, *Ratramne de Corbie: histoire Littéraire et controverses doctrinales* (Paris, 1976), 77–88. I accepted this dating of Ratramnus' treatise in my article, "Figure, Character, and the Glorified Body," see 3 and n. 4.

[7] Gottschalk, *Opusc. theol.* 23, *Œuvres*, ed. Lambot, 324–335, 335–337.

attacking a lost work by the Irish scholar;[8] John Scottus' commentary of c. 862 on the Pseudo-Dionysian *Celestial Hierarchy*, which appears to allude to the controversy;[9] a letter of 853–856 by Hrabanus referring to the mistake of "certain people" who believe that the eucharistic and crucified bodies are identical and to his recently composed (now lost) treatise against this opinion;[10] and Pascasius' defenses of his doctrine that the eucharist contains the incarnate body and blood, in two texts dating to the last years of his life (he died c. 859). The last two named works are the portion of his Matthew commentary on the last supper, written after 849,[11] and a letter of the early to mid 850s sent to Fredugard, probably a monk of St.-Riquier, after Fredugard had queried Pascasius' views.[12] It was most likely the same set of debates that provoked Hincmar to defend the identity of the eucharistic and historical bodies in the *Ferculum Salomonis*, written for Charles the Bald c. 853–856. I suspect Hincmar was already familiar with Pascasius' *De corpore* by c. 845, since, as will be discussed further in the next chapter, allusions to concepts expressed in the treatise seem to appear in the archbishop's poem on Mary, dating to 845–849.[13] But it was not until he wrote the *Ferculum Salomonis* and its prose commentary that he seems to have iso-

---

[8] Adrevald, *De corpore et sanguine Domini contra ineptias Joannis Scoti*, PL 124.947–954. On John Scottus' background and early years in Francia, see O'Meara, *Periphyseon*, 11–12.

[9] Eriugena, *Expositiones in Ierarchiam Coelestem* 1.3, ed. J. Barbet, CCCM 31 (Turnhout, 1975), 17, lines 584–594. See Cristiani, "Controversia eucaristica," 210–213.

[10] "Nam quidam nuper de ipso sacramento corporis et sanguinis Domini non rite sentientes dixerunt, hoc ipsum esse corpus et sanguinem Domini, quod de Maria virgine natum est, et in quo ipse Dominus passus in cruce est et resurrexit de sepulcro. Cui errori, quantum potuimus, ad Eigilum abbatem scribentes restitimus et quod vere credendum est aperuimus": Hrabanus, *Ep.* 56, *MGH Epp.* 5.513.

[11] See Paulus, ed., *Expositio in Matheo*, CCCM 56.viii-ix; see ibid., 26.26–29, CCCM 56B.1288–1298.

[12] Pascasius, *Ep. ad Fredugardum*, CCCM 16.145. Pascasius appended to the letter his exegesis of the last supper according to Matthew. The letter's date has been the subject of some debate, with Paulus assigning it to c. 856 and identifying Fredugard as a monk of St.-Riquier (*CCCM* 16.135, 137), as does Ganz, *Corbie*, 90. The background is clearly outlined in Ganz, *Corbie*, esp. 30–35.

[13] Hincmar, *Carm.* 2, *MGH PLAC* 3.410–412. Although the poem evidently predates the controversy, most of its verses (lines 25–80) are a meditation on the eucharist that agrees with elements of the teachings in Pascasius' *De corpore*. Hincmar traveled with Charles the Bald's court in the early 840s and could easily have read the copy of the treatise that Pascasius gave to the king in 843 or 844. See Paul Edward Dutton and Herbert L. Kessler, *The Poetry and Paintings of the First Bible of Charles the Bald* (Ann Arbor, 1997), 22–23, 29, citing Janet Nelson, "The Intellectual in Politics: Context, Content and Authorship in the Capitulary of Coulaines, November 843," in idem, *The Frankish World, 750–900* (London, 1996), 164–166 (repr. from *Intellectual Life in the Middle Ages: Essays Presented to Margaret Gibson*, ed. Lesley Smith and Benedicta Ward [London, 1992], 1–14).

lated and articulated the main arguments he and Pascasius use against those who deny that the two bodies are identical, while also affirming his own theology of predestination.[14]

Hrabanus' letter, Pascasius' treatise on Matthew, and the letter to Fredugard point to a disagreement among several people about the relationship between the incarnate and eucharistic bodies. Pascasius' letter to Fredugard notes that "many" voice doubt specifically about this aspect of his teachings, and Ratramnus seems to echo that remark when he refers to a quarrel involving enough people to constitute a "schism," about both the eucharist's connection with the historical body and whether or not the eucharistic presence is potentially visible.[15] Although Ratramnus may well distort the character of the disagreement, it is likely that he and the other theologians whose works have just been mentioned took part in the same conflict, one that Pascasius, Hrabanus, and Hincmar's *Ferculum Salomonis* suggest occurred c. 853–856. To see Ratramnus' treatise, too, as a product of this controversy would explain the distance it has from Pascasius' *De corpore*. Ratramnus does not quote from or otherwise show direct knowledge of that tract, never refers directly to Pascasius, in some ways seems to argue past his fellow monk and abbot, and implies that he opposes a group rather than an individual.[16] The later dating would also place Ratramnus' *De corpore* closer to his other theological writings, all produced c. 850 and after. Among them are his treatise on the virgin birth, which again disagrees with Pascasius, and his treatise on predestination, which as already seen basically sides with Gottschalk.[17]

---

[14] Hincmar, *Explan. in ferc. Salom.*, PL 125.817–834; *Carm.* 4.1, *MGH PLAC* 3.414–415. For an apparent reference to the eucharist controversy in an anonymous homiliary from Lyons, see Picasso, "Riti eucaristici," 503 and n.1. The connection between Hincmar's and Pascasius' eucharistic doctrines is briefly discussed in Reil, *Christus am Kreuz*, 68–69.

[15] Pascasius, *Ep. ad Fredugardum*, CCCM 16.145–146, see 153–154, 155; Ratramnus, *De corpore* 2, ed. Van Den Brink, 43. These parallels among the works indicated suggest that the dispute to which Ratramnus alludes was not confined to Corbie and/or Corvey.

[16] See Chazelle, "Figure, Character, and the Glorified Body," 5–9.

[17] On Ratramnus' doctrine of Mary, see idem, *De eo quod Christus ex uirgine natus est*, in *La virginidad de María según Ratramno y Radberto monjes*, ed. J.-M. Canal (Rome, 1968), 32–60. The differing views of Christ in the writings on Mary by Pascasius and Ratramnus — the former giving greater weight to Christ's miracle-working divinity while the latter stresses the corporeality of his humanity – correspond to the differences in their understandings of Christ suggested by their writings on the eucharist and, in Pascasius' case, his commentary on Matthew. In the last-named work, as in the others noted, Pascasius stresses God's ability in Christ to override natural law. See chapter 4 n. 56; Pascasius, *De partu Virginis*, ed. E. A. Matter, *CCCM* 56C (Turnhout, 1985), 47–89, see 11–14.

Although contemporary interest in scriptural and liturgical exegesis created an environment conducive to a dispute of this kind, the most probable scenario seems to me that it was sparked, or at least indirectly influenced, by the confrontations between Hincmar and Gottschalk over divine predestination, in which some of the same and other Carolingian ecclesiastics quickly took sides. It is unclear whether Pascasius himself associated the two issues when defending his eucharist theology in the 850s. A comment in his letter to Fredugard that "so far no one is read to have erred about these things [i.e. scriptural and patristic teachings on the eucharistic presence] other than those who have also erred concerning Christ" may refer to Amalarius (his notion that the eucharist represents the "triform" body of Christ); yet it is perhaps more likely, given when the letter was written, that Pascasius was thinking of Gottschalk's beliefs about the Trinity and predestination. Other passages in the letter and the Matthew commentary recall the discussions of predestination, but there is no certain evidence of what relation, if any, Pascasius saw between the two conflicts.[18] As for Ratramnus, without trying to establish the relative chronology of his *De corpore* and *De praedestinatione*, I think it is possible that the doctrine of the former treatise presupposes ideas set forth in the latter. What is more certain, however, is that Hincmar and Gottschalk connected their disagreements about the two matters. For them, orthodoxy on predestination led to or demanded orthodoxy on the eucharist. Gottschalk observes that he felt compelled to write after he read Pascasius' *De corpore*, apparently not knowing its author's name; possibly it was Hincmar who made a copy available to him, though it may have been Ratramnus.[19] Gottschalk ties his rejection of the Pascasian doctrine of the eucharist to his rejection of the notion that Christ was crucified for all humanity, and he indicates that on both matters he diverges with an unnamed opponent, whom the context indicates is Hincmar.[20] The two concerns are also linked

---

[18] See Pascasius, *Ep. ad Fredugardum*, CCCM 16.169 lines 778–780 (quoting 1 Tim. 2.4); but, on the other hand, note his remark in *In Matheo* 26.28, CCCM 56B.1292 lines 843–845 that Christ shed his blood "for many" (Matth. 26.28), not "for all," since some mortals disobey the gospel and refuse belief in him. The letter to Fredugard ends its excerpt from the treatise on Matthew directly before this comment.

[19] Gottschalk, *Opus. theol.* 23, *Œuvres*, ed. Lambot, 325; Emile Amann, *L'Epoque carolingienne*, vol. 6 of *Histoire de l'église depuis les origines jusqu'à nos jours*, ed. H. Fliche and V. Martin (Paris, 1937), 317.

[20] Gottschalk implies that Hincmar is a target in *Opus. theol.* 23, *Œuvres*, ed. Lambot, 331.

in the commentary on the *Ferculum Salomonis*, while allusions to Hincmar's teachings against Gottschalk's predestination theology appear in his discussion of the eucharist in *De cavendis vitiis et virtutibus exercendis*, written for Charles the Bald in the 860s or early 870s; this treatise confirms the archbishop's continued agreement (at least about the eucharist) with Pascasius.[21] In the decade after the predestination controversy formally ended and possibly even after Gottschalk's death in 868/869, Hincmar still deemed it necessary to remind his monarch of the true faith in both areas of thought, just as in the same years John Scottus Eriugena continued to think about the problems addressed in both quarrels, as shown by his *Periphyseon*, poems, and commentaries on the *Celestial Hierarchy* and John.

Pascasius and Hincmar

Even the second edition of Pascasius' *De corpore*, therefore, probably predates the eucharist controversy itself by seven or more years. As a consequence, my concern here is with that treatise only insofar as it helps elucidate the questions discussed in the 850s and later reverberations of them, especially as they relate to theology of the crucifixion. I begin with the eucharist theology that both Pascasius and Hincmar are known to have defended in the 850s,[22] with Pascasius focusing on the doctrines of his first treatise that are repeated and supported in his later writings. With Hincmar, I take into account his poem and commentary, the *Ferculum Salomonis*, and, though postdating the controversy, the last section of *De cavendis*, the archbishop's longest discussion of the eucharistic presence. As a whole, Section 3 of *De cavendis* offers a rather meandering meditation, carried forward by unidentified patristic sources and echoes of scripture and the liturgy that slide into one another, on the significance of the crucifixion and the consecrated bread and wine to the Christian's longing for heaven. The discussion is molded to the treatise's larger aim of instructing King Charles the Bald about sin, its consequences, and the moral behavior appropriate to his royal position. As Doris Nachtmann has recently demonstrated through her excellent

---

[21] *De cavendis vitiis et virtutibus exercendis* 3, MGH Quellen 16, ed. D. Nachtmann (Munich, 1998), 226–266. On the date, see Nachtmann, ed., ibid., 23–24.

[22] Adrevald's *florilegium* also seems intended to support Pascasius' doctrine, but it is too brief and too reliant on patristic material to indicate clearly its author's views.

edition of the treatise, only a small fraction of the words in the text are actually Hincmar's rather than his sources.[23] Nevertheless, he clearly selected, arranged, and spliced these materials together with a few phrases of his own in order to convey ideas that, as Nachtmann notes, do not precisely align with those of the earlier authorities from whom he borrowed, and that ultimately reflect his own thinking.[24] While it is sometimes hard to sort out Hincmar's doctrinal developments in this treatise and the *Ferculum Salomonis*, and while *De cavendis* shows some distance from the controversy of the 850s, whose issues it does not forcefully address, these works possess enough similarities with Pascasius' to warrant examining them together.

In recognizing that an identity exists between the eucharist and the historical or incarnate, crucified body and blood of Christ, Pascasius and Hincmar uphold the doctrine of the eucharist that most closely approaches popular tendencies in the ninth century to think that the consecrated elements contain or become flesh and blood in a physical sense.[25] Both scholars acknowledge that, after consecration, the eucharist continues to appear as wine and bread while its contents remain spiritual, immaterial, and hence normally imperceptible to the corporeal senses. Nevertheless, for them, in every celebration of the mass bread and wine inwardly become the very body born of Mary, which suffered, died on the cross, and rose from the dead, and the blood that poured from Jesus' side. As Pascasius declares, Christ the tree of life, "whose image was that tree in paradise," is now in the church in his flesh.[26] The flesh and blood that suffered once in the passion are now in the sacrament.[27] For Pascasius, it seems, and perhaps also Hincmar, the body and blood are absent from the eucharist that unbelievers and other sinners receive, who in line with 1 Corinthians 11.28–29 only eat and drink their judgment. In their case, the

---

[23] See Nachtmann, ed., *De cavendis, MGH Quellen* 16.14–23.   [24] See ibid., *MGH Quellen* 16, esp. 4–5.

[25] As suggested, e.g., by Ratramnus' reference to people who hold that Christ's flesh and blood are visibly present in the eucharist (*De corpore* 2, ed. Van Den Brink, 43); and by Gottschalk's account of his experience in Dalmatia, where he met a pagan noble who "bibere me suppliciter petiuit in illius dei amore qui de uino sanguinem suum facit": *Opus. theol.* 23, *Œuvres*, ed. Lambot, 325. An allusion to advocates of the notion that Christ's body is "carnally" present in the eucharist also occurs in Pascasius' letter to Fredugard: *Ep. ad Fredugardum, CCCM* 16.147 lines 66–70. In general, Carolingian Europe was rich in popular practices and beliefs concerning the eucharist's "magical" properties, ideas that survived into later times: see Flint, *Rise of Magic*, esp. 214, 283, 285, 298, 304.   [26] Pascasius, *De corpore* 7, *CCCM* 16.39.

[27] Pascasius, *In Matheo* 26.28, *CCCM* 56B.1293 lines 869–874.

virtus of the sacrament is withdrawn.[28] Yet for those who are cleansed of sins and, therefore, in a state of faith that enables them to receive "spiritually," aware of the immaterial presence, the eucharist is the bread that descended from heaven and the flesh that hung on the cross.[29] In their case, Pascasius contends, the holy spirit creates the true, crucified flesh and blood in the bread and wine by the same power that created true flesh in the Virgin. Christ's passion is "handed over in mystery" and his blood and flesh are "mystically" immolated, since mortals daily sin, but the terms "mystery" and "mystically" serve to underscore the imperceptible quality of the eucharistic presence, not to differentiate it from the body and blood of the crucifixion.[30] In the holy church "that is the body of Christ," Hincmar informs Charles the Bald in *De cavendis*, evidently emending the passage he takes from Leo I, there can be no true sacrifices "unless the true pontiff reconciles us in the propriety and truth of our nature."[31] Although the immaculate lamb is now in heaven with the father, "nevertheless from the same flesh that he assumed from the Virgin is effected the sacrament of propitiation."[32] While both Hincmar and Pascasius also think of the bread and wine as representations of Christ's body and blood, they believe that the eucharist's inner identity with the entities represented – the crucified flesh and blood – distinguishes the sacrament from Old Testament figures

[28] Pascasius, *De corpore* 6, *CCCM* 16.34–37, esp. 35; 8, *CCCM* 16.40–52. The sacrament's *virtus* is evidently the same power that gives life through the fruit of the tree of life: ibid. 1, *CCCM* 16.19. Cf. ibid. 9, *CCCM* 16.54–55; and Hincmar, *De cavendis* 3.2, *MGH Quellen* 16.263 (Prosper): "Nam escam vitae accipit et aeternitatis poculum bibit, qui in Christo manet et cuius Christus inhabitator est. Qui autem discordat a Christo, nec carnem Christi manducat, nec sanguinem bibit *ad vitam* [Hincmarian addition], etiamsi tantae rei sacramentum ad iudicium suae praesumptionis cotidie indifferenter accipiat." It is unclear whether recipients in discord with Christ fail to consume his flesh and blood altogether, or do not receive those substances "to life." Cf. ibid. 3.2, *MGH Quellen* 16.231–232 (Bede).

[29] Pascasius, *De corpore* 1, *CCCM* 16.13–20; 10, *CCCM* 16.68; Hincmar, *Carm.* 4.1, *MGH PLAC* 3.414–415, cf. *De cavendis* 3.1, 2, *MGH Quellen* 16.227, 235–237. On the need for cleansing of sins and faith in order to receive the eucharist properly, e.g. ibid. 2.6, 8, *MGH Quellen* 16.206–207 (Gregory), 221 (Gregory, but with changes apparently by Hincmar shifting the focus to the eucharist). See also Wilmart, "Distiques," 88.

[30] Pascasius, *De corpore* 2, 4, 9, *CCCM* 16.23, 27–28, 52–53 (Bede). See *Ep. ad Fredugardum*, *CCCM* 16.145–147, 149, 151, 159–160.

[31] "Aliter enim in *sancta* ecclesia, quae corpus est Christi, nec rata sunt sacerdotia, nec vera sacrificia, nisi in nostrae proprietate *ac veritate* naturae nos verus pontifex reconciliet et verus inmaculati agni sanguis emundet..." Hincmar, *De cavendis* 3, *MGH Quellen* 16.262. Words in italics note departures, as identified by Nachtmann, from the original text (Leo I).

[32] Ibid. 3.2, *MGH Quellen* 16.262 (Leo I).

of Christ. For Pascasius, the Jews had mere "images" and shadows, pointing towards a reality to come for those who correctly understood the
figures' significance, but possessing nothing of that truth within themselves. Hincmar implies that the ancient Israelites received spiritual yet efficacious versions of the sacraments, a slightly different position from
Pascasius' that is in line with the archbishop's predestination theology – his
belief that redemption is offered to all mortals before and after the incarnation, but access to it requires the sacraments' reception.[33]

In the writings of both Carolingian theologians, the conviction that
every eucharist contains (at least for the faithful) Jesus' one, incarnate body
and its blood partly reflects the influence of Ambrose's doctrine that blood
and flesh are spiritually, invisibly, yet truly present in the wine and bread,
and of the same church father's related concept of the spirituality of Jesus'
resurrected and glorified body. Christ's body in heaven is a spiritual entity
largely assimilated with the divine nature, and therefore capable of being
in two places at once. Without ceasing to be humanity, it lacks the circum-
scription that Ratramnus and Gottschalk appear to attribute to it; as
Hincmar indicates, quoting Ambrose, the incarnate body in the eucharist
is the "nourishment of [Christ's] divine substance."[34] Yet Pascasius and the
archbishop also imply a certain physicality to the eucharistic body and
blood, despite their insistence on the presence's mystery and spirituality,
that distinguishes their thought from Ambrose's and suggests they were
also attuned to Augustine's view of the continued corporeality of body,
including Christ's, in heaven.[35] In Hincmar's *De cavendis*, some of the language in which the eucharist is described might be taken to mean that the
body sacrificed on the cross again dies in the mass, a belief Gottschalk
attacks. "Declare him killed and offer him to be sacrificed in his mystery,"
the archbishop urges Charles the Bald, in passionate exclamations that

---

[33] Pascasius, *De corpore* 5, CCCM 16.31–34; *In Matheo* 26.28, CCCM 56B.1293–1294, 1297. Note, too,
the "image" (*imago*) of Christ offered by the tree of life in paradise (*De corpore* 7, CCCM 16.39).
See Hincmar, *De cavendis* 3.2, MGH Quellen 16.260 (Ambrose, evidently with Hincmarian additions), cf. ibid., MGH Quellen 16.233–234 (Bede, with Hincmarian additions), 254–255 (emending
Augustine); idem, *De praed. Epil.* 6, PL 125.459.

[34] See Hincmar, *De cavendis* 3.2, MGH Quellen 16.257, 259–260 (Ambrose); Pascasius, *De corpore* 5, 6,
CCCM 16.32–34, *Ep. ad Fredugardum*, CCCM 16.153, 155–156. Cf. Ambrose, *De mysteriis* 9.58.

[35] Augustine, esp. *De civ. Dei* 13.20–22, 22.5; de Lubac, *Corpus mysticum*, 147–148; Kelly, *Early
Christian Doctrines*, 478–479. In general, both sides of the Carolingian controversy make use of
both church fathers; see de Lubac, *Corpus mysticum*, 146–152; Chazelle, "Figure, Character, and
the Glorified Body," 34–36.

echo the story of the prodigal son (esp. Luke 15.23): "Kill! That is, believe him dead for sinners!" In the eucharistic offering, Christ the fatted calf is daily immolated "for believers."[36] In Pascasius' *De corpore*, the presence's quasi-physicality is implied in the references to miraculous apparitions at celebrations of the mass, and in claims that the faithful perceive the eucharist's contents in a manner akin to their perception of material things. Thus it is noted that to "see" Christ's flesh in the eucharist is comparable to seeing him on the cross, that recipients learn to "taste" and "see" other than with the physical senses, that to the minds of believers, it is "as if [divine power] showed the same things visibly which it offers inwardly to effect salvation."[37] Such remarks count among the substantial evidence of the growing concern among ninth-century scholars with the role of the sense of sight in Christian devotion, as is also suggested by their discussions of images, crosses, and relics, of the vision of God, and of the liturgy's visual representation of holy actors and events. The scarcity of parallels in Pascasius' letter to Fredugard and commentary on Matthew may be a clue that in those writings he was newly sensitive to Ratramnus' charge that "certain faithful" believe the eucharist's sacred contents to be material and actually visible to the corporeal eyes.[38]

Like Carolingian commentators on the mass liturgy, Pascasius and Hincmar define a function for the eucharist as Christ's body and blood and, at the same time, the commemorative representation of those entities and of the offering on the cross. Along lines seen in the expositions of the mass examined in chapter 4, Pascasius' *De corpore* affirms that the faithful recognize the priest's actions in the mass to resemble Christ's sacrifice in the passion. Furthermore, the bread resembles Christ's body and recalls that he is the bread of heaven, the wine mixed with water in the chalice bears a likeness to the liquid from his side wound, and the many grains and grapes used to make the one bread and the wine recall the unity of the faithful with Christ.[39] In a selection of Augustinian excerpts also found in Florus of Lyons' *De expositione missae*, *De cavendis* implies that the wine is mixed with water as a sign of unity. The wine is the likeness of Christ's blood and the

[36] Hincmar, *De cavendis* 3.2, MGH Quellen 16.247. Cf. Gottschalk, *Opus. theol.* 23, *Œuvres*, ed. Lambot, 331–333.
[37] Pascasius, *De corpore* 1, 3, 8, CCCM 16.15, 24, 42; on apparitions, *De corpore* 14, CCCM 16.85–92, esp. 89–92. See *Ep. ad Fredugardum*, CCCM 16.161; and the dedicatory poem to Charles the Bald, *Carm.* 4, MGH PLAC 3.52–53 line 15.   [38] Ratramnus, *De corpore* 2, ed. Van Den Brink, 43.
[39] Pascasius, *De corpore* 4, 10–11, 13, CCCM 16.28, 65–76, 84.

eucharistic bread and chalice are the "commemoration and annunciation of [Christ's] death."[40] Partly through the same collection of passages from Augustine, Hincmar ties the eucharist's memorial function as much to the future as to the past. Pascasius' treatise on Matthew remarks that the "mystical sacraments [offered] in faith" in the eucharist will no longer be necessary once Christ returns, since then, "what is done now in mystery will be more clearly revealed in the light."[41] But Hincmar, in *De cavendis*, using Augustine or Florus – and possibly influenced by the eschatological focus that the predestination controversy encouraged – links the two experiences more closely, even though he, too, indicates that the eucharist offers only an anticipation of the future glory. The mass elements are a source of hope that already lead minds upwards and serve the church as it waits for Christ to return. What is commemorated and provides hope in the eucharist is above all the blood. The celebration of the eucharist is the basis of ecclesiastical unity until the world ends, insofar as the church drinks "what flowed from Christ's side."[42] Charles the Bald is urged to prepare for that future joy by repenting his sins and receiving in faith this manifestation of Jesus' humility. Through their consumption of the bread and wine the faithful already, in a certain measure, are illumined by the divine light they will contemplate in paradise – also a theme of Hincmar's third treatise – and, it is implied, they enjoy a foretaste of the heavenly feast.[43]

A distinctive feature of Pascasius' argumentation in *De corpore* and the letter to Fredugard is the connection he draws between the eucharist's likeness to or representation of the body and blood – its figural function – and their identity. In ascribing a figural significance to the bread and wine he is partly influenced by an Augustinian doctrine of signs; but the notion that the eucharist's role as figure is compatible with the concept that it actually contains the crucified body and blood finds its primary support in Ambrose's description of Christ as the "figure or character of his [God's] substance" (*figura uel caracter substantiae eius*).[44] Like other patristic and

---

[40] Hincmar, *De cavendis* 3.2, *MGH Quellen* 16.240–241, see 239 n. 509 on sources; ibid. 3, *MGH Quellen* 16.253–254 (Fulgentius), 256–257 (Ambrose). Cf. Hincmar, *Carm.* 2, *MGH*, *PLAC* 3.411 lines 57–60.   [41] Pascasius, *In Matheo* 26.28, *CCCM* 56B.1293 lines 866–867.

[42] Hincmar, *De cavendis* 3.2, *MGH Quellen* 16.242, see 239 n. 509.

[43] Ibid. 3.1, 2, *MGH Quellen* 16.227–228, 244–245 (Augustine), see ibid. 2, *MGH Quellen* 16.202–203 (Gregory).

[44] Pascasius, *De corpore* 4, *CCCM* 16.27–31; *Ep. ad Fredugardum*, *CCCM* 16.146–148 (Ambrose, *De incarnationis Dominicae sacramento* 10, based on a variant of Hebrews 1.3). The definition

early medieval scholars, Pascasius associates the term "character" with the impression made by a stamp or seal. On that basis, he regards a character as a visible sign possessing the same veracity and authority as its source, granted the viewer's ability to distinguish between them.[45] Just as Christ's humanity is the figure and character of his divinity, therefore, according to Pascasius following Ambrose, and written letters are characters that give visible form to the "strength and power and spirit" of spoken letters or words, the eucharist is the figure and also the character of the "truth" of Jesus' flesh and blood. The written text is as "true" as the oral expression it records, while Christ, who "makes himself visible to our senses so that we may grasp the things that are in him," is truly God. Similarly, the eucharistic elements invisibly house the true incarnate flesh and blood because the wine and bread are those entities' figure and character.[46]

The core justification for Pascasius' and also Hincmar's doctrine of the eucharistic presence, however, comes not from any role ascribed to it as a figure / character but from their shared beliefs, which they again understand to agree with patristic teachings, about the nature of God and the correct interpretation of the biblical passages relating to the eucharist's foundation and the uniqueness of Christ's sacrifice. First, God is truth; Pascasius sometimes refers to Christ as "Truth" to confirm this. Therefore, the gospel accounts of Jesus' words at the last supper, identifying the bread and wine as his body and blood (a preference is shown for John), must be accepted as perfectly true. Jesus, the very word spoken in scripture, can have meant nothing else but what he said.[47] Second, as we have already seen from his exegesis of Matthew's passion narrative, Pascasius stresses the concept that divine omnipotence means God in Christ, at the last supper and any other

Pascasius offers of figure, apart from its connection with character, accords with Augustine, *De magistro*, esp. 8.22–9.28, 10.33–13.45; *De doctrina Christiana* 2, esp.1–4.

[45] See N. M. Häring, "*Character, Signum,* and *Signaculum*: die Entwicklung bis nach der karolingischen Renaissance," *Scholastik: Vierteljahresschrift für Theologie und Philosophie* 30 (1955), 482; idem, "St. Augustine's Use of the Word Character," *Mediaeval Studies* 14 (1952), 79–92.

[46] Pascasius, *De corpore* 4, CCCM 16.29–30. See ibid., 3, CCCM 16.24–25, describing the incarnation as a "great sacrament" (*magnum sacramentum*) because of the operation of divinity within humanity in a fashion parallel to the eucharist; and the spiritual meaning of scripture as sacramental because of the invisible working of the holy spirit in the words. Scripture is a sacrament by which the faithful are "fed" and thus gain understanding of Christ. Cf. Chazelle, "Figure, Character, and the Glorified Body," 15–19.

[47] See Pascasius, *De corpore* 1, CCCM 16.15, 18; 12, CCCM 16.80; 19, CCCM 16.104–105 (Augustine); *Ep. ad Fredugardum*, CCCM 16.145, 146, 148, 154, 155, 156; *In Matheo* 2.12, CCCM 56.168, ibid. 26.26, CCCM 56B.1288. See Hincmar, *De cavendis* 3.2, MGH Quellen 16.236–237.

point in history, can and does at times work against the laws of nature he himself established, including the laws governing physical existence. This idea occurs, too, in the surviving verses of Hincmar's *Ferculum Salomonis* and in *De cavendis*. In an Ambrosian passage emended by Hincmar, which recalls the exegesis of John 19.34 in Pascasius' commentary on Matthew, *De cavendis* identifies the water and blood flowing from Christ's side after he died – the phrase, *post mortem Christi*, is a Hincmarian addition – as one of several, miraculous examples of the power of divine grace to override nature.[48] Correspondingly, both Hincmar and Pascasius believe, just as divinity could create something from nothing at the creation, become flesh at the incarnation, and work other miracles through Christ, so is it able to change bread and wine into the very body and blood of the crucifixion, while assuring that those entities remain indivisible and imperceptible to the corporeal senses. Such a transformation happened at the last supper, before Christ even suffered. It recurs in every celebration of the mass at the words of institution, which alone have the power to consecrate the bread and wine, because they are the words of the omnipotent creator.[49]

In *De cavendis* more than in the other writings noted, this unambiguous presentation of divine power is juxtaposed to Jesus' self-abasement, sometimes in ways that evoke the contrast between all-suffering and infinite power in Christ suggested in sections of Hincmar's third treatise. A long passage in *De cavendis* from Augustine's exegesis of Psalm 33 is also quoted in Florus of Lyon's exposition of the mass. It expresses a similar idea to a text from Chrysostom in Hincmar's third treatise, but in both Florus' work and the third treatise the patristic material is used without explicit reference to an identity between the eucharistic and crucified bodies. In *De cavendis*, however, it is evident that Hincmar considers the Augustinian excerpt compatible with his doctrine that the two bodies are identical. The point for the archbishop, it seems, is to highlight the voluntary humiliation the word had to accept in order not merely to die on the cross, but to provide his own flesh and blood as healing food and drink. Like the mother who provides milk for her infant by "incarnating" the bread she ingests,

---

[48] Hincmar, *De cavendis* 3.2, MGH *Quellen* 16.258–261, esp. 261. Cf. idem, *Carm.* 4.1, MGH *PLAC* 3.414–415; *De praed.* 35, PL 125.375A/B; Pascasius, *In Matheo* 27.54, CCCM 56B.1399 lines 4281–4284.

[49] See Pascasius, *De corpore* 1, 15, CCCM 16.13–17, 92–96; *Ep. ad Fredugardum*, CCCM 16.150, 154–156, 169; *In Matheo* 26.26, CCCM 56B.1288–1289; Hincmar, *Carm.* 4.1, MGH *PLAC* 3.415, lines 5–6, 10; *De cavendis* 3.2, MGH *Quellen* 16.236, 256–261 (Ambrose, with emendations).

divine wisdom, equal to the father, descended to earth to become incarnate and "obedient unto death," thus providing mortals with the same
bread of heaven that also feeds the angels. Perhaps the most moving
expression of the conjunction of powerful divinity with mortal humanity
in Hincmar's extant writing on the eucharist comes shortly afterwards,
again from Augustine's commentary on Psalm 33, where Jesus at the last
supper is described as carrying himself in his own hands, a token simultaneously of humility and omnipotence.[50]

And third, for Pascasius as well as Hincmar, every eucharist must
contain the one, crucified flesh and blood because only then is it redemptive. Given, on the one hand, the "truth" of Jesus' words at the last supper –
the bread and wine are truly his body and blood – and, on the other, the
scriptural teachings that his crucifixion was the unique oblation sufficient
for all creation, that having risen from the tomb he can never die again, the
mass must be a sacrifice of the very same, crucified body in order to be
redemptive. In spite of their Augustinian sense of the corporeality of Jesus'
body and blood, Pascasius and Hincmar follow Ambrose's more "spiritual"
perspective closely enough to believe that an identity between the eucharist and the historical body and blood alone reconciles the crucifixion's
uniqueness as a sacrifice with every sinful Christian's need to receive his
sacrificed redeemer in the mass. As both scholars recall, Jesus is the innocent lamb immolated once to atone the father, who now cleanses through
the eucharist because human beings daily sin. Continued access to the
redemption the crucifixion provided is available in baptism, penance, and
especially the consecrated bread and wine: baptism removes the stains of
original sin and sins committed before the sacrament, penance and the
eucharist imitate Jesus' oblation and cleanse of subsequent wrongdoings,
and in the mass the faithful eat and drink the very flesh and blood that
Christ made available on the cross, confirming and strengthening their
union with him.[51] Pascasius, who gives particular weight to the eucharist's

---

[50] Hincmar, *De cavendis* 3.2, *MGH Quellen* 16.242–244 (Augustine, *Enarr. in Ps.* 33.1); see ibid., 3.2,
MGH Quellen 16.251–252. Cf. Florus, *De expositione missae, PL* 119.16–17; Hincmar, *De praed.* 35, *PL*
125.375D-376A (Chrysostom).

[51] Pascasius, *De corpore* 9, *CCCM* 16.52–65 (Bede, Hilar, Gregory I); see ibid. 2, 12, 15, 21, *CCCM*
16.23, 77, 96, 112–113; *Ep. ad Fredugardum, CCCM* 16.148–149, 150–151 (Gregory I), 156; *In Matheo*
26.27–28, *CCCM* 56B.1290, 1293–1294 (Origen). Cf. Hincmar, *De cavendis* 2–3, *MGH Quellen*
16.225–227; ibid. 3, *MGH Quellen* 16.231–233, 238, 246–248, 256–258, 262–266; *Explan. in ferc.
Salom., PL* 125.826–827, 830–832.

ability to join Christians to their savior – mystically, yet in truth since it is in fact his crucified body and blood – indicates in *De corpore* that the church, though Christ's body, does not share the bread and wine's identity with the historical Jesus. Only the sacrament is not only his body but his "flesh." It is by eating the flesh and blood of the crucifixion, though, that the church becomes "from [Christ's] flesh and bones" and "two in one flesh" with him.[52] To deny that what the faithful consume in the eucharist is the incarnate, though imperceptible, body is to deny the completeness of Christ's union with his members.[53]

But while Pascasius' letter to Fredugard and commentary on Matthew may allude to the predestination controversy, neither tract sets his thought about the eucharist clearly in that framework. In Hincmar's *De cavendis*, and more noticeably in his commentary on the *Ferculum Salomonis*, the identity between the eucharist and historical bodies is tied to his predestination doctrine that Christ offers all mortals the chance to persevere in grace and be saved. The divine gift of grace and cleansing of sins is shown to be available to all who, fearing the last judgment, manifest their faith in baptism, frequent penance, and the eucharist. For Hincmar, the eucharist's ability to redeem everyone who receives it in faith, because God willed the salvation of all humanity, depends on its identity with the crucified body and blood.[54] Thus the concept that the eucharist contains the historical entities evidently seems to him confirmation of the church's critical importance to the mortal's quest for salvation, against what Gottschalk was presumed to teach, since the church is the only channel through which Christians, living and dead, may gain access to the one body of the crucifixion that must be received in the mass.[55]

As is true of the third treatise, Hincmar's eucharist writings, more than those of Pascasius, link ecclesiastical authority and the crucifixion's redemptive efficacy above all with the blood received in the chalice. A passage in *De*

[52] Pascasius, *De corpore 7, CCCM* 16.37–40; cf. *In Matheo* 26.29, *CCCM* 56B.1296–1297 (Origen).

[53] See Pascasius, *De corpore* 1, 3, 9, 10–11, 12, 19, 20, 21, *CCCM* 16.19, 25, 55, 57, 61 (Gregory I), 65–73 (Gregory I), 78–79, 101–102, 107, 112–114, 116; *Ep. ad Fredugardum, CCCM* 16.148, 156–157, 172–173 (Ambrose, Hilary); Hincmar, *De cavendis* 3.2, *MGH Quellen* 16.255–256 (Augustine, Prosper, Leo I, Gregory, Ambrose); cf. *De praed. Epil.* 1, *PL* 125.419–420.

[54] Hincmar, *Explan. in ferc. Salom.*, *PL* 125.818B/C, 826–827, 831–832; *Carm.* 4.1, *MGH PLAC* 3.414–415. Cf. *De cavendis* 3.2, *MGH Quellen* 16.246–250 (Augustine, Jerome, Gregory, Bede).

[55] The nature and scope of ecclesiastical authority is generally a pronounced theme of Hincmar's thought. I discuss some aspects in my article, "Archbishops Ebo and Hincmar of Reims and the Utrecht Psalter," *Speculum* 72 (1997), 1055–1077, esp. 1068–1071.

cavendis echoes a theme of Hincmar's treatises on predestination, and has parallels in John Scottus' thought, when it suggests that Jesus' bloodshed was both a sign of the divine love's reach throughout history and the forceful instrument by which he opened hell and released its faithful prisoners.[56] Later in *De cavendis*, the Augustinian analogy between the side wound and the church's origin is developed in a passage that borrows from Leo I and an Easter hymn, with emendations by Hincmar to identify the eucharist with the crucified body and blood more closely than do his sources. The eucharist's origin in the crucified Christ, especially that of the chalice, is directly tied to the church's power as arbiter of the sacraments. The focus is on *Ecclesia*, who receives in her cup the blood and water that flow from the crucified body.[57] Similarly, Hincmar's *Ferculum Salomonis* presents the litter (Canticle 3.9–10) as a foreshadowing of the church, which, in the eucharistic wine, gains the repeated cleansing necessary to salvation; for this is the "living blood of the copious redemption" that Christ, the "immaculate and spotless lamb," poured out on behalf of all humanity.[58] The imagery of the copiousness of Christ's blood and redemption, which the archbishop developed in attacking Gottschalk's predestination theology, not only accords with his belief that the son of God died for all mortals. As his discussions of the eucharist show, it also corresponds to a very real conviction that the blood of the crucifixion is indeed infinite, offering redemption to all, because it is present in every chalice that the church offers in the mass.[59]

Pascasius' opponents

Of the four Carolingian theologians whose extant writings indicate their opposition to the Pascasian doctrine – Hrabanus, John Scottus, Ratramnus, and Gottschalk – the remarks in Hrabanus' surviving letter are too brief to offer us insight into the theological basis of his opinion. With John Scottus, all his extant works that comment on the eucharist, in brief, scattered passages, postdate his *De praedestinatione* and translations of Pseudo-Dionysius, and therefore probably the height of the eucharist controversy.

---

[56] Hincmar, *De cavendis* 3.2, MGH *Quellen* 16.238–240, see 248–249 (Gregory I, Augustine, Jerome).
[57] Ibid. 3.2, MGH *Quellen* 16.261, see nn. 637–639.
[58] See Hincmar, *Explan. in ferc. Salom.*, PL 125.818B, 826C-827B.
[59] See Hincmar, *De cavendis* 3.2, MGH *Quellen* 16.252–253.

They reflect the influence of Greek thought on his views and do not clearly inform us as to how he might have responded to quarrels in the 850s, though they likely offer some insights. These writings – the exposition on the *Celestial Hierarchy*, some related sections of *Periphyseon*, the commentary on John, and several of the poems – indicate his understanding of the eucharist as a mystery that is also a "fact."[60] Not only the historical reality of its institution is recognized, but also its sacral power and the legitimacy of referring to it as Christ's body and blood. For John Scottus, the eucharist is at least as closely connected with the crucified body as is the water of baptism. As he declares in Poems 2 and 8, the "altar of the cross is bathed" in the wave of blood that purges mortals, bringing them to eternal life and deification; Jesus who washes the faithful "from the fount of your side" also offers the "potent antidote" that wards off evil from those who drink.[61] Along lines that in some ways echo the arguments of Pascasius and Hincmar and, correspondingly, Ambrose's spiritualized understanding of Christ's glorified body (though with the claim that this doctrine agrees with Augustine), John Scottus suggests that Jesus' body and blood in heaven are spiritual entities assimilated to his divine nature. They are capable of being "always and everywhere," and hence, it appears, simultaneously in the bread and wine and in the celestial realm. Christ is the unique "mystical lamb" prefigured in the repeated sacrifices of the ancient Israelites, the commentary on John declares. The uniqueness of his sacrifice on the cross means that the mass offers a "spiritual" immolation that the faithful eat "intellectually, not dentally but mentally," a belief shared by Hincmar and Pascasius, despite the corporeality they also seem to attribute to the eucharistic presence.[62]

Yet although some of these comments might imply that John Scottus identified the eucharist with the incarnate and glorified body, a position that distinguishes his teachings from those of Gottschalk and Ratramnus, overall, influenced by Pseudo-Dionysius and a conception of the created universe as primarily meaningful insofar as it is symbolic, his principal

---

[60] John Scottus, *In Ioh.* 6.5–6, SC 180.352–367.

[61] John Scottus, Poem 2, *Carmina*, ed. Herren, 64–67 lines 58–60, Poem 8, ibid., 84–89 lines 72, 76–77.

[62] John Scottus, *In Ioh.* 1.31, SC 180.176–179. See *Periph.* 5, PL 122.992–993, trans. O'Meara, *Periphyseon*, esp. 677–679. Cf. Florus' attack on John Scottus regarding the nature of Christ's resurrected body: *Joannis Scoti Erigenae erroneas definitiones*, PL 119.101–250, at 153–154, referring to John Scottus, *De praed.* 8.4–5, CCCM 50.50–51.

interest in his extant writings on the eucharist seems to be in what it does not contain. His major complaint about the eucharist controversy is that certain participants assert the eucharist to have no significance "beyond itself," presumably meaning beyond its sacred contents, a statement that is probably directed against Pascasius and his allies. For John Scottus, the consecrated bread and wine are transformed into Christ in the unity of his humanity and divinity, and therefore into the body and blood born on earth and risen from the dead, as is not true for Ratramnus or Gottschalk. Yet precisely because Jesus' glorified, human–divine existence is no longer confined to one time or location, the faithful should attend not to the presence within the eucharist but to the greater reality it signifies: the Christ who is, "in the unity of his divine and human substance beyond everything that is perceived by corporeal sense, above everything that is recognized by the power of intelligence, invisible God in each of his natures." Above all else, the eucharist's mystery should lead the faithful to contemplate the son of God and heavenly truth far exceeding the sacrament's boundaries, an experience that occurs now through faith and in a more perfect sense in the future, with the final return to God.[63]

Like his predestination doctrine, John Scottus' eucharist theology, as far as it can be known, ultimately remains isolated from the thought that the Carolingian quarrels inspired in his contemporaries, and it may therefore have been largely incomprehensible to them. Although it shows some affinities with the positions espoused by Pascasius and Hincmar, occasionally approaching their views perhaps more than those of Ratramnus and Gottschalk, it seems clear that John Scottus did not align himself with Pascasius, and conceivably he believed his doctrine closer to that of the monk of Orbais. In their own treatises against the Pascasian doctrine, Ratramnus and Gottschalk maintain that the consecrated bread and wine are truly Christ's body and blood, in accordance with Jesus' words of institution, yet the uniqueness of his sacrifice on the cross means the sacrament cannot contain the incarnate, crucified entities. Both theologians set out this position in tightly structured tracts relying more than those by Pascasius and Hincmar (or the short passages in John Scottus' extant writings) on dialectic and grammatical analysis. Both works show how

[63] John Scottus, *Exp. in Ier. Coel.* 1.3, CCCM 31.16–17. See Pelikan, *Christian Tradition* 3.96; Cristiani, "Controversia eucaristica," 210–213; George S. M. Walker, "Eriugena's Conception of the Sacraments," in *Studies in Church History*, vol. 3, ed. G. J. Cuming (Leiden, 1966), 150–158.

removed their authors' thought was from the pastoral concerns of men like Hincmar and Pascasius, as also seems true for John Scottus, even though in defending the eucharist's contents as Christ's true body and blood Gottschalk refers to his missionary experience in Dalmatia.[64]

In spite of the shared characteristics of Ratramnus' and Gottschalk's writings, their approaches to the eucharist controversy are different enough that, for the most part, it is best to consider them separately. According to Gottschalk, his unnamed opponent, evidently Hincmar, preaches that Christ suffers in every celebration of the mass, and that consequently all the reprobate "have been redeemed, are redeemed, and must be redeemed" through the eucharist. Christians must beware this doctrine, lest the wicked say to the elect, "He suffered once for your sins, he suffers frequently for ours, then to exhaust the sins of many (Hebrews 9.28), now generally for all."[65] Against this notion and the teachings of Pascasius' *De corpore*, Gottschalk asserts, first of all, that since God willed the salvation of the elect alone and Christ died solely for them, they alone receive a eucharistic presence that is salvific – just as his tractates on predestination argue that baptism bestows grace only on the saved. Although he is not clear on the point, he seems to think that the bread and wine become Christ's body and blood for the wicked as for the blessed;[66] but whatever the damned receive in the eucharist brings them not salvation but judgment, in accordance with 1 Corinthians 11.28–29 and with the punishment eternally ordained for them.[67] Both Pascasius and Hincmar claim that the eucharist redeems only those who consume it in faith, and at least Pascasius implies that Christ's body and blood are present in the bread and wine they alone receive. Gottschalk's views are to some extent similar, but with his own predestination theology in mind, he decisively identifies the truly faithful recipients with the few mortals predestined to salvation, while those who receive judgment in the eucharist are the wicked predestined to damnation. For Gottschalk, paying careful attention to the grammar of scripture, Jesus referred to the blessed alone when he said, in John 6.52, "The bread that I give is my flesh for the life of the world." Evoking his doctrine that the reprobate and the elect constitute two separate worlds, he argues that

---

[64] Gottschalk, *Opus. theol.* 23, *Œuvres*, ed. Lambot, 325.   [65] Ibid., 331.

[66] Even the pagan noble Gottschalk spoke with in Dalmatia correctly identified the eucharistic wine with Christ's blood: ibid., 325 lines 9–13, see 324, 328, 330, 333–335.

[67] Ibid., 328, lines 3–5.

John uses the term *mundum* in the singular because the eucharist offers life only to the world of the saved;[68] to it alone Christ "comes everyday with his new body and blood to revive, feed, give drink, and truly . . . renew it."[69] What the damned and the elect consume at the mass is therefore as different as chaff from wheat, dry scrub from fruitful vine,[70] even though which mortals eat and drink to their salvation and which do not will remain unknown until Christ returns.

Gottschalk and Ratramnus evidently consider the terms "flesh" (*caro*) and "body" (*corpus*) synonymous; for Gottschalk, both may be used to speak of the church as well as of the incarnate Christ and the eucharist.[71] Yet in spite of the presence for him of "true" flesh or body and blood in the eucharist, he firmly rejects the idea that even for the elect these can be the body and blood of the crucifixion. In part, his insistence on this point serves to reinforce his contention that the eucharist cannot redeem the wicked, since the sacrament is distanced from the passion that Christ endured only for the elect. Neither through baptism nor through the eucharist may the reprobate escape their destiny of eternal damnation, because even when they receive the eucharistic body and blood they do not have access to the oblation of the cross.[72] But it is also probable that the distinction made by both Gottschalk and Ratramnus between the eucharistic and historical bodies was influenced by their rigid interpretation of divine omnipotence and immutability, which was critical to their defenses of the doctrine of twin predestination. The God of Gottschalk and Ratramnus does not repeat himself, especially when it is so unambiguously (in their view) laid down in scripture that Christ's sacrifice on the cross was unique. As indicated in the epistle to the Hebrews, this is a God who ordained one incarnation and one crucifixion, not many, events that he wills to save only those predestined to salvation. Christ was crucified once for the elect alone, and his torments do not recur in the eucharist.[73]

[68] Gottschalk, *Opus. theol.* 9.3, 23, *Œuvres*, ed. Lambot, 204–205, 328, see 327.
[69] Gottschalk, *Opus. theol.* 23, *Œuvres*, ed. Lambot, 333 lines 26–29.   [70] Ibid., 330.
[71] Ibid., 334–335; see Ratramnus, *De corpore* 25, 71, 72, ed. Van Den Brink, 49, 60–61.
[72] Gottschalk apparently attributes to Hincmar the notion that reception of the eucharist has the same significance for all recipients that the passion has (according to Gottschalk) for the elect alone: *Opus. theol.* 23, *Œuvres*, ed. Lambot, 331 lines 1–8. For Hincmar, however, as indicated above, Christ suffered for everyone, yet the redemption offered through his passion is only received by those who consume the eucharist in a state of faith.
[73] Ibid., 331–332; see Ratramnus, *De corpore* 35–41, ed. Van Den Brink, 51–54.

As this suggests, both Gottschalk and Ratramnus find their primary scriptural justification for differentiating the two bodies in the letter to the Hebrews. The same biblical passages that for Pascasius and Hincmar demonstrate the uniqueness of Christ's sacrifice in the passion and therefore the presence of the incarnate body and blood in the eucharist, for Gottschalk and Ratramnus mean that the eucharistic presence differs from the historical blood and flesh. The exegesis of the last two scholars is strongly influenced by an Augustinian view of the resurrected Jesus as retaining, even in heaven, physical properties he possessed before death, in contrast to the beliefs of Hincmar, Pascasius, and also John Scottus, closer to Ambrose's, that this body is an essentially spiritual entity. For Gottschalk and Ratramnus, it seems, the physical, circumscribable qualities of the body and blood of the crucifixion, resurrection, and ascension mean that they cannot be both the unique oblation of the cross and present in the mass. Otherwise, it must be believed that Christ suffers again in each eucharistic sacrifice, a doctrine that scripture's teachings on the uniqueness of the passion make impossible, but one that Gottschalk accuses Hincmar of defending.[74] Correspondingly, as Gottschalk and Ratramnus both note, echoing the canon of the mass but giving the passage a clearly different exegesis than Pascasius or Hincmar, at the last supper Christ gave his body and blood to his disciples "before he suffered." What he gave, therefore, was not the body that would be crucified.[75] A passage near the end of Gottschalk's *De corpore* further underscores the uniqueness of the crucified flesh and blood, and their physicality, by suggesting that these differ from the eucharist insofar as the "carnate" body alone can be identified as a man.[76]

Nevertheless, more clearly than Ratramnus, Gottschalk posits an essential connection between the eucharist received by the elect and the crucified, incarnate Christ. Again, this supports his doctrine that the crucified body was sacrificed only for those predestined to salvation. Consecrated by the holy spirit, the eucharist of the elect is borne to heaven at the priest's prayer that the gifts be carried to the celestial altar. Just as Jesus gave his

---

[74] Gottschalk, *Opus. theol.* 23, *Œuvres*, ed. Lambot, 331.

[75] Ibid., 329 lines 8–14, see (on what the elect receive) 328, 330, 334–335; Ratramnus, *De corpore* 27–28, ed. Van Den Brink, 50.

[76] Gottschalk, *Opus. theol.* 23, *Œuvres*, ed. Lambot, 334 lines 4–5. Ratramnus hints at the same doctrine: *De corpore* 72, ed. Van Den Brink, 60–61.

body and blood to the disciples at the last supper when he had yet to suffer, so the incarnate, heavenly Christ, his body eternally whole and incorruptible yet circumscribable, bestows the eucharistic body and blood transferred from earth to heaven on the blessed, his church.[77] Through an analogy based on John 12.24–25 and 1 Corinthians 15.35–45, with connections to Augustinian exegesis,[78] it is suggested that the crucified body of Christ, "having been sown in death as a grain or seed of life," rose up like the tree of life to offer its fruit "to those who take it." In consuming the eucharist, the elect alone take or eat this fruit, not the body sacrificed once for all time and resurrected from the dead yet something it produces, which therefore belongs to it.[79] While the heavenly joining of the sacrament with the glorified body is understood to preserve the distinction between them, it also means that the eucharist received from Christ in heaven, Christ himself, and the church that eats to its "remedy" share one "nature." They all deserve the name "body of Christ," as later Carolingian scholars generally agreed, including Pascasius in his *De corpore*. But whereas Pascasius identified the incarnate flesh with the eucharist and suggested that the church was Christ's "body" in a different sense, without clearly indicating how, Gottschalk utilizes the categories of "nature" and "species" in order to define more exactly the relationship among the three entities. Each, he contends, is a different "species" of a single "nature" that is united in one flesh, since Christ possesses only one flesh or body.[80] Flesh (Christ) gives his flesh (the eucharist) to his flesh (the church), all three specially distinct but naturally one.[81] This relationship, which Gottschalk claims to reflect the correct understanding of the claim (taken from Pascasius' treatise but thought to be a direct quotation from Ambrose) that

---

[77] Gottschalk, *Opus. theol.* 23, *Œuvres*, ed. Lambot, 326–328. Whether wicked recipients also receive the transferred entities is unclear. Gottschalk's notion of a transference to the heavenly incarnate Christ is adapted from a passage in Pascasius that he thought came from Augustine. While Pascasius uses the Latin *transferre* to reinforce his claim that the eucharist actually contains the incarnate body, Gottschalk understands the term to affirm the connection yet distinction between these entities. See Pascasius, *De corpore* 7, CCCM 16.38–39; Jean-Paul Bouhot, "Extraits du *De corpore et sanguine Domini* de Pascase Radbert sous le nom d'Augustin," *Recherches augustiniennes* 12 (1977), 119–173, at 138–139.

[78] Augustine, *De Genesi ad litteram* 8.5.9, 11.40.54; *De civ. Dei* 13.20–21.

[79] See Gottschalk, *Opus. theol.* 23, *Œuvres*, ed. Lambot, 328, 329–330. Cf. Pascasius, *De corpore* 7, CCCM 16.38–39.

[80] Gottschalk, *Opus. theol.* 23, *Œuvres*, ed. Lambot, 326–29, 333–334, 337.

[81] Ibid., 335 lines 6–9. See Eph. 5.31–32.

the bread and wine contain the flesh born of Mary,[82] differentiates the eucharist from its Old Testament prefigurations. Unlike the mass elements, it seems, they do not share in the "nature" of Christ's body, being merely figures of the truth to come, a point on which Gottschalk evidently agrees with Pascasius.[83]

Ratramnus' *De corpore et sanguine Domini* opens by describing the recent dispute that led Charles the Bald to order him to write as one between two groups of faithful.[84] Throughout the treatise, it is clear that both groups consist of believing members of Christ's church, or in other words – if there is a connection with his *De praedestinatione* – the elect predestined to salvation. The erroneous teachings of some about the eucharist apparently do not themselves compromise membership in the church, *De corpore* implies, so long as such people have faith in Christ, have been baptized, and believe that the eucharist truly contains his body and blood. Hence although the treatise refers to *fideles* and *credentes* rather than *electi*, its comment that Christ was crucified for the "salvation of believers" (*credentes*)[85] should perhaps be interpreted in light of Ratramnus' and Gottschalk's predestination theology and the notion that Jesus died for the elect. If so, then the "world" for whom Christ died, as noted shortly thereafter in *De corpore*,[86] consists solely of the *credentes*. This would mean that these passages accord with Ratramnus' claim in *De praedestinatione*, quoting Augustine and agreeing with Gottschalk, that the "entire world" of the church is alone saved through Christ, having been elected from the mass of humanity that forms the "damned world."[87] The situation of the damned is not mentioned in Ratramnus' *De corpore*; there is no reference, for instance, even to 1 Corinthians 11.28–29, otherwise so popular a scriptural text in Carolingian writing on the mass and the eucharist. The focus is exclusively on the church consisting of the faithful or blessed who look forward to eternal salvation.

The quarrel that separates the two sets of faithful identified at the outset of Ratramnus' treatise is one over whether Christ's body and blood are present "in truth" in the eucharist, or "in mystery." Those who believe the

---

[82] Gottschalk, *Opus. theol.* 23, *Œuvres*, ed. Lambot, 337, esp. lines 10–13. See Pascasius, *De corpore* 1, *CCCM* 16.15 lines 51–52; cf. Ambrose, *De myst.* 53.

[83] Gottschalk, *Opus. theol.* 23, *Œuvres*, ed. Lambot, 336.

[84] Ratramnus, *De corpore* 2, ed. Van Den Brink, 43.   [85] Ibid. 24, ed. Van Den Brink, 49.

[86] Ibid. 25, ed. Van Den Brink, 49.

[87] Ratramnus, *De praed.* 1, *PL* 121.32B/C; Augustine, *Tract.* 87.2–3.

body and blood are present in truth, he indicates, hold to the Pascasian doctrine that the bread and wine contain the historical, incarnate body and blood. As already noted, Ratramnus believes this position in conflict with the biblical teaching that Christ's sacrifice was unique. Yet although Ratramnus agrees with Gottschalk here, as he does about predestination, he diverges with the monk of Orbais in his concern over what he thinks is a particular facet of the error causing the quarrel: the concept that the eucharistic presence is material and, therefore, sensible. For Ratramnus, the two ideas are interdependent; to claim that the incarnate body and blood are in the sacrament is to believe in a material presence that, at least potentially, is visible to the corporeal eyes, and to combat one doctrine is to confront the other, as well.[88] Nevertheless, it is the notion of a potentially visible presence that most worries him. This is the problem addressed in the first half of his treatise and it is kept in mind throughout the second half, where attention turns to the doctrine that the eucharist contains the incarnate body and blood.

Partly taking a grammatical approach as does Gottschalk in his tracts on the eucharist, Ratramnus hinges his arguments against the visibility of the eucharistic presence on the meanings of "truth" (*veritas*) and "figure" (*figura*).[89] Both words are interpreted in such a way as to make it logically contradictory to think either that the bread and wine are the historical body and blood or that the latter entities are sensibly present. Following Augustine more closely than does Pascasius, with help from Isidor, Ratramnus maintains that the term "figure" denotes only a relationship between two entities with separate existences, a relationship that can therefore be designated by the words "image," "likeness," "pledge," and "sacrament" – though the last term refers to something that is not only an image or likeness, but is also consecrated by the holy spirit.[90] The figure is in its own right a truth, just as is the thing it signifies; an object is a figure if it brings to mind that other, separate existence. To employ one of Augustine's analogies (not one used by Ratramnus, but clarifying his thought), the word "ox" refers to an animal that is itself the sign of an evangelist.[91] Both the ox and the gospel writer exist in reality and the former may function as the sign of the latter, yet it is never identifiable

---

[88] Ratramnus, *De corpore* 2, 5, ed. Van Den Brink, 43, 44. [89] Ibid. 6–8, ed. Van Den Brink, 44.

[90] Ibid. 7, 35–45, 86–89, ed. Van Den Brink, 44, 51–54, 64–65 (Augustine, *Ep.* 98; Isidor, *Etymol.* 6.19.38, 39). See above, n. 44. [91] Augustine, *De doctrina Christiana* 2.10.

with its referent. The ox is never "in truth" the evangelist. Differences between signifier and signified obscure their relationship from the ignorant – for example, many people will not realize that the ox signifies a gospel writer – while the similarities allow this association to be recognized by the knowledgeable. Truth, on the other hand, constitutes something in its own existence. According to Ratramnus' definition, a truthful statement is the "demonstration of something manifest, not veiled by shadow-images but indicated with pure, open, and natural significations, as for example when it is said that Christ was born from the Virgin, suffered, died, and was buried. . . . Here nothing else may be understood than what is said."[92]

Given these definitions, in Ratramnus' view, all the characteristics of a material entity have to be present for it to exist "in truth." More consistently than Pascasius or Hincmar, though, as already noted, he agrees with Augustine and also Gottschalk in conceiving of Christ's incarnate body and blood as corporeal entities even after their resurrection and glorification.[93] For this reason, from his perspective, to assert that they are in the eucharist means that the sacrament ceases to be materially wine and bread, becoming instead physical – hence visible – blood and flesh; and this is to deny the characteristic of the eucharistic presence that Ratramnus most stresses – its spirituality, in contrast to the continued corporeality of Christ's glorified existence. With support from Ambrose, the second half of Ratramnus' *De corpore* affirms that through consecration the bread and wine become body and blood spiritually but "in truth," since they immaterially come to possess every attribute of the body and blood of the glorified savior *except physicality*. Jesus spoke the truth at the last supper, since like the resurrected Christ, the eucharistic presence is immortal, impassible, eternal, and incorruptible.[94] By virtue of this presence of the true, yet immaterial flesh and blood of Jesus, the bread and wine of the mass are sacramental; consecrated by the holy spirit, they bestow eternal life on the faithful recipient. But given Ambrose's confirmation of the eucharist's spiritual nature, Ratramnus argues that, lacking the crucial quality of corporeality, they differ from the "physical" body and blood presently in heaven. Unlike the incarnate Christ, the body and

---

[92] Ratramnus, *De corpore* 8, ed. Van Den Brink, 44.

[93] See ibid. 61–65, ed. Van Den Brink, 58–59 (Ambrose); ibid. 86–97, 100, ed. Van Den Brink, 64–69 (Fulgentius, Augustine).   [94] Ibid. 13, ed. Van Den Brink, 46.

blood of the mass can only be perceived by the mind or soul, not by the corporeal senses.[95]

Virtually every chapter of *De corpore*, though especially its second half,[96] contrasts figure to flesh, image to reality, spiritual to physical in order to highlight the difference between the eucharistic body and blood and the sensible, physical blood and flesh of the crucified and resurrected Jesus, sacrificed once for all time. While Gottschalk allows for a certain connection between the eucharistic and historical bodies through Christ's operation in heaven, Ratramnus only links them insofar as the eucharistic body or flesh is the "figure" of the incarnate truth, a term that for him clearly acknowledges their disjunction. The eucharist is figural, according to Ratramnus' Augustinian understanding of the term, not because it shares that incarnate reality – it does not by the very definition of figure – but solely through their resemblance. The external characteristics of bread and wine and the hidden presence within them, "spiritual" flesh and blood, both bear a likeness to Christ's incarnate body and blood and signify the unity within his body, the church.[97] As independently existing figure and sacrament, the consecrated bread and wine are comparable to the other sacraments of the church, baptism and chrism,[98] and to their Old Testament types. All these things, it seems, are figures or "images" of truth they do not contain, all of them are divinely blessed so as to offer life to believers; the Old Testament prefigurations were the equivalent of the sacraments of baptism and the eucharist available to the faithful Jews living before the incarnation.[99] As Augustine's discussion of sacraments in his letter to Bishop Boniface seems to Ratramnus to affirm, therefore, the eucharist's function as a figure parallels that of the mass liturgy as a whole, the "image" and "representation" of the model of patience on the cross, which inspires the faithful to follow the example of suffering that Christ set in his passion.[100]

It becomes evident toward the end of his treatise that Ratramnus' concern to refute the doctrine of a visible presence in the eucharist and to emphasize its difference, on this basis, from the incarnate body and blood

[95] See ibid. 51–60, ed. Van Den Brink, 55–58 (Ambrose).
[96] Ibid., esp. 50–101, ed. Van Den Brink, 55–69.
[97] Ibid. 40, 73–75, ed. Van Den Brink, 53–54, 61; see ibid. 95–96, 98–100, ed. Van Den Brink, 67–69 (Augustine). [98] Ibid. 17–18, 46 (Isidor), ed. Van Den Brink 47, 54–55.
[99] Ibid. 20–25, ed. Van Den Brink, 48–49.
[100] Ibid. 35–38, ed. Van Den Brink, 51–53 (Augustine).

reflects a deep interest, beyond what is seen in Pascasius' or Gottschalk's eucharist writings but reminiscent of Hincmar, in the relationship between the eucharist's contents and the final vision of the eschaton. In this, his work echoes the discussions of the vision of God that took place within and alongside the deliberations over divine predestination, both issues that are connected with eucharist theology in Hincmar's *Ferculum Salomonis* and *De cavendis*. Towards the end of his *De corpore*, Ratramnus links the terms figure, image, likeness, pledge, and sacrament with the eucharist's role as the figure not only of past truth – the crucified savior – but also of the hidden, supernal reality that will be manifested when the world ends. But whereas Hincmar's *De cavendis* urges Charles the Bald to rejoice in the foretaste of the future that the eucharist offers in the present, the monk of Corbie more forcefully insists on the eucharist's inferiority to the joy of Christ's return, when the blessed will see him "face to face" and behold the "truth itself."[101] The difference in outlook parallels the differences in the two scholars' eucharist and predestination theologies. For Hincmar, the eucharist offers all mortals the chance to be washed of their sins and receive the divine grace available to everyone in the one-time oblation on the cross, since it contains that very flesh and blood. Through the eucharist, any mortal, if he or she has faith, may come in contact with the very body that the blessed will behold in heaven, granted that the eucharistic experience is spiritual and grounded in faith, involving something that remains physically invisible. But Ratramnus' eucharistic doctrine is in line with his concept of God's predestination of the elect to salvation and the wicked to damnation, whether or not it was directly influenced by his participation in the predestination dispute. The eucharist does not provide any opportunity to alter this eternally ordained destiny, established in the unique sacrifice on the cross. Although as a sacrament it bestows eternal life on believers, then, it also reminds them of what happened once in the crucifixion, the source of their grace, and it sustains the church as it awaits the reward promised only to them, which they alone will enjoy and only once humanity's final lot is revealed at the end of time.

[101] "Quoniam hoc proprium salvatoris corpus existit, nec in eo vel aliqua figura, vel aliqua significatio, sed ipsa rei manifestatio cognoscitur, et ipsius visionem credentes desiderant, quoniam ipsum est caput nostrum. Et ipso viso, saciabitur desiderium nostrum. Quoniam ipse et pater unum sunt. Non secundum quod corpus habet salvator, sed secundum plenitudinem divinitatis quae habitat in homine christo": ibid. 97, ed. Van Den Brink, 68; see ibid. 88, 100, ed. Van Den Brink, 64–65, 68–69. Cf. Hincmar, *De cavendis* 3.2, MGH *Quellen* 16.245–246 (Augustine).

Conclusion

For the participants in both sides of the eucharistic controversy, as far as we can judge from their extant writings, and for the authors of the numerous other later Carolingian texts that reflect on the mass liturgy's signification, the eucharist plays a unique role in the church. Picking up on refrains heard in the liturgy, in Hebrews, and in the gospel accounts of the last supper and passion, they generally seem to agree that the consecrated elements are the divinely empowered gifts of the dying Jesus, reminders of his one-time sacrifice and sources of life in the present for those who eat and drink in faith. One of the most prominent themes of this literature is that faithful reception of the sacrament both symbolizes Christians' relation with their heavenly lord and one another and actually joins them together, whether true faith is narrowly identified with the elect, as in Gottschalk's and probably Ratramnus' eucharist theology, or is believed potentially available to all mortals. Whatever the connection envisioned between the body of the church, the body eaten in the mass, and Christ's incarnate body, consumption of the bread and wine reinforces the union created at baptism among the members of the ecclesiastical body and between them and their head.

In addition, the extant treatises that reflect the eucharist controversy all confront, in varying ways, the apparent contradiction between the scripturally based doctrine of the crucifixion's one-time offering and Jesus' speech at the last supper, echoed in the mass, announcing the bread and wine to be his body and blood. While to clarify the relation between the body on the cross and in the eucharist was one aim of Pascasius' *De corpore et sanguine Domini*, this matter became the driving force in the mid-ninth-century debate, and reverberations of it, as of the quarrel over predestination, are evident in later writings by Hincmar and John Scottus. The attempts to explain the nature of the eucharistic presence, by all the theologians studied here, coincide with new consideration of the nature of Christ's body on earth, after the resurrection, and in heaven, its relation to the body of the church, and the experience of the crucified savior available to the faithful through the sacrament compared with that of the end of time.

Despite the usage of some of the same patristic sources, these tangled issues led each participant in the conflict to formulate a eucharist theology not completely like that of any contemporary. Leaving aside John Scottus' thought, which, as far as it is known, has similarities to teachings from both sides of the quarrel as well as its own, distinctive features, the most notable divergence is between the positions of Gottschalk and Ratramnus, on the one hand, and Pascasius and Hincmar on the other. The first two scholars differentiate Christ's body in the eucharist from the essentially corporeal body of the crucifixion and resurrection, though Gottschalk links the incarnate and eucharistic entities more closely than does Ratramnus. Hincmar and Pascasius dwell to a greater degree on the redemptive significance of Jesus' crucified human nature, contending that precisely this suffering, bleeding body, the unique source of remission of sins, is received in the mass.

Yet as might seem paradoxical, given the concern of Hincmar and Pascasius with the suffering Christ and the emphasis of Gottschalk and Ratramnus on the immutability of God's will, the eucharist theology of the first two scholars also grants a clear place to divine omnipotence in determining the sacrament's contents. Christ's status as God and truth incarnate, Pascasius and Hincmar assert, enables him to override even the divinely established laws of nature. This is why his one human nature, transformed after the resurrection into a spiritual entity but still evidently retaining a certain corporeality, can be simultaneously indivisible in heaven and available on earth in every celebration of the mass, including the last supper. As Hincmar, especially, makes clear, though there is a hint of the same idea in Pascasius' letter to Fredugard, the doctrine suggested by 1 Timothy 2.4, that Christ's death offers salvation to all humanity, possesses an unassailable foundation in his eternal divinity. For only a God who is all-powerful can operate against the laws of the physical universe so as to assure that his unique, crucified flesh and blood are present in every consecration of the bread and wine. In Hincmar's writings, more clearly than Pascasius', such beliefs are associated with an emphasis on ecclesiastical authority also found in the archbishop's treatises on predestination (as well as in other works by him). They are tied, as well, to a concept of faithful reception of the eucharist as a precursor to divine illumination that gives the relationship between those two experiences a very different twist from that suggested in Ratramnus' *De corpore.*·

CHAPTER 7

Three later Carolingian crucifixion images

The ninth-century Carolingian empire witnessed a surge in imagery of the crucifixion, the first time in western Europe that this became a significant subject of artistic representation. More than ever before in the west, judging from the available evidence, clergy, monks, and laity desired works of art that would place the crucified Christ before their eyes. While later Carolingian theologians asserted that the seeing of crosses inspired inner contemplation of the crucified savior; debated the relation of the body and blood mentally "beheld" in the eucharist to the visible features of bread and wine; compared remembrance of the crucifixion and the experience of the eucharist with the final vision of God; and examined the role of Holy Week and the mass as visual reminders of the passion, artists provided the faithful with material representations of the sight for which they longed.

Of all the crucifixion images in different artistic media produced in the ninth-century Carolingian church, probably the most remarkable is the ivory presently set into the cover of the early-eleventh-century Pericopes of Henry II (fig. 30).[1] The plaque is generally thought to have been made at the court school of Charles the Bald between 840 and 870, with scholars usually preferring the later to the early years of this period. Although the school's artistic center is uncertain, its work reveals ties to Rheims and

---

[1] Munich, Bayerische Staatsbibliothek, Clm. 4452. The Book of Pericopes was given by Henry II to Bamberg Cathedral shortly before 1014. I am very grateful to Dr. Elisabeth Klemm of the Bayerische Staatsbibliothek, Munich, for arranging for me to study the Pericopes ivory and the cover of the *Codex Aureus* of St. Emmeram (Munich, Bayerische Staatsbibliothek, Clm. 14000) at first hand.

Metz. The Pericopes tablet is one of a group of stylistically and iconographically related depictions of the crucifixion, in various media, typically attributed to Metz, Charles' court school, and sometimes other centers, and broadly dated between c. 840 and the end of the ninth century. No other Carolingian rendering of the passion, however, matches this carving for the complex theological program that its elegant craftsmanship seems to set before the viewer. Most of its individual motifs appear in other Carolingian works of art, but they are brought together into a composition without known, overall model or contemporary parallel.

The unusual crucifixion images of *In honorem sanctae crucis* and the Gellone Sacramentary were possibly influenced by concerns about the relative value of artistic imagery and the written word such as are expressed in the *Opus Caroli regis*. More noticeably, they suggest the impact of the Christology of the passion that took shape in the early Carolingian court, as it confronted Spanish Adoptionism and Byzantine iconodulism. Hrabanus and the sacramentary's designer, both likely to have been familiar with theological developments within Charlemagne's entourage, created unprecedented pictorial forms that integrate text and imagery in ways that seem to underscore their crucified redeemer's union of two natures in one person, thereby providing new visual perspectives on the implications of this fundamental Christian teaching. The Pericopes ivory, too, I think, was influenced by the clarification of dogma spurred by theological controversy in Carolingian scholarly circles, in particular by Hincmar's contributions to the quarrels over divine predestination and the eucharistic presence. As this suggests, the archbishop of Rheims may well have been the ivory's patron. Not only is it possible that its composition owes something to his theological doctrine, however. One further aim of the plaque, I will propose, was to remind Charles the Bald of Hincmar's views on the criteria of virtuous rulership. As Lawrence Nees has argued for the Hercules plaques on the ivory-decorated throne known as the *Cathedra Petri* (fig. 19),[2] here again we may have a work of art commissioned by Hincmar to warn Charles about the demands and risks of secular power, ideas that the archbishop also sought to communicate to the king and other princes in writing.

Before turning to the Pericopes tablet, it is helpful to investigate the intellectual concerns suggested by two manuscript depictions of the crucifixion

---

[2] See Nees, *Tainted Mantle*, esp. Parts 3, 4.

that probably predate its carving. Along with other imagery in the same codices, these probably served, directly or indirectly, as sources for certain of the ivory's pictorial elements, and some lines of thought they imply seem to be related. One is the illustration to Psalm 115 in the Utrecht Psalter (fig. 26), a Rheims production generally dated to 820–835, but which I have recently argued may instead have been made c. 845–855, during the first decade of Hincmar's archiepiscopacy.[3] The second is the crucifixion miniature in the Drogo Sacramentary (fig. 27), produced for Bishop Drogo of Metz most likely after the psalter and usually assigned to the last years of his episcopacy. Work on the sacramentary quite possibly ceased with Drogo's death in 855.[4]

The Utrecht Psalter illustration to Psalm 115

Scholarship on the Utrecht Psalter has long recognized that most of its 166 uncolored, pen and ink drawings offer closely "literal" illustrations of the texts, with individual phrases and sometimes words transposed directly into visual form. Many scenes, however, include some motifs deriving from Christian interpretations of the codex's chiefly Old Testament material. The lord praised by David is frequently portrayed as Christ, the Trinity is

[3] Utrecht, Bibliotheek der Rijksuniversiteit, MS 32, folio 67r; Chazelle, "Archbishops Ebo and Hincmar of Reims." Christian Beutler dates the Pericopes ivory to Louis the Pious' reign (814–840) on the grounds that its style indicates a close relationship with the Utrecht Psalter: *Der Gott am Kreuz: zur Entstehung der Kreuzigungsdarstellung* (Hamburg, 1986), 6. My suggestion that the psalter, like the ivory, may have been produced under Hincmar also takes the two works' stylistic similarities into account. Facsimile of the psalter in *Utrecht-Psalter: vollständige Faksimile-Ausgabe im Originalformat der Handschrift 32, Utrecht-Psalter, aus dem Besitz der Bibliotheek der Rijksunjiversiteit te Utrecht*, 2 vols., Commentary by K. van der Horst and J. A. Engelbregt (Graz, 1984). The illustrations of the Utrecht Psalter were also published earlier; they are probably most accessible in E. T. Dewald, *The Illustrations of the Utrecht Psalter* (Princeton, 1933). For references to other literature on the psalter, see my article and Koert van der Horst, William Noel, Wilhelmina C. M. Wüstefeld, eds., *The Utrecht Psalter in Medieval Art: Picturing the Psalms of David* (Westrenen, 1996).

[4] Paris, BNF, MS lat. 9428, fol. 43v; Facsimile in *Drogo-Sakramentar, Ms. Latin 9428, Bibliothèque nationale, Paris. Vollständige Faksimile-Ausgabe im Originalformat*, 2 vols., ed. F. Mütherich, commentary by W. Köhler (Graz, 1974), on the date, 13–17. Franz Unterkircher, *Zur Ikonographie und Liturgie des Drogo-Sakramentars* (Graz, 1977), 9–11, 18–19 favors a date before 840, but he is not generally followed. More recently, a date of c. 845–855 is proposed by Roger E. Reynolds, "Image and Text: A Carolingian Illustration of Modifications in the Early Roman Eucharistic Ordines," *Viator* 14 (1983), 59–75, esp. 64; and Elizabeth Leesti, "Illustrations in the Drogo Sacramentary (Paris, BNF, MS lat. 9428)" (Ph.D. diss., University of Toronto, 1984), 205; see also idem, "Carolingian Crucifixion Iconography: an Elaboration of a Byzantine Theme," *Revue d'art canadienne / Canadian Art Review* 20 (1993), 3–15.

PATER NOSTER
QUI ES IN CAELIS SCIFICE
TUR NOMEN TUUM · AD
UENIAT REGNUM TUUM ·
FIAT UOLUNTAS TUA

SICUT IN CAELO ET IN TRA
PANEM NOSTRUM COTI
DIANUM DA NOBIS HO
DIE · ET DIMITTE NOBIS
DEBITA NOSTRA ·

SICUT ET NOS DIMITTI
MUS DEBITORIBUS NOS
TRIS · ET NE NOS INDU
CAS IN TEMPTATIONEM
SED LIBERA NOS A MALO ·

INCIPIT SYMBOLU   APOSTOLORUM
CREDO IN DOM PA
TREM OMNIPOTENTEM
CREATORE CAELI ET TERRAE
ET IN IHM XPM FILIUM EIUS
UNICUM DNM NOSTRU ·
QUI CONCEPTUS EST DE SPU
SCO · NATUS EX MARIA UIR

GIN AE · PASSUS SUB PON
TIO PILATO CRUCIFIXUS
MORTUUS ET SEPULTUS · DES
CENDIT AD INFERNA · TER
TIA DIE RESURREXIT A MOR
TUIS · ASCENDIT AD CAELUM
SEDET AD DEXTERAM DI PA

TRIS · OMNIPOTENTIS IN
DE UENTURUS IUDICARE
UIUOS ET MORTUOS ·
CREDO ET IN SPM SCM SCAM
ECCLESIAM CATHOLICAM
SCORUM · COMMUNIO
NEM · REMISSIONEM

Figure 22. Illustration to the Apostles' Creed, Utrecht Psalter, Utrecht, Bibliotheek der Rijksuniversiteit, MS 32, fol. 90 recto

depicted, twice with the Virgin Mary alongside (Gloria, Apostles' Creed; fols. 89v, 90r; fig. 22), and about ten illustrations make typological references to Christian events that the Old Testament texts were understood to prefigure, one being the crucifixion.[5] The psalter contains one depiction of a cross accompanied by the other instruments of the passion (whip, crown of thorns, lance, sponge, lot machine), in the illustration to Psalm 21 (fol. 12r); and it has four representations of the crucifixion itself, two in psalm illustrations: to Psalm 88 (fol. 51v; fig. 23), where the image illustrates verse 39 ("But thou has rejected and despised: thou hast been angry with thy anointed") and/or verse 52 ("Wherewith thy enemies have reproached, O Lord; wherewith they have reproached the change of thy anointed);[6] and to

---

[5] See Koert van der Horst, "The Utrecht Psalter: Picturing the Psalms of David," in *The Utrecht Psalter in Medieval Art,* ed. van der Horst et al., 23–84, at 67–70; Suzy Dufrenne, *Les Illustrations du Psautier d'Utrecht: Sources et apport carolingien* (Paris, 1978), 130–136, 140–150.

[6] Dufrenne links the image mainly with Ps. 88.39, but Augustine's exegesis suggests verse 52 as another possibility: *Enarr. in Ps.* 88.2, CCSL 39, ed. D. E. Dekkers and J. Fraipont (Turnhout,

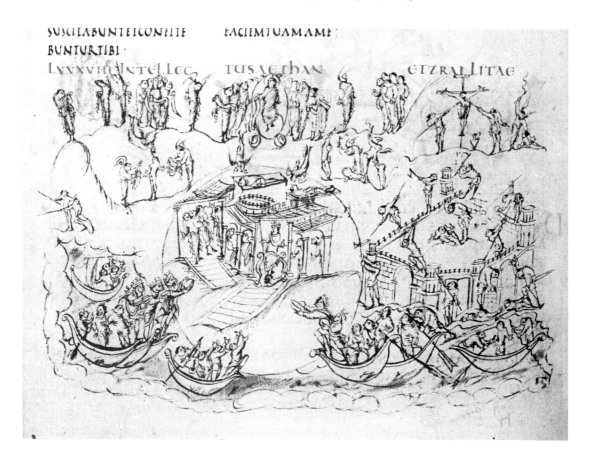

SUSCITABUNTEICONIHE   FACIEMTUAMAME

BUNTURTIBI·

LXXXVIIIINTELLEC   TUSAETHAN   GIZRALITAG

Psalm 115 (fol. 67r; fig. 26). The two remaining crucifixion images accompany texts appended to the psalms: the Canticle of Habbacuc (fol. 85v; fig. 24), and the Apostles' Creed (fol. 90r; fig. 22), a Carolingian addition to the Latin psalter. The last-named picture is both Christian and "literal"; its representations of New Testament events form an essentially literal illustration of the verses' narrative of the same episodes, in keeping with Utrecht's general preference for this type of decoration.

It has been argued that the Utrecht Psalter reflects an earlier tradition for literal illustration of the psalter that also influenced another Carolingian manuscript, the Stuttgart Psalter.[7] Stuttgart is usually dated c. 820–830, partly on the basis of comparison to Utrecht. Similarities with

Figure 23. Illustration to Psalm 88, Utrecht Psalter, Utrecht, Bibliotheek der Rijksuniversiteit, MS 32, fol. 51 verso

1956), 1242–1243; *De civ. Dei* 17.12, *CCSL* 48, ed. B. Dombart and A. Kalb (Turnhout, 1955), 576. Cf. Dufrenne, *Illustrations*, 64–65 and n. 212.

7 Stuttgart, Württembergische Landesbibliothek, Cod. bibl. 2 23; *Der stuttgarter Bilderpsalter. Bibl. Fol. 23, Württembergische Landesbibliothek Stuttgart*, 2 vols., ed. B. Bischoff et al. (Stuttgart, 1965–1968); *The Stuttgart Psalter: Biblia folio 23, Württembergische Landesbibliothek, Stuttgart*, Commentary by E. T. Dewald (Princeton, 1930).

AE·DNSREGNABITIN
AETERNUMEIUITRA·

ETEQUITIBUSEIUSINMA
RE·ETREDUXITSUPER

BULAUERUNTPERSICCUM
INMEDIOEIUS·

CANTICUMABACUC
DNEAUDIUI·
AUDITIONEMTUAMTUA

PROPHETE
IBLABSCONDITAESTFORTI
TUDOEIUS·ANTEFACIEM

IRATUSESDNE·AUTINFLU
MINIBUSFURORTUUS·UEL

Figure 24. Illustration to the Canticle of Habbacuc, Utrecht Psalter, Utrecht, Bibliotheek der Rijksuniversiteit, MS 32, fol. 85 verso

Stuttgart and the Byzantine marginal psalters, the latter showing elements of the same tradition, have been noted in the choices of verses illustrated, the subjects, and occasionally in composition. Florentine Mütherich and more recently Kathleen Corrigan have observed, though, that virtually all the connections between Utrecht and these other ninth-century manuscripts have solely to do with the literal illustrations of Old Testament material, whereas the Byzantine psalters and Stuttgart are also related to one another in some of their Christian typological imagery.[8] In terms of the crucifixion, the event is depicted for Psalm 1.3 in the Stuttgart Psalter (fol. 2r); for Psalms 21.2 and 18–19 in the Khludov (fols. 19r–20r), Pantokrator (fol. 10r),[9] and Stuttgart Psalters (fols. 25v, 27r); for Psalms 45.7 and 68.22 in Khludov (fols. 45v, 67r; fig. 25) and Psalm 68.22 in Stuttgart (fol. 80v); and for Psalm 73.12 in both the Khludov (fol. 72v) and

---

[8] I follow here the summary of the state of research in Kathleen Corrigan, *Visual Polemics in the Ninth-Century Byzantine Psalters* (Cambridge, 1992), 8–9, see 82–83. See, too, van der Horst, "The Utrecht Psalter," 73–76, citing Florentine Mütherich, "Die Stellung der Bilder in der früh-mittelalterlichen Psalterillustration," in *Der stuttgarter Bilderpsalter*, ed. Bischoff et al., 2.151–222. Cf. Dufrenne, *Illustrations*, 140–150. The thesis of a common ancestry between the Byzantine marginal psalters and Utrecht, and of the latter as primarily a copy of a single, early Christian psalter, has been most forcefully advanced by Dufrenne, *Illustrations*. See, though, the reviews of this book by Herbert Kessler, *Art Bulletin* 63 (1981), 142–145, Joachim E. Gaehde, *Kunstchronik* 35 (1982), 396–405.

[9] Khludov Psalter, Moscow, His. Mus. Cod. 129; Pantokrator Psalter, Mt. Athos, Pantokrator 61.

Figure 25. Illustration to Psalm 68, Khludov Psalter, Moscow, State Historical Museum, gr. 129, fol. 67 recto

Pantokrator Psalters (fol. 98r). As this indicates, while crucifixion images illustrate some of the same psalm verses in these books, the scene's locations in Utrecht are without parallel in either Stuttgart or the marginal psalters. Whatever the degree to which Old Testament, literal decoration links Utrecht with the manuscripts just noted, no such connection or common ancestry explains its crucifixion images, and therefore they, at least, are best regarded as the products of independent, Carolingian design decisions.

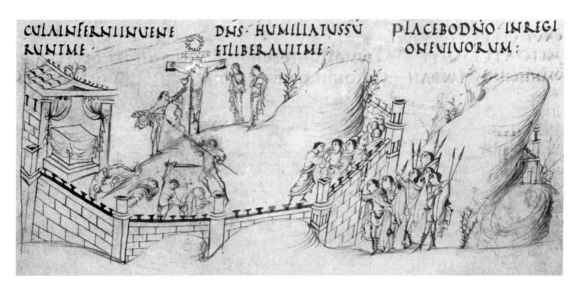

CULAINFERNIINUENE
RUNTME ·

DNS · HUMILIATUSSU
ETLIBERAUITME;

PLACEBODÑO · INREGI
ONEUIUORUM;

Figure 26. Illustration to Psalm 115, Utrecht Psalter, Utrecht, Bibliotheek der Rijksuniversiteit, MS 32, fol. 67 recto

The illustration to Psalm 115 (fig. 26) differs on three main counts from the other pictures of the crucified Christ and from certain design principles otherwise evident in the psalter. First, this is the only representation of the scene with overtly eucharistic details, a chalice held to Christ's side to receive the blood from his wound and a paten piled with hosts. Second, it is the only one in which Jesus' eyes seem closed in death.[10] And third, as educated, ninth-century users of the psalter would surely have recognized, it is the only drawing in the psalter in which the crucifixion is the organizing principle of the entire picture, rather than one among several, separate motifs referring to different portions of the text. The other pictorial forms have been deliberately and meaningfully selected and arranged into a unified composition structured around the crucifix, so that the drawing as a whole – not merely certain parts of it – conveys a coherent, essentially typological message that breaks decisively with the predominance of literal illustration in most of the manuscript. Consequently, no matter what role older models might have played in the rest of the psalter or for some, specific elements of this image, the Psalm 115 picture was most likely conceptualized in its entirety by its Carolingian designer.

In order to assess the signification of this unusual drawing, we must begin with its psalm. The opening verse is numbered 10 in the Vulgate, because in the Hebrew order Psalms 114 and 115 form two parts of the single Psalm 116:

[10] Denoted by short lines, in contrast to the dots used in the psalter's other crucifixion-images; see Haussherr, *Der tote Christus am Kreuz*, 111–114, esp. 113.

10   I have believed, therefore have I spoken; but I have been humbled exceedingly.

11   I said in my excess: Every man is a liar.

12   What shall I render to the Lord, for all the things that he hath rendered to me?

13   I will take the chalice of salvation; and I will call upon the name of the Lord.

14   I will pay my vows to the Lord before all his people:

15   precious in the sight of the Lord is the death of his saints.

16   O Lord, for I am thy servant: I am thy servant, and the son of thy handmaid. Thou hast broken my bonds:

17   I will sacrifice to thee the sacrifice of praise, and I will call upon the name of the Lord.

18   I will pay my vows to the Lord in the sight of all his people:

19   in the courts of the house of the Lord, in the midst of thee, O Jerusalem.

As should be evident from the discussion in chapter 3 of the Gellone Sacramentary miniatures, several aspects of the Utrecht picture for Psalm 115 have clear western or Byzantine precedents. The beardless Jesus, nimbed and robed in a short-sleeved colobium-like garment, hangs stiffly on a cross surmounted by a *tabula ansata*.[11] The victory wreath poised on top of the cross (a motif not seen in earlier crucifixion imagery) probably signifies the continued presence of the divine nature and its victory despite the human mortality. Although neither Longinus nor Stephaton is present (this is the only crucifixion image in Utrecht without those two figures), blood flows from the open wound in Christ's side. Mary and John are both to the cross's right, with the Virgin closest to her son. The hill on which they stand brings their heads nearly, but not quite, level with Christ's, above the other figures in the scene. Both raise their hands to their faces in gestures that suggest thoughtfulness or perhaps grief. The portrayal of Jesus as dead on the cross – the weight of his body pulls slightly down on his arms, his head bows towards his right shoulder (the moment of death described in John 19.30), and his eyes are apparently shut – departs from what has survived of older western imagery, but the second crucifixion initial of the Gellone Sacramentary (fig. 10) possibly showed a dead crucified Christ and the iconography is found on

[11]   Cf. the crucifixion fresco in the Chapel of Theodotus, Sta. Maria Antiqua, Rome (fig. 8).

eighth- and early ninth-century icons from Mt. Sinai.[12] Probably no image of the chalice held to the side of the crucified Jesus – an iconography that first appears in ninth-century Carolingian productions – predates the Utrecht Psalter, but if the manuscript was produced in 845 or later, it postdates the miniatures depicting the eucharistic cup alongside the lamb of God in the Arnaldus Gospels and Bamberg Bible, Tours manuscripts of c. 840,[13] and a chalice is set to the right of Christ in one of the Stuttgart Psalter crucifixion images (fol. 27r).

Like most other drawings of the Utrecht Psalter, the Psalm 115 picture directly illustrates individual words and phrases of the accompanying text, in this case by lending them a Christian interpretation. In accordance with verse 19, the artist has set Christ in an open space surrounded by a polygonal, turreted wall. Mary is the "handmaid" of verse 16. Below the cross and to its left, the male figure dressed in a loincloth is the psalmist; the rope dangling from his left wrist evokes the close of the same verse. The chalice he raises to Christ's side recalls verse 13; the paten and chalice together are reminders of verses 13 and 17, from which the phrases "chalice of salvation" and "sacrifice of praise" are echoed in the Gregorian canon of the mass.[14] In the middle ground of the picture, below David and near the small temple beside him, two dead bodies lie on the ground and a soldier raises his sword to behead a man kneeling at his feet, recalling the saints' deaths of verse 15. To the right, a group of weaponless men dressed in tunics and mantles gaze over the wall at armed soldiers. The foremost figure among the unarmed men touches another's lips in reference, probably, to David's declaration in his "excess" that "every man is a liar" (verse 11). In contrast to the soldiers on both sides of the wall, the weaponless figures in the enclosure, the "courts of the house of the Lord" that form the heavenly Jerusalem, count among the Lord's "people" before whom David proclaims his devotion to Christ, according to verses 14 and 18.

Two critical features of the drawing, however, that are not immediately explained by the psalm itself, prayers of the mass, or known, earlier iconographic traditions for representing the crucifixion, are David's dress in a side-knotted loincloth and the soldier directly below the cross who points

[12] Weitzmann, *Icons*, cat. B.36, 50.

[13] Nancy, Cathedral Treasury, unnumbered MS, fol. 3v; Bamberg, Staatliche Bibliothek, Misc. class. Bibl. 1, fol. 339v; Hubert et al., *L'Empire carolingien*, 132–133 figs. 120, 121.

[14] *Sacramentaire grégorien* 1, ed. Deshusses, nos. 6, 11.

his spear toward the psalmist. Cynthia Hahn has astutely noted that in order to account for these details, it is necessary to interpret the image through the prism of early Christian exegesis of Psalm 115, especially Augustine's *enarratio*.[15] For Augustine, this psalm echoes the "voice of the martyr," that is of believers unafraid to confess their faith, though they may be humbled by tribulation; God will console and strengthen them.[16] The chalice of salvation that David renders to the lord (verse 13) designates the pain of the crucifixion. In line with Matthew 20.21–22, Jesus gives the chalice to others when he asks them to imitate his sufferings, just as do the martyrs in the Utrecht illustration by dying for their beliefs at the same time he dies.[17] Those who embrace not heresy but orthodox belief, according to Augustine, in particular the martyrs, are not only servants of God but sons of his handmaid and mother, whose special status is indicated in the drawing by her elevated position between Jesus and John, the latter her son in a special sense. Together these servants of Christ reside within the "courts of the house of the lord" because they are precious in his sight. The martyrs are lovers of peace as opposed to the lovers of war, Augustine declares, a contrast signified in the psalter drawing by the juxtaposition of the unarmed saints, David, Christ, Mary, and John to their well-armed enemies.[18]

Augustine's exegesis provides the key to understanding David's posture, dress, and relation to the soldier facing him in the illustration.[19] His arms stretch to either side of his body as Christ's arms are extended on the cross, and it is David who wears the perizoma. The loincloth is reminiscent of the one worn by the crucified Jesus in the Utrecht drawing for Psalm 88 (fig. 23) and (it seems, though the image is unclear) in the picture for the Canticle of Habbacuc (fig. 24), both pictures that show him between Longinus and Stephaton. In the Psalm 115 illustration, though, the psalmist rather than his redeemer is threatened by the spear bearer, who points his lance at the

---

[15] *Passio Kiliani ... Passio Margaretae: Faksimile-Ausgabe des Codex, ... MS. I 189 ... aus dem Besitz der Niedersächsischen Landesbibliothek Hannover*, commentary by Cynthia Hahn (Graz, 1988), 116.

[16] Augustine, *Enarr. in Ps.* 115.3–4, CCSL 40, ed. D. E. Dekkers and J. Fraipont (Turnhout, 1956), 1652–1656, at 1654–1655.

[17] See Matthew 20.21–22: "She saith to him [Jesus]: Say that these my two sons may sit, the one on thy right hand, and the other on thy left, in thy kingdom. And Jesus answering, said: You know not what you ask. Can you drink the chalice that I shall drink? They say to him: We can."

[18] See Augustine, *Enarr. in Ps.* 115.5–9, CCSL 40.1655–1656.

[19] Hahn, *Passio Kiliani ...*, 116 and n. 121.

very spot in David's side that corresponds to Jesus' side wound. Raising the cup of the mass, a symbol of the son of God's torments and bloodshed, the half-naked David waits to receive his attacker's blow and spill his own blood, imitating Christ's lowliness and death as well as the humble deaths of the nearby martyrs. In Augustine's words, he is "conformed to Christ through the chalice of salvation."[20] The psalmist faces the same fate as Jesus and the saints because he has spoken the truth. He, too, accepts martyrdom, and the sacrifice he makes in presenting his body to the spear is another way that he pays his "vows to the Lord." By this "sacrifice of praise" and the parallel oblation of the chalice and paten, he renders "to the Lord, for all the things that he hath rendered to me," in answer to the question posed in verse 12. He, too, is Christ's servant and son of his handmaid, manifesting his faith through both his willingness to die for Christ and his participation in the mass. For his imitation of his crucified lord, his "bonds" are broken, whether those of sin or physical life, as they are for the martyrs, and like Mary, John, and the other saints he deserves a place with Christ in the heavenly Jerusalem. Triumph comes out of patience, humility, and even death, just as it did for Christ, as shown by the victory wreath over his head and the chalice catching his salvific blood.

Partly inspired by Augustine's teachings, the designer of the Psalm 115 illustration has transposed into visual form some of the most pronounced refrains in later Carolingian thought about the crucifixion and its relation to penance and the mass. As discussed by Amalarius in his exegesis of the liturgy, Hrabanus in his own liturgical exegesis and sermons for Holy Week, and other ninth-century scholars in a range of writings, the passion involved an oblation of mortal humanity that is recalled and rehearsed in the mass, constitutes the source of the healing food and drink of the eucharist, and presents a model of patience in adversity and of self-sacrifice. Whereas the martyrs follow Jesus by physically dying in his name, other clergy, monks, and laity may do so through faith and virtue, above all humility. They suffer for Christ by humbly repenting their sins and participating in the eucharist as does David in this image, Christ-like – and consequently like the martyrs – in his offering of both the chalice and paten and his own body. The difference between the passive acquiescence to pain and death shown by Christ, David, and the martyr-saints, and the bristling

---

[20] Augustine, *Enarr. in Ps* 115.9, *CCSL* 40.1656.

weapons of their enemies, and correspondingly the implicit contrast between the soldiers' manifestations of violence and faithful participation in the mass, mirror the association of wickedness with armed force and virtue with its renunciation that runs through much of the Utrecht illustration, a theme I more closely explore in a forthcoming article.[21] The designer of the Psalm 115 drawing wanted the psalter's users to reflect on these doctrines as they joined Mary and John in contemplation of the dead Christ, witnessing his bloodshed that simultaneously attests his divinity and suffering sacrifice, and remembering the triumph signified by the wreath above his head. Thus the viewer might be expected to experience contrition for the sins that made the crucifixion necessary. In desiring to be like the saints, David, and Christ, he or she would long for the celestial Jerusalem in which they already reside, where, the canon of the mass reminds believers, the food of Christ's body and blood is perpetually offered at the heavenly altar.

The explicit connection that the illustration draws between Psalm 115, the eucharist, and the crucifixion does not occur in Augustine's exegesis of the psalm, but his comments on the phrase "chalice of salvation" certainly allow for the idea. Further inspiration for the picture obviously lay in the prayers of the mass liturgy, with their echoes of verses 13 and 17, and probably in the large volume of Carolingian literature that refers to the eucharist and its chalice as channels of the redemption achieved in Jesus' death.[22] In particular, the Utrecht picture has been compared with the references to Psalm 115.13 in Pascasius Radbertus' *De corpore et sanguine Domini*. Pascasius connects the verse with Jesus' words of institution in chapter 21 of his treatise's first edition, written in 831–833. The chalice in the psalm is identified

---

[21] "Violence and Virtuous Rulership in the Utrecht Psalter" was delivered at the symposium, *Der illuminierte Psalter: Darstellungsinhalte, Bildgebrauch und Zierausstattung*, October 4–6, 1999, Bamberg, Germany, and will be published in the conference proceedings. See also Corrigan, "Early Medieval Psalter Illustration in Byzantium and the West," in *The Utrecht Psalter in Medieval Art*, ed. van der Horst et al., 85–103, at 101, noting the militaristic character of the Utrecht Psalter decoration.

[22] Note, however, that the Stuttgart Psalter image for the same psalm (fol. 130v) shows David before an altar without depicting the crucifixion. The Harley Psalter (London, BL, Harley MS 603, fols. 59r, 59v), in many respects a copy of Utrecht, illustrates Ps. 115 with a figure holding a large cup up to Christ in majesty and, in a second image, to a standing Christ (no crucifixion). See W. Noel, *The Harley Psalter* (Cambridge 1995), 77, 157–161, figs. 35, 71; idem, "The Utrecht Psalter in England: Continuity and Experiment," in *The Utrecht Psalter in Medieval Art*, ed. van der Horst et al., 121–165, at 136 and fig. 27. Cf. Suzy Dufrenne, *Tableaux synoptiques de 15 psautiers médiévaux* (Paris, 1978), Ps. 115.

as the cup of the mass and a symbol of Christ's passion. Chapter 19 of the revised edition, dating to 843–844, adds a new comment that links the same verse with the passion and the commingling, the addition of a particle of bread to the eucharistic chalice. David's chalice prefigures the "mystery of Christ's passion," Pascasius there states, an event that involved both Christ's flesh and his blood, just as in the cup the blood and body are joined by the mixing of the two elements.[23]

More noticeably, however, the depiction of David raising the chalice and handing the paten from the cross to an altar is reminiscent of the Carolingian mass offertory, when the faithful presented their gifts of bread and wine to the altar.[24] Psalm 115.12 and 17 are echoed in the exegesis of the offertory in Amalarius' *Liber officialis*, where he alludes to the participants' imitation of the crucifixion through their own offerings, the "sacrifice of those who render their prayers to the lord."[25] But a more explicit connection between Psalm 115 and the mass offertory is found in the Prayerbook of Charles the Bald, a Rheims manuscript of 846–869. The prayerbook notes the recitation of verses 12–13 at this point, perhaps their earliest recorded usage for this purpose in a Latin mass. Charles is the person who brings the offering to the altar, much as David, whom Hincmar and other Carolingian clergy often urge their princes to imitate, presents the paten in the psalter drawing.[26]

Where the influence of Pascasius' *De corpore* might seem especially likely is in its arguments that the crucified flesh and blood are contained in the consecrated bread and wine, a doctrine clearly implied in this illustration. Given the specificity of the portrayal of David taking the chalice and paten from Christ on the cross directly to the altar and the centrality of this motif to the picture as a whole, it is difficult not to think that the illustration's designer understood the eucharistic presence much as did Pascasius and wanted to

[23] Pascasius, *De corpore* 19, *CCCM* 16.103 lines 44–49 (addition to second edition); ibid., 21, *CCCM* 16.110 lines 12–16. See Haussherr, *Der tote Christus*, 217–225, esp. 220–225; discussed in Dufrenne, *Illustrations*, 65 and n. 214.

[24] Amalarius, *Liber officialis* 3.19, *ST* 139.317; McKitterick, *The Frankish Church and the Carolingian Reforms*, 144. Cf. Angenendt, "Taufritus" (discussione), *Segni e riti*, 326.

[25] Amalarius, *Liber officialis* 3.19, *ST* 139.311. The offertory is viewed as a reminder of martyrdom and penitential imitation of Christ's death in Amalarius, *Missa expositionis geminus codex*, *ST* 138.262–263.

[26] Jungmann, *Missarum Sollemnia*, 2.58 n.22, as noted by Haussherr, *Der tote Christus*, 222; see Anton, *Fürstenspiegel*, esp. 419–32. On the prayerbook's decoration, Deshman, "Exalted Servant," 385–417.

draw viewers' attention to this concept. Conceivably, the designer thought along such lines without being familiar with *De corpore*, perhaps long before Pascasius wrote, if the psalter was produced c. 820–830 as it is sometimes dated. The iconographic complexity and clear originality of the drawing are certainly evidence of its creator's intellectual independence.

Nevertheless, the correspondence between the eucharist doctrine that the psalter image suggests and Pascasius teaches is so striking as to invite consideration of the possibility of an immediate connection between them. So far as I am aware, though, until Pascasius presented a copy of his treatise to Charles the Bald in 843–844, there is no indication that the work was known outside Corbie and Corvey, the monastery to which it was sent in 831–833. The first unambiguous evidence of discussion of its contents beyond these two monasteries appears only with the controversy of the early to mid 850s; but as remarked in the last chapter, some parallels to Pascasius' ideas are earlier discernible in Hincmar's poem on the Virgin Mary, composed in 845–849. The archbishop's thinking about the eucharist might have tended in this direction without knowledge of his contemporary's tractate; yet it is reasonable to suspect that by the time he wrote his poem, Hincmar had read Pascasius' work, perhaps in the copy given to Charles, whom the future archbishop probably accompanied on the visit to Corbie in late 843 or spring 844.[27] Hincmar's verses dedicate a luxury volume that he commissioned for the new cathedral church of Rheims containing texts on the assumption and Mary's birth, including a letter/sermon on the assumption that he claimed was by Jerome but was actually by Pascasius.[28] Among other themes, the archbishop's poem essentially joins the "Pascasian" doctrine of the assumption with the Pascasian doctrine of the eucharist. The opening and closing verses praise the Virgin for her role in the incarnation and as the *stella maris* holier than the saints. Now in heaven, the mother whom Jesus' words from the cross joined to her new son, John the evangelist, perpetually beholds the face of her heavenly lord.[29] But in between, fifty-five out of the hundred verses

---

[27] See chapter 6 n. 13.

[28] Hincmar, *Carm.* 2, *MGH PLAC* 3.410–412; Pascasius, *Epistula Beati Hieronymi ad Paulam et Eustochium*, ed. A. Ripberger, *CCCM* 56C (Turnhout, 1985), 109–162. See Lambot, "L'homélie du Ps.-Jérôme," 265–282; Barré, "Lettre du pseudo-Jérôme," 203–225. Hincmar's gifts to the cathedral of Rheims, including books of luxury quality, are described in Flodoard, *Historia Remensis ecclesiae* 3, *MGH SS* 13.478–479, 482.

[29] Hincmar, *Carm.* 2, *MGH PLAC* 3.410–412, lines 1–18, 81–94.

focus primarily on the eucharist, commenting on it along lines seen in *De corpore*, though more vaguely than does Pascasius. Hincmar alludes to the sacrament as the source of salvation from the body born of the Virgin and sacrificed on the cross; indicates that in its identity with her offspring, the body eaten in heaven yet also received on earth joins Christians with Christ in one body and flesh and brings glory to the saints; and reflects on the eucharist's mystery and invisibility except to faith, the replication of the passion at the altar where it washes the faithful of sins, and the paradox of Christ's repeated suffering in the mass, even though he cannot die again and his body remains whole.[30] These combined meditations on Mary's holiness and special place in heaven above the other saints, on the crucifixion, and on the eucharist offer, overall, closer comparison to the Utrecht Psalm 115 illustration than does Pascasius' treatise. Again, this does not mean that the psalter must date to Hincmar's archiepiscopacy or that he contributed to its design, for one because it is conceivable that the image preceded the poem and provided inspiration for it, rather than the reverse. Yet it suggests, once more, the value of inquiry into the possibility that the psalter was made under Hincmar. Moreover, recognition of the parallels between the poem and the drawing, whatever the basis of the apparent resemblance between their messages, helps clarify the ideas suggested by the illustration and the unified nature of its composition, the expression of a coherent body of doctrine.[31]

The crucifixion miniature in the Drogo Sacramentary

The stylistic and iconographic connections that modern scholars have observed between the decoration of the Utrecht Psalter and the Drogo Sacramentary, a book probably made for the personal use of Bishop Drogo of Metz (d. 855), support the view that the sacramentary's designer or designers knew the psalter, perhaps because they had some involvement

[30] Ibid., esp. lines 25–80.

[31] If the Utrecht Psalter was produced under Hincmar, the doctrine of Mary expressed in his poem may also shed light on the unusual depictions of her in heaven, in the illustrations to the Gloria and the Apostles Creed (fols. 89v, 90r). Both images are generally described as representations of the Trinity, but this seems misleading, for one because of Mary's prominence in them. The dove of the holy spirit, in both, is associated with her and the infant she carries, underscoring the miracle of the incarnation, the source of her sanctity. Mary looks toward her "heavenly lord," whom she forever beholds, as in Hincmar's poem. Other correspondences with the poem and Pascasius' letter may be disernible and deserve further study.

Figure 27. Palm Sunday initial, Drogo Sacramentary, Paris, Bibliothèque Nationale de France, cod. lat. 9428, fol. 43 verso

in its production before coming to Metz. Familiarity with Utrecht is certainly suggested by the sacramentary's only crucifixion miniature, which appears in one of its forty-one beautifully executed, historiated initials, the "O" of a prayer assigned to Palm Sunday (fol. 43v; fig. 27):

> Omnipotent eternal God, who, as an example of humility for the human race to imitate, made our savior both assume flesh and undergo the cross, grant quickly that we may deserve to have proofs of his patience [suffering] and be partners of his resurrection.[32]

The illumination is preceded by an initial depicting the entry into Jerusalem, for the Palm Sunday procession of palms (fol. 43r), and it is followed by miniatures for Holy Thursday, the Easter vigil, and Easter Sunday. In agreement with the accompanying oration, contemporary sermons for Holy Week, and commentaries on its liturgy, the crucifixion painting of Palm Sunday, which marks the week's beginning, reminds the book's users that they should be aware of the passion's suffering throughout the coming days' commemoration and rehearsal of Jesus' self-abasement. By penitential witness of and obedience to the model he set on the cross, they may expect

---

[32] "Die Dominica in Ramis Palmarum ad Sanctum Iohannem: Omnipotens sempiterne Deus, qui humano generi ad imitandum humilitatis exemplum saluatorem nostrum et carnem sumere et crucem subire fecisti, concede propitius ut et patientiae ipsius habere documenta et resurrectionis consortia mereamur." *Sacramentaire grégorien* 3, ed. Deshusses, no. 4412. I also discuss this miniature in a forthcoming article, "An *Exemplum* of Humility: the Crucifixion Miniature in the Drogo Sacramentary," in *Reading Medieval Images*, ed. E. Sears and T. K. Thomas (Ann Arbor).

to receive the redeeming benefits of his death, mediated to the faithful through the church and her sacraments.

Near the center of the O initial, a nimbed, perizoma-clad Christ is fixed to a cross surmounted by a *tabula ansata*. His eyes are apparently still open, though this is unclear because of the image's small size; yet like the Utrecht drawing for Psalm 115 and also that for Psalm 88, to which the miniature's Christ bears the closest resemblance, the picture shows that he is dying, through the twist of his body and the drop of his head onto his right shoulder. While the head's inclination possibly indicates that he looks at the figures to his right (if his eyes are open), it also recalls his giving up of the spirit, according to John 19.30. These two interpretations should not be viewed as contradictory but rather reflect the polyvalence that, as will be seen, much of the picture seems to possess. As in the Utrecht illustration to Psalm 115, blood pours from the pierced side into a chalice. Mary and John stand on either side of Christ. The Virgin's special importance is implied not by proximity to the cross, as in the psalter, but by her size; next to her son she is the scene's largest figure.[33] Both she and John lift their hands to their faces in gestures of thoughtfulness or grief, as they watch Jesus from hillocks that bring their heads level with his. The remaining figures in the painting all look towards their savior, guiding the viewer's gaze into the center of the O. Two tiny resurrected stand in open coffins to the lower left and right of Christ and lift their arms toward the crucifix above them, recalling the six dead who rise below the crucifix in the Utrecht drawing for the Apostles' Creed (fol. 90r; fig. 22).[34] The wreath hanging above the cross from the upper rim of the O (rather than poised on the cross shaft as in the Utrecht Psalm 115 drawing) is flanked by personifications of the sun and moon,[35] and two half-figures of

[33] In other later Carolingian crucifixion imagery she is usually the same height as John. See for example the Utrecht Psalter illustrations to Ps. 115 and the Apostles' Creed (figs. 26 and 22); and Kornbluth, *Engraved Gems of the Carolingian Empire*, frontispiece, figures 3, 4, 7, 14, 18; Gaborit-Chopin, *Elfenbeinkunst*, 54 fig. 45, cat. 48; 55 fig. 47, cat. 49; 65 fig. 59, cat. 56; 70 fig. 66, cat. 64. She is bigger than John on the Narbonne crucifixion ivory, however (Narbonne, Cathedral Treasury; Gaborit-Chopin, *Elfenbeinkunst*, 52 fig. 43, cat. 45). Her exceptional size in the sacramentary miniature, at least, may also reflect the influence of Augustine's exegesis of John 3 and John 19, referring to her spiritual motherhood of mortals through her son the creator: Augustine, *In Iohannis Evangelium Tractatus*, Tract. 11.6–12.8, esp. 12.8, 119.1–3, *CCSL* 36, ed. R. Willems (Turnhout, 1954), 113–125, 658–659.
[34] Van der Horst, "The Utrecht Psalter," 74 fig. 56.
[35] The sun and moon are standard motifs in crucifixion imagery of the period. See Josef Engemann, "Zur Position von Sonne und Mond bei Darstellungen der Kreuzigung Christi," in *Studien zur spätantiken und byzantinischen Kunst: Friedrich Wilhelm Deichmann Gewidmet*, vol. 3, ed. O. Feld and U. Peschlow (Bonn, 1986), 95–101.

angels look down on Christ, extending hands to him in acclamation. Between the cross and Mary, lower than her because of the undulating ground, stands a nimbed female approximately the same size as John, whom, scholars generally agree, personifies *Ecclesia*. She holds a banner with her left hand and, with her right, raises the chalice to catch the blood from Christ's side wound.

While *Ecclesia* raising the chalice appears in other ninth-century Carolingian crucifixion images, works whose chronological relationship to the Drogo Sacramentary is not completely certain but that most likely postdate it, she does not occur in the Utrecht crucifixion scenes.[36] The image of a female head, possibly personifying the church, near the crucified Christ of the Gellone *Te igitur* offers a certain precedent, but the Drogo Sacramentary's *Ecclesia* with the chalice may well be the first appearance of precisely this motif in Carolingian art. The human figure in the sacramentary miniature whom I have yet to mention also has no clear precedent: the seated old man to the cross's left (viewer's right), whose identity as well as that of the disk or globe in his lap have been the subjects of dispute. In general, he is interpreted as signifying the old order that yields before Christ, whether through defeat or voluntary acceptance of the new faith. Yet whereas one scholar has suggested, along such lines, that he is simultaneously Melchisedech and Drogo with a paten, others have considered the object he holds to be a globe or disk representing the *orbis terrarum*, and they have variously identified him as a personification of Synagogue, Jerusalem, and the Old Law, as the defeated prince of the world, Moses, and the prophet, Osee.[37]

The closest comparison to this figure in the other Drogo Sacramentary miniatures is the *Te igitur* image of Melchisedech (fol. 15v), though the priest-king does not hold a disk or orb and he wears differently colored robes.[38] Both Melchisedech and the figure in the Palm Sunday painting are reminiscent of some of the bearded, robed prophets in the Utrecht Psalter, such as the one before David in the illustration to Psalm 77 (fol. 45r; fig. 28).

---

[36] On this and other aspects of later Carolingian crucifixion iconography, Robert Melzak, "The Carolingian Ivory Carvings of the Later Metz Group" (Ph.D. diss., Columbia University, 1983), 181–198. *Ecclesia* with the chalice is already depicted in a fresco at Bawît, Monastery of Apollo (sixth to seventh century): Schiller, *Ikonographie der christlichen Kunst*, 4.1.39–40, fig. 98.

[37] Sonia Simon, "Studies on the Drogo Sacramentary: Eschatology and the Priest-King" (Ph.D. diss., Boston University, 1975), 69–90, esp. 77–90, with references to earlier literature; the figure is Melchisedech/Drogo. See Leesti, "Illustrations," 122 (the figure is Synagogue/Jerusalem holding an orb); Unterkircher, *Zur Ikonographie*, 18–19 (the figure is Osee holding the *orbis terrarum*).   [38] Cf. Simon, "Studies on the Drogo Sacramentary," 77–90.

Figure 28. Illustration to Psalm 77, Utrecht Psalter, Utrecht, Bibliotheek der Rijksuniversiteit, MS 32, fol. 45 recto

Given these resemblances, as I argue in my article on the miniature, I agree that the old man in the Palm Sunday depiction represents the transition from the old order and its prophets to the new, as does Melchisedech in the *Te igitur* painting, but in this case by portraying Nicodemus.[39]

Of principal significance to my interpretation, and to how the book's users would have most likely understood the miniature, is the gospel reading for the main service of Good Friday: the passion narrative in John 19, which recounts the piercing of Jesus' side and provides the scriptural basis for the portrayal of Mary and John alongside the cross, in both this illumination and other medieval crucifixion imagery.[40] John 19.39–40 states that after Christ died, Nicodemus, "who at the first came to Jesus by night," appeared at the crucifixion site to help Joseph of Arimathea remove the

---

[39] Knut Berg proposed the same identification on different grounds: "Une iconographie peu connue du crucifiement," *Cahiers archéologiques* 9 (1957), 319–328, at 326. Nicodemus is a model viewer of the crucifixion in some later medieval works of art. See Jennifer Sheppard, "A Devotional Diptych of the Resurrection: Oxford, Corpus Christi College MS 2," in *English Manuscript Studies 1100–1700*, ed. Peter Beal and Jeremy Griffiths (Oxford, 1990), 231–256. This reference was provided by an unidentified reader of a draft of my article, "An *Exemplum* of Humility."

[40] See *Ord.* 23, 24, 27–29, 30B-32, *Ordines romani* 3.271–519; Römer, "Liturgie des Karfreitags," 62.

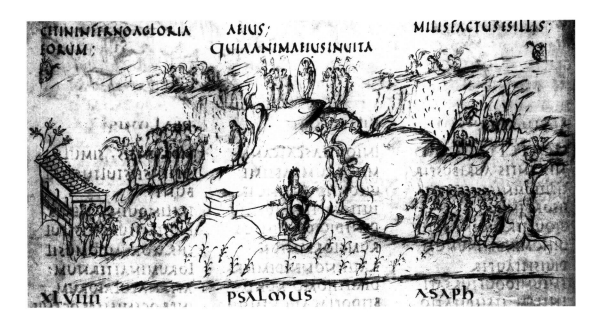

Figure 29. Illustration to Psalm 49, Utrecht Psalter, Utrecht, Bibliotheek der Rijksuniversiteit, MS 32, fol. 28 verso

body and prepare it for burial. According to John 3, where the first meeting with Christ is described, Nicodemus, a Pharisee and "ruler of the Jews" (John 3.1), sought out Jesus as a rabbi, asking the questions that led the latter to compare the forthcoming crucifixion to the story of the brazen serpent.

The Drogo Sacramentary miniature, I suggest, combines evocations of John 3 and John 19. In accordance with John 19.39, Nicodemus waits for the body that still hangs on the cross. His posture reinforces the irony, implicit to John 3, of his relationship with Christ. Seated on the ground like some scholarly men in the Utrecht Psalter,[41] the old man who still lives, a scholar of the old law and ruler of the Jews, seeks instruction from the young crucified king and teacher of the new law. As most modern studies of this miniature have agreed, the object in Nicodemus' lap is probably the *orbis terrarum*, a symbol of dominion also seen in a number of the Utrecht drawings, among them two in which the orb belongs to *Terra* herself (fol. 28v; fig. 29).[42] Its association with Nicodemus accords with his status as a "ruler of the Jews," but, in signifying his rulership, it most likely also reflects Augustine's exegesis of John 3. For Augustine, Nicodemus' rule was

---

[41] E.g. Utrecht Psalter, fol. 6r (Ps. 10; seated men with scrolls), fol. 13r (Ps. 22; David, who is being anointed by an angel).

[42] Ps. 49. Cf. Utrecht Psalter, fol. 10v (Ps. 18, held by a king, possibly David), fol. 53r (Ps. 89, held by *Terra*).

decidedly limited to this earth, since his worldliness meant he was unable to comprehend spiritual things as he talked with Jesus, despite the faith that brought him to turn to the "rabbi."[43] The small oblong object on the ground beside the old man is probably a smoldering torch,[44] an allusion perhaps both to the lights extinguished during the Good Friday liturgy and to the status of the incarnate and crucified Christ, according to John 3.19–21. He is the source of light that overwhelms the shadows of sin and death, rendering – in this image – the light of the torch unnecessary. Nicodemus, who first approached Jesus "by night" and therefore sits on the moon or dark side of the cross, gazes upon the light of revelation whose significance he does not yet fully grasp, because he is still weighed down by earthly matters. (Perhaps this condition explains, too, why he is the only seated person in the scene, and why he sits on the ground.) A further source possibly relevant to understanding his presence in the miniature is the apocryphal Gospel of Nicodemus, a text preserved in several ninth-century Carolingian manuscripts.[45] As in that gospel, so in the sacramentary painting Nicodemus witnesses Christ's passion.[46] The two resurrected dead recall the "many bodies of the saints" that Matthew 27.52 describes rising when Jesus died, and also the promise in John 3.15–16 that all who believe in the crucified son of man will have eternal life. More specifically, though, they may represent the two sons of Symeon identified in Nicodemus' gospel as recipients of that honor.[47]

The liturgical texts of Good Friday and Jesus' speech in John 3 together help elucidate the serpent beneath the crucifix, again a "new" feature of ninth-century Carolingian crucifixion imagery possibly first seen in this miniature.[48] The motif has some connection with the traditional iconography of warriors and saints slaying serpent- and dragon-like demons by means of lances and sometimes cross-staffs,[49] and with the representa-

---

[43] Augustine, *Tract.* 11.3–6, 12.5–6, *CCSL* 36.111–114, 122–124.

[44] It has been compared to the smoking torch Christ holds in the Utrecht Psalter, fol. 9r (Ps. 17): Simon, "Studies on the Drogo Sacramentary," 72–73.

[45] Z. Izydorczyk, ed., *The Medieval Gospel of Nicodemus: Texts, Intertexts, and Contexts in Western Europe* (Tempe, AZ, 1997), 4; idem, *Manuscripts of the "Evangelium Nicodemi": a Census* (Toronto, 1993), 234.   [46] Cf. Nicodemus 5, 7.1, 12.1.   [47] Nicodemus 17.1–3.

[48] For some other examples, see Kornbluth, *Engraved Gems*, frontispiece, figures 14–16, 18–19, 43, 48; Gaborit-Chopin, *Elfenbeinkunst*, 70 fig. 66, cat. 64; 191 cat. 63; Hubert et al., *L'Empire carolingien*, 165 fig. 152.

[49] Carolingian examples include the St. Michael ivory fragment (Leipzig, Museum des Kunsthandwerks; Gaborit-Chopin, *Elfenbeinkunst*, 50 fig. 40, cat. 42; the Arch of Einhard (Paris, BNF, cod. fr. 10440, fol. 45r; fig. 17).

tions, based on Psalm 90.13, of Christ treading on the beasts, a motif that occurs in the Utrecht Psalter as well as on some of the early Carolingian ivories mentioned at the beginning of chapter 3 (see fig. 5).[50] Yet unlike these works of art, the serpent beneath the crucifix clearly ties Satan's defeat to the crucified Jesus. The detail is broadly reminiscent of those contemporary writings that stress the remission of sins and liberation from the devil through Christ's death and bloodshed, but, perhaps more directly, it evokes elements of the Good Friday service. The portion of Habbacuc heard on Good Friday contains the verse, "Death shall go before his face. And the devil shall go before his feet"(Habbacuc 3.5). The Roman liturgy stipulated the subsequent recitation of Psalm 90, a usage Amalarius notes in the *Liber officialis*;[51] but while later Carolingian churches adhered to Roman "Gregorian" custom for many aspects of their ceremony, during the ninth century the practice gradually spread on Good Friday of replacing Psalm 90 with Psalm 139. The latter text, traditionally employed in the Gallican rite, compares the evil men besetting the psalmist to snakes.[52] David's enemies "have sharpened their tongues like a serpent" and have the "venom of asps under their lips," verse 4 declares; yet the "labor of their lips" will overwhelm them and the lord will cast them down (Ps. 139.10–11). Augustine's commentary on the psalm identifies the wicked with their serpent-like tongues as the body of the devil.[53] As suggested by Psalm 139, Augustine's analysis, and the verses from Habbacuc, the sacramentary miniature shows the lord with death "before his face" who has cast down "before his feet" the symbol of Satan and human iniquity.

John 3.14–16, however, suggests yet another level of meaning to the motif. The son of man lifted on the cross, his slumped body a subdued version of the coils at his feet, is the new brazen serpent who overcomes the snake-like devil, just as the one raised in the wilderness vanquished the biting snakes (Numbers 21.9). Again it is useful to consider Augustine's exegesis, which, interweaving the themes of death and sin signified by the snake, suggests that a primary factor linking Christ and the bronze effigy is the former's death. The snake lifted up by Moses is, symbolically, "the death of the lord on the cross" that conquered the death represented by the

---

[50] Utrecht Psalter, fols. 36r (Ps. 64), 53v (Ps. 90).

[51] Amalarius, *Liber officialis* 1.13, *ST* 139.94–95; on the Habbacuc responsory, ibid., 91–92.

[52] Römer, "Liturgie des Karfreitags," 58–59 and n.15.

[53] Augustine, *Enarr. in Ps.* 139.6–7, *CCSL* 40.2015–2016.

"image of the serpent." As the sacramentary picture seems to convey, it is precisely Christ's dying that brings life and "kills death," defeating the "image" of the serpent of sin. Those who desire to be healed of wickedness, according to Augustine, must therefore "set their gaze upon the serpent that the serpent may have no power." While temporal life was restored to the Israelites who beheld the brazen serpent, anyone who looks "with faith upon the death of Christ" – as do Nicodemus and the other figures surrounding the cross in the sacramentary painting, and indeed all the miniature's viewers, joined in contemplating the crucifixion through the oculus-like O – may hope to receive eternal life.[54]

Augustine's analysis of John 3 and the Holy Week liturgy together shed additional light, as well, on Nicodemus' presence beneath the cross. Augustine compares Nicodemus' relationship with Christ – one of faith without yet full understanding – to that of catechumens awaiting baptism, the principal ceremony of the Easter vigil.[55] The catechumen already believes in Christ, yet although he "is not ashamed of the lord's cross," like Nicodemus he is not a full member of the church since Jesus does not yet "trust himself" to him. In the sacramentary miniature, that lack of trust is possibly implied by the bend of the redeemer's body away from Nicodemus and toward *Ecclesia*, symbol of the baptized faithful. As Augustine notes, trust will not occur until, through a humility imitating Christ's humility, demonstrated in the Easter baptism, Nicodemus/the catechumen comes to "understand Christ's flesh" and thus to distinguish earthly from spiritual things. Only then does the new Christian deserve the manna the ancient Israelites received after they crossed the Red Sea, the living bread from heaven that is the eucharistic body and blood.[56]

Insofar as Nicodemus in the sacramentary picture symbolizes the catechumen's condition, he is also emblematic of the situation all Christians occupy during the final week of Lent that begins with Palm Sunday, when they fast and do penitence in wait for their savior's resurrection and the Easter mass.[57] All laity, monks, and clergy and therefore the sacramentary's intended users, including Drogo, are in a sense like the catechumen, since

---

[54] Augustine, *Tract.* 12.11, CCSL 36.126–127. Cf. Simon, "Studies on the Drogo Sacramentary," 73; Stanley Ferber, "Crucifixion Iconography in a Group of Carolingian Ivory Plaques," *Art Bulletin* 48 (1966), 323–334, at 324.   [55] See Cramer, *Baptism and Change*, 137–138.

[56] Augustine, *Tract.* 11.3–6, 12.5–6, CCSL 36.111–114, 122–124.

[57] Cf. Amalarius, *Liber officialis* 1.15, ST 139.107–108; Römer, "Die Liturgie des Karfreitags," 86–89.

they must renew the cleansing received in baptism by humbly repenting the sins that made Jesus' death necessary, before they can merit the newly resurrected body of the Easter eucharist. His body turned towards the miniature's audience while his uplifted hand and eyes direct their gaze towards the crucifix, Nicodemus invites Drogo and other clergy who might have employed this book to contemplate these same truths along with the vision he beholds – a vision that corresponds to the faithful person's inner "seeing" of the crucified lord during Holy Week and, above all, on Good Friday. In some ways, the image leads them to be mindful of Christ's divine omnipotence, attested by the wreath, the reverence of the sun, moon, angels, and other figures in the scene, the resurrection of the dead, and the conquered serpent. But as it would also remind them, the devil's defeat is grounded in Jesus' suffering and death, a model of sacrifice, "patience," and humility, as stated in the prayer alongside the miniature. These are features of his passion that every mortal – even a bishop such as Drogo – must imitate through baptism, the "second baptism" and self-oblation of penitence, the mass, and the passion's liturgical commemoration and reenactment from Palm Sunday to Good Friday. The climax to the Holy Week ceremonial is the *Adoratio crucis*, when Christians behold the image or relic of the cross and prostrate themselves to kiss it, as if, according to Amalarius and other ninth-century interpreters, they see Christ hanging there.[58] By the meditation on the crucifixion to which the Drogo Sacramentary painting already urges them on Palm Sunday, they are drawn to humble, faithful penitence in preparation for Good Friday and then for the ceremonies of baptism and the Easter mass – all rites that the image's designer believed critical to the hope expressed in the painting's oration of becoming "partners of the resurrection," like the two saints who rise from their tombs.

It is possible that the miniature's designer and the sacramentary's users interpreted this image not only in light of Augustinian exegesis and the liturgy of Holy Week, but also of the quarrels over predestination and the eucharist that were probably contemporary with the book's production. Three aspects of the painting deserve to be considered from this perspective. The first is its evident allusion to John 3.14–16, particularly through the images of Nicodemus and the serpent beneath the crucifix, both motifs for which no precedents can be certainly identified. The same scriptural

---

[58] See chapter 3, at n. 125.

passage, it should be remembered, was a major proof text on both sides of the predestination controversy. Hincmar wrote to Amalarius c. 850, by when the latter was in Metz, to request assistance against Gottschalk's teachings.[59] We do not know how Amalarius responded – he may have died before he could do so – but that the archbishop of Rheims called on him and was evidently on good terms with Drogo may signal the agreement of both men with the opposition to Gottschalk.[60] Hence the quarrel over predestination, which initially gained strength in the years during which the sacramentary was probably produced, conceivably encouraged the miniature's designer to create a crucifixion image that plays on the John 3 passage. Furthermore, whether or not the conflict directly influenced the designer, the sacramentary's users in Metz could well have understood the visual allusions to John 3.14–16 in a manner compatible with predestination doctrine, most likely that of Hincmar, who already uses the passage to attack Gottschalk in *Ad simplices*:[61] the hope for redemption rests on faithful witness, like Nicodemus, of the crucified Jesus; the crucifixion offers all humanity the chance to be redeemed, but actually to receive this reward demands a turning in faith to Christ that corresponds to inner contemplation of the new brazen serpent.

Second, the eucharist controversy was perhaps a factor behind at least one of the notable differences between the sacramentary miniature and the Utrecht Psalm 115 illustration: David and *Ecclesia* occupy comparable positions in their respective scenes, but whereas the former holds both a chalice and a paten with bread, *Ecclesia* holds only the chalice. Although the Psalm 115 drawing seems to reflect a doctrine of the eucharist agreeing with Pascasius', the psalter may well have been completed before the dispute over his teachings erupted in the early to mid 850s (whether or not one accepts my proposal that Utrecht may date to 845–855). Hence even if the picture is a clue that its designer was directly acquainted with Pascasius'

---

[59] Ganz, "Theology," *NCMH* 2.769. Amalarius was at one point in his life associated with Troyes and he served as bishop of Lyons from 835–838; but he is generally known as "of Metz" because he spent his last years in that city under the patronage of its bishop, Drogo, dying there in 850–852. After his death the city honored him as a saint: Hanssens, ed., *ST* 138.58–82; Allen Cabaniss, *Amalarius of Metz*, 89–93. A connection with Amalarius' exegesis of the mass has been proposed for the Drogo Sacramentary's ivory covers: Reynolds, "Image and Text," esp. 68–72.

[60] On Hincmar and Drogo, see Flodoard, *Hist. Rem. eccl.* 3.21, *MGH SS* 36.279; Hincmar, *Epp.* 3, 71, *MGH Epp.* 8 (Berlin, 1939), 2, 37.

[61] Hincmar, *Ad simplices*, "Zwei Schriften," ed. Gundlach, 288.

De corpore, like Hincmar's poem on the Virgin the drawing would probably not have been influenced by the controversy itself. In part, the representation of the chalice alone (without paten) in the Drogo Sacramentary miniature coincides with the emphasis generally found in early medieval literature on the redemptive efficacy of Christ's blood. It probably owes something, as well, to the Augustinian exegesis of John 19, where the blood and water from Christ's side wound, the liquids of the eucharist and baptism, are linked with the origin of the church. An additional concern, however, motivated by the quarrel over the eucharist's relation to the historical body and blood, was perhaps to make unambiguous that both elements in the sacrament, flesh together with blood, belong to the one incarnate, crucified Christ. Perhaps such a concern was a factor, too, in the choice to portray him dressed in the perizoma rather than the colobium used for the Psalm 115 illustration, since the reality of his incarnate body is thus more exposed to view. Through both the absence of the eucharistic bread and the depiction of the naked flesh, the designer of the sacramentary image perhaps sought to remind viewers, more clearly than does any Utrecht drawing, that Jesus' body is the sole body of both the crucifixion and the mass. The blood from the side wound is the liquid in the chalice, but no consecrated bread/flesh is seen apart from the sacrifice of the passion, an event whose own historical reality, the picture also recalls, is the theme of the Holy Week liturgy.

Third, the sacramentary illumination differs from the Utrecht Psalm 115 drawing in its announcement of the church's function to provide access to the eucharist and the redemption that the crucifixion accomplished. Standing while Nicodemus sits, on the sun rather than dark side of the cross, holding high her triumphal banner while his torch lies abandoned, *Ecclesia* receives Christ's blood as Nicodemus remains without the eucharist. Whether the inclination of Jesus' head denotes his death or the direction of his gaze, or both, his bending away from Nicodemus and towards the church underscores the difference between them. The church's role as arbiter of the sacraments is perhaps suggested by the Gellone Sacramentary decoration. It is also implicit, again, in the Augustinian exegesis of the blood and water from Christ's side wound, an interpretation often repeated in Carolingian exegesis of the passion; and more generally, Carolingian writings often connect the church's role as mediator of salvation with the sacraments, especially the eucharist. This line of thought, of course, makes particular sense in a sacramentary, especially one intended for so powerful a bishop as Drogo. Yet it is conceivable that the Drogo Sacramentary picture's forceful reference to ecclesiastical power in its triumphant, chalice-bearing *Ecclesia* was once more influenced by the theological conflicts that began in the late 840s. The question of where control over the means of redemption lay gained a new dimension in those years, as Hincmar, Hrabanus, and their allies became convinced that support for Gottschalk's preaching on divine predestination threatened the church as an institution and faith in the sacraments' efficacy. For Hincmar, a similar danger underlay Gottschalk's theology of the eucharist. The archbishop of Rheims countered his opponent's doctrine as early as the *Ferculum Salomonis*, not only by defending the presence of the incarnate flesh and blood in the consecrated bread and wine and linking this doctrine with orthodoxy on predestination. In addition, he directly tied ecclesiastical authority to his understanding of the eucharist's nature, particularly his identification of the crucified Christ's blood with the chalice.[62] Awareness of these issues and ideas may have helped form the intellectual context for the image of *Ecclesia* raising the chalice in the sacramentary miniature, a motif that occurs in other ninth-century Carolingian crucifixion imagery but perhaps first in this painting.

The crucifixion ivory of the Pericopes of Henry II

The imagery of the Pericopes tablet (fig. 30) once more suggests knowledge of the Utrecht Psalter and, further, of the Drogo Sacramentary, either because the plaque's designer studied those manuscripts or because he participated in the production of one or both. But some of the iconographic differences between the ivory and the imagery in these codices imply the carving was also influenced by ideas finding their clearest expression in literature that postdates the psalter and sacramentary, texts written in the late 850s through the early 870s. Among these works are two admonitory tractates by Hincmar for Charles the Bald, one of them his *De cavendis vitiis et virtutibus exercendis*, where the advice to the monarch concerning virtue and vice encompasses the archbishop's longest extant discussion of the eucharist.

---

[62] See chapter 6, at n. 55.

Figure 30. Pericopes of
Henry II, Munich, Bayerische
Staatsbibliothek, Clm. 4452,
ivory cover

Since modern scholars have yet to agree on the identity of several figures
on this ivory, I will begin with the pictorial elements about which more or
less of a consensus exists. The crucifixion scene dominates the top half of
the carving. A nimbed Christ, dressed in the perizoma and bearded, as seems
to be true for all the composition's male figures, hangs on a rough-hewn
cross. The ivory's worn condition makes uncertain whether his eyes are

open or shut, but his body twists slightly at the hips, the weight pulls on his arms, and his head rests on his right shoulder, implying that he gives up the spirit. If his eyes are open, then like the Christ of the Drogo Sacramentary miniature he may also be looking down toward the figures to his right and, below them, the empty sepulchre of his resurrection. Rather than the Virgin and John alone, the ivory artist has depicted John, to the right of the cross, holding his mantle-wrapped hands before his face, and, on the far left of the scene, the group of grieving women whom Mark, Matthew, Luke, and the Gospel of Nicodemus describing as witnessing the crucifixion from a distance.[63] *Ecclesia*, just below the cross and to Christ's right (viewer's left), has a banner in her left hand and the chalice lifted with her right to catch the blood from the side wound. Behind her is the smaller, stocky figure of Longinus, with lance raised. On the opposite side of the cross, Stephaton stands directly in front of John, lifting the sponge-pole to Jesus' mouth; a strikingly large jug of vinegar is set on the ground behind and just below the sponge bearer's feet. Above the cross hover three angels, full-length rather than the half-figures seen in the Drogo Sacramentary miniature. The two on the left carry cloths, while the one to the right, without a cloth, places one hand on the cross. The angels to the far left and right also carry batons whose ends are broken off, making it impossible to be certain what they originally represented. Above the angels, the hand of God appears from a cloud, flanked by wagon-borne personifications of the sun and moon.

At the cross's base, the large, twisted body of the serpent, its jaw gaping, forces down the line of ground below it as if the earth were unable to sustain its weight. Moving downward to the ivory's lower half, we see the three women approaching the empty tomb from the right of the plaque, each carrying a container of spices. They are greeted by the angel with cross staff sitting on the stone before the tomb entrance. The three-storeyed sepulchre behind the angel towers up into the area of the crucifixion, and Longinus' lance traverses the space between the building's dome and the crucified Christ, guiding the viewer's eye from one to the other. Behind the tomb, partly emerging from the acanthus border, are four soldier / guards. One or possibly two are asleep (one clearly uses his hand to support his chin), while the other two partially conceal themselves behind their shields, yet seem to attend to the scene in front of them. Lower still on

---

[63] See Mark 15.40, Matthew 27.55, Luke 23.49, Nicodemus 11.3.1.

the ivory, four figures in different stages of resurrection emerge from a jumbled assortment of open sarcophagi and tombs. Three large figures occupy the lowest tier of imagery, below the rising dead. The half-nude, bearded, reclining male to the left, with horns protruding from his head (one has broken off), is a personification of *Oceanus*. He holds a cornucopia and an overturned vessel from which water spills, as he turns his back to the viewer but looks over his shoulder. The personification of *Terra* in the right-hand corner is similarly naked above the waist. Gazing upward, she holds a cornucopia in her left hand and has two snakes draped over her right forearm, one suckling at her breast. Seated on a cushioned, backless throne, the middle figure of the three, another female who has one breast bared, also looks toward the imagery above, lifting her right hand in a gesture that mirrors that of the hand of God at the top of the ivory. Thus she seems to acknowledge and accept the divine power that descends from the hand of God down through the crucifix, the power that defeats the serpent, raises Christ from the dead, and opens the tombs around her. The most plausible identification of this figure has been proposed by Otto Werckmeister, who argues that she represents the Temple described in Sedulius' *Carmen paschale* and, therefore, the transition from the old law to the new. This interpretation is supported by the formal parallel between her posture and that of Nicodemus in the Drogo Sacramentary crucifixion miniature (fol. 43v; fig. 27). When Christ died, Sedulius states, "that marvelous temple, filled with ancient religion, groaned like a sad foster-child and wept for her own creator, as she beheld the roofs of the great temple fall. When the temple veil rent she immediately showed her bare breast to all, signifying that the secret things within were now to be revealed to the gentiles and all future people of faith."[64]

As other scholars have remarked, the ivory is by the same hand as the back cover of the Paris Psalter or Psalter of Charles the Bald (fig. 31), a carving with imagery derived from the Utrecht illustration to Psalm 50. The Paris Psalter ivory probably dates to 869 or slightly earlier; it is likely that the codex was given to Metz cathedral in that year, to mark Charles'

---

[64] "Tunc illud quoque templum mirabile, plenum religionis antiquae, maioris templi culmina cecidisse conspiciens, uelut alumnus tristis et ingemens proprium defleret auctorem, discusso protinus uelo nudum cunctis pectus ostendit, interiora scilicet euidenter arcana gentibus reseranda significans et populis fideliter adfuturis…" Sedulius, *Carmen paschale*, Op. 5, CSEL 10, ed. J. Huemer (1885), 292 lines 13–18; O. K. Werckmeister, *Der Deckel des Codex Aureus von St. Emmeram: ein Goldschmiedewerk des 9. Jahrhunderts* (Baden-Baden, 1963), 59.

Figure 31. Nathan before David, Psalter of Charles the Bald, Paris, Bibliothèque Nationale de France, cod. lat. 1152, ivory cover

coronation as king of Lotharingia.[65] The Pericopes tablet shares some iconographic and stylistic characteristics with this plaque as with other ivory works assigned to later ninth-century Metz and Charles' court school, particularly those depicting the crucifixion.[66] Correspondences are evident, too, with individual motifs of works in other media usually associated with Charles and dated to the 860s to 870s. The flying angels above the crucifix, for instance, recall not only those in the earlier, Gellone Sacramentary *Te igitur* miniature (fig. 7) and on several Metz crucifixion ivories, but the lower two angels (above the horizontal of the cross) on the second cover of the Lindau Gospels.[67] Personifications of *Oceanus* and *Terra* with similarities to the Pericopes ivory figures appear on some of the Metz crucifixion ivories as well as in the Christ-in-majesty illumination of the Paris Sacramentary fragment and the miniature of the adoration of the lamb in the *Codex Aureus* of St. Emmeram.[68]

The same details of the Pericopes tablet, though, along with others, suggest an especially close relationship with the Utrecht Psalter and Drogo Sacramentary. The representation of the crucified Jesus, Longinus, and Stephaton invites comparison to a number of crucifixion images of the second half of the ninth century, but most noticeably to the same three figures of the Utrecht illustration to Psalm 88 (fol. 51v; fig. 23). This drawing also provides the clearest precedent for the shape and size of the jug at Stephaton's feet, and other Utrecht pictures show *quadriga* similar to those driven by the ivory's personifications of the sun and moon (see fig. 24).[69] The ivory's scene of the women visiting the tomb is close to the Drogo Sacramentary miniature for the Easter mass *ad sanctum Petrum* (fol. 58r), and to the pictures of the same subject in the Utrecht illustrations to Psalm 15 (fol. 8r) and the Apostles' Creed (fol. 90r; fig. 22). The dead emerging

---

[65] Paris, BNF, lat. 1152; van der Horst et al., eds., *The Utrecht Psalter in Medieval Art*, 202 cat. 14. See William J. Diebold, "Verbal, Visual, and Cultural Literacy in Medieval Art: Word and Image in the Psalter of Charles the Bald," *Word & Image* 8 (1992), 89–99, esp. 96 and n. 51; Gaborit-Chopin, *Elfenbeinkunst*, 189, cat. 54.

[66] See Goldschmidt, *Elfenbeinskulpturen* I, e.g. nos. 44, 78, 83, 85, 86, 88, 89, 96b; Melzak, "Carolingian Ivory Carvings"; Amy Vandersall, "The Ivories of the Court School of Charles the Bald" (Ph.D. diss., Yale University, 1965).

[67] New York, Pierpont Morgan Library; Hubert et al., *L'Empire carolingien*, 257 fig. 236.

[68] Paris, BNF lat. 1141, fol. 6r; Munich, Clm. 14000, fol. 6r; Wilhelm Koehler and Florentine Mütherich, *Die karolingische Miniaturen, 5.1: Die Hofschule Karls des Kahlen* (Berlin, 1982), 165, 175, pls. 43b, 47; Hubert et al., *L'Empire carolingien*, 150, 154, figs. 138, 142.

[69] E.g. Utrecht Psalter fols. 37v (Ps. 67), 85v (Habbacuc).

from their graves recall the two resurrected of the sacramentary crucifixion miniature (fol. 43v; fig. 24) and the six such figures of the psalter's drawing for the Apostles Creed. The best comparison to *Oceanus* is probably the river god in the psalter's drawing for Psalm 1 (fol. 1v).[70] The personification of the Temple is reminiscent not only of the Drogo Sacramentary Nicodemus, but also of the image of *Terra* in the Utrecht drawing for Psalm 49 (fol. 28v). Precedents also occur in the Utrecht Psalter for the full-length angels above the cross, though in none of the manuscript's drawings are *Oceanus*, *Terra*, and angels directly associated with the crucified Christ. Finally, the crucifixion painting in the Drogo Sacramentary provides an obvious comparison to the ivory's *Ecclesia* with the chalice, and the crowned figure on the far right of the ivory again bears some resemblance (differently than the Temple) to the sacramentary picture's Nicodemus.[71]

Yet while individually most pictorial elements of the ivory can be related to motifs in the Utrecht Psalter, the Drogo Sacramentary, and sometimes other ninth-century productions, taken as a whole, as noted earlier, the plaque is unique in Carolingian art. The varied ideas about the passion and its significance it seems to express resonate less with scattered details in other artistic productions than with a remarkable array of later Carolingian writings and liturgical sources. Viewed against this material, multiple layers of signification are discernible and were doubtless accessible to the monks, clergy, and nobility such as Charles the Bald who were most plausibly its contemporary viewers, without it being necessary to turn specifically to texts by Hincmar.

It is only possible to point out a few examples of this multivalence here. To begin with, the educated, ninth-century viewer would certainly have recognized the numerous visual references the carving makes to the dramatic conjunction in the crucified Christ of human mortality and triumphant divinity, often by evoking elements of church ritual. The roughly hewn cross, for instance, recalls its origin as the tree of life in Eden that will be beheld again in heaven, and therefore the dying Jesus' own status as the second Adam. These are refrains, it has been seen in earlier chapters, of the *Adoratio crucis*, the Easter ritual, and the feasts of the cross, as well as of an abundance of Carolingian poetry and other literature remembering the cross and crucifixion. The three angels above the cross, linking it with the

[70] See also Utrecht Psalter fol. 54v (Ps. 92).
[71] Cf. Vandersall, "Ivories of the Court School," 98–100.

heavenly realm and hand of God, suggest the continuity between the passion, ascension, return, and the eschatological vision that is similarly implied in the Gellone Sacramentary *Te igitur* miniature (fol. 143v; fig. 7) and some earlier images, such as the fresco above the main apse of Sta. Maria Antiqua, Rome. Like the Gellone angels, they are reminders, too, of the celestial throngs who join the faithful in singing the *Sanctus* of the mass. The threefold refrain of that hymn perhaps helps explain why three angels are depicted on the ivory. In addition, as Werckmeister remarked, they recall the mass prayer asking that God's angel bear the consecrated eucharist to the supernal altar, the blood that pours into *Ecclesia*'s chalice and the body still on the cross, which two of the angels may wait to receive in their cloths.[72] But perhaps they should also be understood to present the crucifix to the surrounding witnesses and the ivory's viewers for adoration, just as the clergy displayed the cross on Good Friday. Again, the *Sanctus* hymn may have been influential; one *ordo* in a northern French manuscript of the second half of the ninth century directs that it be sung by three clergy as the cross is brought forward for the *Adoratio crucis*.[73] The hand that the angel to the right rests on the cross and the cloths carried by the angels to the left and center, in part suggestive of their reverence and wait for Christ's holy body, in the ascension and the mass, conceivably invite thoughts, as well, of the cross's ritual unveiling on Good Friday, a custom first mentioned in the same northern French *ordo*. Placed near the altar for the Adoration, the cross was concealed with cloths that were dramatically pulled away while the *Ecce lignum crucis* was sung.[74] The ritual itself was possibly understood to symbolize the tearing of the temple veil at Christ's death, the episode that Matthew associates with the earth's quaking and the resurrection of the dead (Matth. 27.51–52), and that Sedulius links with the Temple's baring of her breast, in recognition of the divine secrets now revealed to the world.

The evil that the crucifixion defeats is most notably symbolized by the coiled serpent beneath the cross, as in the Drogo Sacramentary Palm

---

[72] "Supplices te rogamus omnipotens deus, iube et perferri per manus angeli tui in sublime altare tuum, in conspectu diuinae maiestatis tuae, ut quotquot ex hac altaris participatione sacrosanctum filii tui corpus et sanguinem sumpserimus omni benedictione caelesti et gratia repleamur." *Sacramentaire grégorien* 1, ed. Deshusses, no. 13. See Werckmeister, *Deckel*, 58.

[73] Ord. 31, *Ordines romani* 3.491–509. The unique manuscript is Paris, BNF lat. 9421, which also contains a copy of the first edition of Amalarius' *Liber officialis*.

[74] Ord. 31, *Ordines romani* 3.498; see Römer, "Liturgie des Karfreitags," 73–74.

Figure 32. Cathedra Petri, *Terra* (right)

Sunday miniature, but other features of the carving reinforce this message. One is the personification of *Terra*. In other Carolingian works of art, including Utrecht, she is portrayed with a variety of attributes, some clearly casting her in a positive light: cornucopias (see fig. 29), children, sometimes at her breasts, and in several cases, more ambiguously, a snake winding up one arm, as she is shown for instance on the *Cathedra Petri* (fig. 32).[75] I have been unable to find another extant, Carolingian depiction of the suckling serpent at her breast, but the motif recurs in the early eleventh-century, illustrated copy at Montecassino of Hrabanus Maurus' *De universo*, an image probably based on a ninth-century exemplar. The Montecassino codex depicts both an ox and a snake drinking from the breasts of a *Terra* with streaming hair, nude from the waist up.[76] Book 12.1 of Hrabanus' treatise, written in 842, indicates that the serpent in this picture symbolizes corruption. Drawing on Isidor's *Etymologiae*,

---

[75] Basilica di San Pietro in Vaticano; Staubach, *Rex Christianus*, fig. 34; Nees, *Tainted Mantle*, fig. 18. See also Utrecht Psalter, fols. 28v (Ps. 49; fig. 26) and 58r (Ps. 101); Koehler and Mütherich, *Karolingische Miniaturen*, 5.1, 165, 175, pls. 43b, 47; Goldschmidt, *Elfenbeinskulpturen* 1, nos. 83, 85, 88; Gaborit-Chopin, *Elfenbeinkunst*, 70 fig. 66, cat. 64.

[76] Montecassino, Archivio e biblioteca dell'abbazia Cod. 132, p. 294; facsimile in *Rabano Mauro, De rerum naturis. Cod. Casin. 132 [dell'] Archivio dell'Abbazia di Montecassino*, commentary by G. Cavallo (Pavone Canovese, 1994). On this manuscript, see also Ferrari, *Liber s. crucis*, 337, with reference to earlier literature. The two animals in the Montecassino image (ox and snake) may represent the clean and unclean animals. I am grateful for this suggestion to an unidentified member of the audience at my paper in Kalamazoo, Michigan, May 2000.

Cassiodorus' exegesis of Psalms 23 and 84, and the *Clavis* of Pseudo-Melito,[77] Hrabanus identifies *Earth* with both good and evil and the latter, in turn, with the serpent. For its role in Adam and Eve's fall, God condemned the snake forever to "eat" earth (Gen. 3.14). *Terra* represents the sinners whom the serpent draws into perdition and on whose iniquities – carnality, false adulation, heresy – it feeds.[78] The Pericopes tablet may associate *Terra* with goodness through her cornucopia, yet it also links her with wickedness – possibly by her almost cowering position and fearful expression as she looks up at the crucifix, as though afraid of the divine power above her, more certainly by the snake that consumes evil from her breast. Given this, her semi-nudity should probably be viewed as an allusion to carnality. Although she lacks the rich clothing and gold cup attributed to Babylon in Apocalypse 17, her appearance may have been partly influenced by the identification there of earthly sinfulness with that city, an idea echoed in *De ciuitate Dei*. [79] As described in Apocalypse 17, Babylon is "the great harlot who sitteth upon many waters" – perhaps the water that on the ivory flows from *Oceanus'* jug toward *Terra's* feet (unlike the Temple, she sits on the ground or possibly in the stream) – the desolate, naked "mother of the fornications, and the abominations of the earth" (Apoc. 17.1, 5, 16).

The oversized pitcher at Stephaton's feet on the ivory, like that in the Utrecht Psalter illustration to Psalm 88 (fig. 23), was probably also intended and understood by educated viewers as a reference to the sins the passion overcame, based on patristic and Carolingian exegesis of the vessel as a symbol of human iniquity, especially though not solely of the Jews.[80] It is worth noting that the vessel clearly has a similar signification in the Khludov Psalter's decoration for Psalm 68.22 (fol. 67r; fig. 25). In an adjoining scene to the crucifixion, a second identical container but larger than the one used by Stephaton, to whom the artist has given Jewish features, serves iconoclasts who whitewash an icon of Christ.[81] For Pascasius Radbertus in his commentary on Matthew, as discussed in chapter 4, the sponge is the

---

[77] Marianne Reuter, *Text und Bild im Codex 132 der Bibliothek von Montecassino, "Liber Rabani de originibus rerum"* (Munich, 1984), 155–156, referring to the connection with the Pericopes ivory motif at n. 354.   [78] Hrabanus, *De universo* 12.1, *PL* 111.331–332.

[79] See e.g. Augustine, *De civ. Dei* 16.4, 17, 18.2.

[80] This may also be true for the large vessel in the crucifixion scene of the mid-ninth-century Metz ivory on Paris, BNF lat. 9388: Gaborit-Chopin, *Elfenbeinkunst*, 55 fig. 47 cat. 49.

[81] Corrigan, *Visual Polemics*, 30.

cup of death from which Christ absorbs all the vices passed on to him in baptism and penance, so that they can be deleted on the cross and "death absorbed into victory." His body emptied the human race's corruption and transformed it into the new wine drunk in paradise.[82] These ideas clarify not merely why the pitcher is so large both in the Utrecht drawing and on the Pericopes ivory – it holds the sins of the entire human race – but the care with which the ivory's designer has arranged motifs, differently than in the psalter illustration. Stephaton's pole guides the viewer's eye from the defeated serpent and the jug of vinegar to Christ's face, where the lance of Longinus draws the gaze from Christ down to *Ecclesia* and, below her, the empty sepulchre. The wine-based liquid in the vessel, poised just above the tail of Satan's serpent, moves through the sponge to Jesus, where it becomes the redeeming blood that flows from his side into *Ecclesia*'s small cup. The Christ who assumes the vinegar of humanity's wickedness into his body, a body that is itself innocent, dies providing a remedy in his blood, the consecrated wine of the eucharist received through the church, and then demonstrates his triumph in the resurrection.

The concept that salvation depends on faithful witness of the crucified, dying lord, another theme of some of the literature discussed in preceding chapters, clearly played a role in the design of the Drogo Sacramentary painting for Palm Sunday (fig. 27). The importance of witness to the resurrection, too, is recalled in the same book's Easter miniatures, both the painting of the three women at the tomb for the mass *ad sanctum Petrum* (fol. 58r), and another D initial depicting Peter before the empty tomb (fol. 56r). But these ideas are given added force on the Pericopes carving simply by the number of figures represented. The sacramentary's crucifixion miniature shows the crucifix along with two angels, sun and moon, *Ecclesia*, Nicodemus, John, Mary, and two risen dead. The ivory, which seems crowded with figures in comparison with other Carolingian crucifixion images, shows the crucified Jesus beheld by the sun and moon, three angels, *Ecclesia*, the seated figure to the far right, Longinus and Stephaton, John, the five women in place of the Virgin alone, four resurrected mortals, Temple, and *Terra*. Furthermore, whereas the Drogo Sacramentary illumination of the three women includes two stunned/sleeping guards and

---

[82] Pascasius, *In Matheo* 27.48, *CCCM* 56B.1388–1390.

none are depicted in the miniature of Peter before the sepulchre or the Utrecht Psalter's depictions of the empty tomb (see fig. 22), the ivory shows four soldiers, at least two joining the women in their witness of the resurrection.[83] The ivory's designer has gone to considerable lengths to multiply the number of people watching these events. At the same time, particularly through the gaze of *Terra* and Temple, the latter's raised hand, and the outward facing *Oceanus*, the viewer's own eye is guided into the image and up toward Christ's sepulchre and the crucifix above. This is perhaps uncovered by the angels, so that it may be beheld by the faithful gathered for the crucifixion and the *Adoratio crucis*, while the hand of God draws the gaze down toward the same scene.

Finally, the Drogo Sacramentary alludes to the resurrection in its crucifixion miniature, and it directly recalls the event in its Easter paintings, just as the Utrecht Psalter represents both episodes; yet the Pericopes ivory sets forth a tightly integrated composition that, again in line with a fundamental concept in so much Carolingian writing about the crucifixion, far more dramatically shows the combined truth of death and its reversal. Christ is the redeemer whose crucifixion is mourned by the women and John. He dies in order to take on humanity's sins and shed his purging blood, an atoning sacrifice offered to the father – the hand above the cross – and available to mortals in the mass. But the defeated serpent, the cross as the tree of life, Jesus' own empty tomb, the graves in the lower register, and other details emphasize his victory. The divine power by which he rose from the sepulchre and raises the dead is implied to be universal, by the sun, moon, *Oceanus*, and *Terra* in the ivory's corners, and it reaches throughout creation's history, from the garden in which the tree of life first stood to the eschaton, foreshadowed in the opening graves that prefigure the final resurrection. Although the composition is divided into different levels, pictorial elements break from one band into another and are juxtaposed to accentuate the work's unity: the apposition of the hand of God to Temple's hand, the gaze of the sun, moon, and the angels downward while Temple

---

[83] Utrecht Psalter fols. 8r (Ps. 15), 90r (Apostles' Creed). Cf. Matthew 28.4, Nicodemus 13.2–3, noting that all the guards became as though dead. The Pericopes tablet's iconography is not unprecedented. One of the guards looks towards the women at the tomb on the ascension ivory of c. 400 in Munich, Bayerisches Nationalmuseum, and in the Rabbula Gospels, Florence, Biblioteca Laurenziana, Cod. Plut. I, 56, fol. 13r; Steigemann and Wemhoff, eds., *799: Kunst und Kultur: Katalog* 2, 689 x.2; Wolfgang Braunfels, *Die Welt der Karolinger und ihre Kunst* (Munich, 1968), fig. 178; Kartsonis, *Anastasis*, fig. 5.

and *Terra* look upward, the line traced by Longinus' spear between the empty sepulchre and the crucifix. This may well be a reason for the unusual, elongated form of Christ's sepulchre. The monument finds an interesting comparison in a building depicted in the frontispiece miniature of the St. Petersburg manuscript of the *Visio Baronti*, a Rheims codex made c. 850, during Hincmar's archiepiscopacy;[84] its height contrasts with the smaller sepulchres depicted in the Drogo Sacramentary and the squat ones in the Utrecht Psalter. The taller structure on the ivory, the symbol of resurrection reaching into the scene of the crucifixion, reinforces the other indications of the connection between the two events. The most noticeably "unifying" element of the carving, though, is the serpent, its coiled body marking the midpoint between the areas of crucifixion and resurrection, and the center of the cross's power that reaches from the heavens to *Oceanus*, *Terra*, and the rising dead.

From what has been said so far it should be apparent that this is a highly idiosyncratic artistic production not fully explicable by reference to any other, single work of art or single text, one, indeed, for which it would be difficult to exhaust the liturgical, scriptural, exegetical, and theological concepts the carving might have suggested to an educated, ninth-century audience. Its creator was himself a scholar. Much as is true of the best later Carolingian exegetes, he skillfully transformed borrowings from and allusions to other visual as well as textual sources into a new composite presenting his own commentary on the crucified Christ, the passion, and its aftermath, and on ecclesiastical ritual honoring those events. But although, again, in order to attribute signification to most of the ivory's pictorial elements or to have some idea of contemporaries' interpretations of them it is unnecessary to appeal to Hincmar, we should recognize how closely aspects of the thinking suggested by this plaque agree with his doctrines studied in previous chapters.

Correspondences may be detected at two points where the archbishop of Rheims' doctrines of predestination and human salvation approach those articulated by John Scottus Eriugena. One is in the ivory's emphasis on the

---

[84] Russian National Library, cod. lat. Oct. v. I. 5, fol. 1v. The manuscript and its imagery are discussed in Lawrence Nees, "The Illustrated Manuscript of the *Visio Baronti* (*Revelatio Baronti*) in St. Petersburg (Russian National Library, cod. Oct. v. 1. 5)," in *Court Culture in the Early Middle Ages*, ed. C. Cubitt (Turnhout, forthcoming). Nees kindly permitted me to read his article before its publication.

vision of God, specifically the crucified and resurrected Christ, and on that experience's connection with faith in the crucified Jesus. While such ideas are also suggested by the Drogo Sacramentary crucifixion miniature, which itself may have been influenced by Hincmarian doctrine, the ivory designer appears to have sought to extend and strengthen references to them. Some of the clearest explorations in later Carolingian literature of the crucifixion's relation to the eternal, heavenly vision occur in the writings by John Scottus and Hincmar discussed in chapters 5 and 6 that date between the late 850s and 870s: John Scottus' poetry and commentary on John, Hincmar's third treatise on predestination, and *De cavendis*. In this context, it is perhaps important to remember the various facets of Augustine's exegesis of the tree of life presented in Hincmar's third treatise, John Scottus' *Periphyseon*, and also Pascasius' *De corpore*. In *Periphyseon* 5, John Scottus links the tree's fruit with the theophany granted the elect and eternal enjoyment of Christ the word; Hincmar and Pascasius, like Gottschalk though with different doctrinal consequences, link it with the mass. For Hincmar and Pascasius, the tree of life is a type of the altar and Christ, and its fruit symbolizes the eucharist that they identify with his incarnate body. This is a pleasure that, according to Hincmar, especially, anticipates the one the saved will know when Christ returns.[85]

Furthermore, while John 3.14–16 was used by participants on both sides in the predestination controversy, some of the most forceful Carolingian exegesis of the passage tying faith to the inner vision of the crucified savior appears in the same writings by John Scottus and Hincmar, especially the former's commentary on John and the latter's third treatise and *De cavendis*. Here again, Hincmar's usage of the biblical verses seems particularly significant. Like *Ad simplices*, though more frequently, the third treatise quotes and cites them to support the doctrine that the crucifixion offers grace to all mortals, yet in order to receive the divine gift they must turn to faithful contemplation of the crucified Jesus. As is perhaps true of the Drogo Sacramentary crucifixion miniature, the Pericopes ivory conceivably juxtaposes the dying Christ to the defeated serpent partly in order to evoke Jesus' position as the new brazen serpent. In this capacity, Hincmar indicates in both the third treatise and *De cavendis*, through the passage from Bede also quoted in *Ad simplices*, Christ saves from eternal death those who

---

[85] See chapter 5, at nn. 119 (Hincmar), 158 (John Scottus); chapter 6, at nn. 26 (Pascasius), 78 (Gottschalk).

"look upon the mystery of the lord's passion" and imitate him by faithful repentance of their sins.[86] Echoing his arguments against Gottschalk, Hincmar's own remarks in *De cavendis*, moving beyond Bede's text, remind Charles the Bald that the life promised in John 3.16 depends on perseverance in faith and good works and faithful reception of the eucharist. This virtuousness, he implies, is grounded in the believer's inner witness of Christ, and the heavenly beatitude thereby earned consists of enjoyment of the tree of life with the angels and saints,[87] a blessing to which the Pericopes ivory clearly alludes.

Second, the universality that the Pericopes ivory attributes to Jesus' death for sin, through its representation of the heavens, *Ocean*, and *Earth*, recalls Hincmar's and John Scottus' different, repeated affirmations of the crucifixion's cosmic impact. In John Scottus' poetry – which Hincmar may well have known and appreciated, whatever his disagreements with some aspects of John Scottus' theology – this idea is developed in dramatic images of the omnipotent, conquering savior, his saving blood and cross signifying his divine majesty, liberation of the underworld, and triumphant resurrection, events that flow into one another and transform the entire universe.[88] In both Hincmar's and John Scottus' thought, the notion of the crucifixion's universal reach that undergirds their defenses of the divine will for the salvation of all human beings is supported by the doctrine of Christ as the new Adam, which the ivory most likely recalled for its contemporary viewers. Christ's death offers redemption to all humanity throughout creation history, because as the second Adam he entirely assumed human nature into his one person; similarly, on the ivory the crucified redeemer hangs on the cross that originated in the garden of Eden, while his resurrection and that of other mortals anticipate the eschaton. The direct descent on the ivory from the crucifixion to Jesus' empty tomb and from there to the prominently depicted, rising dead, in different stages of resurrection, is also reminiscent of Hincmar's insistence that the universal efficacy of Jesus' death and bloodshed is proven in the future resurrection of every mortal, for which the crucifixion and resurrection together

---

[86] Hincmar, *De praed.* 29, *PL* 125.291D-292A; cf. ibid. 28, 285D-286A; and idem, *De cavendis* 3.2, *MGH Quellen* 16.234 (Bede, Hom. 2.18, *CCSL* 122.316).

[87] Hincmar, *De cavendis* 3.2, *MGH Quellen* 16.235. The passage from Bede probably ends at line 4, not line 6 as indicated by Nachtmann, ibid., n. 477. Lines 4–6 are likely Hincmar's direct quotation of John 3.16 (vs. Nachtmann, ibid., nn. 479–480). [88] Chapter 5, at n. 148.

set the stage. All will rise as did Christ and all will then behold their crucified and risen lord, because he died for every human being.[89]

The features of the ivory just discussed sometimes find closer comparisons in Hincmar's work than John Scottus' but the two scholars' thinking on the points noted overlaps enough to make it difficult to argue for the greater influence of one over the other, especially given the problems with any attempt to draw comparisons between written and visual expressions of thought. A possible connection specifically to the archbishop's teachings, however, in particular his ideas about the nature of virtuous, Christian kingship and, relating to this, his doctrine of the eucharist, becomes apparent if we turn now to the two details of the ivory yet to be examined: the standing, veiled woman with a banner and the crowned figure holding a disk, dressed in robes with beaded trim (the only decorated garb on the ivory), and seated beneath a gabled portico, to the far right of the tablet. Here we find the strongest indications that the ivory may have been commissioned by Hincmar with Charles the Bald as its principal intended viewer.

Although the woman with a banner resembles the figures sometimes identified as personifications of Synagogue on Metz crucifixion ivories,[90] at least on the Pericopes tablet, as other scholars have agreed, she is better interpreted as a second representation of *Ecclesia*.[91] Close inspection of the ivory reveals that she originally must have had the identical dress and attributes, except for the chalice, as the *Ecclesia* to the left of the cross; the cross on the banner held by the woman at the right and the knob on the headdress of the one on the left have broken off. The seated figure with the disk is more enigmatic. Most scholars have argued that this is a female personification of a city; usually it is proposed that she is Jerusalem. The identification is mainly based on her female appearance (primarily her beardlessness, whereas all the clearly male figures in the carving seem to be bearded) and on the towers that originally formed her crown's uprights.[92]

---

[89] See chapter 5, at nn. 94, 103 (Hincmar), 139, 156 (John Scottus).

[90] Goldschmidt, *Elfenbeinskulpturen* I, e.g. nos. 78, 83, 85, 86, 88, 89.

[91] Gaborit-Chopin, *Elfenbeinkunst*, 189 cat. 55 (with hesitancy); Vandersall, "Ivories of the Court School," 88–89; Melzak, "Carolingian Ivory Carvings," 192; Goldschmidt, *Elfenbeinskulpturen* I. p. 26, no. 41.

[92] See Gaborit-Chopin, *Elfenbeinkunst*, 189 cat. 55; Melzak, "Carolingian Ivory Carvings," 192; Vandersall, "Ivories of the Court School," 89 (Jerusalem and therefore *Synagoga*, with references to earlier literature).

The majority are now broken, but the original character of the crown is evident when it is seen at first hand. It is important, however, to recognize the figure's distinctiveness among Carolingian images of personified cities or other territory. Similar crowns are worn by Francia and Gothia in the portrait of Charles the Bald in the *Codex Aureus* of St. Emmeram (fol. 5v), and two Utrecht Psalter drawings include depictions of *Terra* that offer other grounds for comparison. In that for Psalm 49 (fol. 28v; fig. 29) she sits wearing a differently styled crown and long robes, holds two wands, and has on her lap two cornucopias and the sphere or disk symbolizing the *orbis terrarum*; this last motif is of relatively the same size as the disk belonging to the Pericopes ivory figure. The illustration to Psalm 89 shows *Terra* without a crown, again holding the *globus* or disk (fol. 53r). On the upper cover of the Drogo Gospelbook, a Metz crucifixion ivory with an as yet undetermined relation to the Pericopes carving, a personification of a region or city, probably Jerusalem, sits to the far right of the crucifix. A wall studded with towers springs from her veiled head and she holds a banner and a knife.[93]

The combination of attributes belonging to the Pericopes ivory figure, though – tower crown, disk, long vestment with decorated borders, and gabled portico – is exceptional. In view of these details, the closest parallels in Carolingian art are representations not of personified regions but of kings. Among them are again a number of drawings in the Utrecht Psalter. The illustration to Psalm 18 (fol. 10v) depicts a king, possibly David, seated within a mandorla; he wears a crown (not with towers) and long vestments, and he holds a cross staff and globe of approximately the same size as the object held by the figure on the ivory. Other Utrecht pictures show David, Saul, and anonymous princes standing or seated beneath gables resembling the one on the ivory. In these images, the roof is clearly a sign of their authority, and thus serves a comparable function to the triangular pediment of the *Cathedra Petri*.[94] In the Utrecht illustration to Psalm 88 (fol. 51v; fig. 23), for example, a beardless, crowned David, seated below a gabled portico, uses his lance to impale an enemy at his feet. The illustrations to Psalms 1, 51, and 151 (fols. 1v, 30r, 91v) depict the ungodly man in the first drawing, portrayed as a prince, and Saul in the other two; they are dressed in long robes, hold swords, sit enthroned beneath or before gabled struc-

---

[93] Paris, BNF, MS lat. 9383; Goldschmidt, *Elfenbeinskulpturen* 1, no. 83; see Melzak, "Carolingian Ivory Carvings," 68–70, 97–98, 182, 191–192, with references to earlier literature.

[94] See Nees, *Tainted Mantle*, 152, 239.

tures, and are accompanied by armed attendants.[95] Similarities are evident, too, between the Pericopes figure and King David on a later ninth-century ivory in Florence.[96] Bearded, crowned, and dressed in long, decorated robes, the psalmist sits on his throne flanked by attendants, a scepter in his right hand and in his left a tiny version of the orb or disk. His body is in frontal view, and like the figure on the Pericopes tablet he turns his head in profile to his right. But the most striking comparisons to the Pericopes ivory motif are the portraits of Charles the Bald in the San Paolo Bible (fol. 1r) and Paris Psalter (fol. 3v; fig. 33), codices made in the late 860s to early 870s. In these two miniatures, the crowned monarch, in long vestments, sits on a throne below a triangular pediment (Bible) or pitched roof (Psalter) and holds a large, circular disk or globe, together with a scepter in the psalter illumination. The orb/disk is adorned with his cruciform monogram in the San Paolo Bible, a cross symbol in the Paris Psalter.[97] Smaller, more clearly spherical and unadorned versions of the emblem of royal office are held by the mounted ruler, probably Charles the Bald though possibly also evoking Charlemagne, of the Louvre's bronze statuette,[98] and by Charles the Bald in his portrait on the backrest of the *Cathedra Petri* (fig. 20).

Despite the evident differences among the spheres and disks belonging to *Terra*, David, and Charles in the images just surveyed, as well as those held by Nicodemus in the Drogo Sacramentary crucifixion miniature and by the seated figure on the Pericopes ivory, Percy Schramm's study has made it clear that they all derive from a pagan classical symbol of the heavens and earth that had been associated with rulers in antiquity.[99] In the

---

[95] I discuss the pictures to Psalms 1, 51, and 151 in my forthcoming article, "Violence and Virtuous Rulership in the Utrecht Psalter."

[96] Florence, Museo Nazionale del Bargello (Coll. Carrand no. 33); Gaborit-Chopin, *Elfenbeinkunst*, 69 fig. 65, cat. 62 (arguing that this is a Rheims work of the last quarter of the ninth century); Goldschmidt, *Elfenbeinskulpturen* I, no. 113 (Metz school; see pp. 57–58).

[97] Rome, Abbazia di S. Paolo fuori le Mura; Paris, BNF, lat. 1152. See Diebold, "Verbal, Visual, and Cultural Literacy"; idem, "The Ruler Portrait of Charles the Bald in the S. Paolo Bible," *Art Bulletin* 76 (1994), 7–18; Hubert et al., *L'Empire carolingien*, 140 fig. 130, 147 fig. 135. The relation between the Pericopes ivory disk and those held by Charles is also noted in Vandersall, "Ivories of the Court School," 116.

[98] Paris, Musée du Louvre; Michael McCormick, "Paderborn 799: Königliche Repräsentation — Visualierung eines Herrschaftskonzepts," in *799: Kunst und Kultur: Beiträge,* ed. Steigemann and Wemhoff, 71–81, pl. 3; Hubert et al., *L'Empire carolingien,* 225 fig. 206; Schramm and Mütherich, *Denkmale der deutschen Könige und Kaiser* 1.267 pl. 58.

[99] Percy E. Schramm, *Sphaira, Globus, Reichsapfel: Wanderung und Wandlung eines Herrschaftszeichens von Caesar bis zu Elisabeth II.* (Stuttgart, 1958), I, 57–59.

Figure 33. Portrait of Charles the Bald, Psalter of Charles the Bald, Paris, Bibliothèque Nationale de France, cod. lat. 1152, fol. 3 verso

San Paolo Bible and Paris Psalter illuminations, the decoration of the sphere or disk with cruciform motifs adds a Christian dimension to the sovereignty the object signifies; Charles reigns on Christ's behalf. [100] No images have survived of any other Carolingian ruler with this emblem of office, though, and the only four extant depictions of Charles the Bald with the attribute – the Louvre statuette, the *Cathedra Petri* carving, and the two

[100] Cf. the inscription below Charles' portrait in the San Paolo Bible (fol. 1r), discussed in Diebold, "Ruler Portrait," 10, 12.

manuscript paintings – were all made c. 860–875, that is in the decade or so prior to his imperial coronation in 875. Although there is no textual evidence he actually possessed such a symbol – it seems to have appeared only in his portraits – the dating of these four images makes it reasonable to suspect that he adopted it as an attribute of his authority around this time, if only for artistic representation, at least partly because of its association with classical, imperial Rome.[101]

Yet even though the figure on the Pericopes tablet therefore has close connections with both antique imagery and other Carolingian works of art, especially depictions of Charles, it is probable that one of its immediate sources was not iconographic but literary: the account of *Tellus* in *De civitate Dei* 7.24. This chapter is part of Augustine's effort in Books 6 and 7 of his treatise to demonstrate the error of Rome's paganism by analyzing the teachings of the pagan classical author, M. Terentius Varro. In Book 7.24, Augustine quotes Varro's description of *Tellus* as the "Great Mother" who is portrayed seated, to show that she is motionless, holding a tambour (*tympanum*) to symbolize the earth, with towers rising from her head.[102] Augustine then proceeds to a lengthy, vigorous condemnation of the goddess' sins. For him, *Tellus* epitomizes the temporal, carnal wickedness of Roman paganism that must be rejected in favor of the true faith alone leading to eternal life.[103]

The formal correspondences between the Pericopes tablet's figure and *Tellus* in *De civitate Dei* make it seem best to identify the former as the latter, in the sense in which Augustine understood the goddess. This interpretation accords with the ivory motif's seated (motionless) position, tower crown, disk, and evidently female face. Possibly, her large size relative to the other figures on the same plane of the composition, except Christ, recalls Varro's identification of her as the "Great Mother"; Varro, Augustine claims, believed that *Tellus* summed up in her one person many deities of the Roman pantheon. *Ecclesia's* banner and the hand she places on the disk reveal that the earthly sovereignty once belonging to this great goddess, as signified by her attributes, particularly the disk, is overcome by Christianity and has passed to the church.

---

[101] See Schramm, *Sphaira, Globus, Reichsapfel*, 58–59.

[102] "Eandem, inquit, dicunt Matrem Magnam; quod tympanum habeat, significari esse orbem terrae; quod turres in capite, oppida; quod sedens fingatur, circa eam cum omnia moueantur, ipsam non moueri." Augustine, *De civ. Dei* 7.24, *CCSL* 47, ed. B. Dombart and A. Kalb (Turnhout, 1955), 205. [103] Ibid. 7.24, 26, *CCSL* 47.205–208, see esp. 208 lines 8–10.

Some aspects of the figure's depiction, however – her robe's decorated borders, the posture reminiscent of ruler portraiture, the gable portico – do not appear strictly relevant to a representation of *Tellus*, while the resemblance they and the disk offer to what are probably contemporary images of Charles seems too marked to have gone unnoticed by members of his entourage or the king himself. Surely he and other contemporary viewers of the ivory would have observed that a special prominence is given to *Tellus* through the way her arm and gable structure overlap the acanthus border,[104] and moreover that she is very royal in appearance. It is difficult not to believe that deliberate, meaningful design choices were at work here. These features, I propose, are clues that an intended effect of this detail was to draw Charles' attention to it and its signification. The image of *Tellus* is quite possibly meant as a reminder or warning directed at the monarch that his very similar portraits advertising his own royal dominion, perhaps especially those that show him with the originally classical, pagan attribute of the disk or sphere, reflect a worldliness rooted in pagan error that has given way to Christ. *Tellus* possesses qualities antithetical to those that Charles should embrace. For the king to glory in such symbols and in the earthly grandeur they signify, the ivory therefore implies, is to separate himself from the salvation to which Christians should aspire by abandoning pride and other sins – a message reinforced on the ivory by *Terra* at the tablet's base, the defeated serpent, and by the vinegar vessel. Redemption is dependent not on mundane honors but on the humility and faith that correspond to witness of the crucified, resurrected Jesus, whose divine conquest of evil is so effectively displayed on this plaque; and it depends on humble submission to the authority that the church possesses from Christ, as indicated by the double representation of *Ecclesia*. It is she who makes available to mortals such as Charles the crucifixion's saving benefits mediated through the liturgy, especially those received in the crucified flesh and blood of the eucharist.

This reading of the Pericopes ivory aligns it with several other artistic productions from Rheims, Metz, and Charles' court school that set before him examples of iniquity he was expected to reject. One is the back cover of the Paris Psalter (fig. 31), which I mentioned earlier is by the same hand as the Pericopes ivory. Like its model, the Utrecht illustration to Psalm 50 (fol.

---

[104] I am grateful to John Contreni for pointing this out to me (oral communication, Kalamazoo, Michigan, May, 2000).

29r), the Paris Psalter ivory shows David as a sinner. He stands beneath a gable portico similar to the one on the Pericopes tablet, admonished by the prophet Nathan for his adultery with Bathsheba and the killing of her husband, Uriah, both of whom are also depicted (2 Kings 11–12).[105] Another such production is the San Paolo Bible, where, as William Diebold has convincingly argued, the series of paintings of Old Testament monarchs presents Charles the Bald with examples of both virtuous kingship, such as Solomon (fol. 188v), and evil rule such as Pharaoh (fol. 21v) and Saul (fol. 83v).[106] A third monument to note is the *Cathedra Petri*. As mentioned in chapter 4,[107] the throne's ivories depict numerous scenes of armed confrontations, often deriving from Utrecht Psalter imagery, that allegorize the struggle between vice and virtue. Charles was evidently meant to identify himself with the forces of goodness and, correspondingly, to join in the opposition to those of sin. Against the background of this interpretation of the friezes, generally accepted by scholars, Lawrence Nees has presented strong arguments for understanding the Hercules plaques beneath the throne's seat as works commissioned by Hincmar in order to set a further, negative exemplar before the Carolingian monarch (fig. 19). The mythical pagan hero's labors carved there constitute a warning directed to Charles of the dangers of "pride and vainglory" that the archbishop associated with the classical tradition.[108]

Whatever the luxury codex for which the Pericopes ivory was intended – an issue I cannot address at this point – it seems likely to me that it was made in the 860s or early 870s, as were the three works of art mentioned above, and at least partly for a comparable purpose: to steer Charles away from sins that the designer identified with bad kingship and towards faith, the sacraments, and acceptance of ecclesiastical guidance. One of the means chosen to communicate this message on the Pericopes carving was a model of evil from *De civitate Dei* that mirrored aspects of the Carolingian ruler's own comportment.

If this was indeed a function of the ivory, then like the works just noted it merits comparison with the ninth-century *Fürstenspiegel* exhorting lay

---

[105] Cf. Deshman, "Exalted Servant," 406–408. On David as an exemplar of virtuous kingship, including the virtue of penitence for his sins, see Anton, *Fürstenspiegel*, esp. 420–432, esp. 426.

[106] Diebold, "Ruler Portrait," esp. 12–14.   [107] Chapter 4, at n. 27.

[108] See Nees, *Tainted Mantle*, 147–168, esp. 167–168, 178–180 on the monument's dating. Nees' reading of the Hercules plaques departs from those proposed by other scholars, but it seems to me the most convincing. For a different theory, see Staubach, *Rex Christianus*, 283–334.

princes to similar behavior.[109] The "mirrors of princes" and related literature by Carolingian authors generally reveal the profound influence of
concepts of Christian virtue and rulership traceable back, to a large extent,
to Augustine's *De civitate Dei*. Often those ideals are articulated by reference to that treatise or other Augustinian sources, especially the description in *De civitate Dei* 5.24 of the true happiness of Christian emperors.[110]
The Carolingian scholar whose development on Augustine's teachings
most closely agrees with the ideas suggested by the Pericopes carving,
however, is Hincmar. The archbishop of Rheims wrote more than any
other contemporary exhorting princes to virtuous governance in forcefully Augustinian terms, and as has already been discussed, he was
emphatic in upholding the power of the church, including the right of
clergy and particularly bishops to advise kings.[111] Furthermore as Nees has
demonstrated, he possessed a pronounced distaste for the trappings of the
pagan Roman *imperium*, which set him at odds with Charles the Bald in the
several years preceding that ruler's acquisition of the imperial title.
Influenced by Augustine, especially *De civitate Dei*, Hincmar considered
pagan Roman culture incompatible with the Christian virtues that led to
salvation. In view of this position he opposed Charles' desire for the imperial throne, urging him to attend instead to his responsibilities as a
Christian king.[112]

Most of Hincmar's writings of admonition were composed for Charles,
his son and grandson. The treatises by the archbishop deserving closest
consideration in relation to the Pericopes ivory are *De cavendis vitiis et virtutibus exercendis*, dating to the 860s or early 870s,[113] and *De regis persona et
regio ministerio* of c. 873, both written for Charles. Of the two solely *De regis
persona*, strictly speaking, belongs to the genre of mirrors of princes, in that
it focuses on the qualities directly pertaining to the royal office. Hincmar
turns to several church fathers, primarily Augustine, in order to outline a
fundamentally Augustinian conception of the nature of Christian monar-

---

[109] See Anton, *Fürstenspiegel*, 132–356.

[110] E.g. the final chapter (17) of Jonas' *De institutione regia* ends by quoting this passage: *SC* 407, ed.
A. Dubreucq (Paris, 1995), 282–284. See Anton, *Fürstenspiegel*, 216–217 and n.402, and on
Augustinian thought and its influence, 47–48, 98–99. Also Nees, *Tainted Mantle*, 77–109.

[111] See Chazelle, "Archbishops Ebo and Hincmar of Reims," 1068–1071, with references to earlier
scholarly literature.

[112] See Devisse, *Hincmar* 2.803–824; Nees, *Tainted Mantle*, 210–211, 243–245; Nelson, *Charles the
Bald*, 235–242.   [113] Nachtmann, ed., *MGH Quellen* 16.23–24 (on the date).

chy. The single most quoted source is *De civitate Dei*. Through this and the other patristic texts used, Charles is reminded that true happiness is impossible for a king who is devoted to the emptiness of temporal glory and unnecessary, belligerent expansion of his dominion, rather than to the opposing virtues that underpin hope for eternal life. Only wars that God sanctions should be waged, and a monarch's focus should instead be on governance with piety, humility, charity, appropriate mercy, and justice, and in the pursuit of peace.[114] *De cavendis*, which as noted in the last chapter is largely a mosaic of unacknowledged scriptural, liturgical, and patristic excerpts, is not concerned with the criteria of good rule, specifically, but seeks to elucidate for Charles the virtues that all Christians must pursue in order to be redeemed and the vices to be avoided.[115] Shifting the emphasis of the largely Gregorian material, Hincmar warns the Carolingian ruler that greed is the foundation of pride, lust, gluttony, and other evils.[116] The first third of the treatise describes the costs to Charles if he does not abandon the sins that bind the mortal to Satan. The second third outlines the route of contrition and humble penitence through which the baptized Christian purges the sinful soul, and it warns the king at painful length of the last judgment and the fires of hell facing those who do not suitably repent, throw off their wicked ways, and persevere in virtue and good works.

What clearly makes *De cavendis* unique among moral tractates for Carolingian princes, and especially significant to interpretation of the Pericopes ivory, is the focus of the last third on the eucharist.[117] The sacrament's nature probably ceased to be an issue of widespread debate after the 850s, but both John Scottus and Hincmar discuss the subject in later writings, in Hincmar's case primarily *De cavendis*. Although John Scottus identifies the eucharist with the crucified and resurrected body, the doctrine he evidently espouses that the Christian must move beyond thoughts of the sacrament's contents in order to contemplate Christ's uncircumscribable divinity, that what lies outside the eucharist's boundaries is more important than what exists within them, seems removed from the identity with the incarnate son of God that the ivory implies, at the very least by the

---

[114] *De regis persona et regio ministerio*, PL 125.833–856. See Anton, *Fürstenspiegel*, 286–287.

[115] Anton, *Fürstenspiegel*, 287.

[116] Hincmar, *De cavendis* 1.2, *MGH Quellen* 16.132–133; see Nachtmann, ed., *MGH Quellen* 16.5.

[117] Hincmar, *De cavendis* 3.2, *MGH Quellen* 16.226–266.

raised chalice. Like the Drogo Sacramentary miniature, the carving may have been intended to recall not simply the connection between the crucified Christ's blood and the eucharistic wine, but also the status of the body still on the cross – again, perhaps significantly, clad in the perizoma – as the one flesh of both the passion and the mass. This perspective on the sacrament accords less with John Scottus' thought than with the doctrine expressed in *De cavendis* as earlier in Pascasius' *De corpore*, commentary on Matthew, and letter to Fredugard, Hincmar's poem on the Virgin, and the *Ferculum Salomonis*. More forcefully than Pascasius' writings, however, or the verses on Mary, both the *Ferculum Salomonis* and *De cavendis* link Pascasius' and Hincmar's theology of the eucharist with the church's authority to mediate redemption to mortals. The Christian virtuousness that Charles the Bald must embrace, Hincmar leaves no doubt in *De cavendis*, has at its core a eucharist governed by the church that contains the incarnate body and blood. To attain the salvation offered every mortal in the passion, Charles among them, requires membership in the church, the exercise of virtue rather than vice, and reception of the eucharist, whose consumption is rendered meritorious through penitence, humility, and orthodox faith, including a correct understanding of the sacrament's nature.[118]

In my view, the Pericopes ivory's depiction of *Ecclesia* before a regal *Tellus* has no closer parallel in contemporary Carolingian thought than Hincmar's Augustinian-based antipathy to pagan, imperial Rome, the disjunction he posits between its culture and the salvation to which the church guides her faithful, and his warnings to Charles prior to the imperial coronation not to allow earthly vanity to blind the monarch to the duties of Christian kingship. Correspondingly, it is unsurprising that other pictorial elements of the plaque evoke important aspects of the teachings on predestination, the crucifixion, the church, and the eucharist that Hincmar communicated to the same ruler. Perhaps, therefore – to point out a few additional ways in which *De cavendis* may shed light on the carving's iconography and on how contemporaries may have understood it – the angels above the cross owe some inspiration to the relationship implied in that treatise, by means of excerpts from Augustine's *enarratio* on Psalm 33, between the eucharist, the incarnate body, and the bread eaten at

---

[118] See chapter 6, at n. 55.

the celestial altar. In line with Hincmar's evident interpretation of Augustine, the ivory's angels and the hand of God may have recalled for Charles, given his knowledge of *De cavendis*, the descent of the word and living bread from heaven to the mortal body on the cross and in the eucharist, as well as the same body's reascent at the ascension and in the mass oblation.[119] Earlier in *De cavendis*, joining passages from Gregory I and Bede, Hincmar places striking emphasis on the angels' presence at the mass ceremony. Charles is warned to avoid the behavior of those who accumulate sins even inside a church and be mindful of the angels attending "with invisible presence on the elect" during the eucharistic celebration, just as heavenly throngs watched over the tomb in which the body lay after the crucifixion. By demonstrating fear and veneration in the angels' presence during the mass, he follows the example of the women who visited the sepulchre, who when they saw the angels (two according to Luke's gospel), "were afraid and bowed down their countenance towards the ground" (Luke 24.5) – much as the two women nearest the tomb are depicted on the Pericopes ivory, with shoulders hunched so that they seem to look downward.[120] Drawing on Bede, Hincmar then claims that the vessels they carried (according to Mark and Luke) symbolize the "golden vials full of odours, which are the prayers of the saints" (Apoc. 5.8) and the heart's purging of sordidness in preparation for the eucharist. In emulation of the women, the archbishop tells Charles (through Bede),

> we gradually spread spices at the lord's tomb when, remembering the passion and death that he accepted for us, we both outwardly show the light of good deeds to our neighbors and we glow inwardly in our heart with the sweetness of pure compunction. This appropriately happens at any hour yet especially when we enter a church to pray, when we approach the altar to consume the mysteries of the lord's body and blood. For if the women sought with such care the dead body of the lord, how much more fitting is it that we, who know him to have risen from the dead, to have ascended into the heavens, to be present everywhere in the power of the divine majesty, assist with every reverence those who watch over him [and] celebrate his mysteries?[121]

If Charles consumes the eucharist with these beliefs in mind and his soul properly cleansed, distancing himself from the evil that brings damnation,

---

[119] Hincmar, *De cavendis* 3.2, MGH Quellen 16.242–244.
[120] Ibid. 2.6, MGH Quellen 16.207–209.   [121] Ibid. 2.6, MGH Quellen 16.210, see 211.

he will enjoy a foretaste of the celestial feast. Hence he will gain the divine illumination that anticipates the vision of God in paradise, Hincmar indicates later in the same treatise, where he will partake of the tree of life in heaven with the angels and the saints.[122] But as the archbishop wants his king to understand, as well, this illumination is only possible for Christian rulers who reject earthly glorification and accept the spiritual guidance of their clergy, the church's representatives, receiving the eucharist in true faith, contrition, and humility. These, too, may well have been among the ideas that Charles pondered as he contemplated the Pericopes plaque and, perhaps guided by Hincmar, sought to understand its multivalent imagery.[123]

Conclusion

The foregoing analysis of the Pericopes ivory explores the possibilities of interpretation more than it attempts to establish definitively its meaning. On the whole, the carving's signification may always be more uncertain than that of the other artistic productions examined in this book. The Gellone Sacramentary, Utrecht Psalter, and Drogo Sacramentary provide us with textual frameworks for their decoration; we can better assess the credibility of different readings by examining the degree to which they

---

[122] See ibid. 3.2, *MGH Quellen* 16.234–235, 242, 245–246 (Augustine, with Hincmar's additions); ibid. 2.3, *MGH Quellen* 16.185–186 (Gregory I).

[123] Given Werckmeister's suggestion that the ivory was possibly made as the back cover for the *Codex Aureus* of St.-Emmeram, whose imagery and *tituli*, apparently written by John Scottus, seem to reflect elements of that scholar's theology, it is intriguing to wonder whether Hincmar might have partly intended the ivory to undermine certain doctrines suggested by the book's illumination. For example, the *Codex Aureus* depicts Charles himself enthroned in resplendent glory, attended by angels, the hand of God over his head, and already evidently enjoying the vision of the end of time (fols. 5v-6r; Hubert et al., *L'Empire carolingien*, 149–150 figs. 137, 138); but the Pericopes ivory situates the angels and the hand of God over the crucified Christ (who died for Charles' sins), seems to warn Charles to avoid the vice of pride, associated with some of his own attributes of earthly rule, and encourages him to recognize that only through the eucharist consumed in faith and humility can he experience an anticipation of the heavenly feast and vision. If a concern to "respond" in this manner to the *Codex Aureus* decoration was an aim in the ivory's production, then in this respect, again, it provides an interesting comparison to the function Nees has proposed for the Hercules plaques on the *Cathedra Petri*: see *Tainted Mantle*, esp. 235–250; Werckmeister, *Deckel*, 58–59, 72–73. Edouard Jeauneau and Paul Dutton have shown that the *tituli* of the *Codex Aureus* miniatures are by John Scottus: "The Verses of the *Codex Aureus* of St.-Emmeram," in E. Jeauneau, *Etudes érigéniennes* (Paris, 1987), 593–638. These issues and others still raised by the *Codex Aureus* as well as the Pericopes tablet clearly need further study.

coincide with accompanying liturgical and biblical texts, as well as with contemporary and earlier scholars' exegesis of the same writings. The ivory lacks a similar, direct association with the written word to assist us in deciphering its pictorial forms. From this perspective, perhaps, only Hrabanus' *In honorem s. crucis* offers truly solid grounds on which to base an iconographic analysis, because of the author's lengthy "declarations" of the meanings of his figures; and even there, as we have seen, we must look outside the material in the treatise to Hrabanus' connections with Alcuin and the early Carolingian court, in order to gain a better understanding of the ideas his work may have been meant to express.

Regardless of these difficulties, however, certain features of the images discussed in chapter 3 and this chapter are clear enough to permit some comparison of the doctrinal orientations they seem to indicate. First, a few points should be apparent at which the thought about the crucified Christ suggested by the imagery of Gellone (in particular its *Te igitur* image, fig. 7) and by Hrabanus' treatise intersects with that implied by the Psalm 115 illustration in the Utrecht Psalter, the Drogo Sacramentary crucifixion miniature, and the Pericopes ivory (figs. 26, 27, and 30). A central concern for the designer of each image was to find suitable artistic means to convey the belief that the crucified Jesus is fully human and fully God. Both the early and the later Carolingian depictions offer decisive reminders that he is the eternal, universal lord: in Gellone and Poem 1 of *In honorem* (fig. 11), his open eyes and unsuffering body; the angels of the *Sanctus* in Gellone; the praise of the divine Christ woven through his body in Hrabanus' poem; the subsequent texts and images of *In honorem* celebrating the cross's and Christ's cosmic rule; the triumphal wreath, hand of God, defeated serpent, adoring angels, sun, and moon, and the rising dead of the images studied in this chapter. Yet while the divinity is therefore kept clearly in view, all these representations are also indicative of efforts by their designers, beyond what is suggested by earlier western crucifixion imagery, to show Jesus' simultaneous possession of true humanity. In the Utrecht Psalter, Drogo Sacramentary, and Pericopes ivory images, the mortality of the human nature is evident from the slumping body, bowed head, and in at least one case closed eyes, a detail possibly found earlier in Gellone's second crucifixion illumination (fig. 10). In Hrabanus' *In honorem* and the Gellone Sacramentary, the mortal humanity is evoked partly through the accompanying texts, and both Hrabanus and the Gellone artist chose to depict

Christ wearing the perizoma, as did the artists of two of the three later Carolingian images examined, perhaps in order to emphasize the human flesh's reality.

In addition, each image invites the viewer to attend to the connection between the crucifixion and the liturgy – the rites of Holy Week and Easter, especially the *Adoratio crucis* of Good Friday, other ceremonies of cross worship, baptism, the mass. Unlike Pascasius and some of his contemporaries, earlier Carolingian theologians did not try to define in exact terms the eucharist's relation to the incarnate body, and it is therefore understandable that neither Gellone nor *In honorem* implies a position on this issue. Yet even so, the Gellone *Te igitur* illumination is grounded in the belief, consistently held throughout this period, that the consecrated bread and wine commemorate the sacrifice of the cross and contain the body and blood of Christ; and like the Drogo Sacramentary and Pericopes images, though not as starkly, it seems to link the eucharist to ecclesiastical authority.

Still, the differences in theological perspective between the images investigated in chapter 3 and those discussed in this chapter are more striking than the similarities. The Gellone Sacramentary, probably made for Notre-Dame of Cambrai in 790–c. 804, was perhaps sent to Gellone with Benedict of Aniane's struggle against Adoptionist heterodoxy in mind. Its miniatures reveal a highly innovative artist's search to communicate ideas about the Virgin Mary, baptism, and the crucifixion that may have been influenced by the theological deliberations at Charlemagne's court over the nature of Christ and possibly, as well, those over the role of images and the relative value of artistic representation and the written word. Pictorial forms that in some respects were apparently without precedent, and that were perhaps intended to gain iconic value from their tight integration with texts, highlight the union of divinity and humanity in Jesus' one person. In a manner that recalls the anti-Adoptionist doctrines of Alcuin and Paulinus, the joining of the two natures is implied to have begun with the conception in Mary, Jesus' royal mother, and to continue beyond the crucifixion and resurrection to his return. This union is indicated to be critical to the salvific efficacy of both baptism and – in line with the teachings of the *Opus Caroli regis* on the eucharist – the bread and wine that the church offers the faithful in the mass.

In honorem sanctae crucis, perhaps completed little more than a decade after the Gellone Sacramentary reached Aquitaine, is a didactic treatise revealing Hrabanus' impressive command of both a classical literary genre and Christian dogma, knowledge he must have largely acquired from his teacher, Alcuin. The treatise's *carmina figurata* have no match in earlier or later writings of this form. Their unique intricacy and the range of insights they present concerning the physical universe, scriptural exegesis, number symbolism, and other topics, testimony to the high levels of learning attainable in the early years of the Carolingian *renovatio*, were most likely important reasons for Hrabanus' life-long pride in his work and for its popularity among his contemporaries, as well as in subsequent centuries. These factors, however, do not obscure the similarity of some of his doctrinal concerns to those of the designer of the Gellone Sacramentary illuminations. At the core of *In honorem* is an interest in the divine savior's triumph over sin/death/Satan, the cross's manifestation of his eternal, universal majesty, and in the function of the cross's form as both sacred letter and image, traditional beliefs widely explored in early and later Carolingian literature. In addition, though, Hrabanus' texts and figures, especially the figure of Poem 1, like the Gellone decoration, were probably affected by the theological outlook of Charlemagne's entourage. Conceivably the treatise has some connection with the discussions of the role of artistic images, their relation to consecrated things and to written language; but what is clearer is the impact of the concerns about Christological orthodoxy. Much as in Gellone, though by different means – taking advantage of the special intersection of image and text in the *carmen figuratum* – Hrabanus demonstrates that Christ's mediatorship is the basis of mortals' hopes for salvation as well as of the cross's sanctity.

The Utrecht Psalter, the Drogo Sacramentary, and the Pericopes ivory, however, belong to cultural environments shaped, in the ninth-century empire, by the wider diffusion of schools, teachers, and students involved in intensive study of patristic and classical literature, the Bible, and the liturgy.[124] Among the symptoms of these developments are the rise in copying of older texts and in the amount of original writing in Latin and the vernacular. An increasing volume of poetry, scriptural commentaries, homiletic collections, and studies of the liturgy and the sacraments by

---

[124] Beyond the other secondary literature cited in chapter 4 relating to these developments, see Rosamond McKitterick, *The Carolingians and the Written Word* (Cambridge, 1989); idem, ed., *Carolingian Culture*; idem, ed., *The Uses of Literacy in Early Medieval Europe* (Cambridge, 1990).

Carolingian authors give new consideration to the passion's meaning, nature, and purpose. So also do the writings that stem from the theological conflicts examined in chapters 5 and 6, quarrels internal to the Carolingian realms that placed new pressure on participants to attend closely to scriptural and liturgical exegesis, and to the patristic sources offering assistance in these tasks.

The extensive research by Carolingian churchmen into the Bible and the liturgy, and into the patristic writings that could help them elucidate scripture, church ritual, and doctrinal issues, promoted three, additional phenomena relevant to this chapter. One, noted in chapter 4, is attentiveness to the passion's temporal progression and the significance of each stage in Jesus' suffering and dying. A second is the emphasis found in a variety of ninth-century Carolingian texts on the redemptive role of his human mortality, sacrifice, and bloodshed, and on the inspiration to contrition, empathy, and humility provided by his crucified human nature. Although some early Carolingian texts, especially a few by Alcuin, dwell on Christ's death as the source of redemption and an incentive to repentance, such themes are more pronounced in later Carolingian literature; and they tend to be linked with clearer reminders that the benefits of Jesus' death and sacrifice are channeled to mortals through penance, the sacraments, and the church.

The third phenomenon is one to which I have made occasional references in previous chapters, but it needs to be isolated here. This is the growth of interest among ninth-century scholars in the role of the physical sense of sight in Christian devotion, particularly as this applies to the seeing of the crucified and resurrected Jesus. Perhaps an early stage in this development is evident in the *Opus Caroli regis*, in the sharp disjunction Theodulf posits between images, beheld only through the bodily eyes (therefore of little use to Christian devotion), and the interior contemplation of God or the heavenly realm for which the primary aid is scripture. In contrast, Hrabanus' *In honorem s. crucis* clearly assigns a central role to corporeal sight in contemplation of the mysteries revealed through the form of the cross. Similarly, to varying degrees, with the exception of Claudius' letter-treatise to Theutmir, the tractates of the 820s to 840s on images, crosses, and relics of the saints explore the positive value of seeing such objects. Hence some of them stress the recollection of the passion that the cross's sight inspires, especially on Good Friday, even while sometimes expressing antipathy to the veneration of images. Ninth-century exegesis of the liturgy, above all by Amalarius and to a lesser degree that by other scholars, analyzes how, partly through the impact on the sense of sight, the rituals of baptism, Easter, the mass, and Holy Week recall and com-memorate stages in Christ's passion and resurrection. In this context, certain aspects of the Good Friday main service, especially the *Adoratio crucis*, are occasionally identified with the inner vision of the crucified savior. The quarrel over divine predestination led Hincmar to oppose Gottschalk partly by reference to the heavenly vision of God, the faithful person's inner vision of the crucified Christ, suggested in John 3.14–16, and the witness of the returned Christ at the final resurrection. Other Carolingian theologians of the mid ninth century wrote treatises on the celestial vision; its nature is obviously a key issue in the thought of John Scottus Eriugena, and, not discussed in the preceding pages, the genres of dream and vision literature gain new importance in the ninth century. Finally, the controversy over the eucharist encouraged participants to think about the relation between, on the one hand, the features of bread and wine and the reminder they offer of the crucifixion, on the other the body and blood of Christ perceptible to the mind or soul that are housed within them – as all Carolingians believed, whatever their understanding of the precise nature of that presence.

These developments form significant elements of the cultural back-ground to the images investigated in this chapter. Further study would doubtless show this to be true, as well, for other later Carolingian artistic productions. The polyvalent interpretations of the liturgy, the sacraments, and the Bible offered by the three works of art studied here seem to reflect an adeptness in combining allusions to multiple liturgical, exegetical, doc-trinal, and other sources that has more numerous parallels in later than early Carolingian literature. Moreover, in spite of the evident concern with Jesus' humanity shown by the Gellone Sacramentary and *In honorem s. crucis* imagery, the manner in which the crucified human nature is visually recalled is clearly different in the Utrecht Psalter, the Drogo Sacramentary, and on the Pericopes ivory. In Gellone and Hrabanus' treatise, the desire to express the simultaneous presence of both natures seems to have encour-aged efforts to join visual and textual references to each nature as closely as possible, like layered transparencies in an anatomy book. Unlike these works, the images I have analyzed from Utrecht, the Drogo Sacramentary, and the Pericopes ivory do not appear intended to direct meditation specifically to the divinity's union with humanity. Rather, they suggest greater interest in the visible reality of Jesus' suffering – as something to be beheld and contemplated in its own right – and thus greater interest in its significance as an inspiration to repentance, a model for the faithful to emulate, and the source of redemption accessible in the sacraments. Although Christ's possession of two natures is affirmed, the designers chose pictorial details essentially separating the attributes of his humanity from those of his divinity. The viewer is led to consider his human body insofar as it bled and died on the cross, while other aspects of the depiction recall the divine victory over death. The recollection of Jesus' sacrifice, the contrition, the imitation of his exemplary virtue that these representations were no doubt expected to stir are analogous to the impact that contemporary texts ascribe to the sight and adoration of crosses and to the entire liturgy of Holy Week and the mass. All these constitute devotional experiences enabling the faithful to "see" the crucified Christ and, by doing so, inspiring penitence and obedience to his example of humility.

Finally, the images studied in this chapter may have been influenced by the developments in thought that underlay the mid-ninth-century debates over predestination and the eucharistic presence, in particular teachings of Hincmar of Rheims. Given the theological expertise and intellectual independence demonstrated by the creator of the Utrecht Psalter illustration to Psalm 115, it is conceivable that he chose to identify the eucharist with Christ's historical body and blood apart from any knowledge of Pascasius' *De corpore et sanguine Domini*, perhaps before that treatise was written. The drawing may constitute the earliest surviving evidence in Carolingian theology of an interest in clarifying this particular doctrine. Indeed, one can even speculate that Hincmar was inspired to embrace Pascasius' teachings, alluding to them in his poem on the Virgin Mary, through familiarity with an already existing Utrecht Psalter. Nevertheless, it is important not to ignore the possibility that the psalter was made under Hincmar and that the Psalm 115 drawing testifies to his own belief in the eucharist's identity with the crucified blood and flesh. Hence it perhaps reflects the relation between this notion and Mary's special status in heaven implied in his verses honoring her. As for the Drogo Sacramentary miniature, it may have been influenced by the quarrels that the same eucharist doctrine engendered in the 850s. Here, there is possibly a sympathy for Pascasius' ideas that reflects awareness of the controversy over them, while other aspects of the painting, such as the focus brought on *Ecclesia*'s mediation of the sacrament, perhaps attest the concerns about the church's welfare provoked by Gottschalk's doctrine of twin predestination.

More complex parallels to Hincmarian thought, though, are suggested by the Pericopes ivory. To a significant degree, the carving can be interpreted in light of ninth-century Carolingian liturgical practice and commentaries on scripture and the liturgy, and certain aspects of its imagery accord with John Scottus Eriugena's theology where his beliefs approach those of Hincmar. Yet despite the problems in determining the meaning of a work of art divorced from written texts, it is with Hincmar's thinking about predestination, the eucharist, the church, and the principles of virtuous kingship in mind that the Pericopes tablet's elaborate composition is best analyzed. This magnificent carving, quite possibly commissioned by Hincmar for Charles the Bald in the 860s or early 870s, may count among a greater number of artistic productions than yet known offering a pictorial record of the ideas that the archbishop so energetically propounded in his writings, as he sought to convince his contemporaries, most of all his king, of what he was convinced was divinely ordained truth.

CHAPTER 8

Conclusion

Throughout the period covered in this book, from Charlemagne's reign to the end of that of his grandson, Charles the Bald, Carolingian scholars struggled to interpret the Bible and the liturgy, absorb the teachings of the church fathers, employ their own words, those of older writings, and artistic imagery to express the precepts of their religion, and attempt their own answers, sometimes of profound intellectual complexity, to the doctrinal issues of their day. It is true, as modern scholarship has so often asserted, that they lacked the knowledge of Greek philosophical thought and the tools of logical analysis available to later scholastics like Anselm, Abelard, and Thomas Aquinas. But that should not allow us to assume they were less capable of sustained intellectual deliberation and discourse, utilizing the artistic and literary techniques they had mastered and turning for inspiration to the Bible, the liturgy, and the patristic authorities they knew and admired.

Whether eighth- and ninth-century ecclesiastics wrote about the crucifixion or explored its meaning through works of art, their thought remained within certain broad doctrinal perameters inherited from earlier theologians, particularly of the Latin church. With support from scripture, liturgical texts, and patristic sources, they found diverse, visual and verbal means to acknowledge the crucified Jesus' possession of both mortal humanity and immortal divinity, his mediatorship between the earthly and heavenly realms. In both eighth- and ninth-century literature, discussions of the passion's significance range from a focus on the relationship between the two natures, to emphasis on the son of God's divine omnipotence and celestial dominion, to meditation on his wounded, dying human body as the locus of redemption, to variations on these themes. For early as for later Carolingian Christians, these ideas were recalled, "represented," and in a sense reconciled with one another by the ecclesiastical rites in which they all participated. Local and regional customs varied widely and church ceremonial developed remarkably between the eighth and ninth centuries; yet throughout these years, baptism, the mass, and the annual feasts and observations that commemorated Jesus' death, resurrection, and his glorified cross, looking forward to his return, provided a structure of shared ritual lending coherence to the variegated doctrine. The liturgy continually demonstrated the fundamental unity of the participants' beliefs about the crucifixion, even as it itself invited study, interpretation, and pictorial expression of its message.

But while scholars under both Charlemagne and his heirs accepted this basic framework of thought, what their teachings share in common is less remarkable than the rich plurality of ideas that texts and artistic creations show to have flourished within the empire's boundaries. Not only are there distinctions between earlier and later decades; it is important that we attend to the nuances of pictorial and textual expression that differentiate contemporary artistic productions and the writings of theologians at work in the same years, or sometimes individual compositions by a single author. The Gellone and *In honorem s. crucis* decorations seem influenced by a similar interest in affirming Christological orthodoxy, but they adopt dissimilar approaches to this task; the Utrecht Psalter illustration to Psalm 115, the Drogo Sacramentary Palm Sunday image, and the Pericopes ivory may all reflect Hincmarian doctrine, but they suggest their designers' diverse interests, as well, in patristic exegesis, liturgical prayers and readings, doctrinal tractates, contemporary quarrels, and political matters. Correspondingly, in Carolingian literature that discusses the crucifixion, the traditional doctrines outlined in chapter 1 shift in form in the hands of different authors. The textual sources on which they draw, the other issues addressed that lead to thought about the event, and sometimes simply, no doubt, the intellectual preferences of the eighth- and ninth-century writers themselves, lend their reflections on the passion distinctive traits. Perhaps no other theologian of this epoch matches Alcuin in his anxiety over sin's burden; yet even Alcuin expected that the most stained human soul could be washed in Christ's blood. Although Amalarius' *Liber officialis* develops

on an already established notion of the liturgy as the representative commemoration of the sacred past, his enthusiastic exploration of the ceremonies' symbolic mysteries gives this notion an altogether unique
character. Candidus' *De passione Domini* is marked by its sensitivity to Jesus'
paradigmatic suffering and humility. Pascasius' commentary on Matthew
is notable for its skillfully interwoven borrowings from and echoes of older
authorities, and its emphasis on the ability of Christ's humanity, even on
the cross, to override natural law. John Scottus Eriugena's poetry sets out
an incomparable picture of the crucifixion's power to defeat Satan and
empty hell.

The variations in perspective are especially noticeable in the documen-
tation from the four theological controversies that have been my main
focus. In none of these conflicts was the passion the only subject considered; in each, however, it was realized by at least certain scholars that successful argument required clarifying some facet of the dogma that God
chose to save mortals by becoming a man and dying on a cross. The ways in
which the crucifixion is remembered, though, elucidate not only larger,
shared patterns of thought – between the *Opus Caroli regis* and the anti-
Adoptionist literature, between the writings on predestination and on the
eucharist – but also differences. The early Carolingian assaults on Nicea II
and Hispanic Adoptionism agree in their efforts to defend Christ's possession of two natures, yet they differ in how they approach this undertaking.
Theodulf's treatise describes the union of divinity with humanity, manifested in the crucifixion, as the bridge that enables Christians to proceed
from material concerns to the spiritual truths recorded in scripture, and
therefore to Christ as God. In attacking Adoptionism, Paulinus and Alcuin
examine how the crucifixion revealed the union's perfection and, therefore, the humanity's sinlessness, though Paulinus offers more tightly
argued, elegant expositions of these teachings, while Alcuin's less orga-
nized, more passionate defenses of them seem particularly concerned to
demonstrate the harmony between his and patristic thought.

Benedict of Aniane gives still another view of official Carolingian
Christology when he links the union's completeness with the more
"Hispanic" theme of the word's descent from and reascent to the father. In
the quarrels over predestination and the eucharist, attention is again
directed to the passion, on these occasions more clearly because of its function as the source of the redemption mediated in the liturgy and sacra-

ments, and because of disagreements over scriptural and liturgical exegesis. But differences of opinion occur even among individual theologians supposedly on the same "sides" in the debates. Gottschalk's supporters do not completely accept his theology of predestination, including his evidently rigid rejection of the possibility that Christ suffered for other mortals besides the elect. Hincmar follows Hrabanus in upholding the divine will for universal salvation and Christ's death for all humanity, and the archbishop of Reims essentially agrees with Pascasius' doctrine of the eucharistic presence. Yet he moves away from his allies and closer to John Scottus – with whom he differs in other respects – in his special emphasis on the cosmic reach of Christ's suffering and bloodshed and on the passion's connection with the heavenly vision. While Gottschalk and Ratramnus both believe that the eucharist does not contain the incarnate body and blood, they do not have quite the same concept of the relation between those entities; and Ratramnus, like Hincmar, appears more aware of the eucharist as a foreshadowing of the vision of God.

The individuality of the ideas suggested by these texts and images, the range of doctrines that Carolingian participants in the theological disputes could articulate, no matter their misunderstandings of each other's positions, show we are dealing with writers and artistic designers of distinct intellectual dispositions despite the cultural ties that bound them with one another. Although they shared loyalty to the same doctrinal and liturgical traditions traceable back to the church fathers and the Bible, and often had access to similar books and pictorial models, they innovated on those foundations on a scale never before seen in the medieval west. That they so confidently opposed Nicea II and Spanish Adoptionism, so vehemently quarreled over predestination and the eucharist, engaged in dialogue and strife on yet further matters, and presented their varied thinking about their crucified savior in such a wide array of literary and artistic productions belies the still common view of the era's primary scholarly achievement as the preservation and transmission of older learning.

The focus here has been on only a narrowly defined area of eighth- and ninth-century theological discourse and its influence on a few artistic representations of the crucifixion. With both written and iconographic evidence, I have preferred to concentrate on a selection of works than try for a more wide-reaching but necessarily less careful examination of that which has survived. The restricted scope of this investigation has, I hope, made it possible to clarify some aspects of Carolingian belief beyond concepts of the passion's nature and purpose. Nevertheless, it should remain apparent that this period of heightened intellectual activity, especially in terms of theology, has not by any means received the attention that is required from historians for us to comprehend satisfactorily either the evolution of doctrine in the Carolingian church, or its relation to the thought of preceding and subsequent centuries, in the west or Byzantium. Further studies are necessary not only of formal doctrinal treatises but, to a greater extent than attempted here, of the abundant exegetical material, poetry, letters, liturgical books, and other sources not immediately inspired by the contemporary quarrels, yet documents that nonetheless provide insights into theological belief. More investigation is also needed into the complex relationship between the artistic imagery and ideas set forth in writing. While difficulties of access to the extant evidence clearly remain – texts published only in the *Patrologia latina* or only found in manuscripts, works of art unavailable for direct examination and only sporadically if ever reproduced, to name two major problems – they are gradually being eased. New critical editions, manuscript studies, facsimiles, and art historical analyses are appearing at an increasing rate that answer critical questions about the sources, production, and transmission of such materials. It is essential that historians now exploit these more thoroughly in order to elucidate the mental world they reveal. Only by carefully listening to the ideas eighth- and ninth-century scholars and artists sought to convey through prose and verse, passages borrowed from earlier authorities, and images can we hope to understand the intellectual forces that were the fundamental catalyst to the Carolingian *renovatio*.

Select bibliography

Primary sources

The list is limited to printed editions of the principal Carolingian sources used.

Adrevald of Fleury, *De corpore et sanguine Domini contra ineptias Joannis Scoti*, PL
    124.947–954.

Agobard, *Opera Omnia*, CCCM 52, edited by L. Van Acker, Turnhout, 1981.

Alcuin, *Adversus Elipandum libri IV*, PL 101.231–300.

    Adversus Felicem Urgellitanum Episcopum libri VII, PL 101.119–230.

    Carmina, MGH PLAC 1, edited by E. Dümmler, pp. 160–351, Berlin, 1881.

    Carmina rhythmica, MGH PLAC 4.3, edited by K. Strecker, pp. 903–910,
        Berlin, 1923.

    Commentaria in S. Joannis Evangelium, PL 100.737–1008.

    De baptismi caeremoniis, PL 101.611–614.

    De fide sanctae et individuae Trinitatis, PL 101.11–58.

    De virtutibus et vitiis ad Widonem comitem, PL 101.613–638.

    Epistolae, MGH Epp. 4, edited by E. Dümmler, pp. 1–481, Berlin, 1895.

    Expositio in epistolam Pauli Apostoli ad Hebraeos, PL 100.1031–1084.

    Expositio pia ac brevis in psalmos poenitentiales, in psalmum CXVIII et graduales,
        PL 100.569–638.

    Liber contra haeresim Felicis: Edition with an Introduction, edited by G. B.
        Blumenshine, ST 285, Vatican City, 1980.

    Missae, edited by J. Deshusses, "Les messes d'Alcuin," *Archiv für
        Liturgiewissenschaft* 14 (1972), 7–41.

    Versus de patribus, regibus et sanctis euboricensis ecclesiae, edited and translated
        by P. Godman, *The Bishops, Kings, and Saints of York*, Oxford, 1982.

Amalarius, *Opera liturgica omnia*, 3 vol., *ST* 138–140, edited by J. M. Hanssens,
    Vatican City, 1948–1950.

Amolo of Lyons, *Opuscula* 1–2, *PL* 116.97–106.

Angilbert of St.-Riquier, *Carmina, MGH PLAC* 1, edited by E. Dümmler, pp.
    355–366, Berlin, 1881.

    Institutio de Diversitate Officiorum, CCM 1, edited by K. Hallinger, pp. 283–303,
        Siegburg, 1963.

Audradus Modicus, *Liber de fonte vitae, MGH PLAC* 3, edited by L. Traube, pp.
    73–84, Berlin, 1896.

    Carminum supplementum, MGH PLAC 3, edited by L. Traube, pp. 739–745,
        Berlin, 1896.

Benedict of Aniane, *Opuscula* 1–2, *PL* 103.1381–1411.

Bernowin, *Carmina, MGH PLAC* 1, edited by E. Dümmler, pp. 413–425, Berlin, 1881.

Candidus, *Opusculum de passione Domini, PL* 106.57–104.

Carmina Centulensia, MGH PLAC 3, edited by L. Traube, pp. 265–368, Berlin, 1896.

Christian of Stavelot, *Expositio in Matthaeum evangelistam, PL* 106.1261–1504.

Claudius of Turin, *Apologeticum atque rescriptum adversus Theutmirum abbatem*,
    MGH Epp. 4, edited by E. Dümmler, pp. 610–613, Berlin, 1895.

    Enarratio in Epistolam D. Pauli ad Galatas, PL 104.841–912.

Concilium Francofurtense A. 794, MGH Conc. 2.1, edited by A. Werminghoff, pp.
    110–171, Hanover, 1906.

Concilium Parisiense A. 825, MGH Conc. 2.2, edited by A. Werminghoff, pp. 475–551,
    Hanover, 1908.

Concilium Parisiense A. 829, MGH Conc. 2.2, edited by A. Werminghoff, pp. 606–680,
    Hanover, 1908.

Corpus Consuetudinem Monasticarum, vol. 1; *Initia Consuetudinis Benedictinae*, edited
    by K. Hallinger, Siegburg, 1963.

De Conversione Saxonum Carmen, MGH PLAC 1, edited by E. Dümmler, pp. 380–381,
    Berlin, 1881.

Dicta Albini / Dicta Candidi, edited by J. Marenbon, *From the Circle of Alcuin to the*
    School of Auxerre: Logic, Theology and Philosophy in the Early Middle Ages,
    pp. 151–170, Cambridge, 1981.

Drogo-Sakramentar, Ms. Latin 9428, Bibliothèque nationale, Paris. Vollständige
    Faksimile-Ausgabe im Originalformat, 2 vols., edited by F. Mütherich,
    Commentary by W. Köhler, Graz, 1974.

Dungal the Scot, *Responsa contra perversas Claudii Taurinensis episcopi sententias*,
    MGH Epp. 4, edited by E. Dümmler, pp. 583–585, Berlin, 1895.

Liber Adversus Claudium Taurinensem, PL 105.457–530.

Einhard, *Quaestio de adoranda cruce, MGH Epp.* 5, edited by K. Hampe, pp. 146–149, Berlin, 1899.

Florus of Lyons, *Opuscula adversus Amalarium* 1–3, *PL* 119.71–96. *Opusculum* 1 also edited by E. Dümmler, *MGH Epp.* 5, pp. 267–273, Berlin, 1899.

    Opusculum de expositione missae, PL 119.15–72.

    (Pseudo-Remigius), *De tribus epistolis liber, PL* 121.985–1068.

    (Pseudo-Remigius), *Libellus de tendenda immobiliter scripturae veritate, PL* 121.1083–1134.

Gosbert, *Carmen acrostichum, MGH PLAC* 1, edited by E. Dümmler, pp. 620–622, Berlin, 1881.

Gottschalk of Orbais, *Die Gedichte des Gottschalk von Orbais*, edited by M.-L. Weber, Frankfurt am Main, 1992.

    Œuvres théologiques et grammaticales de Godescalc d'Orbais, edited by D. C. Lambot, Louvain, 1945.

Haimo of Auxerre, *Divi Pauli epistolas expositio, PL* 117.361–938.

    Homiliae de tempore, PL 118.11–746.

Heiric of Auxerre, *I Collectanea di Eirico di Auxerre*, edited by R. Quadri, Fribourg, 1966.

    Homiliae per circulum anni, CCCM 116–116B, edited by R. Quadri, Turnhout, 1992–1994.

The Heliand: the Saxon Gospel, translated by G. Ronald Murphy, Oxford, 1992.

Hincmar of Rheims, *De regis persona et regio ministerio, PL* 125.833–856.

    De cavendis vitiis et virtutibus exercendis, MGH Quellen zur Geistesgeschichte des Mittelalters 16, edited by D. Nachtmann, Munich, 1998.

    Carmina, MGH PLAC 3, edited by L. Traube, pp. 406–420, Berlin, 1896.

    Explanatio in ferculum Salomonis, PL 125.817–834.

    De praedestinatione Dei et libero arbitrio, PL 125.65–474.

    Epistolae, MGH Epp. 8.1, Berlin, 1939.

    Ad simplices, edited by W. Gundlach, "Zwei Schriften des Erzbischofs Hinkmar von Reims, II," *Zeitschrift für Kirchengeschichte* 10 (1889), 258–310.

Hrabanus Maurus, *Carmina, MGH PLAC* 2, edited by E. Dümmler, pp. 154–258, Berlin, 1884.

    Commentariorium in Matthaeum, PL 107.727–1156.

    De institutione clericorum libri tres, edited by A. Knoepfler, Munich, 1900 / 1901.

    De videndo Deum, de puritate cordis et modo poenitentiae, PL 112.1261–1332.

Epistolae, edited by E. Dümmler, *MGH Epp.* 5, pp. 379–516, Berlin, 1899.

Homiliae de festis praecipuis, item de virtutibus, PL 110.9–134.

In honorem sanctae crucis, CCCM 100, edited by M. Perrin, Turnhout, 1997. Translated into French by M. Perrin, *Raban Maur, Louanges de la Sainte Croix*, Paris, 1988. Facsimile edition in *Hrabanus Maurus. Liber de laudibus sanctae crucis. Codex Vindobonensis 652 der Österreichischen Nationalbibliothek, Wien. Vollständige Faksimile-Ausgabe.* Graz, 1972.

Liber de sacris ordinibus, PL 112.1165–1192.

John Scottus Eriugena, *Eriugenae Carmina*, edited and translated by M. W. Herren, Scriptores Latini Hiberniae 12, Dublin, 1993.

De praedestinatione, CCCM 50, edited by G. Madec, Turnhout, 1978.

Periphyseon, Books 1–3, CCCM 161–163, edited by E. Jeauneau, Turnhout, 1996–1999. *Periphyseon (De diuisione naturae) Liber 4*, edited by E. Jeauneau with the assistance of Mark Zier, translated by J. J. O'Meara and I. P. Sheldon-Williams, Scriptores Latini Hiberniae 13, Dublin, 1995. The full treatise (Books 1–5) is published in *PL* 122. Translation of the entirety by I. P. Sheldon-Williams, revised by John J. O'Meara, *Eriugena, Periphyseon (Division of Nature)* (Montreal, 1987).

Commentaire sur l'évangile de Jean (In Iohannis Evangelium), SC 180, edited and translated into French by E. Jeauneau, Paris, 1972.

Expositiones in Ierarchiam Coelestem, CCCM 31, edited by J. Barbet, Turnhout, 1975.

Jonas of Orléans, *De cultu imaginum*, PL 106.305–388.

Le métier du roi (De institutione regia), SC 407, edited and translated into French by A. Dubreucq, Paris, 1995.

Joseph the Scot, *Carmina*, MGH PLAC 1, edited by E. Dümmler, pp. 149–159, Berlin, 1881.

Leidrad of Lyons, *Liber de sacramento baptismi*, PL 99.853–872.

Liber Sacramentorum Gellonensis, CCSL 159–159A, edited by A. Dumas, Turnhout, 1981.

Lupus of Ferrières, *Liber de tribus quaestionibus*, PL 119.619–648.

Magnus of Sens, *Libellus de mysterio baptismatis*, PL 102.981–984.

Milo of St.-Amand, *Carmina figurata*, MGH PLAC 3, edited by L. Traube, pp. 561–565, Berlin, 1896.

Odilbert of Mainz, *Erzbischof Odilbert von Mailand über die Taufe*, edited by F. Wiegand. Aalen, 1972, reprint of Leipzig, 1899 edition.

Ordines Romani. Les ordines romani du haut moyen âge, 5 vols., edited by M. Andrieu, Louvain, 1931–1961.

Otfrid of Weissenburg, *Otfrids Evangelienbuch*, edited by O. Erdmann, 4th edition, Tübingen, 1962.

Pascasius Radbertus, *De corpore et sanguine Domini cum appendice epistola ad Fredugardum*, CCCM 16, edited by B. Paulus, Turnhout, 1969.

    De partu Virginis, edited by E. A. Matter, *CCCM* 56C, pp. 5–96, Turnhout, 1985.

    Epistola ad Paulam et Eustochium de Assumptione Sanctae Mariae Virginis, edited by A. Ripberger, *CCCM* 56C, pp. 97–172, Turnhout, 1985.

    Expositio in Matheo Libri XII, *CCCM* 56–56B, edited by B. Paulus, Turnhout, 1984.

Paul the Deacon, *Die Gedichte des Paulus Diaconus: kritische und erklärende Ausgabe*, edited by K. Neff, Munich, 1908.

    "Homéliaire de Paul Diacre," edited by R. Grégoire, *Les Homéliaires du Moyen Age: inventaire et analyse des manuscrits*, pp. 71–114, Rome, 1966.

Paulinus of Aquileia, *Contra Felicem libri tres*, *CCCM* 95, edited by D. Norberg, Turnhout, 1990.

    L'Œuvre poétique de Paulin d'Aquilée, edited by D. Norberg, Stockholm, 1979.

    Liber exhortationis, PL 99.197–282.

Precum libelli quattuor aevi karolini, edited by A. Wilmart, Rome, 1940.

Prudentius of Troyes, *Epistola tractoria*, PL 115.1365–1368.

    De praedestinatione, PL 115.1009–1366.

Quierzy (Frühjahr 853), MGH *Conc*. 3, edited by W. Hartmann, pp. 294–297, Hanover, 1984.

Ratramnus of Corbie, *De corpore et sanguine Domini*, edited by J. N. Bakhuizen Van Den Brink, 2nd edition, Amsterdam, 1974.

    De praedestinatione Dei, PL 121.11–80.

Remigius of Auxerre, *Expositio missae*, (Pseudo-Alcuin) *Liber de divinis officiis* 40, PL 101.1246–1271.

Sacramentaire grégorien, 3 vols., edited by J. Deshusses, Fribourg, 1971–1982.

Sedulius Scottus, *Collectanea in omnes beati Pauli epistolas*, PL 103.9–270.

Theodulf of Orléans, *Carmina*, MGH *PLAC* 1, edited by E. Dümmler, pp. 437–578, Berlin, 1881.

    Opus Caroli regis contra synodum (Libri Carolini), MGH *Leges* 4, *Conc*. 2, *Supplementum* 1, edited by A. Freeman in collaboration with P. Meyvaert, Hanover, 1998.

    De ordine baptismi, PL 105.223–240.

Tusey (22. Oktober–7. November 860), MGH *Conc*. 4, edited by W. Hartmann, pp. 12–42, Hanover, 1998.

Utrecht-Psalter: vollständige Faksimile-Ausgabe im Originalformat der Handschrift 32,
    Utrecht-Psalter, aus dem Besitz der Bibliotheek der Rijksuniversiteit te Utrecht,
    2 vols., *Commentary* by K. van der Horst and J. A. Engelbregt, Graz, 1984.
Valence (8. Januar 855), MGH Conc. 3, edited by W. Hartmann, pp. 347–365, Hanover,
    1984.
Walafrid Strabo, *Libellus de exordiis et incrementis quarundam in observationibus*
    ecclesiasticis rerum, edited by V. Krause, *MGH Capit.* 2, pp. 473–516,
    Hanover, 1897. Translated by A. Harting-Corrêa, *Walafrid Strabo's*
    Libellus de exordiis et incrementis quarundam in observationibus ecclesiasticis
    rerum: a Translation and Liturgical Commentary, Leiden, 1996.

Secondary sources

Amann, Emile, *L'Epoque carolingienne,* vol. 6 of *Histoire de l'Eglise depuis les origines*
    jusqu'à nos jours, edited by A. Fliche and V. Martin, Paris, 1937.
Amos, T. L., "Preaching and the Sermon in the Carolingian World," in *"De ore*
    Domini": Preacher and Word in the Middle Ages, edited by T. L. Amos, E. A.
    Green, and B. M. Kienzle, pp. 41–60, Kalamazoo, 1989.
Anton, Hans Hubert, *Fürstenspiegel und Herrscherethos in der Karolingerzeit,* Bonn,
    1968.
Arnulf, Arwed, *Versus ad picturas: Studien zur Titulusdichtung als Quellengattung der*
    Kunstgeschichte von der Antike bis zum Hochmittelalter, Munich, 1997.
Aulén, Gustaf, *Christus Victor: an Historical Study of the Three Main Types of the Idea*
    of the Atonement, translated by A. G. Hebert, New York, 1956.
Bandmann, Günter, "Früh- und hochmittelalterliche Altaranordnung als
    Darstellung," in *Das erste Jahrtausend: Kultur und Kunst im werdenden*
    Abendland an Rhein und Ruhr, vol. 1, edited by V. H. Elbern, pp. 371–411,
    Düsseldorf, 1962.
Barber, Charles, "The Body Within the Frame: a Use of Word and Image in
    Iconoclasm," *Word & Image* 9 (1993), 140–153.
Barré, Henri, "La lettre du pseudo-Jérome sur l'assomption est-elle antérieure à
    Pascase Radbert?" *Revue Bénédictine* 68 (1958), 203–225.
    Les Homéliaires carolingiens de l'école d'Auxerre, Vatican City, 1962.
Belting, Hans, "Der Einhardsbogen," *Zeitschrift für Kunstgeschichte* 36 (1973), 93–121.
    Likeness and Presence: a History of the Image before the Era of Art, translated
    from the German by E. Jephcott, Chicago, 1994.
Belting, Hans, and Christa Belting-Ihm, "Das Kreuzbild im *Hodegos* des Anastasios
    Sinaites: ein Beitrag zur Frage nach der ältesten Darstellung des toten

Crucifixus," in *Tortulae: Studien zu altchristlichen und byzantinischen Monumenten*, edited by W.N. Schumacher, pp. 30–39, Rome, 1966.

Berg, Knut, "Une iconographie peu connue du crucifiement," *Cahiers archéologiques* 9 (1957), 319–328.

Berndt, Rainer, ed., *Das frankfurter Konzil von 794: Kristallisationspunkt karolingischer Kultur*, 2 vols., Mainz, 1997.

Beutler, Christian, *Der Gott am Kreuz: zur Entstehung der Kreuzigungsdarstellung*, Hamburg, 1986.

Bischoff, Bernhard, "Kreuz und Buch im frühmittelalter und in den ersten Jahrhunderten der spanischen Reconquista," *Mittelalterliche Studien: ausgewählte Aufsätze zur Schriftkunde und Literaturgeschichte*, 3 vols., vol. 2, pp. 284–303, Stuttgart, 1967.

"Wendepunkte in der Geschichte der lateinischen Exegese im Frühmittelalter," *Mittelalterliche Studien: ausgewählte Aufsätze zur Schriftkunde und Literaturgeschichte*, 3 vols., vol. 1, pp. 205–273, Stuttgart, 1966.

"Ursprung und Geschichte eines Kreuzsegens," *Mittelalterliche Studien: Ausgewählte Aufsätze zur Schriftkunde und Literaturgeschichte*, 3 vols., vol. 2, pp. 275–284, Stuttgart, 1967.

Bloch, Peter, "Zum Dedikationsbild im Lob des Kreuzes des Hrabanus Maurus," in *Das erste Jahrtausend: Kultur und Kunst im werdenden Abendland an Rhein und Ruhr*, vol. 1, edited by V. H. Elbern, pp. 471–494, Düsseldorf, 1962.

Blumenshine, Gary B., "Alcuin's *Liber Contra Haeresim Felicis* and the Frankish Kingdom," *Frühmittelalterlichen Studien* 17 (1983), 222–233.

Blumenthal, Uta-Renate, ed., *Carolingian Essays: Andrew W. Mellon Lectures in Early Christian Studies*, Washington, DC, 1983.

Boespflug, F. and N. Lossky, eds., *Nicée II, 787–1987: douze siècles d'images religieuses*, Paris, 1987.

Boinet, A., *La Miniature carolingienne*, Paris, 1920.

Bonner, Gerald, "The Doctrine of Sacrifice: Augustine and the Latin Patristic Tradition," in *Sacrifice and Redemption: Durham Essays in Theology*, edited by S.W. Sykes, pp. 101–117, Cambridge, 1991.

Bouhot, Jean-Paul, "Extraits du *De corpore et sanguine Domini* de Pascase Radbert sous le nom d'Augustin," *Recherches augustiniennes* 12 (1977), 119–173.

"Fragments attribués à Virgile de Thapse dans l'*Expositio missae* de Florus de Lyons," *Revue des études augustiniennes* 21 (1975), 302–316.

Ratramne de Corbie: histoire littéraire et controverses doctrinales, Paris, 1976.

Braunfels, Wolfgang, ed., *Karl der Grosse: Lebenswerk und Nachleben*, 4 vols., Düsseldorf, 1965–1967.

Die Welt der Karolinger und ihre Kunst, Munich, 1968.

Brown, Peter, *The Cult of the Saints: its Rise and Function in Latin Christianity*, Chicago, 1981.

Brunhölzl, Franz, *Histoire de la littérature latine du moyen âge*, vol. 1.2: *La Fondation de l'Europe à l'époque carolingienne*, translated by H. Rochais, Leiden, 1991.

Bullough, Donald, "Alcuin's Cultural Influence: the Evidence of the Manuscripts," in *Alcuin of York: Scholar at the Carolingian Court*, edited by L. A. J. R. Houwen and A. A. MacDonald, pp. 1–26, Groningen, 1995.

Carolingian Renewal: Sources and Heritage, Manchester, 1991.

"The Carolingian Liturgical Experience," *Studies in Church History* 35 (1999), 29–64.

Cabaniss, Allen, "Agobard of Lyons," *Speculum* 26 (1951), 50–76.

Amalarius of Metz, Amsterdam, 1954.

Cappuyns, M., *Jean Scot Erigène: sa vie, son oeuvre, sa pensée*, Louvain, 1933.

"Note sur le problème de la vision béatifique au ixe s.," *Recherches de théologie ancienne et médiévale* 1 (1929), 98–107.

Cavadini, John, *The Last Christology of the West: Adoptionism in Spain and Gaul, 785–820*, Philadelphia, 1993.

"The Sources and Theology of Alcuin's *De Fide Sanctae et Individuae Trinitatis*," *Traditio* 46 (1991), 123–146.

Chavasse, Antoine, *Le Sacramentaire Gélasien (Vaticanus Reginensis 316)*. Tournai, 1958.

"La structure du Carême et les lectures des messes quadragésimales dans la liturgie Romaine," *La Maison-Dieu* 31 (1952), 76–119.

Chazelle, Celia, "Archbishops Ebo and Hincmar of Reims and the Utrecht Psalter," *Speculum* (1997), 1055–1077. Reprinted in *Approaches to Early-Medieval Art*, edited by Lawrence Nees, pp. 97–119, Cambridge, MA, 1998.

"Figure, Character, and the Glorified Body in the Carolingian Eucharistic Controversy," *Traditio* 47 (1992), 1–36.

"Images, Scripture, the Church, and the *Libri Carolini*," *Proceedings of the Patristic, Medieval, and Renaissance Studies Conference* 16/17 (1993), 53–76.

"Matter, Spirit, and Image in the *Libri Carolini*," *Recherches augustiniennes* 21 (1986), 163–184.

"Memory, Instruction, Worship: 'Gregory's' Influence on Early Medieval Doctrines of the Artistic Image," in *Gregory the Great: a Symposium*, edited by J. C. Cavadini, pp. 181–215, Notre Dame, 1996.

"'Not in Painting but in Writing': Augustine and the Supremacy of the Word in the *Libri Carolini*," in *Reading and Wisdom: the De doctrina Christiana of Augustine in the Middle Ages*, edited by E. D. English, pp. 1–22, Notre Dame, 1995.

"Pictures, Books, and the Illiterate: Pope Gregory I's Letters to Serenus of Marseilles," *Word & Image* 6 (1990), 138–153.

Chester, A. N., "Hebrews: the Final Sacrifice," in *Sacrifice and Redemption: Durham Essays in Theology*, edited by S. W. Sykes, pp. 57–72, Cambridge, 1991.

Colish, Marcia L., "Carolingian Debates over *Nihil* and *Tenebrae*: a Study in Theological Method," *Speculum* 59 (1984), 757–795.

Medieval Foundations of the Western Intellectual Tradition, 400–1400, New Haven, 1997.

Collins, Roger, "The Carolingians and the Ottonians in an Anglophone World," *Journal of Medieval History* 22 (1996), 97–114.

Contreni, John J., "Carolingian Biblical Culture," in *Iohannes Scottus Eriugena: the Bible and Hermeneutics*, edited by G. Van Riel et al., pp. 1–23, Louvain, 1996.

Carolingian Learning, Masters and Manuscripts, Aldershot, 1992.

"The Carolingian Renaissance: Education and Literary Culture," in *NCMH* 2, edited by R. McKitterick, pp. 709–757, Cambridge, 1995.

Constantinescu, Radu, "Alcuin et les *Libelli precum* de l'époque carolingienne," *Revue de l'histoire de la spiritualité* 50 (1974), 17–56.

Corrigan, Kathleen, "Text and Image on an Icon of the Crucifixion at Mount Sinai," in *The Sacred Image East and West*, edited by R. Ousterhout and L. Brubaker, pp. 45–62, Urbana, 1995.

Visual Polemics in the Ninth-Century Byzantine Psalters, Cambridge, 1992.

Cramer, Peter, *Baptism and Change in the Early Middle Ages, c. 200–c.1150*, Cambridge, 1993.

Cremer, F. G., "Christian von Stablo als Exeget: Beobachtungen zur Auslegung von Mt. 9, 14–17," *Revue Bénédictine* 77 (1967), 328–341.

Cristiani, Marta, "La controversia eucaristica nella cultura del secolo ix," *Studi medievali*, 3rd series, 9 (1968), 167–233.

"La notion de loi dans le *De praedestinatione* de Jean Scot," *Studi medievali*, 3rd series, 17 (1976), 81–114.

Dahlhaus-Berg, Elisabeth. *Nova antiquitas et antiqua novitas: typologische Exegese und isidorianisches Geschichtsbild bei Theodulf von Orléans*, Cologne, 1975.

Davis, Leo Donald, "Hincmar of Rheims as a Theologian of the Trinity," *Traditio* 27 (1971), 455–468.

De Jong, Mayke, *Samuel's Image: Child Oblation in the Early Medieval West*, Leiden,
        1996.

    "Carolingian Monasticism: the Power of Prayer," in *NCMH* 2, edited by R.
        McKitterick, pp. 622–653, Cambridge, 1995.

de Nie, Giselle, "Iconic Alchemy: Imaging Miracles in Late Sixth-Century Gaul,"
        Studia Patristica 30, pp. 158–166, Louvain, 1997.

    "Seeing and Believing in the Early Middle Ages: a Preliminary
        Investigation," in *Word and Image: the Pictured Word, Interactions* 2, edited
        by Martin Heusser et al., pp. 67–76, Amsterdam, 1998.

    "Word, Image and Experience in the Early Medieval Miracle Story," in
        *Language and Beyond / Le Langage et ses au-delà, Text: Studies in Comparative
        Literature* 17, edited by P. Joret and A. Remael, pp. 97–122, Amsterdam,
        1998.

de Plinval, G. *Essai sur le style et la langue de Pélage, suivi du traité inédit de induratione
        cordis pharaonis*, Fribourg, 1947.

Deshman, Robert, "The Exalted Servant: the Ruler Theology of the Prayerbook
        of Charles the Bald," *Viator* 11 (1980), 385–417.

Deshusses, Jean, "Le sacramentaire de Gellone dans son contexte historique,"
        Ephemerides liturgicae 75 (1961), 193–210.

    "Les sacramentaires: état actuel de la recherche," *Archiv für
        Liturgiewissenschaft* 24 (1982), 19–46.

    "Le 'Supplement' au sacramentaire grégorien: Alcuin ou Saint Benoît
        d'Aniane?" *Archiv für Liturgiewissenschaft* 9 (1965), 48–71.

Deshusses, Jean, and Benoit Darragon, eds., *Concordances et tableaux pour l'étude
        des grands sacramentaires*, 3 vols., Fribourg, 1982–1983.

Devisse, Jean, *Hincmar: archevêque de Reims, 845–882*, 3 vols., Geneva, 1975.

Dewald, E. T., *The Illustrations of the Utrecht Psalter*, Princeton, 1933.

Diebold, William, "The Ruler Portrait of Charles the Bald in the S. Paolo Bible,"
        Art Bulletin 76 (1994), 7–18.

    "Verbal, Visual, and Cultural Literacy in Medieval Art: Word and Image in
        the Psalter of Charles the Bald." *Word & Image* 8 (1992), 89–99.

Dölger, F. J., "Beiträge zur Geschichte des Kreuzzeichens, I–IX," *Jahrbuch für Antike
        und Christentum* 1–10 (1958–1967).

Duchesne, L., *Origines du culte chrétien*, Paris, 1925.

Duclow, Donald F., "Denial or Promise of the Tree of Life? Eriugena, Augustine,
        and Genesis 3: 22b," in *Iohannes Scottus Eriugena: the Bible and
        Hermeneutics*, edited by G. Van Riel et al., pp. 221–238, Louvain, 1996.

Dufrenne, Suzy, *Les Illustrations du Psautier d'Utrecht: sources et apport carolingien*, Paris, 1978.

Tableaux synoptiques de 15 psautiers médiévaux, Paris, 1978.

Dumeige, G., *Nicée II*, Paris, 1978.

Dutton, Paul, *The Politics of Dreaming in the Carolingian Empire*, Lincoln, NE, 1994.

Dutton, Paul Edward and H. L. Kessler, *The Poetry and Paintings of the First Bible of Charles the Bald*, Ann Arbor, 1997.

Elbern, Victor H., *Der eucharistische Kelch im frühen Mittelalter*, Berlin, 1964.

"Der fränkische Reliquienkasten und Tragaltar von Werden," in *Das erste Jahrtausend: Kultur und Kunst im werdenden Abendland an Rhein und Ruhr*, vol. 1, edited by V. H. Elbern, pp. 436–470, Düsseldorf, 1962.

Der karolingische Goldaltar von Mailand, Bonn, 1952.

Engemann, Josef, "Zur Position von Sonne und Mond bei Darstellungen der Kreuzigung Christi," in *Studien zur spätantiken und byzantinischen Kunst: Friedrich Wilhelm Deichmann gewidmet*, vol. 3, edited by O. Feld and U. Peschlow, pp. 95–101, Bonn, 1986.

Ernst, Ulrich, *Carmen figuratum: Geschichte des Figurengedichts von den antiken Ursprüngen bis zum Ausgang des Mittelalters*, Cologne, 1991.

Etaix, R., "L'homéliaire composé par Raban Maur pour l'empereur Lothaire," *Recherches augustiniennes* 19 (1984), 211–240.

"Le recueil de sermons composé par Raban Maur pour Haistulfe de Mayence," *Revue des études augustiniennes* 32 (1986), 124–137.

Fahey, John Francis, *The Eucharistic Teaching of Ratramn of Corbie*, Mundelein, IL, 1951.

Ferber, Stanley, "Crucifixion Iconography in a Group of Carolingian Ivory Plaques," *Art Bulletin* 48 (1966), 323–334.

Ferrari, Michele, "Hrabanica. Hrabans *De laudibus sanctae crucis* im Spiegel der neueren Forschung," in *Kloster Fulda in der Welt der Karolinger und Ottonen*, edited by G. Schrimpf, pp. 493–526, Frankfurt, 1996.

Il "Liber sanctae crucis" di Rabano Mauro: testo-immagine-contesto, Bern, 1999.

Flint, Valerie, *The Rise of Magic in Early Medieval Europe*, Princeton, 1991.

Freeman, Ann, "Additions and Corrections to the *Libri Carolini*: Links with Alcuin and the Adoptionist Controversy," in *Scire Litteras: Forschungen zum mittelalterlichen Geistesleben*, edited by S. Krämer and M. Bernhard, pp. 159–169, Munich, 1988.

"Carolingian Orthodoxy and the Fate of the *Libri Carolini*," *Viator* 16 (1985), 65–108.

"Further Studies in the *Libri Carolini*, I and II," *Speculum* 40 (1965), 203–289.

"Scripture and Images in the *Libri Carolini*," in *Testo e immagine nell'alto medioevo*. Settimane di studio del Centro Italiano di Studi Sull'Alto Medioevo, 41, pp. 163–195, Spoleto, 1994.

"Theodulf of Orléans and the *Libri Carolini*," *Speculum* 32 (1957), 663–705.

Fried, Johannes, "Fulda in der Bildungs- und Geistesgeschichte des früheren Mittelalters," in *Kloster Fulda in der Welt der Karolinger und Ottonen*, edited by G. Schrimpf, pp. 3–38, Frankfurt, 1996.

Frolow, A., *La relique de la vraie croix: recherches sur le développement d'un culte*, Paris, 1961.

Gaborit-Chopin, Danielle, *Elfenbeinkunst im Mittelalter*, translated from the French by G. Bloch and R. Beyer, Berlin, 1978.

Ganz, David, *Corbie in the Carolingian Renaissance*, Sigmaringen, 1990.

"The Debate on Predestination," in *Charles the Bald: Court and Kingdom*, edited by M. T. Gibson and J. L. Nelson, revised edition, pp. 281–302, Aldershot, 1990.

"Theology and the Organisation of Thought," in *NCMH* 2, edited by R. McKitterick, pp. 758–785, Cambridge, 1995.

Geiselmann, J. R., *Die Eucharistielehre der Vorscholastik*, Paderborn, 1926.

Gero, Stephen, "The *Libri Carolini* and the Image Controversy," *Greek Orthodox Theological Review* 18 (1973), 7–34.

Gibson, Margaret T. and J. L. Nelson, eds., *Charles the Bald, Court and Kingdom*, revised edition, Aldershot, 1990.

Gillmeier, Aloys, *Der Logos am Kreuz: zur christologischen Symbolik der älteren Kreuzigungsdarstellung*, Munich, 1956.

Giron, Maria Angeles Navarro, *La carne de Cristo: el misterio eucharistico a la luz de la controversia entre Pascasio Radberto, Ratramno, Rabano Mauro y Godescalco*, Madrid, 1989.

Gjerlow, Lilli, *Adoratio crucis: the Regularis Concordia and the Decreta Lanfranci*, Oslo, 1961.

Godman, Peter, *Poetry of the Carolingian Renaissance,* London, 1985.

Poets and Emperors: Frankish Politics and Carolingian Poetry, Oxford, 1987.

Godman, Peter, and R. Collins, eds., *Charlemagne's Heir: New Perspectives on the Reign of Louis the Pious,* Oxford, 1989.

Göhler, Hulda, "Das Christusbild in Otfrids Evangelienbuch und im *Heliand*," *Zeitschrift für deutsche Philologie* 59 (1935), 1–52.

Goldschmidt, Adolph, *Die Elfenbeinskulpturen aus der Zeit der karolingischen und sächsischen Kaiser, VIII.-IX. Jahrhundert,* vol. 1, Berlin, 1914.

Gorman, Michael, "The Commentary on Genesis of Claudius of Turin and
    Biblical Studies under Louis the Pious," *Speculum* 72 (1997), 279–329.
    "Wigbod and Biblical Studies under Charlemagne," *Revue Bénédictine* 107
    (1997), 40–76.

Grégoire, Réginald, *Les Homiliaires du Moyen Age: inventaire et analyse des
    manuscrits*, Rome, 1966.

Haendler, Gert, *Epochen karolingischer Theologie: eine Untersuchung über die
    karolingischen Gutachten zum byzantinischen Bilderstreit*, Berlin, 1958.

Häussling, Angelus Albert, *Mönchskonvent und Eucharistiefeier: eine Studie über die
    Messe in der abendländischen Klosterliturgie des frühen Mittelalters und zur
    Geschichte der Messhäufigkeit*, Münster, 1973.

Hahn, Cynthia, *Passio Kiliani . . . Passio Margaretae: Faksimile-Ausgabe des Codex, . . .
    MS. I 189 . . . aus dem Besitz der Niedersächsischen Landesbibliothek Hannover,
    Kommentarband*, Graz, 1988.

Hartmann, Wilfried, *Die Synoden der Karolingerzeit im Frankenreich und in Italien*,
    Paderborn, 1989.

Haseloff, Günther, *Der Tassilokelch*, Munich, 1951.

Hauck, Karl, ed., *Das Einhardkreuz: Vorträge und Studien der Münsteraner Diskussion
    zum arcus Einhardi*, Göttingen, 1974.

Haussherr, Reiner, *Der tote Christus am Kreuz: zur Ikonographie des Gerokreuzes*,
    Bonn, 1963.

Head, Thomas, *Hagiography and the Cult of Saints: the Diocese of Orléans, 800–1200*,
    Cambridge, 1990.

Hefélé, Charles-Joseph, *Histoire des conciles d'après les documents originaux*, vols.
    3–4, Paris, 1909–1911.

Heitz, Carol, "Architecture et liturgie processionelle à l'époque préromane,"
    Revue de l'art 24 (1974), 30–47.
    L'architecture religieuse carolingienne: les formes et leurs fonctions, Paris, 1980.
    Recherches sur les rapports entre architecture et liturgie à l'époque carolingienne,
    Paris, 1963.

Henry, Patrick, "Images of the Church in the Second Nicene Council and in the
    Libri Carolini," in *Law, Church, and Society: Essays in Honor of Stephan
    Kuttner*, edited by K. Pennington and R. Somerville, pp. 237–252,
    Philadelphia, 1977.

Hillgarth, J. M., ed., *Christianity and Paganism, 350–750: the Conversion of Western
    Europe*, 2nd. revised edition, Philadelphia, 1986.

Hubert, Jean, J. Porcher, and W. F. Volbach, *L'Empire carolingien*, Paris, 1968.

Ineichen-Elder, Christine E., "The Authenticity of the *Dicta Candidi, Dicta Albini,* and some Related Texts," in *Insular Latin Studies: Papers on Latin Texts and Manuscripts of the British Isles, 550–1066,* edited by M.W. Herren, pp. 179–193, Toronto, 1981.

  "Candidus-Brun von Fulda: Maler, Lehrer und Schriftsteller," in *Hrabanus Maurus und seine Schule,* edited by W. Böhne, pp. 182–192, Fulda, 1980.

Iogna-Prat, Dominique, C. Jeudy, and G. Lobrichon, eds., *L'Ecole carolingienne d'Auxerre: de Murethach à Remi, 830–908, Entretiens d'Auxerre 1989,* Paris, 1991.

Izydorczyk, Z., *Manuscripts of the "Evangelium Nicodemi": a Census,* Toronto, 1993.

  ed., *The Medieval Gospel of Nicodemus: Texts, Intertexts, and Contexts in Western Europe,* Tempe, AZ, 1997.

Jeauneau, Edouard and P.E. Dutton, "The Verses of the *Codex Aureus* of St.-Emmeram," in E. Jeanneau, *Etudes érigéniennes* (Paris, 1987), 593–638.

Jungmann, J. A., *Missarum Sollemnia: eine genetische Erklärung der römnischen Messe,* 2 vols., 4th. expanded edition, Vienna, 1958.

Kantorwicz, Ernst, *Laudes Regiae: a study in Liturgical Acclamations and Mediaeval Ruler Worship,* Berkeley, 1946.

Kartsonis, Anna, *Anastasis: the Making of an Image,* Princeton, 1986.

Kelly, J. N. D., *Early Christian Doctrines,* New York, 1978.

Kessler, Herbert L., "*Facies bibliothecae revelata*: Carolingian Art as Spiritual Seeing," in *Testo e immagine nell'alto medioevo,* Settimane di studio del Centro Italiano di Studi Sull'Alto Medioevo, 41, pp. 533–594, Spoleto, 1994.

  "Real Absence: Early Medieval Art and the Metamorphosis of Vision," in *Morfologie sociali e culturali in Europa fra tarda antichità e alto medioevo,* Settimane di studio del Centro Italiano di Studi Sull'Alto Medioevo, 45, pp. 1157–1211, Spoleto, 1998.

Klingenberg, Heinz, "Hrabanus Maurus: *In honorem sanctae crucis,*" in *Festschrift für Otto Höfler zum 65. Geburtstag,* vol. 2, edited by H. Birkhand and O. Schwantler, pp. 273–300, Vienna, 1968.

Köhler, Wilhelm, *Die karolingischen Miniaturen,* vols. 1–3, Berlin, 1930–1960.

Köhler, Wilhelm, and Florentine Mütherich, *Die karolingischen Miniaturen,* vols. 4–6, Berlin, 1971–1994.

Kolping, A., "Amalar von Metz und Florus von Lyon," *Zeitschrift für katholische Theologie* 73 (1951), 424–464.

Kornbluth, Genevra, *Engraved Gems of the Carolingian Empire,* University Park, PA, 1995.

Ladner, Gerhart B., "Medieval and Modern Symbolism: a Comparison," *Speculum* 54 (1979), 223–256.

"St. Gregory of Nyssa and St. Augustine on the Symbolism of the Cross," in *Late Classical and Mediaeval Studies in Honor of Albert Mathias Friend, Jr.*, edited by K. Weitzmann, pp. 88–95, Princeton, 1955.

Laistner, M. L. W., "A Ninth-Century Commentator on the Gospel according to Matthew," *Harvard Theological Review* 20 (1927), 129–149.

Lambot, D.C., "L'homélie du Ps.-Jérôme sur l'assomption et l'évangile de la nativité de Marie d'après une lettre inédite d'Hincmar," *Revue Bénédictine* 46 (1934), 265–282.

Lasko, Peter, *Ars sacra, 800–1200*, 2nd edition, New Haven, 1994.

Leclercq, Jean, "Les *Munimenta Fidei* de Saint Benoit d'Aniane," *Analecta Monastica* ser. 1.20 (1948), 21–74.

Leesti, Elizabeth, "Carolingian Crucifixion Iconography: an Elaboration of a Byzantine Theme," *Revue d'art canadienne / Canadian Art Review* 20 (1993), 3–15.

"Illustrations in the Drogo Sacramentary (Paris, Bibliothèque Nationale, MS lat. 9428)," Ph.D. dissertation, University of Toronto, 1984.

Leroquais, Victor, *Les Sacramentaires et les missels manuscrits des bibliothèques publiques de France*, 3 vols., Paris, 1924.

Levitan. W., "Dancing at the End of the Rope: Optatian Porfyry and the Field of Roman Verse," *Transactions of the American Philological Association* 115 (1985), 245–269.

Lewis, Suzanne, "A Byzantine *Virgo Militans* at Charlemagne's Court," *Viator* 11 (1980), 71–93.

Lubac, Henri de, *Corpus mysticum: l'eucharistie et l'église au moyen âge*, 2nd revised edition, Paris, 1949.

Marenbon, John, *From the School of Alcuin to the Circle of Auxerre: Logic, Theology and Philosophy in the Early Middle Ages*, Cambridge, 1981.

"John Scottus and Carolingian Theology: from the *De Praedestinatione*, Its Background and Its Critics, to the *Periphyseon*," in *Charles the Bald: Court and Kingdom*, edited by M. T. Gibson and J. L. Nelson, pp. 303–25, Aldershot, 1990.

Markus, Robert, ed., *Augustine: a Collection of Critical Essays*, Garden City, NY, 1972.

Matter, E. Ann, "Theological Freedom in the Carolingian Age: the Case of Claudius of Turin," in *La Notion de liberté au Moyen Age: Islam, Byzance, Occident*, Penn-Paris-Dumbarton Oaks Colloquia, 4, pp. 51–60, Paris, 1982.

McCormick, Michael, *Eternal Victory: Triumphal Rulership in Late Antiquity, Byzantium and the Early Medieval West*, Cambridge, 1986.

"The Liturgy of War in the Early Middle Ages: Crisis, Litanies, and the Carolingian Monarchy," *Viator* 15 (1984), 1–23.

McKeon, P. R., "The Carolingian Councils of Savonnières (859) and Tusey (860) and Their Background," *Revue Bénédictine* 84 (1974), 75–110.

McKitterick, Rosamond, ed., *The New Cambridge Medieval History,* vol. 2: *c. 700–c. 900.* Cambridge, 1995.

ed., *Carolingian Culture: Emulation and Innovation*, Cambridge, 1994.

The Carolingians and the Written Word, Cambridge, 1989.

"Charles the Bald (823–877) and His Library: the Patronage of Learning," *English Historical Review* 95 (1980), 28–47.

The Frankish Church and the Carolingian Reforms, 789–895, London, 1977.

The Frankish Kingdoms Under the Carolingians, 751–987, London, 1983.

ed., *The Uses of Literacy in Early Medieval Europe*, Cambridge, 1990.

McLaughlin, R. Emmet, "The Word Eclipsed? Preaching in the Early Middle Ages," *Traditio* 46 (1991), 77–122.

Melzak, Robert, "The Carolingian Ivory Carvings of the Later Metz Group," Ph.D. dissertation, Columbia University, 1983.

Meyer, Hans Bernhard, "Alkuin zwischen Antike und Mittelalter: ein Kapitel frühmittelalterlicher Frömmigkeitsgeschichte," *Zeitschrift für katholische Theologie* 81 (1959), 306–350, 405–454.

"*Crux decus mundi*: Alkuins Kreuz- und Osterfrömmigkeit," in *Paschatis sollemnia. Studien zu Osterfeier und Osterfrömmigkeit*, edited by B. Fischer and J. Wagner, pp. 96–107, Basel, 1959.

Moos, Peter von, "Gottschalks Gedicht *O mi custos* – eine *confessio*," *Frühmittelalterliche Studien* 4 (1970), 201–230, 5 (1971), 317–358.

Moreton, B., *The Eighth-Century Gelasian Sacramentary: a Study in Tradition*, Oxford, 1976.

Morin, D.G., "Un traité pélagien inédit du commencement du ve siècle," *Revue Bénédictine* 26 (1909), 163–188.

Morrison, Karl, *The Mimetic Tradition of Reform in the West*, Princeton, 1982.

Tradition and Authority in the Western Church, 300–1140, Princeton, 1969.

Müller, Hans-Georg, *Hrabanus Maurus – De laudibus sanctae crucis*, Ratingen, 1973.

Murphy, G. Ronald, *The Saxon Savior: the Germanic Transformation of the Gospel in the Ninth-Century Heliand*, New York, 1989.

Mütherich, Florentine, "Die Elfenbeinschmuck des Thrones," in *La cattedra lignea di S. Pietro in Vaticano*, edited by M. Maccarrone et al., pp. 253–273, Vatican City, 1971.

Nees, Lawrence, "Art and Architecture," in *NCMH* 2, edited by R. McKitterick, pp. 809–844, Cambridge, 1995.

    A Tainted Mantle: Hercules and the Classical Tradition at the Carolingian Court, Philadelphia, 1991.

    "Theodulf's Mythical Silver Hercules Vase, *Poetica vanitas*, and the Augustinian Critique of the Roman Heritage," *Dumbarton Oaks Papers* 41 (1987), 443–451.

Nelson, Janet L., *Charles the Bald*, London, 1992.

    The Frankish World, 750–900, London, 1996.

    "The Lord's Anointed and the People's Choice: Carolingian Royal Ritual," in *Rituals of Royalty, Power and Ceremonial in Traditional Societies*, edited by D. Cannadine and S. Price, pp. 137–180, Cambridge, 1987.

    Politics and Ritual in Early Medieval Europe, London, 1986.

Nineham, D. E., "Gottschalk of Orbais: Reactionary or Precursor of the Reformation?" *Journal of Ecclesiastical History* 40 (1989), 1–18.

Noble, Thomas F. X., *The Republic of St. Peter: the Birth of the Papal State, 680–825*, Philadelphia, 1984.

Noble, Thomas F. X. and T. Head, eds., *Soldiers of Christ: Saints and Saints' Lives from Late Antiquity and the Early Middle Ages*, University Park, PA, 1995.

Nordhagen, Per Jonas, *The Frescoes of John VII (A.D. 705–707) in Santa Maria Antiqua in Rome*, Rome, 1968.

O'Meara, John J., *Eriugena*, Oxford, 1988.

    Studies in Augustine and Eriugena, ed. T. Halton, Washington, DC, 1992.

Paxton, Frederick, *Christianizing Death: the Creation of a Ritual Process in Early Medieval Europe*, Ithaca, NY, 1990.

Pelikan, Jaroslav, *The Christian Tradition, a History of the Development of Doctrine*, vols. 1–3, Chicago, 1971–1978.

Rabe, Susan A., *Faith, Art, and Politics at Saint-Riquier: the Symbolic Vision of Angilbert*, Philadelphia, 1995.

Rädle, Fidel, "Gottschalks Gedicht an seinen letzten Freund," in *Scire Litteras: Forschungen zum mittelalterlichen Geistesleben*, edited by S. Krämer and M. Bernhard, pp. 315–325, Munich, 1988.

Rathofer, Johannes, *Der Heliand: theologischer Sinn als tektonische Form: Vorbereitung und Grundlegung der Interpretation*, Cologne, 1962.

Raw, Barbara C., *Anglo-Saxon Crucifixion Iconography and the Art of the Monastic Revival*, Cambridge, 1990.

Reil, Johannes, *Christus am Kreuz in der Bildkunst der Karolingerzeit*, Leipzig, 1930.

Die frühchristlichen Darstellung der Kreuzigung Christi, Leipzig, 1904.

Reuter, Marianne, *Text und Bild im Codex 132 der Bibliothek von Montecassino, "Liber Rabani de originibus rerum,"* Munich, 1984.

Reynolds, Roger E., "Image and Text: a Carolingian Illustration of Modifications in the Early Roman Eucharistic *Ordines*," *Viator* 14 (1983), 59–75.

"The Organisation, Law and Liturgy of the Western Church, 700–900," in *NCMH* 2, edited by R. McKitterick, pp. 587–621, Cambridge, 1995.

Riggenbach, Eduard, *Historische Studien zum Hebräerbrief,* vol. 1: *Die ältesten lateinischen Kommentare zum Hebräerbrief*, Leipzig, 1907.

Rivière, Jean, *Le Dogme de la rédemption au début du moyen-âge*, Paris, 1934.

Römer, Gerhard, "Die Liturgie des Karfreitags," *Zeitschrift für katholische Theologie* 77 (1955), 39–93.

Sansterre, Jean-Marie, "Entre *koinè méditerranéene*, influences byzantines et particularités locales: le culte des images et ses limites à Rome dans le haut moyen âge," in *Europa medievale e mondo bizantino: contatti effettivi e possibilità di studi comparati*, edited by G. Arnaldi and G. Cavallo, pp. 109–124, Rome, 1997.

"L'image blessée, l'image souffrante: quelques récits de miracles entre Orient et Occident (vie–xiie siècle)," *Bulletin de l'Institut historique belge de Rome* 69 (1999), 113–130.

"La vénération des images à Ravenne dans le haut moyen âge: notes sur une forme de dévotion peu connue," *Revue Mabillon*, n.s. 7 (= t. 68) (1996), 5–21.

Schade, Herbert, "Die *Libri Carolini* und ihre Stellung zum Bild," *Zeitschrift für katholische Theologie* 79 (1957), 69–78.

Schaller, Dieter, "Der junge 'Rabe' am Hof Karls des Grossen," in *Festschrift Bernhard Bischoff zu seinem 65. Geburtstag dargebracht*, edited by J. Autenrieth and F. Brunhölzl, pp. 123–141, Stuttgart, 1971.

"Die karolingischen Figurengedichte des Cod. Bern. 212," in *Medium Aevum Vivum, Festschrift für Walther Bulst*, edited by H. R. Jauss and D. Schaller, pp. 22–47, Heidelberg, 1960.

"Poetic Rivalries at the Court of Charlemagne," in *Classical Influence on European Culture, A.D. 500–1500*, edited by R. R. Bolgar, pp. 151–157, Cambridge, 1971.

Scheffczyk, L., *Das Mariengeheimnis in Frömmigkeit und Lehre der Karolingerzeit*, Leipzig, 1959.

Schiller, Gertrud, *Iconography of Christian Art*, vol. 2, translated by J. Seligman, Greenwich, CT, 1972.

Schmitt, Jean-Claude, "L'Occident, Nicée II, et les images du VIIIe au XIIIe siècle," in *Nicée II, 787–1987: douze siècles d'images religieuses*, edited by F. Boespflug and N. Lossky, pp. 271–301, Paris, 1987.

Schramm, Percy Ernst, *Sphaira, Globus, Reichsapfel: Wanderung und Wandlung eines Herrschaftszeichens von Caesar bis zu Elisabeth II*, Stuttgart, 1958.

Schramm, Percy Ernst, Hermann Fillitz, and Florentine Mütherich, *Denkmale der deutschen Könige und Kaiser*, 2 vols., vol. 1: Schramm and Mütherich, *Ein Beitrag zur Herrschergeschichte von Karl dem Grossen bis Friedrich II, 768–1250*, 2nd expanded edn., Munich, 1981.

Schrimpf, Gangolf, "Der Beitrag des Johann Scottus Eriugena zum Prädestinationsstreit," in *Die Iren und Europa im früheren Mittelalter*, vol. 2, edited by H. Löwe, pp. 819–865, Stuttgart, 1982.

"Die ethische Auseinandersetzung zwischen Hraban und Gottschalk um die Prädestinationslehre," in *Hrabanus Maurus und seine Schule*, edited by W. Böhne, pp. 164–174, Fulda, 1980.

Das Werk des Johannes Scottus Eriugena im Rahmen des Wissenschaftsverständnisses seiner Zeit, Münster, 1982.

Schwartz, J., "Quelques sources antiques d'ivoires carolingiens," *Cahiers archéologiques* 11 (1960), 145–162.

Sears, Elizabeth, "Louis the Pious as *Miles Christi*: the Dedicatory Image in Hrabanus Maurus' *De laudibus sanctae crucis*," in *Charlemagne's Heir: New Perspectives on the Reign of Louis the Pious*, edited by P. Godman and R. Collins, pp. 605–628, Oxford, 1990.

Segni e riti nella chiesa altomedievale occidentale, 2 vols., Settimane di studio del Centro Italiano di Studi Sull'Alto Medioevo, 33, Spoleto, 1987.

Semmler, J., "Die Beschlusse des Aachener Konzils im Jahre 816," *Zeitschrift für Kirchengeschichte* (1963), 15–82.

Sepière, Marie-Christine, *L'Image d'un Dieu souffrant: aux origines du crucifix*, Paris, 1994.

Simon, Sonia, "Studies on the Drogo Sacramentary: Eschatology and the Priest-King," Ph.D. dissertation, Boston University, 1975.

Smith, Julia M. H., "Religion and Lay Society," in *NCMH* 2, edited by R. McKitterick, pp. 654–678, Cambridge, 1995.

Spilling, Herrad, *Opus Magnentii Hrabani Mauri in honorem sanctae crucis conditum, Hrabans Beziehung zu seinem Werk*, Frankfurt, 1992.

Staubach, Nikolaus, *Rex Christianus: Hofkultur und Herrschaftspropaganda im Reich Karls des Kahlen*, Cologne, 1993.

Steenbock, Frauke, "Kreuzförmige Typen frühmittelalterlicher Prachteinbände," in *Das erste Jahrtausend: Kultur und Kunst im werdenden Abendland an Rhein und Ruhr*, vol. 1, edited by V. H. Elbern, pp. 495–513, Düsseldorf, 1962.

Steigemann, Christoph, and Matthias Wemhoff, eds., *799: Kunst und Kultur der Karolingerzeit, Karl der Grosse und Papst Leo III. in Paderborn: Katalog der Ausstellung Paderborn 799*, 2 vols. and *Beiträge*, Mainz, 1999.

Stock, Brian, *The Implications of Literacy: Written Language and Models of Interpretation in the Eleventh and Twelfth Centuries*, Princeton, 1983.

Stratmann, Martina, "Briefe an Hinkmar von Reims," *Deutsches Archiv* 48 (1992), 37–81.

Sullivan, Richard, "The Carolingian Age: Reflections on Its Place in the History of the Middle Ages," *Speculum* 64 (1989), 267–306.

ed., *The Gentle Voices of Teachers: Aspects of Learning in the Carolingian Age*, Columbus, OH, 1995.

Suntrup, Rudolf, "Präfigurationen des Messopfers in Text und Bild," *Frühmittelalterliche Studien* 18 (1994), 468–528.

"*Te igitur*-Initialen und Kanonbilder in mittelalterlichen Sakramentarhandschriften," in *Text und Bild: Aspekte des Zusammenwirkens zweier Künste im Mittelalter und früher Neuzeit*, edited by C. Meier and U. Ruberg, pp. 278–382, Wiesbaden, 1980.

Szarmach, Paul E., "The Latin Tradition of Alcuin's *Liber de Virtutibus et Vitiis*, cap. xxvii–xxxv," *Mediaevalia* 12 (1989, for 1986), 13–41.

Szövérffy, Joseph, *Die Annalen der lateinischen Hymnendichtung, ein Handbuch*, vol. 1: *Die lateinischen Hymnen bis zum Ende des 11. Jahrhunderts*, Berlin, 1964.

"*Crux Fidelis* . . .: Prolegomena to a History of the Holy Cross Hymns," *Traditio* 22 (1966), 1–41.

Hymns of the Holy Cross, Brookline, MA, 1976.

Taeger, Burkhard, ed., *Der Heliand: Studienausgabe in Auswahl*, Tübingen, 1984.

Zahlensymbolik bei Hraban, bei Hincmar – und im "Heliand"?: Studien zur Zahlensymbolik im Frühmittelalter, Munich, 1970.

Tavard, George H., *Trina deitas: the Controversy Between Hincmar and Gottschalk*, Milwaukee, 1996.

Teyssèdre, B., *Le Sacramentaire de Gellone et la figure humaine dans les manuscrits francs du VIIIe siècle, de l'enluminure à l'illustration*, Toulouse, 1959.

Tiralla, Hugo, *Das augustinische Idealbild der christlichen Obrigkeit als Quelle der "Fürstenspiegel" des Sedulius Scottus und Hincmar von Reims*, Anklam, 1916.

Unterkircher, Franz, *Zur Ikonographie und Liturgie des Drogo-Sakramentars*, Graz, 1977.

van der Horst, Koert, William Noel, Wilhelmina C. M. Wüstefeld, eds., *The Utrecht Psalter in Medieval Art: Picturing the Psalms of David*, Westrenen, 1996.

van der Meer, Frederik, *Maiestas Domini: Théophanies de l'Apocalypse dans l'art chrétien*, Vatican City, 1938.

Vandersall, Amy, "The Ivories of the Court School of Charles the Bald," Ph.D. dissertation, Yale University, 1965.

Vogel, C., *Medieval Liturgy: an Introduction to the Sources*, revised and translated by W. G. Storey and N. K. Rasmussen, Washington, DC, 1986.

Walker, George S. M., "Eriugena's Conception of the Sacraments," *Studies in Church History*, vol. 3, edited by G. J. Cuming, pp. 150–158, Leiden, 1966.

Wallace-Hadrill, J. M., *The Frankish Church*, Oxford, 1983.

Wallach, Luitpold, *Alcuin and Charlemagne: Studies in Carolingian History and Literature*, Ithaca, NY, 1959.

Diplomatic Studies in Latin and Greek Documents from the Carolingian Age, Ithaca, NY, 1977.

Weitzmann, Kurt, *The Monastery of Saint Catherine at Mount Sinae: the Icons*, vol. 1: *From the Sixth to the Tenth Century*, Princeton, 1976.

Wenger, Luke, "Hrabanus Maurus, Fulda, and Carolingian Spirituality," Ph.D. dissertation, Harvard University, 1973.

Werckmeister, Otto Karl, *Der Deckel des Codex Aureus von St. Emmeram: ein Goldschmiedewerk des 9. Jahrhunderts*, Baden-Baden, 1963.

Wilmart, André, "Distiques d'Hincmar sur l'eucharistie? Un sermon oublié de S. Augustin sur le même sujet," *Revue Bénédictine* 40 (1928), 87–98.

Precum libelli quattuor aevi karolini, Rome, 1940.

"Prières médiévales pour l'adoration de la croix," *Ephemerides liturgicae* 46 (1932), 22–65.

Wirth, Jean, *L'Image médiévale: naissance et développements (VIe-XVe siècle)*, Paris, 1989.

Index

Scriptural references